A.R. GURNEY
Collected Plays Volume III
1984–1991

812

GUR

A Smith and Kraus Book
Published by Smith and Kraus, Inc.
177 Lyme Road, Hanover, NH 03755

First Edition: May 2000
10 9 8 7 6 5 4 3 2 1

The Library of Congress Cataloging-In-Publication Data
Gurney, A.R. (Albert Ramsdell), 1930–
A.R. Gurney Collected Plays Volume III: 1984–1991. —1st ed.
384 p. cm. — (Contemporary playwrights series)
ISBN 1-57525-197-3 (cloth) ISBN 1-57525-198-1 (pbk.)
I. Title. II. Series.
PS3557.U82A6   1995
812'.54—dc20   95-19638
CIP

A.R. GURNEY

Collected Plays Volume III
1984–1991

CONTEMPORARY PLAYWRIGHTS
SERIES

SK
A Smith and Kraus Book

CONTENTS

THE COCKTAIL HOUR

To My Family

INTRODUCTION

This play provided one of those rare and lucky experiences in the theatre when you get the right director, an ideal cast, and the perfect place to iron out the kinks—the Old Globe Theatre in San Diego. Oddly enough, it was pretty much slammed by the San Diego critics, but some New York producers liked it anyway and bravely brought it in. The Promenade Theatre in New York provided a fine home for it for several months, before it moved on to successful runs at the Kennedy Center and in Los Angeles. The original actors stayed with it during these various venues, having managed to create on stage a matchless feel for the dynamics of family life. Other excellent productions sprang up in Boston and Chicago, and the play subsequently had considerable life in the regional theatres. *The Cocktail Hour,* even in its title, works with and against the conventional Wasp stereotypes, and if audiences were beginning to become dismissive of this particular ethnic group, here they seemed willing to respond affectionately. Ostensibly, the play would seem to be in the mode of the old-fashioned, drawing-room comedy, but I like to think that its self-reflexiveness, where it constantly comments on itself, gives it a more contemporary flavor and enables an audience to collaborate actively with what is happening on stage.

ORIGINAL PRODUCTION

The Cocktail Hour had its world premiere at the Old Globe Theatre, San Diego, California, in June, 1988. It was first produced in New York City by Roger L. Stevens, Thomas Viertel, Steven Baruch and Richard Frankel at the Promenade Theatre, where it opened on October 20, 1988. It was directed by Jack O'Brien, the scenery and costumes were by Steven Rubin, lighting by Kent Dorsey, the managing director was Thomas Hall and the production stage manager, Douglas Pagliotti. The cast, in order of appearance, was as follows:

Bradley . . . . Keene Curtis
John . . . . Bruce Davison
Ann . . . . Nancy Marchand
Nina . . . . Holland Taylor

CHARACTERS

BRADLEY
ANN: his wife
JOHN: their son
NINA: their daughter

SETTING

The play takes place during early evening in early fall in the mid-seventies, in a city in upstate New York.

AUTHOR'S NOTE

The set is basically realistic, but should also be vaguely theatrical, reminding us subliminally of those photographs of sets of American drawing-room comedies in the thirties or forties, designed by Donald Oenslager or Oliver Smith. In any case, it is a lovely step-down living room, with an arched entrance leading to a front hall, and perhaps the start of a staircase. There is an antique writing desk, a working fireplace with a mantelpiece, a fire bench, and a pretty good Impressionist painting hanging over it. The Upstage wall is full of good books, all hard-back, some leatherbound sets, some large art books, all neatly organized. The room also contains a baby grand piano on which are a number of black-and-white family photographs framed in silver or leather: portraits of children, snapshots of children at sports, pictures of dogs, large group shots of families, an occasional faded photograph of a nineteenth century couple. Downstage, of course, is a large, comfortable couch with a coffee table in front of it, along with several comfortable chairs and a moveable footstool. There might be a corner china cabinet displaying excellent china. All the furniture looks old and waxed and clean. There's a thick, warm Persian rug on the floor. Through the windows, a few barren branches are seen in the early evening light. The overall effect should not be opulent or grandiose or particularly trendy, but rather tasteful, comfortable, and civilized, an oasis of traditional warmth and solid good taste, a haven in a heartless world. On the coffee table, noticeably set apart from the china ashtrays and other objects, is a thick manuscript in a black cover.

ACT I

At rise: The stage is empty. The light from the windows indicates early evening, early fall. After a moment, Bradley enters, carrying a silver ice bucket. He is in his seventies and very well-dressed. He is followed by his son, John, who is in his early forties and more informally dressed. John carries a silver tray with several liquor bottles and glasses on it.

BRADLEY: *(Turning on the light in the hall.)* This is what's called bringing the mountain to Mohammed.

JOHN: Right.

BRADLEY: Otherwise we'd have to trek all the way back to the pantry whenever we needed to return to the well.

JOHN: Makes sense to me.

BRADLEY: *(Setting down the ice bucket on the table behind the couch.)* Of course when we had maids, it was different. You could just push the buzzer, and say bring this, bring that, and they'd bring it.

JOHN: *(Setting down the tray.)* I remember.

BRADLEY: Not that they could mix a drink. They couldn't make a martini to save their skin. But they could make ice, bring water, pass cheese. It was very pleasant.

JOHN: Before the war.

BRADLEY: That damn war. Those Germans have a lot to answer for. Well. Let's see…What are we missing?…Have we got the lemon for your mother's martini?

JOHN: *(Taking it out of his pocket.)* It's right here, Pop.

BRADLEY: Your mother likes a small twist of lemon in her martini.

JOHN: I know.

BRADLEY: And my Cutty Sark scotch.

JOHN: Oh yes.

BRADLEY: *(Looking at the label.)* It' s a good scotch. Not a great scotch, but a good one. I always enjoy the picture on the label. The American clipper ships were the fastest in the world. Magnificent vessels. Beautifully built. Made our country great.

JOHN: The "Cutty Sark" was English, Pop.

BRADLEY: I know that. I'm speaking generally.

JOHN: Actually the clipper ships only lasted a few years.

BRADLEY: Not true.

JOHN: Only a few—before steam.

BRADLEY: Not true at all.

JOHN: I think so, Pop.

BRADLEY: I wish your brother were here. He'd know. He knows all there is to know about boats.

JOHN: *(Going to bookcase.)* I'll look it up.

BRADLEY: Never mind. I said, *never mind.* We are not going to waste the evening in pedantic arguments.

(John returns from the bookcase.)

BRADLEY: Now look what I did. I brought out a whole bottle of soda water. Automatically. Thinking your brother *would* be here. Won't drink anything else. Never did.

JOHN: Smart man.

BRADLEY: I telephoned him yesterday. Tried to get him to come up. "Come on, Jigger," I said. "Join us. John's coming. Your sister will be here. We'll all have cocktails and your mother will provide an excellent dinner. You can play the piano. We'll all gather around the piano and sing. Bring Sylvia, if you want. Bring the children. I'll pay for the whole thing." But no. Wouldn't do it. Jigger's a very positive person, once he's made up his mind.

JOHN: It's a tough trip for him, Pop.

BRADLEY: I know that.

JOHN: He's working weekends now. They've put him back in sales.

BRADLEY: We all have to sell. One way or another.

JOHN: He's looking for another job.

BRADLEY: I know all that. You don't need to tell me that. I'm in touch with him all the time. *(He returns to the bar.)* What'll you have, by the way?

JOHN: Some of that soda water, actually.

BRADLEY: You?

JOHN: That's what I'll have.

BRADLEY: You're the one who likes to tuck it away.

JOHN: Not tonight.

BRADLEY: And why not, may I ask?

JOHN: It makes me say and do things I'm sorry for later.

BRADLEY: That's the fun of it.

JOHN: Not for me.

BRADLEY: You're not in difficulty, are you?

JOHN: No.

BRADLEY: You're not in one of those organizations that make you give it up?

JOHN: I just like to keep a lid on myself, Pop.

BRADLEY: Suit yourself. *(Pours him a glass of soda water.)* Soda water it is. What is it Lord Byron tells us? "Let us have wine and women, mirth and laughter; sermons and soda water the day after"…Maybe you'll change your mind later on.

JOHN: Maybe I will.

BRADLEY: *(Now pouring his own scotch and water very carefully.)* Of course, nobody drinks much these days. At least not with any relish. Marv Watson down at the club is now completely on the wagon. You sit down beside him at the big table, and what's he drinking? Orange juice. I said, "Am I confused about the time, Marv? Are we having breakfast?" Of course the poor thing can't hear, so it doesn't make any difference. But you go to parties these days and even the young people aren't drinking. I saw young Kathy Bickford at the Shoemaker wedding. Standing on the sidelines, looking very morose indeed. I went up to her and said, "What's that strange concoction you've got in your hand, Kathy?" She said, "Lemon Squirt," I said, "What?" She said, "Sugar-free, noncarbonated Lemon Squirt." So I said, "Now, Kathy, you listen to me. You're young and attractive, and you should be drinking champagne. You should be downing a good glass of French champagne, one, two, three, and then you should be out there on that dance floor, kicking up your heels with every usher in sight And after you've done that, you should come right back here, and dance with me!" Of course, she walked away. *(He finishes making his drink.)* They all walk away these days. I suppose I'm becoming a tiresome old fool.

JOHN: Hardly, Pop.

BRADLEY: Yes, well, I can still keep the ball in the air, occasionally. I gave a toast at the Shoemaker's bridal dinner. It went over very well.

JOHN: Mother told me.

BRADLEY: Oh yes. I made a few amusing remarks. I complimented the bride. You know Sarah Shoemaker? She's terribly tall. She towers over the groom. So I began by saying she stoops to conquer.

JOHN: That's a good one, Pop.

BRADLEY: Yes, they liked that. I can still get on my feet if called upon. They still want me to be the Master of Ceremonies at the annual fund raiser for the art gallery. They still ask me to do that.

JOHN: That's great, Pop.

BRADLEY: Of course, we all know what Emerson says, "The music that can deepest reach, and cure all ills, is cordial speech." Doesn't Emerson tell us that?

JOHN: I think he does, Pop.

BRADLEY: You're the publisher in the family. You should know.

JOHN: *(Going to bookcase again.)* Let me look it up.

BRADLEY: It doesn't matter.

JOHN: It'll be right here, in Bartlett's. *(Takes down a book.)*

BRADLEY: No! We are not going to destroy the rhythm of the conversation with a lot of disruptive excursions to the bookcase.

JOHN: *(Putting the book back.)* O.K.

BRADLEY: Besides, I know Emerson said it. I'm positive.

JOHN: O.K., Pop.

(Bradley sits in what is obviously his special chair.)

BRADLEY: *(After a pause.)* Well. Your mother tells me you've written a play.

JOHN: That's right.

BRADLEY: Another play.

JOHN: Right.

BRADLEY: *(Indicating manuscript on table.)* Is that it?

JOHN: That's it.

BRADLEY: Do you think this one will get on?

JOHN: I think so.

BRADLEY: Some of them don't, you know.

JOHN: I know that, Pop.

BRADLEY: I don't mean just yours. Apparently it's a very difficult thing to get them done.

JOHN: That's for sure.

BRADLEY: Of course nobody goes to the theatre any more. Ted Moffatt just made a trip to New York to see his new grandson. I said, "Did you go to the theatre, Ted? Did you see any new plays?" He said he did not. He said all they do these days in the theatre is stand around and shout obscenities at each other. And then take off their clothes. Ted said he wouldn't be caught dead at the theatre. And Ted was once a big theatre-goer.

JOHN: There's some good stuff down there, Pop.

BRADLEY: For you, maybe. Not for me. *(Pause.)* We liked that play of yours we saw in Boston.

JOHN: Thanks.

BRADLEY: Done at some college, wasn't it?

JOHN: Boston University.

BRADLEY: We liked that one. Your mother particularly liked it. She thought it was quite amusing.

JOHN: Tell the critics that.

BRADLEY: Oh well, the critics. They're not infallible.

JOHN: I'll keep that in mind, Pop.

(Pause.)

BRADLEY: We liked that little play of yours we saw in New York a couple of years ago.

JOHN: I thought you *didn't* like it.

BRADLEY: No, we did. Miserable little theatre. Impossible seats. Impossible bathrooms. But the play had charm.

JOHN: Thanks, Pop.

BRADLEY: Or at least the actress did. What was her name again?

JOHN: Swoosie Kurtz.

BRADLEY: Yes. Swoosie Kurtz. Amusing name. Amusing actress. I hear she's gone on to do very well. Your mother saw her on television.

JOHN: She's great.

BRADLEY: Lovely profile. Lovely shoulders. She was very attractive in your play.

JOHN: I'll tell her.

BRADLEY: Yes, do. Tell her your father liked her very much. *(Pause. He eyes the manuscript on the coffee table.)* And now you've written another one.

JOHN: Tried to.

BRADLEY: Looks a little long.

JOHN: They'll make me cut it.

BRADLEY: I hope they make you cut it a good deal.

JOHN: They probably will.

BRADLEY: Nobody likes long plays.

JOHN: I know that, Pop.

BRADLEY: Everyone likes to get it over with promptly, and go home to bed.

JOHN: I know.

BRADLEY: Will Swoosie Kurtz be in this one?

JOHN: I doubt it.

BRADLEY: I hope you get someone who's just as much fun.

JOHN: This play's a little different, Pop.

BRADLEY: Different? How is it different?

JOHN: It's not as light as the others.

BRADLEY: Don't tell me you're getting gloomy in your middle years.

JOHN: Not gloomy, exactly, Pop.

BRADLEY: Are people going to scream and shout in this one?

JOHN: They might raise their voices occasionally.

BRADLEY: Are they going to take off their clothes?

JOHN: No, they won't do that, I promise.

BRADLEY: Put Swoosie Kurtz in it. She wouldn't shout. Though I suppose I wouldn't mind if she took off her clothes.

(Pause.)

JOHN: This one's about us, Pop.

BRADLEY: Us?

JOHN: The family.

BRADLEY: Oh really?

JOHN: This one cuts pretty close to home.

BRADLEY: Oh well. I understand that. You have to deal with what you know. I do it when I'm toastmaster. I sometimes mention your mother. I refer occasionally to you children. At the Shoemaker's wedding, I told an amusing story about Jigger.

JOHN: This one's about you, Pop.

BRADLEY: Me?

JOHN: You.

BRADLEY: Just me?

JOHN: No, no. Mother's in it, of course. And Nina. And Jigger's referred to a lot. And I put myself in it. But I think it centers around you.

BRADLEY: Me.

JOHN: I thought I better tell you that, Pop.

BRADLEY: And it's going on?

JOHN: It's supposed to.

BRADLEY: In New York?

JOHN: That's the talk.

BRADLEY: When?

JOHN: Soon. Supposedly.

(Pause.)

BRADLEY: Do you use our names?

JOHN: Of course not, Pop.

BRADLEY: But it's recognizably us.

JOHN: By people who know us.

BRADLEY: What about people who don't know us?

JOHN: They'll sense it's a personal play.

(Pause.)

BRADLEY: I suppose you make cracks.

JOHN: Cracks?

BRADLEY: Wisecracks. Smart remarks.

JOHN: Not really.

BRADLEY: "Not really." What does that mean, "not really"?

JOHN: I just try to show who we are, Pop.

BRADLEY: Oh, I'm sure. I know what you write. I remember that crack you made about your grandmother in one of your plays.

JOHN: What crack?

BRADLEY: You know very well what crack. You poked fun at her. You ridiculed her. My dear sweet mother who never hurt a fly. That gracious lady who took you to the Erlanger Theatre every Saturday afternoon. That saint of a woman without whom you wouldn't even know what a play *was!*

JOHN: I didn't ridicule her, Pop.

BRADLEY: People laughed. I was there. I heard them laugh at your grandmother. Complete strangers roaring their heads off at my poor dear mother—I can't discuss it.

JOHN: Come on, Pop.

BRADLEY: I don't think you've written anything in your life where you haven't sneaked in a lot of smart-guy wisecracks about our family and our way of life.

JOHN: Please, Pop…

BRADLEY: That story you wrote at boarding school, that show you did at college…

JOHN: You never came to that show.

BRADLEY: I didn't want to come. I knew, I *knew* what you'd say.

JOHN: It was just fun, Pop.

BRADLEY: Oh yes? Well, your idea of fun and my idea of fun are very different. My idea does not include making fools out of your family.

JOHN: Oh Jesus.

BRADLEY: And don't swear! It's demeaning to both of us.

JOHN: O.K., O.K. I'm sorry.

(*Pause.*)

BRADLEY: And you've found producers for this thing?

JOHN: Yes.

BRADLEY: They'll lose their shirt.

JOHN: Maybe.

BRADLEY: They'll go completely bankrupt.

JOHN: Come on, Pop.

BRADLEY: What did that critic say about your last play? What was his remark?

JOHN: He said we weren't worth writing about.

BRADLEY: There you are. You see? Nobody cares about our way of life.

JOHN: I care, Pop.

BRADLEY: You? You've never cared in your life. You've gone out of your way *not* to care. Where were you for our fortieth anniversary? Where were you for my seventy-fifth birthday?

JOHN: You said not to come.

BRADLEY: I didn't want you snickering in the corner, making snide remarks. Oh God, I should have known. I should have known that's why you came up here this weekend. Not to visit your parents in their waning years. Not to touch base with the city that nourished you half your life. Oh no. Nothing like that. Simply to announce that you plan to humiliate us all in front of a lot of strangers in New York City.

JOHN: I came home to get your permission, Pop.

BRADLEY: My permission?

JOHN: I haven't signed any contract yet.

BRADLEY: Then don't.

JOHN: *(After a moment.)* All right, I won't.

BRADLEY: How can I give my permission for a thing like that?

JOHN: All right, Pop.

BRADLEY: How can I approve of someone fouling his own nest?

JOHN: I don't foul—

BRADLEY: How can I possibly seal my own doom?

JOHN: Oh, come on, Pop.

BRADLEY: I suppose I have no legal recourse.

JOHN: The play's *off,* Pop.

BRADLEY: I mean, you don't need to write plays anyway. You have a perfectly good job in publishing.

JOHN: That just keeps me going, Pop.

BRADLEY: It's a fine job. It's a solid, dependable, respectable job.

JOHN: It's not what I really want to do.

BRADLEY: Well, do it anyway. Most men in this world spend a lifetime doing what they don't want to do. And they work harder at it than you do.

JOHN: Come on, Pop…

BRADLEY: After I'm dead, after your mother's dead, after everyone you can possibly hurt has long since gone, then you can write your plays. And you can put them on wherever you want—New York, Hollywood, right here in Memorial Auditorium, I don't care. But not now. Please.

JOHN: O.K.

BRADLEY: I'm tired.

JOHN: O.K., Pop.

BRADLEY: I'm not well.

JOHN: I know, Pop.

BRADLEY: I'm not well at all.

JOHN: Case closed, Pop. Really.

BRADLEY: Thank you very much.

> *(Pause. They are awkward alone.)*

BRADLEY: Sure you don't want a drink?

JOHN: No thanks.

> *(Pause.)*

BRADLEY: Where's your mother?…Suddenly I thoroughly miss your mother. *(Going to doorway, calling off.)* Darling, where are you?

ANN'S VOICE: *(Offstage.)* I'm bringing cheese!

BRADLEY: *(To John.)* She's bringing cheese. *(Eyeing manuscript.)* Did you tell her about this play?

JOHN: Yes.

BRADLEY: Did she read it?

JOHN: She said she didn't want to.

BRADLEY: Why not?

JOHN: I'm not sure.

BRADLEY: That's the trouble. We never are, with your mother.

> *(Ann enters, carrying a plate of crackers and cheese. She is a lovely woman, richly and fashionably dressed.)*

ANN: There.

> *(Both men immediately get to their feet.)*

ANN: I think I may have established a modicum of order in the kitchen.

> *(She waits for John to move his script out of the way, then puts the plate of hors d'oeuvres on the coffee table.)*

ANN: And now I can at least pretend to relax.

BRADLEY: What would you like to drink, darling?

ANN: *(Crossing to close the curtains.)* After almost fifty years of marriage, you know very well what I'd like.

BRADLEY: After almost fifty years of marriage, I know very well always to ask.

ANN: Then I'd like a very dry martini with plenty of ice…

ANN AND BRADLEY: …and a small twist of lemon.

BRADLEY: Thy will be done. *(He goes to the bar, mixes the drink carefully for her.)*

ANN: *(To John, after she has partially pulled the curtains.)* Don't ask me when we'll eat. We are flying on a wing and a prayer in the dinner department.

JOHN: Who've you got out there, Mother? Mildred? Agnes? Who?

ANN: Neither one. Mildred has broken her hip, and Agnes has gone to meet her maker.

JOHN: Aw…

ANN. What I have, out there, is Agnes's cousin's niece, who arrived in a snappy red convertible, and whose name is Cheryl Marie, and who I suspect has never made gravy in her life.

JOHN: We should have just made dinner ourselves, Mother.

ANN. Oh yes. "Ourselves." I've heard that one before. "Ourselves"… "Ourselves" means me. It means that yours truly is slaving away out there while the rest of you are enjoying the cocktail hour in here. No thank you, John. I believe in paying people to do things occasionally, even if the person paid happens to be named Cheryl Marie. *(She sits on the couch.)*

BRADLEY: *(Handing her a drink.)* Here you are, darling.

ANN: Thank you, dear. *(To John.)* No, I'm sorry. The cocktail hour is sacred, in my humble opinion. Even when your father and I are home alone, we still have it. In the kitchen. While I'm cooking. *(She holds out her hand automatically for a cocktail napkin.)*

BRADLEY: *(Handing her a stack of cocktail napkins.)* That's why we did the kitchen over. So we could have it in there.

ANN: I know you children all think you're too busy to have it.

BRADLEY: You're missing something.

ANN: I think so, too.

BRADLEY: *(Joining Ann on the couch.)* We're never too busy for the cocktail hour.

ANN: It allows people to unwind.

BRADLEY: It allows people to sit down together at the end of the day…

ANN: To talk things over…Settle things down…

BRADLEY: The bishop used to say—remember this, darling?—Bishop Dow used to say when he came here for dinner that the cocktail hour took the place of evening prayers.

ANN: Well, I don't know about that.

BRADLEY: No, he did. That's what he said.

ANN: Well, all I know is I cherish it. And now I want to know what I've already missed.

JOHN: Nothing.

BRADLEY: We had a brief discussion of the contemporary theatre.

JOHN: Which terminated rather abruptly.

ANN: *(Looking from one to the other.)* Oh. *(Pause.)* Who'll have some brie? Bradley?

BRADLEY: No, thank you.

ANN: John?

JOHN: *(Pulling up a footstool.)* Thanks.

ANN: I must say I love the theatre.

BRADLEY: Used to love it.

ANN: It used to be very much a part of our lives.

BRADLEY: Years ago. Before the Erlanger Theatre was torn down.

ANN: All the plays would come here.

BRADLEY: All the good plays.

JOHN: I remember…

ANN: Such wonderful plays. With such wonderful plots. They were always about these attractive couples…

BRADLEY: And the husband would have committed some minor indiscretion…

ANN: Normally the wife did, darling.

BRADLEY: No, no. I think it was he…

ANN: She did it more, sweetie. The *wife* was normally the naughty one.

BRADLEY: Well, whoever it was, they were all very attractive about it. And they'd have these attractive leading ladies…

ANN: Gertrude Lawrence, Ina Claire, Katharine Hepburn…

BRADLEY: They'd all come here…

JOHN: I remember your talking about them…

BRADLEY: Your mother played tennis with Hepburn at the Tennis Club.

ANN: Oh, I think we hit a ball or two…

BRADLEY: Your mother beat her.

ANN: Oh, I don't think I *beat* her, Bradley.

BRADLEY: You beat Katharine Hepburn, my love.

ANN: I think we might have played a little doubles, darling.

BRADLEY: You beat Hepburn, six-three, six-four! *That* I remember!

ANN: Well, maybe I did.

BRADLEY: And we met the Lunts.

ANN: Oh, the Lunts, the Lunts…

BRADLEY: They were friends of Bill Hart's. So we all met at the Statler for a cocktail. After a matinee.

ANN: They were terribly amusing.

JOHN: I remember your telling me about the Lunts.

BRADLEY: They could both talk at exactly the same time…

(They do this, of course.)

ANN: Without interrupting each other…

BRADLEY: It was uncanny…

ANN: They'd say the wittiest things…

BRADLEY: Simultaneously…

ANN: And you'd understand both…

BRADLEY: It was absolutely uncanny.

ANN: Of course they'd been married so long…

BRADLEY: Knew each other so well…

ANN: They made you feel very sophisticated.

(They both unconsciously cross their legs at the same time.)

BRADLEY: *(Touching her hand.)* They made you feel proud to be married.

ANN: Absolutely. I totally agree. *(Pause.)* I wish you'd write plays like that, John.

BRADLEY: Won't do it. Refuses to. Simply doesn't want to.

ANN: But I mean, there's a real *need.* Jane Babcock went to Connecticut last weekend to visit her old roommate from Westover, and they thought they'd go into New York to see a play. Well, they looked in the paper and there was absolutely nothing they wanted to see. Finally, they decided to take a chance on one of those noisy English musicals. But when they called for tickets the man said he was going to charge them three dollars extra. Just for telephoning. When they were calling long distance anyway. Well, that did it, of course. They went to the movies instead. And apparently the movie was perfectly horrible. People were shooting each other—in the *face!*…and using the most repulsive language while they were doing it, and the audience was composed of noisy teen-agers who screamed and yelled and rattled candy wrappers all around them. Finally they walked out and drove back to New Canaan, thoroughly disappointed with each other and the world. Jane said they really didn't snap out of it until they had cocktails.

BRADLEY: It's all over. The life we led is completely gone.

ANN: Jane said if one of your plays had been on, John, they would have gone to that. And paid the extra three dollars, too.

JOHN: *(Glancing at Bradley.)* My plays are a sore subject, Mother.

ANN: Oh dear.

BRADLEY: A very sore subject.

ANN: Yes, well, it seems that John at least makes some attempt to write about things we know.

BRADLEY: Oh yes. Undercutting, trivializing…

ANN: Oh now, darling…

BRADLEY: *(Looking warily at manuscript.)* What's it called, this play?

JOHN: It's called *The Cocktail Hour,* actually.

BRADLEY: It's called the *what?*

JOHN: *The Cocktail Hour.*

BRADLEY: That's a terrible title.

ANN: Oh now, sweetheart…

BRADLEY: Terrible.

JOHN: Why is it terrible?

BRADLEY: To begin with, it's been used.

JOHN: That's *The Cocktail PARTY,* Pop. That's T.S. Eliot.

BRADLEY: Even worse. We walked out on that one.

ANN: This is *The Cocktail HOUR,* darling.

BRADLEY: Doesn't make any difference.

ANN: No, it does. A cocktail *party* is a public thing. You *invite* people to a cocktail party. A cocktail *hour* is family. It's private. It's personal. It's very different.

BRADLEY: Nobody will know that. It will confuse everyone. They'll come expecting T.S. Eliot, and they'll get John. Either way, they'll want their money back.

JOHN: They won't want anything back, Pop. I'm putting it on the shelf. Remember?

ANN: On the shelf?

BRADLEY: Where I hope it will remain for a very long time.

ANN: Is that the solution?

BRADLEY: That's the solution. We've agreed on that, that's what we've agreed on. *(He goes into the hall to check the barometer.)*

ANN: Oh dear. *(Pause.)* How's Ellen, by the way?

JOHN: Fine.

ANN: I wish she had come along.

JOHN: She had a conference today, Mother.

ANN: Oh, I think that's wonderful. I wish I'd had a job when I was young.

BRADLEY: *(From the hall.)* All changing, all going…

ANN: And how are the children?

JOHN: Fine. Getting on. Growing up. Charlie already plans to go all the way out to the University of Colorado.

BRADLEY: All gone…Married couples leading totally different lives. Children scattered all over the map…

ANN: I wish you'd brought them all along.

BRADLEY: *(Returning to the room.)* I wish Jigger had come.

ANN: I wish everyone had come. John's family, Jigger's…

BRADLEY: We could have made this a family reunion.

JOHN: Which is another play by T.S. Eliot.

BRADLEY: *(Crossing to piano.)* I don't care about that. All I know is that if Jigger had come, we'd be gathered around that piano right now. We'd be singing all the old songs: *Kiss Me, Kate—Southern Pacific…*

JOHN: It's *"South" Pacific,* Pop.

BRADLEY: Whatever it is, Jigger could play it. I miss him. I miss him terribly.

ANN: We miss *all* the family, Bradley. Everyone.

BRADLEY: Yes. That's right. Of course. *(To John, indicating the photographs on the piano.)* You have that lovely wife, you have those fine, strapping children, do you ever write about them? Do you ever write about how hard your wife has worked over those children? Do you ever tell how your son pitched a no-hitter in Little League? How your sweet Elsie won the art prize? Do you ever write about your brother winning the Sailing Cup? Do we ever hear anything good in your plays? Oh no. Instead you attack your parents in their old age.

JOHN: It's not an *attack,* Pop.

ANN: *(Quickly.)* What if you turned it into a book, John? Books aren't quite so public. Billy Leeming wrote some book about *his* parents, and our local bookstores didn't even bother to carry it. Is it all right if he puts us in a book, Bradley?

JOHN: I can't write it as a book.

ANN: You can certainly try. *(To Bradley.)* It seems a shame to waste all that work.

BRADLEY: *(Looking out a window.)* Where's Nina? Where's our daughter? She's normally right on time.

ANN: I think she had to do something with Portia. She'll be here. Meanwhile, I'd like another drink, Bradley. A weak one—but nonetheless, another.

JOHN: I'll get it.

ANN: No, your father likes to get it.

BRADLEY: While I still can. *(He bends over to get her glass with some difficulty.)*

JOHN: Your back O.K., Pop?

ANN: He's got a pinched nerve.

BRADLEY: Your mother thinks it's a pinched nerve.

ANN: Dr. Randall thinks it's a pinched nerve.

BRADLEY: Well, I think it's something far more serious.

JOHN: What do you think it is, Pop?

BRADLEY: Never mind. We'll call it a pinched nerve because that makes people more comfortable. We'll settle for a pinched nerve. *(He goes to mix Ann's drink.)*

ANN: *(Silently mouthing the words to John.)* It's a pinched nerve.

BRADLEY: *(Mixing her drink.)* And when I was in the hospital with double pneumonia, it was just a cold. I was lying there half-dead with a temperature of one hundred and four, and people would telephone, very much concerned, and your mother would say, "Oh, he's fine, he's perfectly fine, it's just a cold." When they're lowering me into my grave, she'll tell all my friends that it's hay fever. *(He works on her drink.)*

ANN: *(Eyeing the manuscript.)* I suppose I should at least read the thing.

JOHN: Don't if you don't want to.

ANN: Maybe if I read it, it wouldn't seem so frightening.

BRADLEY: Who's frightened? Nobody's frightened.

ANN: Trouble is, it's always so painful, John. Reading your things. And seeing them acted, it's even worse. With all those people *watching.*

BRADLEY: It won't be acted.

ANN: But it should be *done,* Bradley.

BRADLEY: Not this one, please.

ANN: But he's written it. It's his *career.*

BRADLEY: *(As he stirs Ann's drink.)* It's not his career. Publishing is his career. That's what's paid the bills and brought up those children. That, and considerable help from you and me. What we're talking about here is an amusing little hobby which probably costs more than it brings in. Which is fine. We all have hobbies. I like my golf. I like to travel. But I don't use my hobby to attack my parents or make them look foolish in the eyes of the world.

(Ann finally gets her drink out of his hands.)

JOHN: It's not a hobby! And I don't attack!

BRADLEY: Well, I don't care. I don't want to be on some stage. I don't want to have some actor imitating me. I've got very little time left on this earth…

ANN: Oh, Bradley…

BRADLEY: Very little. Much less than anyone thinks.

ANN: Now stop that, Bradley.

BRADLEY: And I don't want people laughing at me, or critics commenting about me, or the few friends I have left commiserating with me in these final days. I don't want that, John. I'm sorry. No. *(He crosses to sit in his chair.)*

ANN: One thing, John. If you don't do it, you won't get your name in the paper. And that's a good thing, in my humble opinion. I've never liked the publicity which happens with plays. It always seemed slightly cheap to me.

BRADLEY: Of course it is.

ANN: And it's dangerous. People read your name, and think you're rich, and rob you. Peggy Fentriss had her name in the paper for her work with the Philharmonic, and when she went to Bermuda, these burglars backed up a whole truck They even took a grapefruit she left in the refrigerator.

BRADLEY: *(Suddenly.)* What do you stand to lose if you don't put this thing on?

JOHN: *(Ironically.)* Just my life, that's all, Pop. Just my life.

BRADLEY: Money. I'm talking about money. How much money would you make on it?

JOHN: You can't tell, Pop.

BRADLEY: Give me an educated guess.

JOHN: Oh…A little. If we're lucky.

BRADLEY: "A little. If we're lucky." What kind of an answer is that? No wonder you never went into business.

JOHN: I don't *know*, Pop.

ANN: I don't see why we have to talk about money, Bradley.

BRADLEY: What's the average amount of money you've made on your other plays?

JOHN: Average?

BRADLEY: Give me an average amount…Five thousand? Ten? What?

JOHN: Pop…

BRADLEY: *(Crossing to the desk.)* I will give you a check for twenty thousand dollars right now for not putting on that play.

ANN: Bradley!

BRADLEY: Twenty thousand dollars… *(He sits down at the desk, finds his checkbook, makes out a check.)*

JOHN: Oh, Pop…

ANN: *(Putting down her drink.)* Twenty *thousand!*

BRADLEY: You can't cash it, of course, till Monday, till I've covered it from savings, but I am hereby giving you a check.

JOHN: I don't want a check.

BRADLEY: Well, you might as well take it, because if you don't, I'll simply leave you twenty thousand extra in my will.

ANN: Oh, Bradley, now stop it!

BRADLEY: *(Holding out the check to John.)* Here. It's a good deal. You'll be twenty thousand to the good, and you can still put the thing on after I'm dead.

JOHN: *(Walking away from it.)* Pop, I can't…

BRADLEY: *(Following him.)* And if you invest it, you'll have the interest besides, which you wouldn't have otherwise.

ANN: I can't stand this

JOHN: I don't want that money, Pop!

BRADLEY: And I don't want that play! I want some peace and privacy in the few days I have left of my life. And I'm willing to pay for it. Now there it is. *(Puts the check on the table by his chair.)* If you have any business sense at all, you'll take it. And if you don't want it for yourself, then give it to your children, who I hope will show more respect for you in your old age than you've ever shown for me.

JOHN: Oh, Pop, oh, Pop, oh, Pop…

(Nina's voice is heard from the hall.)

NINA'S VOICE: Hello!

ANN: Ah. There's Nina. (Calling off.) We're having cocktails, dear! (To others.) I think it might be time to change the subject.

(Nina enters, well-dressed, attractive, mid-forties, removing her raincoat.)

NINA: (Kissing her mother.) I'm terribly sorry I'm late. Portia's in trouble again.

ANN: Oh no.

JOHN: Who's Portia?

NINA: (Kissing her father.) She was up all night, wandering from room to room, sighing and groaning.

ANN: Oh no.

BRADLEY: That sweet Portia.

JOHN: Who's Portia?

NINA: And we also think there's something radically wrong with her rear end.

(She tosses her raincoat on the banister.)

ANN: Oh no.

BRADLEY: Poor thing.

JOHN: Who the hell is *Portia*?

NINA: (Kissing her brother.) Portia is our new golden retriever, and we're very worried about her.

BRADLEY: Portia is a brilliant beast. You should write a play about Portia.

JOHN: I could call it *Practical Dogs*. As opposed to *Practical Cats*. By T. S. Eliot.

BRADLEY: What would you like to drink, Pookins?

NINA: Just white wine, please.

JOHN: I'll get it, Pop.

BRADLEY: (Crossing to bar.) *I'll* get it. I'm still capable of officiating at my own bar.

NINA: Plenty of rocks, please. And plenty of soda water. My stomach is in absolute knots.

JOHN: Over Portia?

BRADLEY: Portia is superb. I adore Portia.

NINA: Over everything.

ANN: Poor Nina, and her nervous stomach.

NINA: Let's not talk about my stomach, Mother. Let's talk about John. I hear you've written another play, John. (Sitting on the couch.)

BRADLEY: We're not discussing it.

NINA: Why not?

ANN: It's a sore subject.

NINA: Why?

ANN: Apparently it's primarily about you-know-who.

NINA: Oh. *(Pause. She sees it on the coffee table.)* Is that it?

ANN: That's it.

(Nina gingerly lifts the cover and looks inside.)

NINA: *(Reading.)* The Cocktail Hour. Hmmm.

BRADLEY: Stupid title.

NINA: They'll confuse it with Eliot.

BRADLEY: Exactly, Pookins.

NINA: Is it going on?

BRADLEY: No.

ANN: Maybe not.

JOHN: I came up to ask his permission.

BRADLEY: And I said no.

NINA: Hmmm.

BRADLEY: *(Bringing her a glass of wine.)* Here's your wine, darling.

NINA: Thank you. *(Pause.)* Is Mother in it?

ANN: Apparently I am.

NINA: Is Jigger?

BRADLEY: I hope not. *(He sits in his chair.)*

JOHN: Well, he is. In a way.

NINA: Are you in it, John?

JOHN: I'm afraid I am.

BRADLEY: I think we've said enough on the subject. I want to know where Ed is, Pookins. I thought Ed would be with you.

NINA: Ed's in New York. On business for the bank.

BRADLEY: I see. Well, we'll miss him.

ANN: *(Now doing her needlepoint.)* Oh yes. We'll miss Ed.

NINA: *(To John.)* Am I in it?

JOHN: I think Pop wants us to change the subject.

BRADLEY: Thank you, John.

NINA: I just want to know if I'm *in* it.

JOHN: Yes, you are.

NINA: Oh God.

BRADLEY: Tell us about the children, Pookins. I want to hear about my grand-children.

NINA: They're all fine, Pop. *(She picks up script, holds it to her ear.)*

ANN: What are you doing, dear?

NINA: I think I heard this thing ticking.

ANN: *(Laughing.)* That's funny.

NINA: Do you think we should drop it in a big bucket of water?

BRADLEY: I think we should change the subject. Tell me about Andy. Does he like his job?

NINA: He likes it fine, Pop. *(To John, as she thumbs through the script.)* I hate to think what you do to me in this thing.

JOHN: You come out all right.

NINA: I'll bet. Am I the wicked older sister?

JOHN: No.

NINA: Am I the uptight, frustrated, bossy bitch?

JOHN: No, no.

NINA: Well, what am I, then?

JOHN: Actually, you play a relatively minor role.

ANN: Sounds like you're lucky, dear.

BRADLEY: Tell me about Wendy. Is Wendy doing well at Williams? Does she still want to be in business?

NINA: Do I get a *name*, at least? What's my name here?

JOHN: I call you Diana.

ANN: Diana?

JOHN: *(To Nina.)* Isn't that what you used to wish your name was? The Goddess Diana, Protectress of Wild Animals

ANN: I knew a Diana Finch once. She used to climb down drainpipes and hang around drugstores. No, I don't like the name.

NINA: Well, it's better than *Nina,* Mother. Which means little Ann. Little you. Sweet little carbon copy.

BRADLEY: I asked you a question about Wendy, Pookins.

NINA: *(Impatiently.)* She's fine, Pop. *(She continues to thumb.)* I only see about ten pages of Diana here, *(More thumbing.)* and in the second act, less than that.

JOHN: It's what's known as a supporting role.

NINA: Supporting? What do I support?

ANN: I imagine all of us dear. You give us all support. Which is true.

BRADLEY: May we talk about something else?

NINA: Do I get to bring in trays? Or do I just carry a spear?

JOHN: You come and go.

NINA: Come and go? Mostly go, I'd say, thank you very much. *(Reads.)* "Diana exits huffily." Oh boy, there it is. "Huffily." Jesus, John. *(She gets up huffily.)*

BRADLEY: All right, then. *(He goes to the bookcase, gets a large volume—Life's Pictured History of World War II—and takes it to a chair in the front hall where he begins to thumb through it determinedly.)* While all of you continue to concentrate on one very tiresome subject, I will try to exercise my mind. Let me know, please, if, as, and when you're willing to broaden the discussion. *(He turns his back on the group.)*

NINA: I just think it's interesting I always play a minor role in this family.

ANN: That's not true, darling.

JOHN: You were the one who always owned the dogs.

ANN: We gave you that lovely coming-out party.

JOHN: You got that trip to Europe.

ANN: You had the most beautiful wedding...

BRADLEY: *(From the hall.)* You got my mother's tea set after she died, Pookins.

JOHN: Jigger and I used to call you the Gravy Train Girl.

NINA: Well, not any more, apparently.

ANN: Maybe you're lucky to get off the hook, dear.

NINA: Oh boy, John. I swear. It's the old story. Once again, you and Jigger, who never show up here, who come up once a year for a day or two, *if* we're lucky, when we have to drop everything we're doing and rush to be at your beck and call—once again, you two end up getting all the attention, whereas I, I, who have remained here since I was married, who have lived here all my *life*...who see Mother and Pop at least once a week, who have them for Christmas and Thanksgiving and even *Easter*, for God's sake...I, who got Pop to go to a younger doctor...I, me, who drove Mother all over town for *weeks* after her cataract operation...who found them a new cleaning woman when their old one just walked *out!*...once again I am told I play a goddamn minor ROLE!

ANN: Now, now...Now, now.

BRADLEY: *(From the hall.)* You've been a wonderful daughter, Pookins.

NINA: *(Crossing to the bar.)* Wonderful or not, I need another drink.

ANN: Be careful, darling. Your stomach.

NINA: Oh, what difference does that make? Who cares? I just play a minor role. If I get ulcers, they're minor ulcers. If I die, it's a minor death.

JOHN: Nina, hey, lookit. I kept trying to build up your part.

NINA: I'll bet.

JOHN: I did. But I never got anywhere.

NINA: Why not?

JOHN: I never could get your number.

BRADLEY: *(From the hall.)* I don't know why anybody has to get anybody else's number.

JOHN: No, I mean, you always seem so content around here.

NINA: Con*tent?*

JOHN: Good husband. Good kids. Good life. You always came out seeming so comfortable and at home.

BRADLEY: *(From the hall.)* I should damn well hope so.

NINA: *Me?* Is this *me* you're talking about? Comfortable and at home?

ANN: He's giving you a compliment, dear.

NINA: Is he? Is that a compliment? Comfortable and at home? Oh boy, that's a laugh. That's a good one, John. Boy, you've really painted me into a corner. Ask Dr. Randall how comfortable I am. Ask him to show you the X-rays of my insides. He'll show you what it's like to be at home.

BRADLEY: *(Coming back in.)* Pookins, sweetheart…

NINA: *(Revving up.)* Do you know anything about my *life,* John? Have you ever bothered to inquire what I *do* around here, all these years you've been away? Did you know that I am Vice-President of the S.P.C.A.?

ANN: *And* on the hospital board. *And* the School for the Blind. *And* the gift shop at the gallery…

NINA: Did you know that I am interested in seeing-eye *dogs,* John? Did you know that? I am profoundly interested in them. I'm good with dogs, I'm the best, everyone says that, and what I want to do more than anything else in the world is go to this two-year school in Cleveland where you do nothing but work with seeing-eye dogs.

ANN: You can't just commute to Cleveland, darling.

NINA: I *know* that, Mother.

JOHN: Why can't you?

NINA: Because I have a husband, John. Because I have a—*life!*

BRADLEY: And a very good life it is, Pookins.

NINA: I mean, what am I supposed to *do,* John? Start subsidizing Eastern Airlines every other *day?* Live in some *motel?* Rattle around some strange city where I don't know a *soul?* Just because I want to work with…because I happen to feel an attachment to…oh God. *(She starts to cry.)*

BRADLEY: *(Going to her.)* Oh now, Pookins…Now stop, sweetie pie…

ANN: I didn't realize people could get quite so upset about dogs.

BRADLEY: It's not dogs, it's John. *(Wheeling on John.)* You see what happens? You arrive here and within half-an-hour, you've thrown the whole family into disarray. It's happened all your life. Par for the course, my friend.

Par for the course. *(Comforting Nina.)* Now calm down, sweetheart. He's not going to do the play anyway.

NINA: *(Breaking away.)* Well, he should! He should do one about *me!* You've never written about me, John. Ever. Why don't you, some time? Why don't you write about a woman who went to the right schools, and married the right man, and lived on the right street all the days of her life, and ended up feeling perfectly terrible! *(She runs out of the room and upstairs.)*

BRADLEY: There you are, John. You satisfied? Will you put that in your play? Or do you still want to concentrate all your guns on your dying father? *(He goes out after Nina, calling.)* Wait. Nina. Pookins Sweetheart... *(He follows her off and upstairs.)*

(Pause.)

ANN: *(Holding out her glass.)* I might have just a splash more, John.

JOHN: *(Taking her glass.)* O.K., Mother.

ANN: Just a splash. I'm serious.

JOHN: *(Mixing it.)* Right.

ANN: You're not having anything?

JOHN: Can't seem to get away with it these days, Mother.

ANN: What does that mean?

JOHN: Very quickly, I turn into an angry drunk.

ANN: Good heavens. Why is that?

JOHN: I don't know... *(Looks where his father has gone.)* I guess I'm sore about something. *(Pause.)* Is he as sick as he says he is, Mother?

ANN: You know your father.

JOHN: He keeps saying he's dying.

ANN: He's been saying that for years. He announced it on his fortieth birthday. He reminds us of it whenever he gets a cold. Lately, when we go to bed, he doesn't say "goodnight" any more. He says, "goodbye," because he thinks he won't last till morning.

JOHN: But you think he's O.K.?

ANN: I think...No, I *know,* we all know, that he has a blood problem, a kind of leukemia, which seems to be in remission now. Somehow I don't think that will kill him. Something else will.

JOHN: You think my play will?

ANN: *He* seems to think it will.

JOHN: Oh God...

ANN: And *you* must think it might, John. Otherwise you never would have bothered to clear it with him.

JOHN: I almost wish I hadn't.

ANN: I'm glad you did. It shows you have strong family feelings.

JOHN: Family feelings, family feelings! The story of my life! The bane of my existence! Family feelings. Dear Mother, dear Pop. May I have permission to cross the street? May I have permission to buy a car? Would you mind very much if I screwed my girl?

ANN: Now that's enough of that, please.

JOHN: Well, it's true! Family feelings. May I have your approval to put on a play? Oh God, why did I come here? Why did I bother? Most playwrights dish out the most brutal diatribes against their parents, who sit proudly in the front row and applaud every insult that comes along. Me? Finally—after fifteen years of beating around the bush—I come up with something which is—all right, maybe a little on the nose, maybe a little frank, maybe a little satiric at times—but still clearly infused with warmth, respect, and an abiding affection, and what happens? I'm being censored, banned, bribed not to produce.

ANN: I still wish you'd make it a book.

JOHN: Oh, Mother...

ANN: No, I'm serious. Books are quieter.

JOHN: I can't write books

ANN: You work on them all the time.

JOHN: But I can't write them.

ANN: Plays are so noisy.

JOHN: I know.

ANN: They cause such attention.

JOHN: I know.

ANN: I don't mean just for us. I mean for you, as well.

JOHN: I know, Mother.

ANN: Those reviews must hurt terribly. The bad ones.

JOHN: They do.

ANN: All coming out together. Wave after wave. Every little suburban newspaper putting in its two-cents worth. And they can all be so mean.

JOHN: Right.

ANN: Book reviewers seem kinder, somehow. You have the feeling that people who write books get their friends to review them.

JOHN: Yes...

ANN: But not with plays. I mean, who *are* those people who review plays? What do they do when they're not sitting around criticizing?

JOHN: I hear some of them are decent folks, Mother.

ANN: They well may be, but I don't think they have the faintest notion what you're writing about.

JOHN: Sometimes they don't seem to.

ANN: They don't like us, John. They resent us. They think we're all Republicans, and all superficial, and all alcoholics.

JOHN: I know.

ANN: *(Taking a sip; with a twinkle.)* Only the latter is true.

(John laughs, possibly hugs her.)

ANN: I also think...

JOHN: What?

ANN: Never mind.

JOHN: No, come on, Mother. What?

ANN: I also think he's scared you'll spill the beans.

JOHN: The beans?

ANN: The beans.

JOHN: What beans?

ANN: Oh, John, face it. Everyone's got beans to spill. And, knowing you, you'll find a way to spill ours.

JOHN: I'm simply trying to tell the truth, Mother.

ANN: Fine. Good. But tell the truth in a *book*. Books take their time. Books *explain* things. If you have to do this, do it quietly and carefully in a book.

JOHN: I can't, Mother.

ANN: You can try.

JOHN: I *can't*. Maybe I'm a masochist, but I can't seem to write anything but plays. I can't write movies or television. I'm caught, I'm trapped in this old medium. It's artificial, it's archaic, it's restrictive beyond belief. It doesn't seem to have anything to do with contemporary American life. I feel like some medieval stone cutter, hacking away in the dark corner of an abandoned monastery, while everyone else is outside, having fun in the Renaissance. And when I finish, a few brooding inquisitors shuffle gloomily in, take a quick look, and say, "That's not it. That's not what we want at all!" Oh, God, why do I do it? Why write plays? Why are they the one thing in the world I want to do? Why have I always done them?

ANN: Not always, John. You used to write the most marvelous letters, for example. From camp. From boarding school...

JOHN: But I wrote plays long before that. Long before I could even write, I put on plays.

ANN: Oh well. Those things you did down in the playroom.

JOHN: They were *plays,* Mother. I'd clear the electric trains off the ping-pong table so it could be a stage. And I'd use up all the crayons in the house doing the scenery. And use up all my allowance bribing Nina and Jigger to be in them.

ANN: And then you'd drag your father and me down and we'd have to sit through the damn things.

JOHN: But they were plays, Mother.

ANN: Yes, I suppose they were.

JOHN: What were they about, Mother? Do you remember?

ANN: I do not.

JOHN: My psychiatrist keeps asking me what they were about. He says they could open a few doors for me, but I've blocked them all.

ANN: I wish you'd block that psychiatrist.

JOHN: But if there was a pattern to the plots, if there was some common theme to what I was doing, it would...

ANN: It would what?

JOHN: Explain things...I wish you could remember.

(Pause.)

ANN: You always gave yourself a leading part, I remember that.

JOHN: I'll bet.

ANN: And it seems to me you always played this foundling, this outsider, this adopted child...

JOHN: Is that true?

ANN: I think so. Your father and I would roll our eyes and think, what have we wrought. I mean, on you'd come, this poor prince who'd been adopted by beggars. Or else...

JOHN: What?

ANN: I remember one particularly silly one. You were the court jester. You put on a bathing suit and a red bathing cap and started dancing around, being very fresh.

JOHN: Hold it. Say that again. What did I wear?

ANN: You wore your little wool bathing trunks from Best and Company, and Nina's red bathing cap.

JOHN: *The Red-Headed Dummy.*

ANN: I suppose.

JOHN: No, I mean that was the title of my play: *The Red-Headed Dummy!* It's coming back!

ANN: Well, whatever it was, I remember it went on for*ever!* It made us late for dinner somewhere.

JOHN: Good God, Mother, I suddenly realize what I was doing in that play.

ANN: Well, *I* certainly don't.

JOHN: I think I know! And I think my shrink would agree!

ANN: I'm all ears.

JOHN: It's a little Freudian, Mother. It's a little raw.

ANN: Then I'm not terribly interested. *(Pause.)* What?

JOHN: What I was doing was parading my penis in front of my parents.

ANN: Oh, John, honestly.

JOHN: I was! The bathing suit, the red cap, *The Red-Headed Dummy!* Get it? I was doing a phallic dance.

ANN: John, don't be unattractive.

JOHN: No, no, really. I was playing my own penis. Smart kid, come to think of it. How many guys in the world get a chance to do that? Especially in front of their parents.

ANN: I think it's time to turn to another topic.

JOHN: No, but wait. Listen, Mother. I'll put it in a historical context. What I was doing was acting out a basic, primitive impulse which goes back to the Greeks. That's how comedy *originated,* Mother! The phallic dance! These peasants would do these gross dances in front of their overlords to see what they could get away with! And that's what I was doing, too, at three-years-old! Me! The Red-Headed Dummy! Dancing under the noses of my parents, before they went out to dinner! Saying, "Hey, you guys. Look. Look over here. I'm here, I'm alive, I'm wild, I have this penis with a mind of its own!" That's what I was doing then! That's what I've always done! That's what I'm doing right now, right in this room! And that's why I have to write plays, Mother. I have to keep doing it.
(Long pause.)

ANN: Are you finished, John?

JOHN: For now, at least.

ANN: All right, then, I want to say this: I don't like all this psychological talk, John. I never have. I think it's cheap and self-indulgent. I've never liked the fact that you've consulted a psychiatrist, and your father agrees with me. It upsets us very much to think that the money we give you at Christmas goes for paying that person rather than for taking your children to Aspen or somewhere. I don't like psychiatrists in general. Celia Underwood went to one, and now she bursts into tears whenever she plays bridge. Psychiatrists make you think about yourself too much. And about the bedroom too much. There's no need!

JOHN: Mother—

ANN: No, please let me finish. Now I want you to write, John. I think sometimes you write quite well, and I think it's a healthy enterprise. But I think you should write *books*. In books, you can talk the way you've just talked and it's not embarrassing. In books, you can go into people's minds…Now we all have things in our lives which we've done, or haven't done, which a book could make clear. I mean, I myself could tell you…I could tell you…I could tell you lots of things if I knew you would write them down quietly and carefully and sympathetically in a good, long book…
(Bradley enters.)
BRADLEY: What book?
ANN: We were just talking about the value of a good book, dear.
BRADLEY: *(Crossing to his chair.)* I agree with you. I'm reading the Bible now, John. I keep it right by my bed. It's surprisingly good reading. And excellent insurance.
ANN: How's Nina? And where's Nina?
BRADLEY: Nina is fine. Nina is dealing with a slight confusion in the kitchen.
ANN: *(Jumping up.)* I knew it. I could feel it in my bones. Tell me what happened.
BRADLEY: There was a slight misunderstanding about the oven.
ANN: Explain that, please.
BRADLEY: The oven was inadvertently turned off.
ANN: You mean that beautiful roast of beef…
BRADLEY: Is at the moment somewhat underdone.
ANN: Oh, I could cry.
BRADLEY: Now don't *worry*, darling. The oven is now working overtime. And there's even talk of Yorkshire pudding.
ANN: How can that creature make Yorkshire pudding if she can't cook a simple roast?
BRADLEY: Because I asked her to, darling. And because I presented her with another package of peas from the deep freeze.
ANN: Why more peas? What happened to the peas she had?
BRADLEY: I'm afraid there was a lack of attention to the right rear burner, darling.
ANN: Oh, I can't *stand* this! We'll be lucky if we eat by nine! I should have known never to take a chance on someone named Cheryl Marie! *(She hurries out, ad-libbing about the roast beef.)*
BRADLEY: *(Calling after her.)* Her name is Sharon, dear. *Sharon* Marie. *(Pause; to John.)* Do you have any servants in this play of yours?
JOHN: Not really.

BRADLEY: "Not really?" What does that mean, "Not really?" Does your producer have to pay for a maid or not?

JOHN: No, he doesn't, Pop.

BRADLEY: Probably just as well. Knowing you, you'd get them all wrong anyway.

JOHN: Thanks.

BRADLEY: Well, I mean, nobody understands how to treat servants today. Even your mother. She was born with them, they brought her breakfast in bed until she married me, and I'm afraid she takes them too much for granted. Your generation is worse. You don't even seem to know they're there. Now I went out just now and spoke personally to Sharon Marie. I inquired about her life. And because I took the time to converse with her, because I made her feel part of the family, you may be sure we will have a much more delicious dinner.

JOHN: And because you tipped her twenty bucks.

BRADLEY: Yes. All right. I did that, too. Because I firmly believe good service is important. You can't live without servants. At least you can't live well. Civilization depends on them. They are the mainstay of intelligent life. Without them, you and I would be out in the kitchen right now, slicing onions and shouting over the Dispose-All, and none of this would be taking place at all.

JOHN: You're probably right.

BRADLEY: Of course I'm right. (Pause.) I did something else while I was out there, besides buttering up Sharon Marie.

JOHN: What else did you do?

BRADLEY: I put in a call to your brother.

JOHN: Ah.

BRADLEY: Couldn't get him, of course. He's still with a client. Seven-thirty on a Saturday night. Yes, well, we all have to work. We all have to put our shoulder to the wheel. No substitute for good hard work. When the head of General Motors dies, they hire a new office boy.

JOHN: You think that's true, Pop?

BRADLEY: Of course it's true. Or was, until your friend Roosevelt came along and gave everyone a free ride.

JOHN: Hey, now wait a minute...

BRADLEY: I can't discuss it. Anyway, I spoke to Sylvia. She expects Jigger home any minute, and then he'll call.

JOHN: Good.

BRADLEY: So when he calls, we can all talk to Jigger. If we can't gather around a piano, we can still gather around a telephone.

JOHN: Fine.

(Bradley goes to the bar to make himself another drink.)

BRADLEY: I wish you'd have a drink.

JOHN: No thanks, Pop.

BRADLEY: It will still be quite a while before we eat.

JOHN: I can last.

BRADLEY: *(As he makes his drink.)* I hate to drink alone.

JOHN: That's O.K.

BRADLEY: As you know, I have very firm rules about alcohol. Never drink before six. Never drink after dinner. And never drink alone. You make me feel like an old souse.

JOHN: I'll have wine, then, Pop.

BRADLEY: Good. It's a convivial thing, drinking together. Even if it's just white wine.

JOHN: Have you got any red there, Pop?

BRADLEY: Red?

JOHN: I don't like white that much.

BRADLEY: You mean I have to go all the way out and open a whole new bottle of red wine?

JOHN: O.K., Pop. A drop of scotch, then.

BRADLEY: *(Pours a glass.)* A little scotch. *(Pours a strong one.)*

JOHN: A *little,* Pop? That looks like a double.

BRADLEY: You can't fly on one wing.

JOHN: Fly? Should I fasten my seat-belt?

BRADLEY: Maybe I just want to have a good, healthy belt with my older son before the evening's over.

JOHN: O.K. *(Raises his glass to his Father, takes a sip. It is obviously strong.)* Ah.

BRADLEY: *(Looking at the check.)* I notice my check is still there.

JOHN: I don't want it, Pop.

BRADLEY: Take it. I insist.

JOHN: I don't want it.

(Pause.)

BRADLEY: *(Settling into his chair.)* Tell me a little more about your play.

JOHN: *(On the couch.)* It's not going on. I promise.

BRADLEY: I just want to know a little more about it.

JOHN: Pop, we'll just get into trouble…

BRADLEY: No, no, we're mature individuals. We're having a drink together at the end of the day…For example, does it have a plot?

JOHN: Not much of one, actually.

BRADLEY: I like a good plot.

JOHN: I can't seem to write them.

BRADLEY: I remember learning at Yale: there are three great plots in Western literature: *Oedipus Rex*, *Tom Jones* and I forget the third.

JOHN: Ben Johnson's *Volpone*.

BRADLEY: No, it wasn't that.

JOHN: According to Coleridge, those are the three great plots.

BRADLEY: No, no.

JOHN: I've just *edited* a textbook on Coleridge, Pop.

BRADLEY: Well, you're still wrong.

JOHN: *(Starts getting up.)* I could look it—

BRADLEY: No!

JOHN: O.K.

(Pause. They drink.)

BRADLEY: So you don't have a plot.

JOHN: Not much of one.

BRADLEY: You don't try to drag in that business about our family having Indian blood, do you?

JOHN: *Do* we?

BRADLEY: We do not. *(Pause.)* Though some people keep saying we do.

JOHN: What people?

BRADLEY: Your cousin Wilbur, particularly. He used to bandy it about. But it's an absolute lie. There is no Indian blood in our branch of the family. I want that absolutely understood before I die.

JOHN: O.K.

BRADLEY: Your Great-uncle Ralph may have had a relationship with an Indian woman, but that was it.

JOHN: Did he?

BRADLEY: *May* have. Besides, she was an Indian princess. She was very well-born. According to your grandmother, she was quite beautiful. And she sewed very well.

JOHN: Sowed corn?

BRADLEY: Sewed moccasins. I don't know what she sewed. The point is that Indian blood never came down through our line. Harry Blackburn down at the club constantly brings it up. He says it accounts for our affinity for alcohol. It's not funny, and I told him so, and if he mentions it again, I'm going to punch him in the nose.

JOHN: Take it easy, Pop.

BRADLEY: Anyway, if you bring up that Indian blood stuff in your play, you are simply barking up the wrong tree.

JOHN: I never thought of it, Pop.

BRADLEY: Good. *(He crosses to sit next to John on the couch.)* Did you bring up your grandfather's death?

(Pause.)

JOHN: Yes.

BRADLEY: I knew you would.

JOHN: I don't make a big deal of it.

BRADLEY: I don't know why you have to make any deal of it at all.

JOHN: I think it helps say who we are.

BRADLEY: You're always harping on it. It seems to be an obsession with you.

JOHN: I just refer to it once, Pop.

BRADLEY: How? What do you say?

JOHN: Oh, well…

BRADLEY: I want to know what you say about my father.

JOHN: I say he was a good man, a kind man, one of the best lawyers in town…

BRADLEY: True enough…

JOHN: A leader in the community. A pillar of the church…

BRADLEY: True…All true…

JOHN: Who, one day, for no discernible reason, strolled down to the edge of the Niagara River, hung his hat, his coat, and his cane on a wooden piling, and then walked into the water and drowned himself.

(Pause.)

BRADLEY: That's what you say in your play?

JOHN: That's what I say, Pop.

(Pause.)

BRADLEY: He left a note.

JOHN: I didn't know that, Pop.

BRADLEY: Oh yes. there was a note in his breast pocket. Addressed to me and my mother. I have it in my safe deposit box.

JOHN: I didn't know he left a note.

BRADLEY: You can have it when I die. *(Pause.)* He says there will be enough money to support my mother and to send me through college. *(Pause.)* Which there was. *(Pause.)* Then he says he's terribly, terribly sorry, but he's come to the conclusion that life isn't worth living any more. *(Pause Bradley turns away from John, takes out a handkerchief and dries his eyes.)*

JOHN: Oh, Pop.

BRADLEY: Churchill had those dark moments.

JOHN: So does my son Jack.

BRADLEY: Jack too? That sweet Jack?

JOHN: He gets it in spades.

BRADLEY: Of course, it's just…life, isn't it? It's part of the equation. The point is, we don't complain, we deal with it. We divert ourselves. We play golf, we have a drink occasionally.

JOHN: We write plays.

BRADLEY: Well, we do *something*. What does that sweet Jack do?

JOHN: Builds model airplanes.

BRADLEY: Oh that poor boy. That poor, poor boy.

JOHN: Yeah, I know.

    (Pause.)

BRADLEY: And your play gets into all this?

JOHN: A little.

BRADLEY: Sounds like a very depressing play.

JOHN: It has its darker moments.

BRADLEY: But no plot.

JOHN: Not really. No.

BRADLEY: *(Getting up.)* Seems to me, you have to have some twist or something. I mean, it's your business, not mine, but it seems to me you need some secret or surprise or something. I thought all plays had to have that.

JOHN: Actually, there is. A little one. At the end of the first act.

BRADLEY: What is it?

JOHN: Oh well.

BRADLEY: Tell it to me.

JOHN: You don't want to hear, Pop.

BRADLEY: Tell it to me anyway.

JOHN: You'll just get angry, Pop.

BRADLEY: I want to hear it. Please.

    (Pause.)

JOHN: All right At the end of the first act, I have this older man…

BRADLEY: Me. I'm sure it's me.

JOHN: It's you and it's not you, Pop.

BRADLEY: What does this fellow do?

JOHN: He tells his older son…

BRADLEY: You.

JOHN: *Partly* me, Pop. Just *partly*.

BRADLEY: Tells his son what?

JOHN: The father tells his son that he doesn't believe...

BRADLEY: Doesn't believe what?

JOHN: Doesn't believe his son is his true son.

BRADLEY: WHAT?

JOHN: He says he thinks his wife once had an affair, and the son is the result.

BRADLEY: That is the most ridiculous thing I ever heard in my life!

JOHN: I knew you'd get sore.

BRADLEY: Of course I'm sore. Who wouldn't get sore? Where in God's name did you get such a ridiculous idea?

JOHN: I don't know. It just happened. As I was writing.

BRADLEY: Thank God this play is not going on! It's demeaning to me, and insulting to your mother! Why in heaven's name would you ever want to write a thing like that?

JOHN: Because I don't think you ever loved me, Pop.

(A telephone rings offstage.)

BRADLEY: That's Jigger.

(The telephone rings again, as Bradley hurriedly exits off and up the stairs. Then a half-ring. Bradley's voice is heard answering from offstage.)

BRADLEY'S VOICE: Hello?...

(John sits on the couch, looking after his Father, then looking at his glass.)

END OF ACT I

ACT II

Immediately after. John is sitting on the couch. His glass is now empty. Nina comes in with a plate of carrot sticks and celery.

NINA: Here are more munchies. It might be a little while before we eat.

JOHN: What's new with Jigger?

NINA: I don't know. I just had a chance to say hello. But I know how these things work. Mother will get on the phone in their bedroom, and Pop will be on the extension in the guest room, and everyone will talk at once. *(She finds her glass.)* Don't you want to get in on the act?

JOHN: I'll wait till things settle down.

NINA: We're lucky that whoosie out there in the kitchen missed up on the meat. I told her we'll be a minimum of twenty minutes during which time she can at least *think* about making gravy.

JOHN: You know. I just thought: isn't this familiar?

NINA: What?

JOHN: This. You and me. Sitting here. Stomach growling. Waiting to eat.

NINA: Because of the cocktail hour…

JOHN: Because of Jigger.

NINA: It wasn't always Jigger.

JOHN: Most of the time it was. I was the good little boy, remember? I'd dash home, do my homework, wash my hands, brush my hair, sit here all during cocktails, and then just as we were about to eat, Jigger would call to say that he was still at some game or something.

NINA: Sometimes.

JOHN: All the time. So you'd dig into another one of your Albert Payson Terhune dog books, and Mother and Pop would have another drink and talk about their day, and I'd just sit here stewing.

NINA: That's your problem.

JOHN: Well, it was the maid's problem, too, remember? All those maids, over the years, coming to the doorway in their rustly, starchy uniforms and saying, "Dinner is served, Missus" and Mother would say, "Give us five more minutes, Mabel, or Jean, or Agnes, or whatever your name is this month," but it would be five, it would be fifteen, it would be half an *hour,* before Jigger got home and our parents would rise from the couch and stagger into the dining room to eat.

NINA: They never staggered, John.

JOHN: No, you're right. They held it beautifully. The cook held dinner beautifully. And the maid kept the plates warm. The cocktail hour kept all of life in an amazing state of suspended animation.

NINA: But oh those meals! Remember those *meals?* Three courses. Soup, a roast, home-made rolls, a home-made dessert! Floating Island, Brown Betty, Pineapple Upside Down Cake...

JOHN: Stewed prunes...

NINA: Only occasionally. And even that was good!

JOHN: Maybe. But how did those poor souls put up with us night after night? Well, of course, they didn't. They lasted a month or two and then quit, one after the other. We were lucky that one of them didn't appear in the doorway some night with a machine gun and mow us all down!

NINA: Oh, honestly, John. We were good to everyone who worked for us. We'd always go out in the kitchen and make a huge fuss.

JOHN: Oh sure, and cadge an extra cookie while the poor things were trying frantically to clean up. Oh God, Nina, what shits we were about maids!

NINA: We drove them to church, we paid their medical bills... *(She takes her shoes off and sprawls on the couch.)*

JOHN: We were shits! When Grandmother died, she left five hundred dollars to each of the three maids that had served her all her life, and the Packard to the chauffeur.

NINA: Mother made it up to them.

JOHN: Oh sure. She tried. And they tried to make it up to themselves all along the way. Remember the one who stole all that liquor? Or the one who started the fire, smoking in the cedar closet? Or the one who went stark raving mad at breakfast and chased Mother around with a butter knife? Oh they had their moments of revenge. But we still built our life on their backs. Has it ever occurred to you that every dinner party, every cocktail hour, good Lord, every civilized endeavor in this world is based on exploiting the labor of the poor Cheryl Maries toiling away offstage.

NINA: Her name is Shirley Marie. *(Pause.)* I think. *(Pause.)* And she's exploiting *us.* She's probably getting fifty bucks for three hours work, when Mother and I did most of it anyway.

JOHN: There you go. Now we're exploiting each other. Pop always carries on about the importance of civilized life, but think of what it costs to achieve it. Between what Freud tells us we do to ourselves, and what Marx tells us we do to each other, it's a wonder we don't crawl up our own assholes.

NINA: Nicely put, John. All I know is, according to your good wife, Ellen, whenever you and she give a party in New York, you're the first one to want to hire some poor out-of-work actor to serve the soup.

JOHN: Yeah, I know. It's a shitty system, but I can't think of a better one.

NINA: *(Getting up, making another drink.)* I think you're a shit, John. I'll say that much.

JOHN: What else is new?

NINA: No, I mean now. Tonight. For this.

JOHN: For this?

NINA: Coming up here. Stirring things up. With your play.

JOHN: This is probably one of the most decent things I've ever done.

NINA: Badgering two old people? Threatening them with some ghastly kind of exposure in the last years of their lives?

JOHN: I came here to get their permission.

NINA: You came here to stir things *up,* John. You came here to cause trouble. That's what you've done since the day you were born, and that's what you'll do till you die. You cannot let people alone, can you? A rainy day, a Sunday afternoon, every evening when you finished your homework, off you'd go on your appointed rounds wandering from room to room in this house, teasing, causing an argument, starting a fight, leaving a trail of upset and unhappy people behind you. And when you finished with all of us, you'd go down in the kitchen and start on the cook. And when the cook left, you'd tease your teachers at school. And now that you're writing plays, you tease the critics! Anyone in authority comes under your guns. Why don't you at least be constructive about it, and tease the Mafia or the C.I.A., for God's sake? *(She sits in a chair opposite him.)*

JOHN: Because I'm not a political person.

NINA: Then what kind of person *are* you, John? Why are you so passionately concerned with disturbing the peace? I mean, here we are, the family at least partially together for the first time in several years and possibly the last time in our lives, and what happens: you torment us with this play, you accuse us of running a slave market in the kitchen, you make us all feel thoroughly uncomfortable. Have you ever thought about this John? Has it ever come to mind that this is what you do?

JOHN: Yes.

NINA: Good. I'm so glad. Why do you suppose you do it?

JOHN: *(Moving around the room.)* Because there's a hell of a lot of horseshit around, and I think I've known it from the beginning.

NINA: Would you care to cite chapter and verse?

JOHN: Sure. Horseshit begins at home.

NINA: He's a wonderful man.

JOHN: He's a hypocrite, kiddo! He's a fake!

NINA: Sssh!

JOHN: Talk about civilization. All that jazz about manners and class and social obligation. He's a poor boy who married a rich girl and doesn't want to be called on it.

NINA: That is a lie! He was only poor after his father died!

JOHN: *(With increasing passion.)* Yes, well, all that crap about hard work and nose to the grindstone and burning the midnight oil. What is all that crap? Have you ever seen it in operation? Whenever I tried to call him at the office, he was out playing golf. Have you ever *seen* him *work?* Has he ever brought any work *home?* Have you ever heard him even talk on the *telephone* about work? Have you ever seen him spade the garden or rake a leaf or change a light bulb? I remember one time when I wrote that paper defending the New Deal, he gave me a long lecture about how nobody wants to work in this country, and all the while he was practicing his putting on the back lawn!

NINA: He's done extremely well in business. He sent us to private schools and first-rate colleges.

JOHN: Oh, I know he's done well—on charm, affability, and Mother's money— and a little help from his friends. His friends have carried him all his life. They're the ones who have thrown the deals his way. You ask him a financial question, he'll say, "Wait a minute, I'll call Bill or Bob or Ted."

NINA: Because that's *life,* John! That's what business *is!* The golf course, the backgammon table at the Mid-Day Club, the Saturn Club grille at six— that's where he *works,* you jerk!

JOHN: Well then that's where his family is, not here! Did he ever show you how to throw a ball or dive into a pool? Not him. Mother did all that, while he was off chumming it up with his pals. All he ever taught me was how to hold a fork or answer an invitation or cut in on a pretty girl. He's never been my father and I've never been his son, and he and I have known that for a long time. *(Pause. He sits exhaustedly on the piano bench.)*

NINA: Well. he's been a wonderful father to me.

JOHN: Maybe so. And maybe to Jigger. I guess that's why I've teased both of you all my life. And why I tease everybody else, for that matter. I'm jealous. I'm jealous of anyone who seems to have a leg up on life, anyone who seems to have a father in the background helping them out. Hell, I even tease my own children. I've bent over backwards to be to them what my father never was to me, and then out of some deep-grained jealousy that they have it too good, I tease the pants off them.

NINA: Jesus, John, you're a mess.

JOHN: I know. But I'd be more of one if I didn't write about it.

NINA: Well, write as much as you want, but don't go public on this one.

JOHN: I've already said I won't.

NINA: I'm not sure I believe you, John. You're too angry. You'll change a few words a few names and out it will come.

JOHN: Nina, I promise…

NINA: Then how come that check is still there? Mother told me about the check, and there it is. How come?

JOHN: I don't want it.

NINA: *(Brings it to him.)* Take it, John. Take it, just so I'll be sure. I know you're gentleman enough not to do it if you take the dough.

JOHN: I'll never cash it. *(He takes the check.)*

NINA: I don't care, but it's yours now, and the play stays in your desk drawer now, until they're both dead. And until *I'm* dead, goddamnit.

JOHN: *(Putting the check in his wallet.)* Or until he changes his mind.

NINA: Fair enough. *(She returns to the couch for more food.)*

JOHN: *(Putting his wallet away.)* Actually I'm kind of glad it's not going on, Nina.

NINA: Why?

JOHN: Because, to tell you the truth, I haven't got the plot right yet.

NINA: What's wrong with it?

JOHN: I dunno. It's not right yet. It's not true yet. There's a secret in it somewhere, and I haven't quite nailed it down.

NINA: What secret?

JOHN: Oh, simply the secret of what went wrong between my father and me. Where, when, why did he turn his countenance from me? There must have been a point. Did I wake him too early in the morning with my infant wails before one of those constantly replaceable nurses jammed a bottle in my mouth? Or rather *refused* to jam a bottle in my mouth because I wasn't crying on schedule?

NINA: Here we go…

JOHN: Or when I was displayed to family and friend, did I embarrass him by playing with my pee-pee?

NINA: John, you have an absolute obsession with your own penis.

JOHN: Or—*I* know! Maybe this is what I did: I made the unpardonable mistake of contradicting him—of looking something *up* in the Book of

Knowledge, and proving him wrong—no, not wrong, that makes no difference, right or wrong,—what I did was destroy the "rhythm of the conversation," maybe that s what I did wrong!

NINA: Oh good Lord…

JOHN: Yes well, I'd love to know what I did to have him say to himself—and to *me!*—"I don't know this boy. This is not my son." Because he's said it as long as I can remember.

NINA: And if he ever told you he loved you, you'd immediately do some totally irritating thing to make him deny it.

JOHN: You think so?

NINA: I know so. If he killed the fatted calf, you'd complain about the cholesterol.

JOHN: Jesus, Nina.

NINA: You would. I've got your number, John, even if you don't have mine. For instance, I know why you're writing this goddamn play.

JOHN: Why?

NINA: *(Hurriedly, as she puts on her shoes.)* You're writing it because he's dying. You're writing it because you love him. You're writing it to hold onto him after he's gone.

(Ann comes in.)

ANN: John, don't you want to speak to your brother before your father hangs up.

JOHN: Sure. *(He angrily grabs some carrots and goes off upstairs.)*

ANN: *(Distractedly.)* Well, that's that.

NINA: What?

ANN: *(Vaguely.)* I'd like a splash more, please, Nina.

NINA: *(Getting Ann's glass, going to the bar.)* All right.

ANN: Just a splash. I'm serious.

NINA: All right.

ANN: *(Sinking onto the couch.)* I give up.

NINA: What's the *trouble*, Mother?

ANN: Jigger. Jigger's the trouble. He wants to move to California.

NINA: What?

ANN: He wants to pick up stakes and move. Wife, children, off they go.

NINA: What's in California?

ANN: A job. A new job. There's a man out there who builds wooden boats, who wants Jigger to work for him. For half of what he's making now.

NINA: But why?

ANN: Because he wants to. He says it's something he's always wanted to do.

NINA: He's always liked boats.

ANN: Don't I know it. That canoe he built in the basement. Those sailboats out on the lake…

NINA: *(Joining her on the couch.)* Which had to be *wood*, remember? No fiberglass allowed. All that labor every spring, because only wood sat naturally on the water…

ANN: Between his boats and your dogs we hardly had time to think around here.

NINA: He felt free on the water. I wish I felt free about something.

ANN: Well I hear they feel free about everything in California.

NINA: And he's just…going?

ANN: Says he is. Says he plans to buy one of those grubby vans, and lug everyone out, like a bunch of Oakies. Your father is frantically trying to talk him out of it.

NINA: *(Musingly.)* I should just go to Cleveland to that dog school.

ANN: Oh, Nina. Think of Ed.

NINA: I *have* thought of Ed. We've talked about it. He says, do it. Which makes it all the harder.

ANN: I should hope so.

NINA: Still. Maybe I should. I should just do it. What would you say if I did it, Mother?

ANN: Go to *Cleve*land?

NINA: Three days a week.

ANN: Just to be with *dogs?*

NINA: To *work* with them, Mother.

ANN: I've never understood your fascination with dogs.

NINA: I don't know. When I'm with them, I feel I'm in touch with something…basic.

ANN: Horses I can understand. The thrill of riding. The excitement of the hunt. The men.

NINA: The men?

ANN: There used to be a lot of attractive men around stables.

NINA: Mother!

ANN: Just as there are around garages today.

NINA: Are you serious?

ANN: But I don't think they hang around kennels.

NINA: I'm interested in *dogs,* Mother.

ANN: I know you are, darling, and I don't think that's any reason to change your life. I mean if you had met some man…

NINA: Mother, have you ever watched any of those Nature things on TV?

ANN: I love them. Every Sunday night…

NINA: I mean, you see animals, birds, even insects operating under these incredibly complicated instincts. Courting, building their nests, rearing their young in the most amazing complex way…

ANN: Amazing behavior…

NINA: Well, I think people have these instincts, too.

ANN: Well, I'm sure we do, darling, but…

NINA: No, but I mean many more than we realize. I think they're built into our blood, and I think we're most alive when we feel them happening to us.

ANN: Oh well now, I don't know…

NINA: I feel most alive when I'm with animals, Mother. Really. I feel some instinctive connection. Put me with a dog, a cat, anything, and I feel I'm in touch with a whole different dimension…It's as if both of us…me and the animal…were reaching back across hundreds of thousands of years to a place where we both knew each other much better. There's something there, Mother. I know there's something there.

ANN: Oh Nina, you sound like one of those peculiar women who wander around Africa falling in love with gorillas.

NINA: Maybe I do. *(Pause.)* I hope I do. *(Pause.)* I'd rather sound like that than just an echo of you, Mother.

ANN: Well. I think we're all getting too wound up over boats and dogs. People, yes. Boats and dogs, no. The whole family seems to be suddenly going to pieces over boats and dogs.

NINA: And plays, Mother.

ANN: Yes. All right. And plays.

(Bradley comes in from upstairs.)

BRADLEY: We've lost him.

ANN: Oh now, darling.

BRADLEY: We've lost him.

ANN: Oh no.

BRADLEY: I'll never see him again.

ANN: Oh, darling.

BRADLEY: I'll be lucky if he comes to my funeral.

ANN: Now, now. I'll tell you one thing. A good *meal* will make us all feel much better.

NINA: I'll tell Shirley.

BRADLEY: Her name is Sharon.

ANN: I still think it's Cheryl.

NINA: Well, whatever it is, I'll tell her we're ready to *eat!* *(She goes out.)*

(Bradley goes to the bar.)

ANN: I wouldn't drink any more, sweetie. We're about to eat.

BRADLEY: I need this.

ANN: How about some wine with dinner? We'll have that.

BRADLEY: Wine won't do it.

ANN: Oh, Bradley…

BRADLEY: *(Moving around the room.)* I've lost my son. My son is moving three thousand miles away. I'm too old and sick and tired to go see him. And he'll be too tied up in his work to come see me.

ANN: *(Following him.)* Oh now, sweetheart…

BRADLEY: There are men, there are men in this world whose sons stay with them all the days of their lives. Fred Tillinghast's sons *work* with him every day at the office. He has lunch with them at noon, he has cocktails with them at night, he plays golf with them on weekends. They discuss everything together. Money, women, they're always completely at ease. When he went to Europe, those boys went with him and carried his bags. What did he do to deserve such luck? What did he do that I didn't? I've given my sons everything. I gave them an allowance every week of their lives. I gave them stock. I gave them the maximum deductible gift every Christmas. And now what happens? I reach my final years, my final moments, the nadir of my life, and one son attacks me while the other deserts me. Oh, it is not to be borne, my love. It is not to be borne. *(He sinks into his chair.)*

ANN: Oh, now just wait, Bradley. Maybe John is talking him out of it.

BRADLEY: John?

ANN: John always had a big influence on him.

BRADLEY: John? Jigger and John have fought all their lives. *I'm* the influence. I'm the father. What can John possibly say that I haven't said?
(John enters quickly.)

JOHN: I told him he should go.

BRADLEY: You didn't.

ANN: John!

JOHN: Sure. I said, go on. Make your move!! How many guys in the world get a chance to do what they really want?

BRADLEY: I should never have let you near the telephone.

ANN: I'm not sure that was entirely helpful, John.

BRADLEY: He has a fine job where he is.

JOHN: Pushing papers around a desk. Dealing with clients all weekend.

BRADLEY: That's an excellent job. He has a decent salary. He's made all sorts of friends. I got him that job through Phil Foster.

JOHN: You might as well know something else, Pop. I got him this new one.

BRADLEY: You?

JOHN: I put him on to it. The boatyard is owned by a college classmate of mine. I read about it in the *Alumni Review* and got an interview for Jigger.

BRADLEY: Why?

JOHN: Because he was miserable where he was.

BRADLEY: I should have known you were behind all this…

JOHN: He hated that job, Pop. Now he can work with boats, and join the Sierra Club, and do all that stuff he loves to do.

BRADLEY: It was none of your damn business.

JOHN: He's my brother!

BRADLEY: I'm his father! Me!

(Nina enters.)

JOHN: Well, I'm glad he's going, Pop. And I think Nina should work in Cleveland, too…I think you should, Nina.

NINA: I think I will.

ANN: Oh Nina, no!

BRADLEY: That's ridiculous.

JOHN: So what if Ed has to cook his own spaghetti occasionally…

NINA: He'd do it gladly.

BRADLEY: Nonsense. Ed can't cook spaghetti…

NINA: No. I think I'll do it. I think I'll go. I'll stay there, and study there, and come home when I can. Put that in your play and write it, John.

JOHN: Maybe I will.

NINA: Sure. Have the goddess Diana come downstage and plant her feet, and give this marvelous speech about seeing-eye dogs, which will bring the audience rising to its feet, and cause your friends the critics to systematically pee in their pants!

ANN: That's not attractive, Nina.

JOHN: I don't know. I kind of liked it.

BRADLEY: You kind of like playing God around here, don't you?

ANN: Yes, John, I really think you should stop managing other people's lives.

BRADLEY: Yes. Do that in your plays if you have to, not in real life.

JOHN: Oh yeah? Well, I'm glad we're talking about real life now, Pop. Because that's something we could use a little more *of*, around here. Hey. Know what? The cocktail hour is over, Pop. It's dead. It's gone. I think Jigger sensed it thirty years ago, and now Nina knows it too, and they're both *trying* to put something back into the world after all these years of a free ride.

BRADLEY: And you? What are you putting back into the world?

JOHN: Me?

BRADLEY: You.

JOHN: I'm writing about it. At least I have the balls to do that.

BRADLEY: Leave this room!

ANN: Oh Bradley...

JOHN: Maybe I should leave altogether.

BRADLEY: Maybe you should.

NINA: Oh Pop...

JOHN: *(Grabbing his bag in the hall.)* Lucky I didn't unpack...

ANN: John, now stop...

JOHN: *(Throwing on his raincoat.)* Call Ellen, Nina. Tell her I'm coming home. Say I'm being banished because of my balls!

BRADLEY: I will not allow you to speak vulgarities in this house.

JOHN: Balls? Balls are vulgar?

ANN: Now that's enough.

JOHN: *(Coming back into the room.)* Does that mean you don't have any, Pop? Does that mean we should all just sit on our ass and watch the world go by?

ANN: *(Going to front hall.)* I think it's time to eat.

BRADLEY: I'll tell you what it means. It means that vulgar people always fall back on vulgar language.

ANN: *(Beckoning to Nina.)* What's the food situation, Nina?

BRADLEY: It means that there are more important things in the world than bodily references.

ANN: *(At the doorway.)* Food! Yoo-hoo, everybody! Food!

BRADLEY: It means that your mother and I, and your grandparents on both sides, and Aunt Jane and Uncle Roger and Cousin Esther, and your forbears who came to this country in the seventeenth *century* have all spent their lives trying to establish something called civilization in this wilderness, and as long as I am alive, I will not allow foul-minded and resentful people to tear it all down. *(He storms off and upstairs.)*
(Long pause.)

ANN: Well. You were right about one thing, John: the cocktail hour is definitely over.

NINA: Um. Not quite, Mother.

ANN: What do you mean?

NINA: Come sit down, Mother.

ANN: Don't tell me there is more bad news from the kitchen.

NINA: *(Going to her.)* The roast beef is a little the worse for wear.

ANN: What?

NINA: The roast is ruined.

ANN: No.

NINA: Sheila got confused.

ANN: Sheila?

NINA: It's *Sheila* Marie. I know, because I just made out her check and said she could go.

ANN: What did she do?

NINA: She thought that microwave thing was a warming oven. It came out looking like a shrunken head.

ANN: Oh, I can't *stand* it!

NINA: The peas are still good, and I found some perfectly adequate lamb chops in the freezer. They won't take too long.

ANN: Thank you, darling. Would you tell your father? I imagine he's upstairs in the television room, cooling off on the hockey game.

NINA: *(Taking one of the hors d'oeuvres plates.)* I'll take him up some cheese, just to hold him. *(She goes off and upstairs.)*

ANN: *(Calling after her.)* You're a peach, Nina. You really are. Those dogs don't deserve you. *(Pause.)* That was an absolutely lovely rib roast of beef.

JOHN: I'm sure.

ANN: Twenty-eight dollars. At the Ex-Cell.

JOHN: I can believe it.

ANN: I suppose Portia might like it. Nina can give it to Portia.

JOHN: Good idea.

    (Pause.)

ANN: *(Beginning to clean up.)* I don't know why I'm talking to you, John. I'm very angry. You've caused nothing but trouble since the minute you arrived.

JOHN: Story of my life.

ANN: I'm afraid it is.

JOHN: I wish I knew why.

ANN: Isn't that what your psychiatrist is supposed to explain, at one hundred dollars a throw?

JOHN: He never could.

ANN: Then I was right: They're a waste of money. *(She starts out.)* I'd better check on those lamb chops.

JOHN: Mother…

    (She stops.)

JOHN: Since I've been here, I've discovered a big problem with this play of mine.

ANN: I'd say it had lots of problems. In my humble opinion.

JOHN: Well, I've discovered a big one. It's missing an obligatory scene.

ANN: And what in heaven's name is that?

JOHN: It's a scene which sooner or later has to happen. It's an essential scene. Without it, everyone walks out feeling discontent and frustrated.

ANN: I suppose you mean some ghastly confrontation with your father.

JOHN: Hell no. I've got plenty of those.

ANN: You've got too many of those.

JOHN: I'm thinking of a scene with you, Mother.

ANN: With me?

JOHN: That's what's been missing all my life, Mother.

ANN: Oh, John, please don't get melodramatic. *(She starts out again.)*

JOHN: I've also discovered why it's been missing.

ANN: Why?

JOHN: Because you don't want it to happen.

ANN: I'll tell you what I want to have happen, John. I want us all to sit down together and have a pleasant meal. That's all I want to have happen at the moment, thank you very much.

JOHN: *(Leading her to the couch.)* Oh come on, Mother. Please. This is the ideal moment. Pop's sulking upstairs. Nina's busy in the kitchen. And you and I are both a little smashed, which will make it easier. Tell me just one thing.

ANN: What thing?

JOHN: What went wrong when I was very young. Something went wrong. There was some short circuit…some problem…something…What was it?

ANN: I don't know what you're talking about.

JOHN: Come on, Mother. Please. Think back.

ANN: *(Getting up.)* John, I am not going to sit around and rake over a lot of old coals. Life's too short and I'm too old, and thank you very much. *(She goes out to the kitchen.)*

JOHN: *(Calling after her.)* And once again, there goes the obligatory scene, right out the door!

(A moment. Then Ann comes back in, putting on an apron.)

ANN: You got lost in the shuffle, John. That's what went wrong. I mean, there you were, born in the heart of the Depression, your father frantic about money, nurses and maids leaving every other day—nobody paid much attention to you, I'm afraid. When Nina was born, we were all dancing around thinking we were the Great Gatsby, and when Jigger came along, we began to settle down. But you, poor soul, were caught in the middle. You lay in your crib screaming for attention, and I'm afraid you've been doing it ever since.

JOHN: That's it?

ANN: That's it. In a nutshell. Now I feel very badly about it, John. I always have. That's why I've found it hard to talk about. I've worked hard to make it up, I promise, but sometimes, no matter how hard you work, you just can't hammer out all the dents. *(She turns to leave again.)*

JOHN: Exit my mother, after a brief, unsatisfactory exchange…

ANN: That's right. Because your mother is now responsible for a meal.

JOHN: *(Blocking her way.)* I can see the scene going on just a tad longer, Mother.

ANN: How?

JOHN: I think there's more to be said.

ANN: About what?

JOHN: About you, Mother.

ANN: Me?

JOHN: You. I think there's much more to be said about you.

ANN: Such as?

JOHN: Such as, where were you, while the king was in the counting house and the kid was in his cradle?

ANN: I was…here, of course.

JOHN: Didn't you pick me up, if I was screaming in my crib?

ANN: Yes. Sometimes. Yes.

JOHN: But not enough?

ANN: No. Not enough.

JOHN: Why not?

    (Pause.)

ANN: Because…because at that point I was a little preoccupied.

JOHN: With what?

ANN: Oh, John.

JOHN: With what?

ANN: I don't have to say.

JOHN: With *what*, Mother?

    (Pause.)

ANN: I was writing a book.

JOHN: You were what?

ANN: I was sitting right at that desk, all day, every day, writing a big, long book. It took too much of my time, and too much of my thoughts, and I'm sorry if it made me neglect you…I've never told anyone about that book.

JOHN: Doesn't it feel good to tell me?

ANN: Not particularly. No. *(She sits at the desk.)*

JOHN: What happened to it?

ANN: I burned it.

JOHN: You burned it?

ANN: All six hundred and twenty-two pages of it. Right in that fireplace. One day, while your father was playing golf.

JOHN: Why?

ANN: Because I didn't like it. I couldn't get it right. It was wrong.

JOHN: Wow, Mother!

ANN: I know it. *(Pause.)* But then we had Jigger, and that took my mind off it.

JOHN: What was the book about, Mother?

ANN: I won't tell.

JOHN: Oh, come on.

ANN: I've never told a soul.

JOHN: One writer to another, Mother.

ANN: Never.

JOHN: You mean, the book you wrote instead of nursing me, the book that took my place at your breast...

ANN: Oh, John, really.

JOHN: The six hundred page book that preoccupied your mind during a crucial formative period of my own, I'll never get to know about. Boy. Talk about hammering out dents, Mother. You've just bashed in my entire front end.

(Pause.)

ANN: I'll give you a brief summary of the plot.

JOHN: O.K.

ANN: Brief. You'll have to fill things in as best you can.

JOHN: O.K. *(He quickly gets a chair from the hall, and straddles it, next to her.)*

ANN: *(Taken aback.)* First, though, I will have a splash more.

JOHN: Sure.

ANN: Just a splash. I'm serious.

JOHN: All right, Mother. *(He hurriedly mixes her martini.)*

ANN: I mean, it's no easy thing to tell one's own son one's innermost thoughts. Particularly when that son tends to be slightly critical.

JOHN: I won't criticize, Mother. I swear. *(He brings her her drink and again straddles the chair beside her.)*

ANN: *(After taking a sip.)* All right, then. My book was about a woman.

JOHN: A woman.

ANN: A governess.

JOHN: A governess?

ANN: A well-born woman who goes to work for a distinguished man and supervises the upbringing of his children.

JOHN: Sounds like *Jane Eyre.*

ANN: If you make any cracks, I won't tell you any more.

JOHN: Sorry, Mother. It sounds good.

ANN: Now, this woman, this governess, does *not* fall in love with her employer. Unlike Jane Eyre.

JOHN: She does not?

ANN: No. She falls in love with someone else.

JOHN: Someone else.

ANN: She falls in love with a groom.

JOHN: A groom?

ANN: A very attractive groom. At the stable. Where she keeps her horse.

JOHN: I'm with you, Mother.

ANN: She has a brief, tempestuous affair with the man who saddles her horse.

JOHN: I see.

ANN: Well, it doesn't work out, so she terminates the affair. But the groom gets so upset, he sets fire to the stable.

JOHN: Sets fire.

ANN: The fire symbolizes his tempestuous passion.

JOHN: I see.

ANN: Naturally, she rushes into the flames to save the horses. And she gets thoroughly burned. All over her face. It's horrible.

JOHN: She is punished, in other words, for her indiscretion.

ANN: Yes. That's right. That's it exactly. But finally her wounds heal. The doctor arrives to take off the bandages. Everyone stands around to see. And guess what? She is perfectly beautiful. She is even more beautiful than she was before. The children cluster around her, the master of the house embraces her, and so she marries this man who has loved her all along. You see? Her experience has helped her. In the long run. *(Pause.)* Anyway, that's the end. *(Pause.)* You can see why I burned it. *(Pause.)* You can see why I haven't told anyone about it, all these years. *(Pause.)* It's terribly corny, isn't it?

JOHN: No, Mother.

ANN: It's silly.

JOHN: No, it says a lot. *(He kisses her on the cheek.)*

ANN: John, you're embarrassing me.

JOHN: No, really. It's very touching.

ANN: Well, I never could get the *feelings* right. Especially with that groom. That passion. That tempestuous passion. Those…flames. I could never get that right in my book.

JOHN: I never could either, in a play.

ANN: Oh, it would be impossible in a play.

JOHN: Maybe.

ANN: That's why I wish you would write a good, long, wonderful book. *(She gets up.)* And now I really ought to give Nina a hand with supper.

JOHN: Mother, one more question…

ANN: You've asked too many.

JOHN: About the groom.

ANN: Ah, the groom.

JOHN: What happened to him?

ANN: Oh heavens. I can't remember. I think I sent him off to Venezuela or somewhere.

JOHN: In the book?

ANN: In the book.

JOHN: But what happened in life, Mother.

ANN: In *life?*

JOHN: Where did he go? Who was he?

ANN: I never said he *existed,* John. This…groom.

JOHN: But he did, didn't he? You met him before you had me. And he left after I was born. And you sat down and wrote about him. Now come on. Who was he?

ANN: John…

JOHN: Please, Mother. Tell me.

ANN: It was over forty years ago…

JOHN: Still, Mother. Come on. Whom did you base him on?

ANN: Oh, John, I don't know…Maybe I'm getting old…or maybe I've had too many cocktails…but I'm beginning to think I based him on your father. *(She starts out as Bradley comes in.)*

BRADLEY: Based what on me?

ANN: My life, darling. I've based my life on you. *(She kisses him and goes out.)* *(Pause.)*

BRADLEY: Your mother always knows when to walk out of a room.

JOHN: My mother is full of surprises.

BRADLEY: Well, she instinctively senses when a man needs to do business with another man. And out she goes.

JOHN: We're going to do business, Pop?

BRADLEY: *(Going to his chair.)* We're going to talk seriously. And I hope when you have to talk seriously with one of your sons, your sweet Ellen will bow out just as gracefully.

JOHN: What's on your mind, Pop?

BRADLEY: First, I'd like a glass of soda water, please.

JOHN: I'll have one, too.

BRADLEY: Good. Time for sermons and soda water, eh?

JOHN: It sure does feel like the day after. *(John fixes the two drinks.)*

BRADLEY: John: you and I spoke angry words to each other a while back. It was most unfortunate. I blame you, I blame myself, and I blame alcohol. There's nothing more dangerous than a lengthy cocktail hour.

JOHN: I apologize, Pop. I got carried away.

BRADLEY: We both got carried away. We screamed and shouted, didn't we? Well, at least we didn't take off our clothes.

JOHN: Here's your soda water, Pop.

BRADLEY: Thank you, John. You know what I did upstairs instead of watching the hockey?

JOHN: What?

BRADLEY: I sat and thought. I thought about all of you. I thought about...my father. Do you suppose all families are doomed to disperse?

JOHN: Most of them do, Pop. Eventually. In this country.

BRADLEY: You don't think it's...me?

JOHN: No, Pop.

BRADLEY: People seem to want to leave me. There seems to be this centrifugal force.

JOHN: That's life, Pop.

BRADLEY: Well, whatever it is, I can't fight it any more...When I was upstairs, I telephoned Jigger. I called him back.

JOHN: Oh yes?

BRADLEY: What is it Horace Greeley tells us? "Go west, young man"? Well, he's young. It's there. I gave him my blessing.

JOHN: *(Sitting near him.)* That's good, Pop.

BRADLEY: "The old oak must bend with the wind...or break..." *(Looks at John.)* Isn't that from Virgil?

JOHN: I think it's T.S. Eliot.
(Both laugh.)

JOHN: But don't look it up.
(They laugh again.)

BRADLEY: Maybe I've loved him too much. Maybe I've loved him at your expense. Do you think that's true?

(Pause.)

JOHN: *(Carefully.)* I don't know…

BRADLEY: Maybe he's trying to get away from me. What do you think?

JOHN: I think… *(Pause.)* I think maybe he's trying to get away from all of us. I think maybe I got him to go because I was jealous. Hell, I think we all put our own spin on the ball—you, me, Nina, Mother—and guess what: it no longer matters. Jigger likes *boats,* Pop. He likes working with *wood.* Maybe he'll build a new clipper ship.

BRADLEY: Well, the point is, he'll be happy there. Sailing. He's a magnificent sailor. Remember right here on Lake Erie?

JOHN: I remember…

BRADLEY: I could sit in my office and look out on the lake, and sometimes I think I could actually see his sails…

JOHN: Yes…

BRADLEY: Of course, that friend of yours is hardly paying him a nickel out there. Hardly a plug nickel. And they'll have to buy a house. I mean, they all can't live in that stupid van. Even after he sells his house here, he'll need a considerable amount of additional cash. So I told him I'd send him a check. *(Bradley begins to look at, around, and under the table next to him for the check he gave to John.)* And I told him the cupboard was a little bare, at the moment. A little bare. I'm no longer collecting a salary, as you know, and I do need to keep a little cash on hand these days. Doctors…Pills…If I should have to go into the hospital…

(John takes the check out of his wallet, hands it to Bradley.)

JOHN: Here you go, Pop.

BRADLEY: *(Taking it.)* Thank you, John. *(Pause.)* I mean, I refuse to sell stock. I can't do that. When I die, I want your mother to have…I want all of you to have…I've got to leave something.

JOHN: I know, Pop.

(Nina comes on.)

NINA: I think we're almost ready to eat. Just so you'll know. *(She takes the hors d'oeuvre plate, starts out.)*

JOHN: We're discussing the National Debt.

NINA: Oh. *(Then she stops.)* Come to think of it, Pop, you could do me one hell of a big favor.

BRADLEY: What, Pookins?

NINA: *(Going to him.)* I wonder if I might ask for a little money.

BRADLEY: Money?

NINA: *(Sitting on the arm of his chair.)* For Cleveland. Tuition. Travel. Living expenses. It costs money to change your life.

BRADLEY: I'm sure that Ed…

NINA: Ed would subsidize my commuting to the moon, if I asked him. Which is why I won't. I want to get back on the gravy train for a while, Pop. I'll borrow from you and pay you back, once I have a job. It's as simple as that.

BRADLEY: We'll work out something, Pookins. I promise.

NINA: Oh thanks, Pop. I knew you would. *(Kisses him, and starts to exit gloatingly.)* And as for you, John, I think you should get yourself a good dog. I'll tell you why but first I have to toss the salad. *(She goes off.)*

BRADLEY: I suppose she'll want at least twenty as well.

JOHN: She might.

BRADLEY: And she should get it. It's only fair.

JOHN: Right.

BRADLEY: I am *not* going to cut into capital.

JOHN: I know…

BRADLEY: My father used to tell me every moment of his life…

JOHN: I know…

BRADLEY: Even as it is, I'm cutting close to the bone…

JOHN: You'll live, Pop.

BRADLEY: No, I won't. I'll die. But I'll die fair. I'll add twenty extra for you in my will. That's a promise. I'll call Bill Sawyer first thing.

JOHN: Thanks, Pop.

BRADLEY: So: You all get exactly the same amount of money.

JOHN: That's right.

BRADLEY: Jigger gets his boats…Nina gets her dogs…

JOHN: Right, Pop…

BRADLEY: And all I have to worry about is that damn play.

JOHN: It's not going on, Pop.

BRADLEY: *(Getting up.)* If only you'd put in some of the good things. The singing around the piano, for example. That was good. Or the skiing. That was very good. That's when we were at our best.

JOHN: It's hard to put skiing on the stage, Pop.

BRADLEY: You could talk about it. You could at least mention it.

JOHN: I do, actually. I bring it up.

BRADLEY: You do? You mention the skiing?

JOHN: The skiing and the piano both.

BRADLEY: Do you think you could mention anything else?

(Ann's voice is heard from offstage.)

ANN'S VOICE: I'm about to light the candles!

BRADLEY: *(Calling off.)* Two more minutes, darling! Just two! *(To John.)* I mean, if I were writing the darned thing, I'd want to prove to those critics we *are* worth writing about. I'd put our best foot forward, up and down the line.

JOHN: I have to call 'em as I see 'em, Pop.

BRADLEY: That's what I'm afraid of.

(Ann appears at the door.)

ANN: Now Nina has just whipped together a perfectly spectacular meal. There's even mint sauce to go with the lamb chops. Now come on, or it will all get cold.

BRADLEY: Just a minute more, my love. We're discussing the future of American drama.

ANN: Couldn't you discuss it in the dining room?

BRADLEY: I'm not sure I can.

ANN: Well hurry, or Nina and I will sit down and dig in all by ourselves.
(She goes off. John takes a necktie out of his jacket pocket, and begins to put it on, looking in a wall mirror.)

BRADLEY: What happens at the end of this play? Do you have me die?

JOHN: No, Pop.

BRADLEY: Sure you don't kill me off?

JOHN: Promise.

BRADLEY: Then how do you leave me in the end?

JOHN: I'm not sure now.

BRADLEY: You could mention my charities, for example, you could say I've tried to be very generous.

JOHN: I could…

BRADLEY: Or you could refer to my feelings for your mother. You should say I've adored her for almost fifty years.

JOHN: I'll think about it, Pop…

(Nina enters.)

NINA: Those lamb chops are just lying there, looking at us! *(Nina exits. Ann's laughter is heard offstage.)*

BRADLEY: I suppose what you need is a kicker at the end of your play.

JOHN: A kicker?

BRADLEY: When I give a speech, I try to end with a kicker.

JOHN: A kicker.

BRADLEY: Some final point which pulls everything together.

JOHN: In the theatre, they call that a button.

BRADLEY: Well, whatever it is, it makes people applaud.

JOHN: You can't *make* people applaud, Pop…

BRADLEY: You can generate an appreciative mood. I mean, isn't that what we want, really? Both of us? In the end? Isn't that why I make speeches and you write plays? Isn't that why people go to the theatre? Don't we all want to celebrate something at the end of the day?

JOHN: I guess we do.

BRADLEY: Of course we do. In spite of all our difficulties, surely we can agree on that. So find a good kicker for the end.

JOHN: Kicker, kicker, who's got the kicker?

BRADLEY: *(Picking up the script gingerly, like a dead fish, and handing it to him.)* Meanwhile, here. Put this away somewhere, so it doesn't dominate the rest of our lives.

JOHN: *(Taking it.)* O.K., Pop.

BRADLEY: *(Turning off various lights.)* Because there are other things in the world besides plays…

JOHN: Pop…

BRADLEY: Good food…congenial conversation…the company of lovely women…

JOHN: I've just thought of a kicker, Pop.

BRADLEY: Now *please* don't settle for some smart remark.

JOHN: Pop, listen. Remember the plot I was telling you about? Where the older son thinks he's illegitimate?

BRADLEY: *(Starting out.)* I can't discuss it.

JOHN: No, no, Pop. Wait. Please. Here's the thing: suppose in the end, he discovers he's the true son of his father, after all.

(Bradley stops, turns, looks at him.)

BRADLEY: That just might do it.

(Ann comes in again.)

ANN: Now come ON. Nothing can be more important than a good meal. Bring the tray, please, John, so that we don't have to stare at a lot of old liquor bottles after dinner. *(To Bradley, taking his arm.)* Wait till you see what Nina has produced for dessert…

BRADLEY: *(As he goes, over his shoulder, to John.)* …I still don't like your title, John. Why don't you simply call it *The Good Father?*…

(John stands, holding his play, watching his parents go off, as the lights fade quickly.)

THE END

THE GOLDEN AGE

INTRODUCTION

Sometimes a writer can be seduced to respond to feelings inspired by a literary work, rather than by an experience in life. In the case of *The Aspern Papers* by Henry James, I was taken enough by the plot to try to do my own version. The trouble is, it's both inhibiting and dangerous to compete with a masterpiece, particularly when you're transposing a murky and complicated piece of fiction to the very different demands of the stage. Still, after several earlier try-outs, I thought we had it licked when, with a snappy cast and sumptuous set, we opened at the Kennedy Center to excellent reviews. On to New York we went, only to be soundly trounced by most of the critics. It didn't help that my genteel effort opened the same week as David Mamet's exuberantly vulgar *Glengarry Glen Ross. The Golden Age,* with its small cast and single set, has since been done to some success by various other theatres, but looking at it now, I think it's a tough nut to crack. I don't think I ever managed to find the right combination of suspense, melodrama, and social comedy which might have made it more exciting, possibly because it came more out of Henry James than out of my own bones.

ORIGINAL PRODUCTION

The Golden Age was first presented at the Greenwich Theatre, in London, in the spring of 1980. It was directed by Alan Strachan, with the following cast:

Virginia	Angela Thorne
Tom	Vincent Marzello
Isabel	Constance Cummings

It was somewhat revised, and produced in the fall of 1983 at the Kennedy Center, in Washington, D.C., by Roger Stevens and Ralph G. Allen. It was directed by John Tillinger; the set was by Oliver Smith; the lighting by Arden Fingerhut; and the costumes by Jane Greenwood. This same production opened at the Jack Lawrence Theatre, in New York City, in April, 1984, produced by Nicholas Benton, Stanley Flink, and Brent Peek. The cast was as follows:

Virginia	Stockard Channing
Tom	Jeff Daniels
Isabel	Irene Worth

(The play was first done as a staged reading at The Aspen Playwrights Conference in 1979, with Barbara Babcock, Peter Maloney, and Celeste Holm, directed by William Shorr.)

CHARACTERS
VIRGINIA
TOM
ISABEL HASTINGS HOYT

SETTING
The front room of the second floor of a brownstone house on the upper East
Side of New York. Suggested by a story of Henry James. The room should be
presented on enough of an angle so that we see at least part of a front window, and an entrance from the hall, where we may also see a section of the
staircase, leading up to other rooms, and down to the kitchen, dining room,
and front door. Dominating the room, however, upstage, should be a large
archway, leading to the back section of this floor. The archway has heavy dark
red plush curtains, to be easily opened and closed.

The room is filled with fine old antique furniture. The walls are covered
with paintings—oils, still lifes, etchings, and prints. The effect should be one
of cluttered, complicated old elegance.

TIME
Spring and Summer, today

ACT I

At rise: The room is empty. The light from the window suggests afternoon, late spring. The curtains for the upstage archway are closed. After a moment, voices of a man and a woman are heard from the left—the ad-lib chatter of two people coming up the stairs. Virginia comes in from the right. She is a plain, rather awkward woman, simply dressed, probably in a sweater and skirt. There's something vague about her, and something nervous. She glances around the room, at the closed curtains particularly, and then turns, back toward the hall.

VIRGINIA: Come in.

(*Tom comes in from the hall. He is a nice-looking guy, youngish, well-dressed. He has a camera slung over his shoulder, like a tourist. He looks around.*)

TOM: (*Enthralled.*) Oh boy.

VIRGINIA: I know it.

TOM: Fabulous room.

VIRGINIA: This is the front room.

TOM: (*Indicating curtains.*) And through there is…what?

VIRGINIA: The back room.

TOM: Oh. Right.

VIRGINIA: No, actually, it was the library.

TOM: Was?

VIRGINIA: She had it done over.

TOM: The lady who lives here?

VIRGINIA: Exactly. She had slipcovers made for all the books.

TOM: No.

VIRGINIA: No. I'm teasing. (*Pause.*) She had it made into her bedroom.

TOM: Ah.

VIRGINIA: She even has a bathroom in there, and a dressing room in back, so she can be all on one floor.

TOM: I see. You mean, because she's so…

VIRGINIA: So what?

TOM: Well I mean, isn't she quite…

VIRGINIA: Quite what?

TOM: Well. Old.

VIRGINIA: Not at all! (*Pause.*) Oh she says she is, but she really isn't. (*Pause.*) I keep telling her she's ageless. She's as beautiful as ever, and she's got a mind like a steel trap.

(Pause.)

TOM: I'd like to meet her.

VIRGINIA: Who wouldn't?

TOM: Could I?

VIRGINIA: Oh no.

TOM: I couldn't?

VIRGINIA: Out of the question. She's given up meeting people.

TOM: Why? Are they too much for her?

VIRGINIA: No. She's too much for them. Now she won't even read her mail. She makes me send it back.

TOM: I know.

VIRGINIA: You wrote her?

TOM: Twice. They both came back unopened.

VIRGINIA: There you are.

(Tom shrugs, looks around.)

TOM: Great stuff, anyway.

VIRGINIA: The loot?

TOM: The furniture.

VIRGINIA: She calls it her loot.

TOM: Well it's great old stuff.

VIRGINIA: Do you think we're a little cluttered?

TOM: Oh no.

VIRGINIA: She keeps saying how cluttered we are.

TOM: I like it.

VIRGINIA: She says this is what you get when you've owned five houses.

TOM: Five?

VIRGINIA: At one time.

TOM: No.

VIRGINIA: Yes.

TOM: May I ask where?

VIRGINIA: Oh gosh. Let me think. There was this, of course, here in New York. And one out in Long Island. And one in the Adirondacks, for the fishing. That's what? Three. Oh, and one in South Carolina. I don't know. Anyway, five.

TOM: And everything ended up here?

VIRGINIA: Oh not everything. Just what didn't get away.

TOM: I see.

VIRGINIA: She says she's a dark star.

TOM: A what?

VIRGINIA: A dark star. She read this article in the New York Times Magazine
    Section which said that when a universe collapses, all these *things* collect
    around a dark star.

TOM: Oh yes?

VIRGINIA: You can't even see the star, but you know it's there, because all these
    things keep gravitating to it.

TOM: Hmmm.

VIRGINIA: Like this furniture. *(Pause.)* And me. *(Pause.)* And now you.
    (Pause. He looks at her.)

TOM: And you're the housekeeper.

VIRGINIA: Sort of.

TOM: Personal secretary, then.

VIRGINIA: Sort of that, too.

TOM: Companion? Nurse?

VIRGINIA: Not *nurse*. She doesn't need a *nurse*. *(Pause.)* No, actually, I'm her
    granddaughter.

TOM: *Grand*daughter?

VIRGINIA: That's what I am.

TOM: You mean, she's your *grandmother?*

VIRGINIA: Absolutely.

TOM: Wow.

VIRGINIA: I know it.

TOM: Hmm. And you stop by during the day?

VIRGINIA: I live here.

TOM: All the time?

VIRGINIA: All the time.

TOM: Just you and she.

VIRGINIA: Just us. Oh, we had a cat. But it got away.

TOM: You do the shopping and cooking and stuff?

VIRGINIA: Try to.

TOM: She's lucky.

VIRGINIA: Why?

TOM: To have you. In this day and age.

VIRGINIA: Why?

TOM: I mean her own grand-daughter.

VIRGINIA: I'm lucky to have her.

TOM: Oh. Sure.

VIRGINIA: Well. You've seen the downstairs, and you've seen this. Now you'd better go.

TOM: What if you told her I was writing an article? About these old brownstones?

VIRGINIA: Oh she knows that.

TOM: Knows it?

VIRGINIA: She guessed. When I told her you were at the door, and wanted to see the house, she said you probably wanted to write something.

TOM: What else did she say?

VIRGINIA: Oh just…show him in. Show him around. And show him out. *(Pause.)*

TOM: That's what she said, huh?

VIRGINIA: That's what she said. So shall we go?

TOM: *(Indicating camera.)* May I at least take a picture?

VIRGINIA: No.

TOM: Just one picture.

VIRGINIA: I said No.

TOM: Just to have something to hold onto.

VIRGINIA: Please.

TOM: Look, I can't just walk away from this.

VIRGINIA: Oh there are plenty of other brownstones in New York.

TOM: I'm not only interested in the house.

VIRGINIA: You're not?

TOM: No. I'm interested in what it contains.

VIRGINIA: You mean, the loot?

TOM: No, I'm interested in the…aura.

VIRGINIA: The aura?

TOM: The mystery. The magic. There are echoes here. Glimmerings of a golden age. I'm ultimately interested in…something else.
(The curtains part to reveal a spectacular old woman standing in the archway.)

ISABEL: He's ultimately interested in me.

VIRGINIA: Gram! I thought you wanted to stay out of it.

ISABEL: Well now I've decided to get into it.

TOM: *(Exultantly.)* I knew you were still alive!

ISABEL: Well at least I try to give that general effect.

VIRGINIA: *(Going to her.)* Gram, this is…

ISABEL: Don't bother to introduce us. I'll forget his name. He already knows mine.

TOM: Well I…

ISABEL: Of course you do. You've looked me up.

(Pause.)

TOM: Isabel Hastings Hoyt.

ISABEL: *(Majestically holding out her hand.)* How do you do.

(Tom goes to shake it.)

ISABEL: Be careful. It's an antique.

TOM: I'm really glad to meet you, Mrs. Hoyt.

ISABEL: You should be. I'm a rare bird. It must be like shaking hands with a whooping crane.

VIRGINIA: Where would you like to sit, Gram?

ISABEL: I seem to be heading toward that chair. *(She begins to make her way downstage toward a particular chair.)*

VIRGINIA: Would you like some help, Gram?

ISABEL: No thank you. I'm still afloat. Just throw me a line if I miss my mooring. *(To Tom, as she moves by him.)* I feel like the old Mauretania, dragged out of mothballs. I need paint, I'm listing to starboard, I probably leak. But I'm still operating under my own steam.

VIRGINIA: You certainly are, Gram.

ISABEL: Oh yes. I'm still able to slide into a slip. *(She waves Virginia away.)* Without tugs. Without a pilot. *(She reaches her chair.)* There. Now. All engines reverse. *(She backs up, settles into her chair.)* Ah. *(To Virginia.)* Now you can add a few fenders.

(Virginia props her up with pillows.)

ISABEL: *(To Tom.)* And if you think that was complicated, wait till I try to get up.

VIRGINIA: Oh Gram, you're marvelous.

ISABEL: Virginia, dear girl, that light. Can you move it? There's no point in having me look as if I were sitting in the dentist's chair. Unless this man is a dentist. Are you a dentist, sir?

VIRGINIA: *(Moving the light a little.)* He's a writer, Gram. Remember?

ISABEL: He can be both. Everyone writes these days. Including dentists. *(To Tom.)* Are you serious about your writing?

TOM: I want to be, Mrs. Hoyt.

ISABEL: *(To Virginia.)* Is he fun to be with? Is he bright and amusing?

VIRGINIA: I haven't noticed, Gram.

ISABEL: Then he's not really serious. *(To Tom.)* You're a—graduate student.

TOM: I used to be. But I gave it up.

ISABEL: I don't believe you. I can smell an academic a mile away.

TOM: Oh well, I teach a course on American Literature three nights a week at Hunter College.

ISABEL: *(To Virginia.)* You see?

TOM: But that's just to make ends meet.

ISABEL: Oh I don't like academics. They're all so hungry.

TOM: Some of them are pretty well fed these days.

ISABEL: For life, man. They're hungry for *life.* They suck your blood. Which would finish me, since I have very little left.

VIRGINIA: Oh Gram…

ISABEL: Now a real writer brings *in* life. He creates it.

TOM: That's why I want to be one. That's why I've come to New York.

ISABEL: Then do it, man! On your own! Don't lean on an old woman!

VIRGINIA: *(Low to Tom.)* Maybe you'd better go.

ISABEL: When I want people to go, I tell them, which is one of the few advantages of being old.

VIRGINIA: All right, Gram.

ISABEL: And I'm still not in love with that light. *(To Tom.)* Irene Castle always kept the light a little to her left. She felt it made her look more beautiful.

VIRGINIA: *(Moving the light again.)* Don't talk so much, Gram. You'll get tired.

ISABEL: It's where you keep putting that light. There's a writer here. Please try to keep me reasonably mysterious. Like the Oracle of Delphi.

VIRGINIA: *(Adjusting the light once again.)* I'll try, Gram.

ISABEL: *(To Tom.)* I met her, you know.

TOM: Irene Castle?

ISABEL: The Oracle of Delphi.

VIRGINIA: Oh Gram…

ISABEL: *(Insistently.)* I met the Oracle. On a trip to Greece with the Van Dusens. They wanted to consult her about the stock market. It was stupid of them. They had no sense of history. Neither did the Oracle. She gave them all the wrong tips.

VIRGINIA: Ssshhh. You're all wound up.

ISABEL: I am, aren't I? I feel like some bit of fluff out of Booth Tarkington, all dizzied up for the first date. Go make us a drink.

VIRGINIA: I'll make tea, Gram.

ISABEL: Tea? For a writer? Real writers like liquor.

VIRGINIA: At four in the afternoon?

ISABEL: At four in the morning. *(To Tom.)* What kind of drink would you like, sir?

TOM: *(Looking from one to the other.)* Oh I don't really…

ISABEL: *(To Virginia.)* Make him a Brandy Alexander. Make me one, too.

VIRGINIA: I don't know how to make Brandy Alexanders, Gram.

ISABEL: Then learn. Read a book. Read Hemingway's *A Moveable Feast.* He describes one in there.

VIRGINIA: Oh Gram…

ISABEL: Or at least he describes something which sounds absolutely delicious. Make whatever it is he describes.

VIRGINIA: Gram, what are you up to?

ISABEL: I am getting you out of the way, dear girl, so I can put this man on the spot.

VIRGINIA: Oh Gram…

ISABEL: Without you saying "Oh Gram" every other minute. Now go. Shoo. Goodbye.

(Virginia goes off, toward downstairs and kitchen, very reluctantly. Isabel is suddenly all business.)

ISABEL: Pull up that chair where I can see you.

TOM: All right.

ISABEL: Now sit in it.

(Tom does. She looks him over.)

ISABEL: A writer, eh?

TOM: Hope to be.

ISABEL: Were you a bad teacher?

TOM: No, I was good. Last year I won a teaching prize for my "contagious enthusiasm."

(Isabel laughs.)

TOM: *(Adds embarrassedly.)* Quote unquote.

ISABEL: In what subject?

TOM: American literature. Mid-Twentieth century. What I call the Golden Age.

ISABEL: Why are you giving it up?

TOM: Oh I'm not. Really. I just want to dig deeper. I want to be where it was. I want to look at things more directly.

ISABEL: Seems odd you'd want to start by writing gossip.

TOM: Oh, hey, listen: I intend to make this a big article.

ISABEL: What makes you think you'll get anything big from me.

TOM: Because you knew some of the finest writers of your time, Mrs. Hoyt, and I figure if I can get closer to them, work with them, work with you, then I'll be able to connect.

(Pause.)

ISABEL: How did you turn me up?

TOM: Well ever since I came to town, I've been poking around the Twenties collection in the New York Public Library. And I keep coming across your name.

ISABEL: My name was bandied about.

TOM: It sure was.

ISABEL: I'm in several books.

TOM: So I discovered.

ISABEL: I'm in the index of two.

TOM: Yes.

ISABEL: Out of print, I suppose. Most of them.

TOM: All of them.

ISABEL: I'm not in paperback?

TOM: Not you.

ISABEL: I would have loved to be in paperback. Think of being taken on the bus, carried to the beach.

TOM: I can't see it, Mrs. Hoyt. You're hardback, all the way.
        (Pause.)

ISABEL: Did you find out much about me, from these books?

TOM: Not much. They kept a respectful distance.

ISABEL: They put me at most of the parties.

TOM: Yes.

ISABEL: I was there.

TOM: I'm sure you were.

ISABEL: And I gave the best ones, by far.

TOM: I read about them...

ISABEL: Am I still in the Social Register?

TOM: They list you as dead.

ISABEL: Those stinkers! That's because I refused to subscribe.

TOM: You're listed as dead there, and dead one other place, but I couldn't find an obituary in the Times.

ISABEL: I'd be in the Times. Certainly I'd be there.

TOM: I know, Mrs. Hoyt. So I was at a loss where to turn next.

ISABEL: You probably decided I was babbling away in some nursing home.

TOM: I did. I almost gave up on you.

ISABEL: Faint heart ne'er won fair lady.

TOM: I know. And then I came across your picture.

ISABEL: Where?

TOM: In the old Life magazine.

ISABEL: Ah. The old Life...

TOM: *(Indicating archway.)* You were standing in that doorway, waving good-bye.

ISABEL: I remember. I was giving a party for Scott Fitzgerald before he went back to France. Some photographer got wind of it.

TOM: In the picture, were you waving goodbye to Fitzgerald?

ISABEL: I was not. I was waving goodbye to the photographer. I was saying, "Scram, please. This is a private party." Which I ought to say to you.

TOM: Well all I know is you looked absolutely spectacular in that dress.

ISABEL: I did, didn't I?

TOM: And that kept me going.

ISABEL: But where? How did you find the house? I never gave out the address, and the telephone's unlisted.

TOM: Ah well. A few weeks ago at Hunter we were doing *Moby Dick*. And a student came up with the mailing list for Save The Whales.

ISABEL: Oh the whales, those poor whales. I give them five dollars every Christmas.

TOM: So it said. And there was your address.

ISABEL: And here you are. To harpoon me.

TOM: Oh no. Just to tell the world what it's been missing.
(Pause.)

ISABEL: Help me up. I want to stagger majestically around the room.
(Tom helps her up, stays standing himself.)

ISABEL: Thank you. *(She walks, turns, looks at him.)* Are you a pansy?

TOM: No!

ISABEL: Be frank.

TOM: I'm not, Mrs. Hoyt.

ISABEL: Too bad. It's the pansies who have good taste.

TOM: Oh I've got good taste. Why do you think I'm here?

ISABEL: All right. Let's see if you do. What do you think is the best thing here?

TOM: The best?

ISABEL: The very best. My most prized possession.

TOM: Let me look.

ISABEL: Yes. You look.
(He looks around. She watches him.)

TOM: This cabinet looks pretty good.

ISABEL: The doors are fake.

TOM: Fake?

ISABEL: Look inside. You'll see new wood.

TOM: How about this chair?

ISABEL: Just a copy.

TOM: I'm surprised.

ISABEL: I like fake things. They're stronger. You can use them. You can sit on them. And you don't feel so badly when they break.

TOM: Is everything here fake?

ISABEL: Not at all.

TOM: There are some good things?

ISABEL: The best. Open your eyes.

TOM: *(As he moves around.)* Am I getting warmer?

ISABEL: No.

TOM: Then I give up.

ISABEL: You've seen it. You've looked right at it.

TOM: I'm sorry.

ISABEL: I'll give you a hint. The best thing here is downstairs.

TOM: In the front hall?

ISABEL: In the kitchen.

TOM: In the kitchen?

ISABEL: Trying to make Brandy Alexanders.

(Pause.)

TOM: Oh. Of course.

ISABEL: By far the best thing I possess.

TOM: Right. Oh sure.

(Pause.)

ISABEL: Well I have to decide whether to let you into my life. You're attractive, but at my age that's not supposed to make much difference. Tell me one more thing about yourself that will absolutely bowl me over.

TOM: *(Carefully.)* I come from Saint Paul, Minnesota.

(Pause.)

ISABEL: I don't believe you.

TOM: It's true.

(Pause.)

ISABEL: Scott Fitzgerald came from Saint Paul, Minnesota.

TOM: He's my favorite author. I identify with him completely.

(Pause.)

ISABEL: I knew him quite well.

TOM: That's why I'm here.

(There is the sound of something breaking, off right. Tom notices it, Isabel doesn't seem to.)

ISABEL: Well you'd better go.

TOM: Go?

ISABEL: Go.

TOM: But what about our Brandy Alexanders?

ISABEL: See if you can survive without one.

TOM: But she's down there, making them.

ISABEL: She's down there, drinking them.

(Another louder crash off left.)

ISABEL: The Golden Sauce. One of the things that has come down to us from the Golden Age. *(She hoists herself out of her chair.)*

TOM: You mean she...

ISABEL: I mean that dear girl has a slight difficulty with the bottle.

TOM: Then why did you let her start?

ISABEL: As if I could make her stop...Now hurry down the hall, and you won't embarrass her.

TOM: Couldn't I...?

ISABEL: No you couldn't. Please go.

TOM: *(Taking his raincoat.)* But what about the article?

ISABEL: *(Drawing herself up.)* Article, sir? Do you think for one minute I would let you write a magazine article?

TOM: You wouldn't?

ISABEL: I would not. I am worthy of an entire book!

(Pause.)

TOM: I'll come back tomorrow.

ISABEL: That would be fine.

(She waves him off, watches him disappear down the stairs. We hear the outside door slam. Then she walks slowly toward the hall, calling softly.)

ISABEL: Virginia...Virginia...See if you can make coffee, please...We have things to discuss.

(The lights fade. Music comes up, preferably the old Paul Whiteman recording of "Poor Butterfly." As the lights come up, we hear the sound coming from an old Capehart gramophone somewhere in the room. After a moment, Virginia comes in from the hall, in a less frumpy dress. She looks around, as if to make sure the coast is clear, then calls off.)

VIRGINIA: Come in.

(Tom comes in, carrying a bunch of flowers.)

TOM: Thank you. *(He looks around for Isabel.)*

VIRGINIA: I turned on the Victrola just to get you in the mood. It's "Poor Butterfly"—Gram's favorite song.

TOM: Oh.

VIRGINIA: Are you in the mood now?

TOM: Yes.

VIRGINIA: Then I'll turn it off. *(Turning off the victrola.)* Would you like something to drink? Tea? Coffee? Or a Brandy Alexander?

TOM: No thanks. This is a working day.

VIRGINIA: Yes. The situation is slightly different from yesterday, isn't it?

TOM: Oh yes.

VIRGINIA: Your reception, and everything.

TOM: I'll say.

VIRGINIA: Today you're getting the red carpet treatment.

TOM: Seems so. *(Remembering flowers.)* Oh. I brought these.

VIRGINIA: They're lovely!...For Gram?

TOM: For—both of you.

VIRGINIA: *(Takes them.)* I'll take them in. *(Starts for curtains, then stops.)* Oh. Gram asked me to call your attention to that painting. You might look at it while I'm gone. *(She indicates an oil portrait on the wall.)*

TOM: This?

VIRGINIA: It's somebody famous.

TOM: Who?

VIRGINIA: Guess.

TOM: Hmmm...A nude study...of a male.

VIRGINIA: Focus on the face.

(She goes out through the curtains with the flowers. He studies the painting. She comes back in.)

VIRGINIA: She says thank you for the flowers.

TOM: She's very welcome... *(Indicating the painting.)* Who is this? The face is vague.

VIRGINIA: I think it's Fitzgerald.

TOM: No!

VIRGINIA: I think it is.

TOM: You think? You think your grandmother owns a portrait of F. Scott Fitz*gerald* in the *nude?*

VIRGINIA: I think she painted it.

TOM: *Painted* it? Her*self?*

VIRGINIA: Oh she painted lots of famous people. She has this studio up on the fourth floor. Where she painted.

TOM: I don't believe it. Fitzgerald would never have posed in the nude. He was a very fastidious guy.

VIRGINIA: Then maybe it's Walter Babcock McCoy.

TOM: Who's Walter Babcock McCoy?

VIRGINIA: Don't you know?

TOM: Doesn't ring a bell.

VIRGINIA: I think he wrote plays.

TOM: Sounds like old melodramas.

VIRGINIA: That's it. Rip-roaring melodramas.

TOM: And he posed for her.

VIRGINIA: Everybody did.

TOM: Except Fitzgerald.

VIRGINIA: Ask her.

TOM: I will. I intend to. *(Pause. He glances toward the curtains.)* As soon as she comes out.

VIRGINIA: Oh she's not.

TOM: Not coming out?

VIRGINIA: Not today.

TOM: Why? She's not sick, is she?

VIRGINIA: She's *fine*. She's perfectly fine. She just doesn't want to see you until we've established some ground rules.

TOM: Ground rules?

VIRGINIA: She says whenever you have a working relationship, it's a good idea to spell things out from the word Go.

TOM: Spell things out.

VIRGINIA: Otherwise, she says there's bound to be trouble. Once, on Long Island, she brought in this man to work around the house, and she forgot to spell things out, and he managed to ruin all the plumbing.

TOM: Hey, I'm not a plumber!

VIRGINIA: That's the point. Neither was the man.

TOM: *(Glancing toward curtains.)* All right. Ground rules.

VIRGINIA: *(Producing a piece of blue note paper.)* Actually, she gave me this list.

TOM: A list.

VIRGINIA: As you know, as I think she may have told you, I have a slight…problem. I have this tendency to…retreat. And she thinks I should learn to deal with things more directly.

TOM: O.K. Fine. Let's do it.

VIRGINIA: All right. Now. The first thing she writes, in capital letters, is HOW MUCH.

TOM: How much?

VIRGINIA: *(Showing him the list.)* See? Capital letters. "HOW MUCH." *(Pause.)*

TOM: Oh. How much do I want to know.

VIRGINIA: No, that's not it. Because there's a little dollar sign here. After the HOW MUCH. Isn't that a little dollar sign? I think it is.

TOM: So she means how much...

VIRGINIA: Money.

> *(Pause.)*

TOM: She means how much...

VIRGINIA: Will you pay.

TOM: For what?

VIRGINIA: For what she gives you.

> *(Pause.)*

TOM: Is she serious?

VIRGINIA: I think she is.

TOM: I haven't thought about money.

VIRGINIA: Well she has.

> *(Pause.)*

TOM: Well, what does she suggest?

VIRGINIA: Suggest?

TOM: On that list.

VIRGINIA: Oh. *(She refers to the list.)* She writes fifty.

TOM: Fifty dollars.

VIRGINIA: Fifty percent.

TOM: Of *what?*

VIRGINIA: Of what you make. From your book.

TOM: *(Laughing.)* Would you tell her I don't even have a publisher yet?

VIRGINIA: Oh she knows that. This is for when you get one.

TOM: Fifty percent...That's quite a chunk...

VIRGINIA: She says this will be a major best seller.

TOM: How does she know?

VIRGINIA: Because she knows the world. And she knows books. And she knows what the world wants to read in books.

TOM: *(Shrugging tolerantly.)* O.K. Fine. We split the pie fifty fifty. Let's hope.

> *(Virginia checks off that item on her list, moves on to the next.)*

VIRGINIA: All right. Next. She writes "Advance."

TOM: Advance?

VIRGINIA: She wants an advance.

TOM: *(Laughing.)* She does, does she? How much?

VIRGINIA: Ten thousand dollars.

TOM: Ten thousand *dollars?*

VIRGINIA: Before she opens her mouth.

TOM: That's ridiculous.

VIRGINIA: She says Gloria Swanson got twice that.

TOM: She knows I don't have ten thousand dollars.

VIRGINIA: She knows a publisher does.

TOM: I don't *have* a publisher.

VIRGINIA: Then go *get* one.

TOM: How can I just *get* one?

VIRGINIA: You can tell them what you've got.

TOM: What have I got?

VIRGINIA: You've got *her,* when she's got ten thousand dollars.

TOM: *(Getting up; exasperatedly.)* Oh look, Miss…Miss…

VIRGINIA: Please call me Virginia.

TOM: All right, Virginia, look…

VIRGINIA: And can I call you…what?

TOM: Tom. The name's Tom. Look…

VIRGINIA: I mean it's silly not to. We're going to be seeing a lot of each other.

TOM: *(Driving through.)* Look. Virginia! Please! No publisher is going to look at me unless I've got something concrete. Tell your grandmother that, please.

VIRGINIA: Oh she knows that. She's not dumb.

TOM: Well then what's she got to *show* for ten thousand dollars?

VIRGINIA: That painting, for one thing.

TOM: Which is a nice amateur portrait of some man…

VIRGINIA: It's not amateur!

TOM: …who wrote old plays…

VIRGINIA: It's a first-rate painting!

TOM: All right, it's terrific. But it's not Fitzgerald. And it's not worth ten thousand dollars.

VIRGINIA: She *realizes* that. *(She opens a worn manila folder.)* That's why I'm supposed to show you this…And this…and this… *(She lays out a series of documents on the coffee table between them, as if she were trumping him in bridge.)*

TOM: What are those!

VIRGINIA: She says read 'em and weep.

(Tom picks up the documents one by one.)

TOM: A postcard…Depicting an old sailing schooner… *(Reads the other side.)* Signed a "Joseph C."…"Dear Isabel: Thank you for an immensely reinvigorating weekend. I will always remember sitting on your veranda, under

a vast swarm of stars, watching the small boats bobbing on the bay..."
(Looks at her.) Joseph C?

VIRGINIA: She says the ship is significant.

(Pause. He turns over the card.)

TOM: Joseph *Con*rad?

VIRGINIA: I think so.

TOM: You *think* so? You think she may have reinvigorated Joseph Conrad?

VIRGINIA: May have.

TOM: *(Looking at next document.)* A sheet of music...a score sheet...entitled "Isabel"... *(Reads the lyrics.)* "Isabel...I wish you well, my love...But what the hell, my love. *(He looks at her.)* Sounds like Cole Porter.

VIRGINIA: That could be it.

TOM: Your *grand*mother has a *lost* song written about her by Cole Porter?

VIRGINIA: She said there's something on the back.

TOM: *(Looking on the back.)* With additional lyrics by T.S. Eliot.

VIRGINIA: That's it.

TOM: *(Shaking his head.)* I don't believe this.

VIRGINIA: Don't, then. *(She gathers up the remaining items.)*

TOM: Wait.

(She stops.)

TOM: What else is there?

VIRGINIA: You won't believe it.

TOM: Give me a chance. I'll...try.

(She looks at him, then slowly hands him another photograph; he looks at it carefully.)

TOM: A small man...And a big woman...By a pool... *(He looks at her, looks at photograph again.)* I want to say it's...Calvin Coolidge and Edith Wharton! In bathing suits!

VIRGINIA: Then say it.

TOM: These faded old photographs. It's hard to tell. He seems...to be...goosing her.

VIRGINIA: I think he is.

TOM: Calvin Coolidge is goosing Edith Wharton?

VIRGINIA: Apparently they had this game...

TOM: *(Now on his feet, holding the documents.)* But Jesus! This stuff is fabulous.

VIRGINIA: You see? You see what I'm talking about?

TOM: Does she have any stuff on Fitzgerald? Any of his writings, for example.

There's supposed to be some lost things he wrote when he was in New York.

VIRGINIA: Then she might have it.

TOM: Might?

VIRGINIA: Now don't distract me. I'm supposed to talk about money. She says none of these things, separately, is worth a huge amount. But you put them together, and you add all the other things she has—why then you have your Golden Age. And any decent publisher will want to pay for it.

TOM: *(Poring over documents.)* This is incredible…

VIRGINIA: *(Returning to her list.)* Now here's where I get very confused. She wrote down all these things like "movie sales" and "television specials," and she wants to be out in a nice, cheap paperback within the year.

TOM: Never mind! I agree to it all! *(Gathering up documents, starting for the door.)* Let me get cracking, then!

VIRGINIA: No! Wait! *(She holds out her hand.)* She wants those things back. Nothing is to leave this house.

TOM: Why not?

VIRGINIA: Because people will steal it and copy it.

TOM: Look, I'll keep a tight watch.

VIRGINIA: *(Determinedly, holding out her hand.)* She doesn't want Edith Wharton Xeroxed. Particularly in a bathing suit.

TOM: Look, I swear—

VIRGINIA: *(Shaking her head.)* Think of the Pentagon Papers. May I have them back, please?

TOM: But how will the publishers know?

VIRGINIA: She says you can *tell* them. Verbally. Using words.

(He hands them back.)

TOM: But they won't believe me.

VIRGINIA: Tell them to trust you. As we do. Tell them the Golden Age, like all great civilizations, was based on trust. *(She takes the photographs and puts them back into the folder.)* And then tell them to make out a cashier's check for ten thousand dollars.

TOM: Look, Virginia, I may be new in town, but I know it won't work.

VIRGINIA: Won't work?

TOM: I won't get a nickel out of any publisher unless I have something specific in hand.

VIRGINIA: Oh yes. Here. Show them this. *(She produces another piece of blue note paper.)*

TOM: *(Reading.)* "To whom it may concern. This man is writing a book about me. It will be worth at least ten thousand dollars up front." Signed, Isabel Hastings Hoyt.

VIRGINIA: She said that should do it. And this. *(She hands him a photograph.)*

TOM: *(Looking at it.)* Her picture. From the old Life. Waving goodbye.

VIRGINIA: Isn't she lovely? It's my favorite, of all the snapshots.

TOM: This is the picture that cheered me on.

VIRGINIA: Then it should cheer on the publishers, too. Tell them as soon as she gets that check, she'll sing like a canary.

TOM: *(Putting the note and picture in his pocket.)* I'll tell them she's waving goodbye to Fitzgerald. That might open a few doors.

VIRGINIA: Or else you might mention Walter Babcock McCoy.

TOM: Who? *(Glances at painting.)* Oh right.

VIRGINIA: Good. Just wait, then, while I tell Gram it's a deal.

TOM: One thing, Virginia.

VIRGINIA: *(Stopping.)* What?

TOM: I have to say this: I'm amazed the way she likes money.

VIRGINIA: She *hates* money. She thinks money is the root of all evil!

TOM: Well, she sure likes to rake it in.

VIRGINIA: That's because she needs it!

TOM: Come on! She must be sitting on a small fortune.

VIRGINIA: She doesn't have a nickel.

TOM: With this house? This furniture?

VIRGINIA: It's not *hers!*

TOM: What??

VIRGINIA: She's in hock up to her elbows!

TOM: I don't believe you.

VIRGINIA: It's true! Everything here is tied up in some dumb historical trust…

TOM: But still, the income…

VIRGINIA: …lasts only as long as she lives!

TOM: O.K., but…

VIRGINIA: Oh you dope! Don't you *see?* She wants the money for me!

TOM: For you?

VIRGINIA: *(Voice breaking.)* She's decided she's dying…And she wants me taken care of after she's gone…

(She turns and exits through the curtains. Tom stands amazed, and then goes out as the lights dim. Lights come up on Isabel, entering through the curtains, carrying a teetering stack of old shoe boxes. It is late afternoon.)

ISABEL: Now here are some more, since you didn't like the last batch. God knows what's in them, but they're from the twenties. *(She sets boxes on chaise and discovers Tom isn't in the room. She starts to the hall looking for him.)* Where are you?

(Tom comes in from the hall, with a portable tape recorder.)

TOM: I thought we'd try this again. It might help you focus.

ISABEL: On what?

TOM: The Golden Age.

(Isabel crosses to chaise, sits and starts going through the shoe boxes. Tom sits on the footstool and sets up the recorder.)

ISABEL: I don't see why you want to call your book *The Golden Age*. It's a cliché, after all. Everyone's always using it. The Golden Age of this, The Golden Age of that. The other day I heard a man on the news talking about the Golden Age of television. *(She laughs.)*

TOM: I don't care. It's what I want.

ISABEL: Just because it's gone doesn't mean it's golden. Those awful wars, that ghastly depression…

TOM: I'm thinking of the time between.

ISABEL: You think the twenties were golden?

TOM: For some. For you.

ISABEL: What makes you say that?

TOM: Because you still shine, Mrs. Hoyt.

ISABEL: And you are a charmer, sir. *(Isabel might wear reading glasses, and uses a magnifying glass as she sifts through things. Tom, in more informal clothes, sits close to her, holding a microphone for a tape recorder.)* All right. Let's focus on the Twenties. *(She pokes among her boxes.)* The Twenties…the Twenties… *(She finds a box. She shuffles through the box.)* Aiken…Locust Valley…New York. Let's concentrate on New York.

TOM: O.K.

ISABEL: *(Taking out a letter.)* Here is a letter signed, I think it's "L," from someone who is apologizing for spilling the soup.

TOM: Who was "L"?

ISABEL: I have no idea. I remember the soup, I don't remember who spilled it. It could have been Lawrence.

TOM: D. H. *Lawrence?*

ISABEL: D. H. or T. E. One of the two. No, it wasn't T. E. He went back to Arabia. It might have been Gertrude.

TOM: Gertrude Lawrence spilled the soup?

ISABEL: Oh dear, I don't know. The point is the soup. And someone is sorry for spilling it. Actually, they shouldn't be sorry, whoever it was. We had a lot of soup. And a lot of spillings. I think we all spilled so much because we drank so much. We had to. We had such terrible soup. We had these miserably unhappy Irish cooks whom we'd drag along from house to house, winter and summer. They weren't interested in soup. Neither were we. So they'd make it, and we'd spill it. And of course when we did, there would be a rather standard pattern. The women would shriek, the men would groan, chairs would scrape, the maids would cluck. There would be all this dabbing with napkins. And all sorts of insane suggestions about what to do with the tablecloth. People would throw salt on it, and champagne, and send to the kitchen for baking soda. It made an absolute mess. No one would settle down till the salad, and even during the dessert— *(She stops, eyes the microphone.)* I can't go on.

TOM: You're getting tired?

ISABEL: *(Indicating the microphone.)* No, no, it's that thing. I can't stand it being pointed at me. Particularly at my mouth. I'm never quite sure where it's been.

TOM: All right. *(He turns off the recorder.)* I'll take notes. *(He picks up a notebook and pencil.)* Go on.
(Pause.)

ISABEL: Now I've lost the thread. You see? You see what happens? You try to record things, to pin them down, and you lose them completely. It's called the Hindenberg Effect. Or the Hawthorne Effect. I knew Hindenberg. He had an excellent cook. I never knew Hawthorne, of course, but I imagine his food was abominable. *(Pause.)* Oh dear. Now I'm completely lost.

TOM: You were right in the middle of dessert.

ISABEL: Let's leave the table, and go to another room.

TOM: Tell me about Fitzgerald.

ISABEL: Tell me about your wife.

TOM: I don't have a wife.

ISABEL: I'll bet you did. In Minnesota.

TOM: That's ancient history.

ISABEL: So is Fitzgerald.

TOM: Mrs. Hoyt…

ISABEL: Fair's fair. We used to have a rule on Long Island. Eleanor Roosevelt made it up. If one person went skinny dipping, everyone did.

TOM: *(Writing again.)* Eleanor Roosevelt went skinny-dipping?

ISABEL: Only at night. And only when William Faulkner wasn't there.

TOM: Why wouldn't she do it with Faulkner?

ISABEL: I don't know. It had something to do with his position.

TOM: His position?

ISABEL: On the Negroes, dear boy. I don't know. I've forgotten…

TOM: *(Putting down his pencil.)* Mrs. Hoyt, do you realize how frustrating this is?

ISABEL: Frustrating?

TOM: Everything you tell me kind of peters out…Everything is full of vague possibilities which don't materialize.

ISABEL: That's life, dear boy. That's how it goes.

TOM: Mrs. Hoyt, let me remind you of something. I'm working on spec here. Do you understand what that means? I am *speculating* on you. I'm not getting a nickel for doing this. Nothing. No publisher has been willing to cough up one red cent until we produce something tangible and concrete. And what's happening? You won't let me take anything out of the house, and you won't give me anything serious to write about, and you get dicey when I even ask. Now I'm *betting* on you, Mrs. Hoyt. I'm putting my life on the line here. I came to New York, and I tracked you down, and I dug you *up,* because I think you've got something to tell the world, Mrs. Hoyt. And what do you give me? A lot of broad, unsubstantiated talk about spilled soup and skinny-dipping! Jesus, Mrs. Hoyt, you are letting me *down!*

(Pause.)

ISABEL: I've been naughty, haven't I?

TOM: Yes you have.

ISABEL: I'll try to be a good girl.

TOM: Thank you.

ISABEL: At least I'll do the best I can.

TOM: Thank you very much.

ISABEL: Then, as they say, shoot.

TOM: Tell me about Fitzgerald.

ISABEL: Oh poor, dear Fitzgerald. Don't you think he's been pretty well pawed over by now?

TOM: I'm not sure, Mrs. Hoyt. Some scholars think there are pieces of his writing yet to be discovered.

ISABEL: Really…

TOM: Things he wrote in New York. Around the time you knew him.

ISABEL: Mercy…

TOM: In fact, you know what I think?

ISABEL: Tell me…

TOM: I think there may be a whole section of *The Great Gatsby* lying around somewhere.

ISABEL: Heavens.

TOM: That's what I think. There's a gap in that book, Mrs. Hoyt. Every time I teach it, I sense it. There's a lost chapter…a section…even a paragraph which would make the whole thing hang together.

ISABEL: Ah. And if you found that, you'd really strike gold, wouldn't you?

TOM: It would be the answer to a dream. So anything you can tell me about Fitzgerald might help.

(Pause.)

ISABEL: Are you interested in a long lost romance?

TOM: Yes!

ISABEL: Between a great writer and an impressionable young girl?

TOM: Yes. Oh Yes. That's it! Tell me all about it.

ISABEL: Well. I met him when I was on tour with Maud Adams.

TOM: You were once an actress?

ISABEL: Once and always, sir. And apparently I was so enchanting that he asked me to star in his new play.

TOM: You mean there's a long-lost play?

ISABEL: Well it's long, but it's not lost. I have several copies.

TOM: Of a play? By Fitzgerald?

ISABEL: Fitzgerald? Who said anything about Fitzgerald? I've been talking about Walter Babcock McCoy.

(Pause.)

TOM: Oh.

ISABEL: You've heard of him?

TOM: Oh sure.

ISABEL: He was a wonderful playwright. We used to call him the real McCoy.

TOM: The real McCoy…

ISABEL: He wrote these marvelous melodramas, full of exciting scenes which never meant anything. Oh I adored him. There is no love like the first love.

TOM: But there must have been others.

ISABEL: Oh well, there was one. But I hate to talk about him.

TOM: Because it's so painful?

ISABEL: Because it's so boring. He was my husband.

TOM: *(Disappointed again.)* Oh.

ISABEL: Roger Hoyt. He promised me the moon if I'd leave the stage and marry him.

TOM: So you did…

ISABEL: Well I married him, but I never left the stage. I simply learned to play another part.

TOM: The loving wife?

ISABEL: Exactly! And Roger was marvelous—in the supporting role. Together we put on a splendid show.

TOM: But it wasn't enough...

ISABEL: Well I thought it was. Until I remembered something.

TOM: You remembered you were a woman.

ISABEL: I remembered I was a mother.

TOM: I forgot there were children.

ISABEL: So did I. But we had two. And we hired various sympathetic souls to take care of them. Then one day, after I had finished painting, and Roger had come in from hunting, I said, "Roger, where are the children? We have these children somewhere. We should be seeing them."

TOM: What did he say?

ISABEL: He said, "You're quite right." So we arranged a time. We had them all gussied up and trotted in. And there we all were. Eyeing each other. It was ghastly.

TOM: So what did you do?

ISABEL: I got a game.

TOM: Game?

ISABEL: I got a game. I said to Roger, "You play games, I play games, these children should play games."

TOM: What did he say?

ISABEL: He said, "You're quite right again." So I sent away to Schwartz. "Help. For heaven's sake, send me a game." And when the children came in, I said, "Here, children. Here's a game. Play it." But then, oh dear, they began to argue. And I said, "Children, don't fight, don't argue. Just play the game." Finally Roger said, "If you children don't stop fighting, I'm leaving this room." But they didn't. So he did.

TOM: He walked out of the room?

ISABEL: He walked out of the house.

TOM: You mean, he left?

ISABEL: Forever.

TOM: My God, you must have felt absolutely defeated.

ISABEL: I felt absolutely delighted. He gave me a handsome settlement, and we'd meet occasionally for lunch in New York.

TOM: And now you were free.

ISABEL: As a bird.

TOM: Enter Fitzgerald, am I right? *(Pause.)* Mrs. Hoyt? *(No answer.)* Would you at least tell me what happened to your husband? And the children?

ISABEL: They died.

TOM: How?

ISABEL: I don't want to talk about it any more.

TOM: Please, Mrs. Hoyt…

ISABEL: I don't. And I won't.

TOM: So I can't write a book about any of that?

ISABEL: No you can't.

(Virginia comes in, carrying a cat.)

VIRGINIA: Look what Virginia dragged in.

ISABEL: Good heavens.

VIRGINIA: I was planting myrtle in the garden and there it was. It came back.

ISABEL: So it did.

VIRGINIA: But isn't it amazing? It survived the whole winter.

ISABEL: Someone else probably took care of it.

VIRGINIA: Maybe. *(Going out.)* Or maybe it got along by itself. I'll give it some milk. *(She goes off, right.)*

ISABEL: *(Shaking her head.)* Not the same cat.

TOM: What?

ISABEL: Not the same cat at all. That's an entirely different cat.

TOM: You're sure?

ISABEL: Of course. I know a cat when I see one. *(Pause.)* But I hope you noticed something just then, sir.

TOM: Noticed what?

ISABEL: Something besides that cat.

TOM: Such as what?

ISABEL: For example, I hope you noticed the time.

TOM: *(Checking his watch.)* Four-thirty in the afternoon.

ISABEL: And guess who isn't wandering around the house with a glass in her hand at four-thirty in the afternoon.

TOM: *(Looking toward left.)* You're right.

ISABEL: And guess who's putting things into the garden.

TOM: It's great, it's wonderful.

ISABEL: And guess who's looking more relaxed and calm and beautiful with every passing day. People notice her on the street now. Last week a masher approached her in the grocery store.

TOM: Really?

ISABEL: Oh yes. It's all very exciting. Are you in love with your wife?

TOM: Me?

ISABEL: You. Do you plan to go back to her?

TOM: We don't get along any more.

ISABEL: Why not?

TOM: She says I roll around in books like a dog in dead fish.

ISABEL: Sounds like a very graphic lady.

TOM: She says I'm lost in the lost generation. Maybe she's right. Maybe I'm so much in love with the past that I can't love anything else.

(Pause.)

ISABEL: Oh dear.

TOM: Yes, well I don't like the present very much, Mrs. Hoyt. I think we're a greedy, vulgar society and we're spinning out of control. Now you stood in the doorway of something different, Mrs. Hoyt. You guarded it, Fitzgerald wrote about it, and there was something *there!*

(Pause.)

ISABEL: Would you like me to tell you something Fitzgerald never mentions?

TOM: Sure.

ISABEL: All right. I'll look back through this doorway, and tell you what *I* see behind me.

TOM: Go ahead.

ISABEL: First, of course, I see one hell of a good party.

TOM: Yes. Fitzgerald saw that.

ISABEL: Oh yes. And he saw that behind every good party is a woman.

TOM: Now we're cooking…a beautiful woman…

ISABEL: No, not a beautiful woman, a smart woman. And behind that woman was money.

TOM: Fitzgerald saw all that.

ISABEL: But that's where he stopped. He never saw that behind the money was always something else.

TOM: A lover?

ISABEL: A list.

TOM: *(Looking up.)* A what?

ISABEL: A list. I believe you've seen my lists.

TOM: I believe I have.

ISABEL: Well then you should know that behind the Golden Age was a good long list. Of things for other people to do. Buy this, serve that, plant this, fix that. With one good list, we could juggle two, three, five houses in the sir, without skipping a beat. We could equip and feed and move an army without losing a mitten. With lists in hand, we crossed rivers, scaled mountains, and established civilizations which lasted all summer long… *(Pause.)* And behind these lists…Would you like to know what was behind these lists?

TOM: Yes I would.

ISABEL: Behind these lists were the slaves.

TOM: The slaves?

ISABEL: The slaves, the slaves. Those poor half-literate Irish girls stumbling up the backstairs after midnight, setting their alarms for the crack of dawn. Those dogged English grooms, already up to curry and saddle those horses we decided not to ride. Those glorious Italians, continually weeding the gardens. The Polish laundress, the German who fixed the pump for the pool, the Scottish nurse—oh those people, those dear people. They made your Golden Age, my dear. They built it from the bottom up. They came in through the Golden Door and they kept the whole thing going. They're not in those boxes, and they won't be in your book, but they were there, all through it. Oh heavens! Oh mercy! I remember them all! Alice and Jean and Vito and Mrs. Veele. I remember them, more and more. I dream of them. Who did we think we were? What did we think we were doing? Bossing those people around.

TOM: You're a regular Marxist, Mrs. Hoyt.

ISABEL: I don't know what I am. I do know we made unconscionable use of other people.

TOM: Oh but hell, Mrs. Hoyt. We do that today. It's always done. All civilizations rest on the backs of somebody's labor.

ISABEL: Maybe so. But no civilization likes to know about it. Which is why I want you to write a good, easy, chatty book which will sit on every coffee table in the country, and make us all a great deal of money.

TOM: Fitzgerald would never have settled for that.

ISABEL: Oh well. Fitzgerald…

(Virginia comes in from the hall, carrying a tray and a glass of medicine.)

VIRGINIA: Are you getting tired, Gram? Remember what the doctor said.

ISABEL: It's rather nice to forget. *(She toasts Tom with the medicine, then drinks it.)*

VIRGINIA: Well I'm starting your dinner. We'll have to eat a little early if we're going to watch the Yankee game.

ISABEL: All right, dear.

(Virginia goes out, Isabel watches her. Tom is forced to. Finally.)

ISABEL: Have you met a nice girl since you've come to town?

TOM: Actually yes.

ISABEL: Some student in class? Batting her eyes?

TOM: No actually, a teacher. She does a course on the Brontes, right down the hall.

ISABEL: The Brontes? Oh dear. That means you're terribly involved.

TOM: I was, Mrs. Hoyt. But lately things are petering out.

ISABEL: Why?

TOM: I don't know…To be honest, Mrs. Hoyt, I'm kind of hung up on you. *(Pause.)*

ISABEL: I'll tell you three more things before I make my exit.

TOM: Good.

ISABEL: Things which are not for publication. Things which are private. Things which have to do with feelings.

TOM: O.K.

ISABEL: First, I'll tell you what happened to my husband.

TOM: Roger?

ISABEL: I don't believe you were ever introduced.

TOM: Mr. Hoyt, then.

ISABEL: Thank you. He was murdered.

TOM: Murdered?

ISABEL: Oh we didn't call it that in those days. We called it a hunting accident. He went hunting with the Vice President of the United States, and the Vice President shot Roger.

TOM: No.

ISABEL: Yes. It seems they both had feelings about the same chorus girl. Apparently the Vice President's feelings were stronger.

TOM: Boy.

ISABEL: The second thing: my children. The older—a boy—was drowned in a sailing accident off Northeast Harbor. He had feelings of independence. He liked to be alone on the water, and in the end, he was.

TOM: I'm sorry.

ISABEL: The other—a lovely girl—had feelings of inferiority. "Don't be silly," I'd say. "Go out. Have fun." So she tried. She went to a party after the war, and met a soldier. Nine months later she produced Virginia. They say the war ended the depression. Not for her it didn't. Not by a long shot…And would you like to know my own feelings about all of this?

TOM: No need, Mrs. Hoyt.

ISABEL: Then I'll simply tell you this. When the war was over, I retired. Totally and completely. I didn't like what I saw behind me, and I certainly didn't like what I saw coming up. *(She gets up.)* I'm now making a farewell appearance just to get money. *(She starts for her room.)*

TOM: *(Getting up.)* But you said there were three things.

ISABEL: *(Going to the hall, looking up the stairs.)* I happen to have a studio on the top floor.

TOM: I know.

ISABEL: It has a bed, a desk, and its own bath. Fitzgerald stayed there.

TOM: Did he?

ISABEL: Would you like to stay there while you write our book?

TOM: Of course!

ISABEL: Fine. Move in any time you want.

TOM: Thank you very much!

ISABEL: But that's not the third thing.

TOM: Not the third thing?

ISABEL: This Bronte woman…Are you sure you're no longer running her around the moors?

TOM: I'm sure.

ISABEL: Then the third thing is written on that blue piece of paper on the table by the hall.

TOM: *(Hurriedly crossing, picking up the paper, reading aloud.)* Angelo de Vita. 310 West 46th Street. *(Looks at her.)* Does he have something to do with Fitzgerald?

ISABEL: He does not. He is the owner of a nice little Italian restaurant on the West Side. His father—no, his *grand*father—used to be our gardener, and when he retired, I gave him some money so his children could make a fresh start. Now you go downstairs, and tell that lovely girl to stop cooking, and put on a pretty dress, and come out to dinner with you at Angelo's. And tell Angelo to send me the bill. And order the soup. Angelo makes good soup. *(She starts in.)*

TOM: Mrs. Hoyt—

(She stops, turning in the doorway.)

TOM: Did Fitzgerald write anything in the studio?

ISABEL: Oh yes.

TOM: Do you have what he wrote?

ISABEL: Oh yes.

TOM: Is it…important?

ISABEL: Everything Fitzgerald wrote is important. But so is the soup. So don't spill it. Goodnight.

(She goes out through the curtains. Tom stands looking after her, then exits into the hall.)

END OF ACT I

ACT II

Night, as indicated from the window. One light is on in the room, and a light in the hall. Voices, as Virginia and Tom come up the stairs. Virginia comes in and turns on another light. She now looks very pretty, in a pretty dress. Tom wears the same clothes.

VIRGINIA: Here kitty, kitty, kitty.

TOM: *(In doorway.)* Maybe it's still downstairs.

VIRGINIA: It adores Gram.

TOM: She doesn't seem to reciprocate.

VIRGINIA: Oh phooey. She just gets mad because it won't always do what she wants. *(Looks at him.)* Anyway, come in.

TOM: *(Coming in hesitantly; indicating the curtained area.)* Won't we wake her up?

VIRGINIA: Oh no. She sleeps like a top. Come on. *(She turns on another light.)* That was fun.

TOM: Nice little restaurant. Good food.

VIRGINIA: Which you weren't supposed to pay for.

TOM: I like to think I can pick up a tab.

VIRGINIA: Well she'll be furious. She'll insist on writing you out a check.

TOM: Why?

VIRGINIA: She just will. She wants the whole evening to be on her. *(She finds another piece of blue note paper on a table.)* Oh look, she even left this.

TOM: A list?

VIRGINIA: Just a note. *(Reads.)* "Brandy in the cabinet, cigars in the humidor." *(Turns to him.)* Have some brandy and cigars.

TOM: No thanks.

VIRGINIA: *(Going to highboy.)* Oh come on. It's fabulous brandy. I ought to know.

TOM: No, really.

(Virginia brings out a brandy bottle and a large snifter on a silver tray.)

VIRGINIA: If you're worrying about me, don't, that's all. I'm fine. I got through cocktails without a cocktail, didn't I? I got through dinner without wine. I can certainly get through the rest of the evening watching a good man enjoy good French brandy.

TOM: O.K.

(She pours him a snifter.)

VIRGINIA: Guess who gave her this?

TOM: Who?

VIRGINIA: Trotsky.

TOM: Back off.

VIRGINIA: Yes he did. One winter, she rented a villa in Cuernavaca so they could argue politics, and he brought her a case of brandy as a house present. *(Hands it to him.)* Here. Have some of Trotsky's brandy.
(Tom takes it, drinks.)

TOM: Mmmm. I'll drink it, even if I don't believe it.

VIRGINIA: Isn't it fabulous? Now a cigar.

TOM: No cigar, thanks.

VIRGINIA: *(Goes to humidor.)* Oh you've got to have one of these. *(Returns with cigar.)* Guess who sent her these?

TOM: Can't imagine. Churchill?

VIRGINIA: No. She and Churchill didn't get along. They disagreed about the Italian campaign.

TOM: Uh huh.

VIRGINIA: No actually, Freud sent her these cigars.

TOM: *(Laughing.)* Come off it.

VIRGINIA: *(Unwrapping cigar, lighting it for him.)* Sigmund Freud sent her these cigars. *Ask* her, if you don't believe me. He wanted to psychoanalyze her, but she said let sleeping dogs lie, and he sent her these cigars just the same. Now enjoy it, for heavens sake.
(Tom takes the cigar.)

VIRGINIA: There. Is that fabulous? Or not?

TOM: *(Puffing.)* It's fabulous. Everything seems fabulous tonight. It's like walking into one of those storybooks where the pictures pop up. This, the brandy, the dinner, the studio… *(He looks at her.)* You.

VIRGINIA: Me?

TOM: You. *(He sits down beside her on the couch.)* You're fabulous, too.

VIRGINIA: Thank you very much.

TOM: I mean it. There's been a kind of glow around you all evening.

VIRGINIA: A glow?

TOM: A golden glow.

VIRGINIA: Oh phooey. That's because you haven't seen enough of your Bronte woman.

TOM: Maybe. *(Pause.)* Or maybe not.

VIRGINIA: Well it's certainly been a long time since I've seen a man.

TOM: You seem to have survived pretty well without one.

VIRGINIA: Just lately. I used to be obsessed with men.

TOM: You?

VIRGINIA: Oh sure. Even when I was eight, I ran away with the gardener's son out in Long Island. We got as far as the gatehouse.

TOM: Big deal.

VIRGINIA: And I've been married twice.

TOM: Married?

VIRGINIA: Twice. I swear. The first was an Englishman. Gram had thrown me into this girls' boarding school in Switzerland, and he started hanging around, and I thought, my God, what's this? Something that doesn't giggle and borrow my bra. So I left school and married him. Trouble was, he started giggling and borrowing my bra.

TOM: Oh Jesus.

VIRGINIA: So Gram sent him a huge check, which is what he wanted all along, and that ended that.

TOM: One down, one to go.

VIRGINIA: Number two was a truck driver.

TOM: Come on.

VIRGINIA: Number two drove trucks. I came back here, and Gram got me a job in the Metropolitan Museum, cataloguing Greek art in the cellar. One day this man delivered a crate. We opened it up. It was a second rate copy of the Discus Thrower. I looked at the statue, and looked at the man, and went off with the real thing.

TOM: To Greece?

VIRGINIA: No, no. To a split-level in the suburbs of Toledo. And he'd be gone days at a time. So I'd sneak a tad of sherry into my morning coffee and when he came back, I wasn't in much shape to defrost his chicken pot pies. So he'd throw them at me.

TOM: The discus thrower…

VIRGINIA: I'll say. The real thing can *hurt*…So Gram sent *him* a check, and a few more to the various institutions which tried to dry me out, and a few more after that to the psychiatrists who finally gave up and sent me back here to her.

TOM: Oh boy, oh boy.

VIRGINIA: You can see why Gram needs money. I've been kind of expensive, over the years. *(Pause.)* Have some more brandy.
(He gets some.)

TOM: But you're O.K. now, I hope.

VIRGINIA: Oh I don't know. I'm so dependent on other things: Men. Liquor. My grandmother. I wish I could be…

TOM: What?

VIRGINIA: Free. *(Pause.)* Once Gram wrote a letter to Jung about me.

TOM: *(Ironically.)* Why not the best?

VIRGINIA: Exactly. And Jung wrote back that I had a Rapunzel complex.

TOM: Which means…?

VIRGINIA: Oh gosh. Let's see. How does it go? I'm the princess in the enchanted tower, guarded by the old crone, and I'm waiting for some prince to climb up and carry me off in all directions.

TOM: Ah.

VIRGINIA: Even now, that's what he'd say I'm doing. I'm letting down my hair. So you have something to hold onto when you climb up and set me free.

TOM: Do you think that's true?

(Pause.)

VIRGINIA: It's hard to know what's true. And what isn't.

TOM: So I'm discovering…What does your grandmother think?

VIRGINIA: Oh she got mad at the old crone part and refused to pay the bill.

TOM: *(Laughing, sets drink down.)* Well I'd better get going.

VIRGINIA: Why?

TOM: Otherwise, I'd kiss you.

VIRGINIA: What's wrong with that?

TOM: Nothing. Except that it wouldn't stop there. Before long, the prince would be begging the princess to go to bed with him.

VIRGINIA: No harm in asking.

TOM: I *can't*, Virginia.

VIRGINIA: Because of your wife?

TOM: Because of your grandmother. In her *house?* After all she's *done?*

VIRGINIA: That's why she's done it.

(Pause.)

TOM: Say that again.

VIRGINIA: She wants you to.

TOM: Why?

VIRGINIA: She thinks it's important. She says when you've fallen off a horse, sooner or later you've got to get back into the saddle.

(Pause.)

TOM: Hmmm.

VIRGINIA: You see?

TOM: I see.

VIRGINIA: It's as simple as that.

TOM: And I'm the horse, eh?

VIRGINIA: Oh well…

TOM: Not the prince, just the horse.

VIRGINIA: Your cigar's gone out. Here. *(She lights a match for his cigar.)*

TOM: *(Refusing the light.)* Kind of puts a man under the gun, doesn't it? Being told he's a horse.

VIRGINIA: It's just a metaphor.

TOM: Maybe she thinks I'm some sort of stud. Which I'm not.

VIRGINIA: Of course you're not. *Lit*erally.

TOM: I mean, is that why she wanted to pay the bill? Just for that? Do I get a tip if I'm good? Is she waiting to give me a carrot?

VIRGINIA: She's not waiting. She's sound asleep.

TOM: Well I have to say I'm not that kind of guy.

VIRGINIA: I told her that.

TOM: And what did she say?

VIRGINIA: She said…I can't remember what she said.

TOM: Come on, Virginia. What did she say?

(Isabel enters through the curtains in exotic black lounging pajamas.)

ISABEL: I said they're all the same.

TOM: Men? Or horses?

ISABEL: Both.

VIRGINIA: Gram, you're supposed to be asleep.

ISABEL: I'm looking for my book.

VIRGINIA: Please go to bed, Gram.

ISABEL: I can't. I got too involved in the ballgame. Reggie Jackson hit his second home run in the bottom of the tenth, and now I need my book to put me to sleep. *(She looks around.)*

TOM: So you think men are like horses, Mrs. Hoyt.

VIRGINIA: Don't, Tom.

ISABEL: Oh absolutely. And I think every woman should know how to ride.

TOM: Did you?

ISABEL: Of course. Side-saddle. On a great, golden gelding.

TOM: And you taught Virginia?

ISABEL: Everything she knows.

TOM: What did you tell her to do when the horse balks, Mrs. Hoyt? Isn't that what horses do occasionally? Don't they balk?

ISABEL: They most certainly do. You can be cantering toward a fence, and they simply refuse. They won't go over.

TOM: And what do you do then?

ISABEL: You show him who's boss. You use a switch. If you have one.

TOM: And if you don't have one?

VIRGINIA: I can't stand this. *(She walks away.)*

ISABEL: *(To Tom.)* You turn him around, squeeze with your knees, and try again.

VIRGINIA: Could we change the subject, please?

TOM: *(Pressing home.)* What if he still won't do it, Mrs. Hoyt? What if he's not some overbred English gelding you can put through his paces? What if he's a proud American mustang, fresh from the prairies, and not yet ready to be broken in!

ISABEL: Ah, then you simply distract him.

TOM: How?

ISABEL: Give the gentleman more brandy, Virginia.

TOM: No thank you.

ISABEL: *(Crossing to victrola.)* Now in my day, whenever we got into trouble… *(She fusses with victrola.)* whenever the conversation took a peculiar turn…whenever there was some awkwardness in the air…why then an orchestra would strike up somewhere…
(Music comes up: "Poor Butterfly.")

ISABEL: And we'd dance…Dance with him, Virginia.

VIRGINIA: No thank you, Gram.

ISABEL: Then I'll have to. *(She stands by the victrola, holding out her arms.)* Well, sir. How long do you intend to remain skulking in the stag line?
(Tom reluctantly crosses to her.)

ISABEL: Fitzgerald used to give a little bow.
(Tom does.)

ISABEL: And then we'd dance.
(They dance.)

ISABEL: Oh, you're wonderful.
(They dance more. She does a little spin.)

ISABEL: Come here, I'll show you something that Adele Astaire taught me.
(They dance more.)

ISABEL: He's getting good, Virginia. You don't know what you're missing.

VIRGINIA: I'll sit this one out, Gram.

ISABEL: Well then turn it off, quickly, before I start doing a mad, frantic Charleston on top of that table.
(Virginia turns off the music. The dancing stops; Isabel turns to Tom.)

ISABEL: Well. Have I distracted you?

TOM: *(Panting.)* I'll say.

ISABEL: Good. Then I'll go to bed if I can find my book.

VIRGINIA: What were you reading, Gram?

ISABEL: I'm not sure. You see how vague I am? I think it was *The Great Gatsby*. I had just gotten to that long section where Gatsby takes Daisy up to his room, and they spend this marvelous night together. Oh I'm furious. It's by far the best part of the book.

TOM: There's no such section in *Gatsby*, Mrs. Hoyt.

ISABEL: There most certainly is. Fitzgerald gave it to me in manuscript, and I've read it many times. It's superb. Best thing he did. Pulls out all the stops. Look on my desk, Virginia. *(To Tom.)* And you, sir. Look on the table in the hall.

TOM: I will. But there's no such thing in all Fitzgerald. *(He goes out.)*

VIRGINIA: Gram, what are you up to?

ISABEL: *(Quickly; to Virginia.)* Get back on your horse.

VIRGINIA: What?

ISABEL: And give him a glimpse of the barn.

VIRGINIA: The barn?

ISABEL: Something he wants! On the other side of the fence! Have you forgotten everything about riding?

(Tom comes back in.)

TOM: It's not out there.

ISABEL: *(Whispering; to Virginia.)* A glimpse of the barn, and he'll go right over.

TOM: I said it's not out there, Mrs. Hoyt.

ISABEL: What isn't?

TOM: Your Fitzgerald.

ISABEL: Was I reading Fitzgerald?

TOM: You said you were.

ISABEL: I must have been dreaming.

TOM: Oh.

ISABEL: Dreaming, reading, it's all the same. Actually, I must have been reading Walter Babcock McCoy. And he's right by my bed, where he belongs. *(She starts out.)* Goodnight, all. *(She exits through the curtains.)*

VIRGINIA: *(Picking up the empty brandy glass and the ashtray.)* Well, I'll clean up.

TOM: She's got it, doesn't she?

VIRGINIA: *(As she works.)* She certainly does! Now where's that cat?

TOM: No, I mean she's got the lost chapter.

VIRGINIA: Here kitty, kitty, kitty.

TOM: Unless she was teasing.

VIRGINIA: It must be in with her.

TOM: The manuscript?

VIRGINIA: The *cat.* Here kitty, kitty, kitty…Well I give up. *(She starts out.)*

TOM: She said Fitzgerald stayed in the studio.

VIRGINIA: I guess he did.

TOM: Did she visit him there?

VIRGINIA: She painted him there.

TOM: Did she sleep with him there?

VIRGINIA: Oh stop.

TOM: She slept with him, and he wrote about it, and she's got what he wrote.

VIRGINIA: You'd better go. *(She starts out.)*

TOM: Wait.

> *(She stops.)*

TOM: Can I at least finish my brandy?

> *(Pause.)*

VIRGINIA: All right. *(She comes back in, pours him another; holds the bottle.)*

TOM: She's sitting on something, isn't she?

VIRGINIA: You think so?

TOM: I know so. She's sitting on something big. *(Pause.)* Isn't she?

> *(Pause.)*

VIRGINIA: Yes.

TOM: What's she sitting on?

VIRGINIA: She's sitting on a golden egg, Tom.

TOM: Knew it.

VIRGINIA: That's because you're so smart, Tom. And I hope you're also smart enough to remember what happened when they started messing around with the goose.

> *(Pause.)*

TOM: *(Swirling his brandy.)* Have you seen the manuscript?

VIRGINIA: *(Taking a glass.)* I'm going to have one of these.

TOM: Don't.

VIRGINIA: Then stop.

TOM: At least tell me if you've seen it.

> *(Pause.)*

VIRGINIA: No.

TOM: Sure you have. Have you read it?

VIRGINIA: No.

TOM: But you've seen it.

VIRGINIA: *(Pouring herself a glass.)* One more word, and I drink this, Tom. I swear.

(Pause.)

TOM: All right. I'll stop.

VIRGINIA: Honestly.

TOM: I said I'll stop.

(Long pause; they eye each other.)

TOM: Just tell me what it looks like.

VIRGINIA: *(Raising her glass.)* I warned you.

(Pause.)

TOM: That is your choice.

(Virginia looks at him.)

TOM: I mean, you wanted to be free…You're a human being, after all. *(Pause.)* Not a horse.

(Pause.)

VIRGINIA: I know it. *(Pause. She takes a good, long defiant slug of the brandy.)*

TOM: *(Trying to stop her.)* Oh hey… *(Pause.)* I just wanted to know what it *looked* like.

VIRGINIA: You tell me.

TOM: Let's see…What would it look like?…It's an old black loose-leaf notebook…

VIRGINIA: That's it.

TOM: Is that what it looks like?

VIRGINIA: Isn't that what all old manuscripts look like? *(She pours herself another drink.)*

TOM: An unpublished chapter…from *The Great Gatsby.* I knew it!

VIRGINIA: Of course you did.

TOM: It would solve everything. It would make that whole strange book come suddenly clear!

VIRGINIA: Possibly.

TOM: And it would deal with sex. Fitzgerald was a prude about sex. This would be the first and only time he wrote about it!

VIRGINIA: Probably.

TOM: Sure! And can you imagine what he did with it? That glittering prose! Oh Jesus, this is a major find! And—and it means that your grandmother, Isabel Hastings Hoyt, was at least a partial model for Daisy Buchanan, who happens to be the most enticing woman in all American literature!

VIRGINIA: Naturally.

TOM: Of course! Sex! Sex! Sex is at the heart of the Golden Age! She said it was Marx, but it's Freud! Oh my God! This is stupendous! And it's all right there, a black book!

VIRGINIA: Obviously.

> *(Pause. He looks at her.)*

TOM: What happens to it?

VIRGINIA: Happens?

TOM: After she dies?

VIRGINIA: Oh.

TOM: What happens?

VIRGINIA: *(Carefully.)* It would come to me. It would be the one thing I'd get.
> *(Pause.)*

TOM: *(Looking at her.)* Daisy Buchanan's grand-daughter.

VIRGINIA: *(Curtseying.)* How do you do. Of course, she might be pulling your
leg.

TOM: Yeah…

VIRGINIA: It might not be Fitzgerald at all.

TOM: Hmmm.

VIRGINIA: It might be something else entirely.

TOM: Might be…

VIRGINIA: It might be an old story, for example. By Henry James. Or it might
be a play.

TOM: A play…

VIRGINIA: By Shaw. Or Philip Barry. Or Eugene O'Neill. Or it might be just
an old melodrama, by Walter Babcock McCoy.

TOM: You mean she might be playing games.

VIRGINIA: Might be.

TOM: Just fooling around.

VIRGINIA: Might be.

TOM: Maybe she got the idea from me, and is just using it to egg me on.

VIRGINIA: Maybe.

TOM: But why?

VIRGINIA: Oh that's easy. Because you're so attractive, Tom. She's pretending
you're Gatsby, and I'm Daisy, and she's doing everything she can to repeat
the past.

TOM: Well you tell her, please, that some critics say Gatsby never sleeps with
Daisy. He was too honorable a man.

VIRGINIA: That's fascinating. Goodnight. *(She starts turning off the lights.)*

TOM: Anyway, I can't imagine your grandmother shacking up with Fitzgerald.

VIRGINIA: Oh I can. I'm sure she was very discreet about it. She probably for-
tified herself with a drink or two. And waited till everything was pitch

dark. But then I can see her tip-toeing upstairs to the studio, and slip-ping into his bed. If she were asked. Here kitty, kitty, kitty.

TOM: *(Carefully.)* I think the cat might be up in the studio.

VIRGINIA: You really think so?

TOM: I really do.

(He looks at her, goes on up the stairs. She turns out the last of the lights, as we black out. In the darkness, over the speakers, we hear the sound of the last chorus of the last aria in Aida: "O Terra Adio." The lights come up slowly. Isabel sits in her chair, in her shawl, listening to the opera from her old Capehart radio-victrola. After a moment, Virginia and Tom appear in the doorway, left. They wear informal clothes. They watch her. Then Tom goes on upstairs. Virginia remains. She holds a blue piece of note paper. She watches her grandmother fondly, then comes into the room.)

VIRGINIA: You wanted to see me, Gram?

ISABEL: *(Holding up her hand.)* Ssshh. *(She speaks the final words of Amneris along with the singer.)* "Pace…Pace…Pace t'imploro…Pace…Pace…"
(We hear applause and an announcer's voice from the radio.)

ANNOUNCER'S VOICE: And the golden curtain descends on the final act of Aida…

ISABEL: *(Joining him.)Aida,* by Guiseppi Verdi. *(She gestures for Virginia to turn off the radio.)* The Met's last broadcast.

VIRGINIA: *(Fixing her pillows.)* Oh they're already on tour, Gram. They'll be back next fall.

ISABEL: I won't.

VIRGINIA: Stop it, Gram.

ISABEL: Yes, well, that rich, deep, contralto voice was the Princess Amneris, sealing herself up in a tomb, so Aida, her slave girl, can go free.

VIRGINIA: That's not quite it, Gram.

ISABEL: What do you mean?

VIRGINIA: Aida joins her lover in the tomb. And Amneris goes free.

ISABEL: Are you sure?

VIRGINIA: I think so.

ISABEL: Of course Verdi wrote it when he was very old. He must have been losing his grip. Much as I adore Verdi. I met him, you know.

VIRGINIA: You didn't meet Verdi, Gram.

ISABEL: I most certainly did. I was traveling through Parma with my mother, and we met this nice old man with a beard who kissed me on the top of my head. That was Verdi. I'm practically positive. Unless it was Michaelangelo.

VIRGINIA: *(Hugging her.)* Oh, Gram. I love you…

ISABEL: You should listen to Verdi. He wrote operas about liberation. Even his name meant freedom. They'd write it on walls.

VIRGINIA: *(Indicating blue piece of paper.)* You left this note on the stairs, Gram. *(She reads.)* "Please stop by."

ISABEL: Oh yes. You're so popular now, I have to waylay you.

VIRGINIA: Now, Gram.

ISABEL: Well you are. Come, sit down beside me. You're the belle of the ball. You should hire a social secretary.

VIRGINIA: We were taking a walk, Gram. It's a lovely day.

ISABEL: I'm glad you're getting out.

VIRGINIA: So am I.

ISABEL: Now see that he takes you around.

VIRGINIA: Around?

ISABEL: Shows you off. Introduces you to his friends. Soon you'll be having a perfectly marvelous time.

VIRGINIA: I *am* having a marvelous time, Gram.

ISABEL: Oh I know you are. But it would be even more marvelous if you met more people.

VIRGINIA: Oh well.

ISABEL: No, really. Take him out of the paddock and onto the trail.

VIRGINIA: He's not a horse, Gram.

ISABEL: Well he doesn't seem to be a writer. I have not heard the typewriter banging away recently. That's not what I've heard banging away.

VIRGINIA: He's hit a snag, Gram.

ISABEL: Of course he has. He's met you. He's been distracted from his labors by a beautiful woman. Why don't you put him back to work?

VIRGINIA: I can't just—

ISABEL: Of course you can. I had to do the same thing with Picasso. We had a hell of a row, but he took it right in stride, and afterwards he painted the Guernica.

VIRGINIA: Oh, Gram…

ISABEL: No, I'm serious. Go meet more men. And when you're shaking hands, and saying goodbye, say it very softly, so they have to lean over to hear you. Then they'll know that you're free and clear for the summer season.

VIRGINIA: I don't care about being free and clear for the summer season.

ISABEL: Well you should. And you should send this one back to his book, so you'll have money to enjoy it.

VIRGINIA: Oh Gram, why did you encourage us, if you're breaking it up?

ISABEL: I thought it would do you good.

VIRGINIA: It has. I haven't had a drink in weeks.

ISABEL: Fine. That means it took.

VIRGINIA: Took?

ISABEL: Like a vaccination, dear. A touch of the serum, so you don't get the real disease. Oh it might hurt a little, it might itch, but that only means it took, my love. It makes you immune.

VIRGINIA: I don't want to be immune.

ISABEL: Of course you do. What is a woman unless she's free? And how can she be free if she's tied to one man?

VIRGINIA: That's your philosophy, Gram.

ISABEL: It most certainly is. I've had eighty years to work it out.

VIRGINIA: Well it's not mine.

ISABEL: Well it ought to be, by now.

VIRGINIA: Well it isn't. I'm a different generation, Gram. I have my own ideas. I think…I think…I think I love him, Gram.

ISABEL: That's an insidious word.

VIRGINIA: Not to me.

ISABEL: Well it is to me. I've learned to distrust it completely.

VIRGINIA: I haven't.

ISABEL: Then it's time you did. It seems to me we've heard that song before.

VIRGINIA: I know…

ISABEL: It seems to me the orchestra played that particular tune in Switzerland. And Toledo. And various other spots in the free world.

VIRGINIA: But this is different.

ISABEL: It certainly is. This one is younger than you are.

VIRGINIA: Nobody cares about that any more, Gram. Not if you're in love.

ISABEL: Is he? Has he said so?

VIRGINIA: No. But there's something between us, Gram. Something special. I can tell.

ISABEL: You don't think it's something to do with me?

VIRGINIA: No.

ISABEL: You don't think he sees you as a way to get to me?

VIRGINIA: No!

ISABEL: Does he ask about me?

VIRGINIA: Sometimes.

ISABEL: What do you tell him?

VIRGINIA: I tell him what I know.

ISABEL: Does he talk about the black book?

VIRGINIA: No.

ISABEL: Virginia…

VIRGINIA: Once in a while.

ISABEL: What do you tell him?

VIRGINIA: I tell him not to talk about it.

ISABEL: Why don't you tell him there isn't one?

VIRGINIA: Oh, Gram…

ISABEL: Why don't you?

VIRGINIA: Because I don't dare.

ISABEL: Sweetheart, I *know* this man. I've met him before. He comes out of the west, all energy and charm, and he's wonderful to go around with for a while. But he's hungry, my love. He wants more than you or I could ever give him. He could break your heart.

VIRGINIA: I don't care. I'm not you, Gram. I'm different. And I need him.

ISABEL: *(With a sigh.)* Oh dear. Then we might have to change course.

VIRGINIA: What will you do?

ISABEL: Sound him out.

VIRGINIA: How?

ISABEL: I'll talk to him.

VIRGINIA: Talk to him?

ISABEL: Just talk.

(Pause.)

VIRGINIA: All right.

ISABEL: Would you get him, please?

VIRGINIA: Now?

ISABEL: Why not now?

VIRGINIA: He's got a class on Monday. He has to prepare.

ISABEL: So do I. Send him down.

(Pause.)

VIRGINIA: All right. *(She goes to the hallway and calls.)* Tom!

ISABEL: *(To herself.)* Tom, Tom, the piper's son…

TOM'S VOICE: Yo?

VIRGINIA: Gram wants to see you.

TOM'S VOICE: Be right down.

VIRGINIA: He's coming down, Gram.

ISABEL: I'll bet he is. Why don't you go make tea?

VIRGINIA: I want to be here, Gram.

ISABEL: Make tea. No tea-bags, either. Give it time. Let it steep.

VIRGINIA: I'm staying here, Gram.

ISABEL: And why is that?

VIRGINIA: So you won't bully him, Gram.

ISABEL: I see.

VIRGINIA: Oh please, Gram. Don't ruin it, please! I don't care why he's here, or what he wants. Just let him last a little longer. I'm so scared of being left alone!

ISABEL: And are you scared, if you make tea, of being left alone with the sherry?

VIRGINIA: I'll make tea, Gram. I'll make the best tea you ever had.

(She turns to go out as Tom appears in the door, carrying the cat. He is in his shirt-sleeves.)

TOM: *(To Virginia.)* Our friend seems to want to go out.

VIRGINIA: I'll take her. *(She takes the cat from Tom, and hurries off downstairs.)*

TOM: *(To Isabel, coming into the room.)* Great cat.

ISABEL: I don't have time to discuss cats. *(Indicating chair.)* Pull up your chair. Let's lay our cards on the table, you and I.

TOM: Fair enough.

ISABEL: Not so long ago, I told you some of my deepest feelings. Do you remember?

TOM: Yes.

ISABEL: Well now I'd like you to tell me yours. About my granddaughter.

(Pause.)

TOM: Ah.

ISABEL: Yes. Ah.

TOM: I like her.

ISABEL: How much?

TOM: A lot.

ISABEL: Do you love her?

TOM: I've only known her a couple of months.

ISABEL: She says she loves you.

TOM: Well I…don't know, Mrs. Hoyt.

ISABEL: You'd know if you loved her.

TOM: I'll tell you this: every time I'm with her, I like her more.

ISABEL: More than your wife, shivering in Minnesota? More than that poor creature, wandering around the moors, teaching the Brontes?

TOM: Your granddaughter's different.

ISABEL: I'll say she is.

TOM: She's special. There's something about her…

ISABEL: There certainly is. *(Pause.)* All right, now, be quiet, because I'm changing my mind. Which at my age is very difficult to do.

(She thinks. He watches her.)

ISABEL: There. I've changed it.

TOM: You have?

ISABEL: Yes. I've come to a decision. I've decided to let you marry my grand-daughter.

TOM: Marry her?

ISABEL: That's what I've decided. She seems to be instinctively monogamous, like a mallard duck, or I suppose I should say a swan.

TOM: Mrs. Hoyt…

ISABEL: Now as you know, I'm not particularly fond of marriage. But I have known several people who liked it. The Lunts, for example, absolutely swore by it, and in times of trouble, we might as well look to the Lunts. So what I have decided is that you should marry my granddaughter, and live with us here, and support her by finishing that book. *(Pause.)* You may reply.

TOM: I'm still married, Mrs. Hoyt.

ISABEL: I know you are. Technically. But nowadays I hear you can order a divorce over the telephone.

TOM: I'm not ready to get married again.

ISABEL: Of course you're not. Neither am I. But apparently she is. And so we've got to be good sports about it.

TOM: Mrs. Hoyt, please—

ISABEL: No, no. Now listen. I've thought it through. It'll be fun actually. You can have the run of the house. You can chase each other around in your pajamas, which I used to do with Bertrand Russell. We'll be aggressively domestic. We'll have meals together! We'll eat leftovers and talk about laundry! Oh I can't wait! You can teach in the morning, and write our book in the afternoon, and we'll all live happily ever after.

TOM: Does she know about this?

ISABEL: Of course not. Good heavens. But I know she wants it. I'm sure of that.

TOM: Mrs. Hoyt. I'm extremely fond of your granddaughter, but I can't marry her. I've already made a mess of marriage. I'm sorry, but the answer is no.

ISABEL: This reminds me of the secret negotiations after World War One. I was there, you know.

TOM: You were at Versailles?

ISABEL: Oh yes. They had to decide what to do with the Ottoman Empire. We called it talking Turkey.

TOM: *(Shaking his head.)* Talking Turkey…

ISABEL: Oh yes. And I'll tell you all about it if you marry my granddaughter.

TOM: Mrs. Hoyt, I swear to you here and now, I'll do everything I can to take care of your granddaughter.

ISABEL: Take care of her?

TOM: That I swear.

ISABEL: You mean make her your mistress?

TOM: I mean take care of her. She'll be my friend.
      (Pause.)

ISABEL: Well then, I want you to ease her into the world. Find her a job. Where you teach, maybe. In the library. *Some*thing.

TOM: Sure.

ISABEL: And finish that *book.*

TOM: I'll try, Mrs. Hoyt.

ISABEL: You see there isn't much money, and she'll be all alone, and I'm terribly concerned how she'll survive.

TOM: *(Touching her hand.)* I'll do my best, Mrs. Hoyt. I promise.

ISABEL: Thank you. And because you said that, I want to give you something.

TOM: Give me something?

ISABEL: I'll give you something right now. Please go to my desk.

TOM: All right. *(He does.)*

ISABEL: And look in the right drawer...

TOM: Right drawer...All right. *(He does.)*

ISABEL: And see if you can find my checkbook and my fountain pen.

TOM: Your checkbook?

ISABEL: I want to give you a check. It won't be much. But it will help you to tide her over.

TOM: You're talking about money.

ISABEL: What else is there to talk about at this point?

TOM: Something profoundly important to American culture.

ISABEL: Sounds like money to me.

TOM: I'm talking about the black book, Mrs. Hoyt.

ISABEL: Oh that.

TOM: Yes that. Give me that, Mrs. Hoyt, and let me publish it, and your granddaughter would be set up for life.

ISABEL: I said I was dreaming. Don't you remember?

TOM: I don't think you were.

ISABEL: Then I made it up. It was just something to keep you around. I'm sorry. That was naughty. I apologize.

TOM: I don't believe that either.

ISABEL: All right. What if I have what you say I have.

TOM: I know you do.

ISABEL: And what if I don't want it published?

TOM: Then of course we'd wait.

ISABEL: Until what?

TOM: Your…demise.

ISABEL: You mean when I kick the bucket?

TOM: All right. Yes.

ISABEL: What if I still don't want.

TOM: Oh Mrs. Hoyt…

ISABEL: Don't you think, dear man, there are some things in this world better left unsaid? Suppose Scott Fitzgerald thought that. Suppose I think so too.

TOM: Suppose you're wrong. Standards change. Suppose Fitzgerald would be proud to have it published now.

ISABEL: And who decides?

TOM: Me. Let me. Oh come on, Mrs. Hoyt, please. You've got a momentous piece of literature waiting in the wings. You've got America's finest writer, in his finest work, bringing it all together for the first and last time! You've got the heart of the matter in that book, Mrs. Hoyt. The absolute center of the Golden Age. Let me just look at it! Let me just see!
(Pause.)

ISABEL: I'm suddenly very tired.

TOM: Then let's talk about it tomorrow.

ISABEL: Not tomorrow.

TOM: Name the time then.

ISABEL: Never.

TOM: Never?

ISABEL: Never again.

TOM: Then what do I do?

ISABEL: Love her, if you can. Care for her. Make her happy. And I promise that one day she'll bring you whatever she gets from me.

TOM: You mean…wait.

ISABEL: That's it.

TOM: Just wait.

ISABEL: And hope. And be a good boy.

TOM: No.

ISABEL: No?

TOM: Let me propose another deal…Suppose I leave. Take a break. Take a breather.

ISABEL: Where would you go?

TOM: Home, maybe. Back to Minnesota.

ISABEL: To your wife?

TOM: To my roots.

ISABEL: Oh I knew it.

TOM: It's hard to hang around if I'm not trusted.

ISABEL: *She* trusts you.

TOM: You don't.

ISABEL: You'd shatter her!

TOM: She always has you.

ISABEL: Not always, sir.

TOM: Then show me the book.

ISABEL: *(Drawing herself up.)* There are certain expressions which I hear have wormed their way onto the stage. I'll use one now. You are a *shit,* sir!

TOM: Oh no.

ISABEL: Oh yes. You are blackmailing me!

TOM: Blackmail…Who's blackmailing who around here? Oh boy, I've found the Golden Age, all right! Right here in this room! You've got lists, games, manipulations! Hell, what am I? Just another slave? Just another flunky you've brought around the house to fix the plumbing!

ISABEL: *(Pointing to the door.)* Get out.

TOM: Gladly! *(He starts for the door.)*

ISABEL: Wait.

(He stops; she leans on chair.)

ISABEL: Before you do, I have to ask you to do me one more favor.

TOM: What is it?

ISABEL: Call the doctor. His number is by the telephone in the hall.

(She almost collapses. Tom comes to help her, calling "Virginia! Virginia!" The lights go to black. Almost immediately the lights come up again. It is late at night. A couple of lights are on in the room, and another in the hall. Virginia comes out from Isabel's room. Tom leans on hall doorjamb. They look at each other.)

TOM: How is she?

VIRGINIA: Fine. Perfectly fine.

TOM: I just got rid of the doctor.

VIRGINIA: She hates doctors.

TOM: He thinks she should go to the hospital.

VIRGINIA: That's why she hates them.

TOM: Well he thinks she should.

VIRGINIA: Well she won't. And I don't blame her. She'd last about a week.
(She starts to break down. He makes a move toward her. She holds up her hand.)

VIRGINIA: I'm perfectly fine. *(She glances toward brandy, glances away.)* And so is she. She's sound asleep. He gave her a pill.

TOM: You should go to bed yourself.

VIRGINIA: I will. I plan to. *(Pause.)* Where's the cat?

TOM: I have no idea.

VIRGINIA: I haven't seen it in ages.

TOM: *(Putting an arm around her.)* Ssshh. It'll turn up.

VIRGINIA: What did you say to her?

TOM: Me?

VIRGINIA: What did you *say?*

TOM: I simply said…

VIRGINIA: You asked for the black book, didn't you?

TOM: I asked to see it, yes.

VIRGINIA: Why?

TOM: It just came up.

VIRGINIA: You promised never to mention it.

TOM: It just came *up*. And hell, why not? I mean, is it a crime to love litera-ture around here? Is it a major crime to want to preserve the past?
(Pause.)

VIRGINIA: She wants you out of the house.

TOM: I'm all packed.

VIRGINIA: She never wants to see you again.

TOM: Ditto.

VIRGINIA: I had to beg her to let you stay even tonight.

TOM: I'm only staying because of you. Tomorrow I'm off. Oh boy, and glad to go. I'm ready for some good fresh air. *(Pause.)* You should be, too.

VIRGINIA: Me?

TOM: I hope you'll get out, too.

VIRGINIA: Oh well.

TOM: I'm serious. I hope we can still see each other. In the real world.

VIRGINIA: She said you were going home.

TOM: I'm not sure I can.

VIRGINIA: Because of her?

TOM: Because of you.

VIRGINIA: Oh stop.

TOM: I just got all riled up over a few pieces of paper which probably don't exist anyway.

VIRGINIA: You don't care about that any more?

TOM: I couldn't care less. I swear. I care about you.

(Pause.)

VIRGINIA: She made me get it out.

TOM: What?

VIRGINIA: She made me put it into her hands. She wanted to hold it.

TOM: Well it's important to her, at least.

VIRGINIA: Oh yes. She wouldn't let go. Finally she got so sleepy I could take it away.

TOM: Well, keep an eye on it. It might be your meal ticket some day.

VIRGINIA: No.

TOM: No?

VIRGINIA: She wants me to burn it.

TOM: *Burn* it?

VIRGINIA: Tomorrow morning. When she wakes up. I'm to burn it in her fireplace, systematically, page by page, right in front of her eyes.

TOM: *Why?*

VIRGINIA: Because she doesn't want you to get your hands on it.

TOM: Oh my lord.

VIRGINIA: She thinks that's all you care about.

TOM: Yeah well you tell her from me that I'm through with Fitzgerald and old manuscripts and literature in general. I plan to go back to graduate school and get a degree in computer science! It makes no never mind to me whether she burns it, or uses it for scratch paper for her goddamn lists, or—you won't do it, will you?

VIRGINIA: Do what?

TOM: Burn it.

VIRGINIA: I'll have to.

TOM: She'll change her mind in the morning.

VIRGINIA: I don't think so.

TOM: Then persuade her.

VIRGINIA: Why?

TOM: So you can have it.

VIRGINIA: I don't want it.

TOM: But you'll need it.

VIRGINIA: Oh I don't know, Tom. Maybe I'd be better off without it.

TOM: Oh Jesus.

VIRGINIA: I mean it's caused nothing but trouble.

TOM: You're right. You're absolutely right. It's stood between us from the word go. It. It. It. Seems all we talk about is IT…Where is it, by the way?

VIRGINIA: What?

TOM: Maybe you should go get it.

VIRGINIA: I will not.

TOM: Maybe we should look at it.

VIRGINIA: Tom!

TOM: While she's asleep.

VIRGINIA: Are you out of your mind?

TOM: Just to get it out of our systems.

VIRGINIA: Oh please.

TOM: I think she wants us to.

VIRGINIA: She does not!

TOM: Subconsciously. That's why she got it out. So we could look at it. That's what her buddy Freud would say.

VIRGINIA: I think you're wrong.

TOM: Let me just glance at it. Before it goes.

VIRGINIA: I said NO, Tom. No. Period.

TOM: Oh God in heaven! What do I do?

VIRGINIA: Maybe you should just go to bed, Tom.

TOM: Go to *bed?* With that about to be *burned?* Virgil would have burned the *Aeneid* if they hadn't stopped him! Byron's wife burned his *diaries* because no one intervened! And you sit there and tell me to go to bed.

VIRGINIA: All I know is I'm exhausted.

(Pause.)

TOM: You're right. Forgive me. Come on. We'll go to bed.

VIRGINIA: I'm not coming up, Tom.

TOM: What?

VIRGINIA: I'm not coming up.

TOM: Why not?

VIRGINIA: I don't want to.

TOM: One last time. In the studio.

VIRGINIA: No.

TOM: I'll come to your room then.

VIRGINIA: I won't be there, Tom.

TOM: Won't be there?

VIRGINIA: I'm sleeping on the couch back in her dressing room.

TOM: Why?

VIRGINIA: Because she asked me to.

TOM: WHY?

VIRGINIA: Maybe she thinks you'll steal it, Tom.

TOM: She said that?

VIRGINIA: She said lots of things.

TOM: And what did you say? *(Pause.)* Did you say I wouldn't?

VIRGINIA: No.

TOM: Good God, Virginia! Who do you think I *am?*

VIRGINIA: I don't know.

(Tom stares at her, then turns and storms out of the room and up the stairs. Virginia stands up, looks after him, turns off the lights by a main switch, next to the curtains, and goes in, slowly. The only light in the main room now comes from the hall and through the window. After a moment, we hear Tom angrily coming down the stairs. He carries a stuffed laundry bag, and a suitcase. As he passes the doorway, he calls into the room.)

TOM: I'll get the rest of my stuff in the morning! *(He continues angrily with his stuff out of sight beyond the door. Another moment. Then he reappears at the doorway. More quietly.)* I said, goodbye. *(He looks in to the room.)* Virginia? *(He stands in the doorway for a moment. Then he takes a step into the room. He calls quietly towards Isabel's room.)* Virginia.

(No answer. He looks around the room, comes in a little further. He looks towards Isabel's room, starts for it. His shoes make a noise. He sits on a chair and carefully takes off his shoes. He moves quietly, threading his way through the furniture to Isabel's doorway. He pauses near the doorway, unable to make up his mind. Then he slips quietly in. A long moment. Then he reappears stealthily. A large, black, worn loose-leaf notebook tied with ribbons is now in his hands. Slowly, he makes his way toward the hallway, left. He stumbles over something, says, "Damn cat." He gets to the hall. He puts the book very carefully on a table by the hall. He finds a match, lights it, begins to untie the ribbons. Suddenly all the lights in the room go on, full blaze. Isabel stands framed in her doorway, one hand on the lightswitch, the other holding a small shotgun. She wears a long white nightgown, and she looks wildly spectacular.)

ISABEL: *(Pointing the gun at him; hissing.)* Leave. That. Alone.

TOM: Mrs. Hoyt...

ISABEL: Leave it *alone.*

TOM: *(Indicating camera.)* I was only—

ISABEL: Take off your clothes.

TOM: What?

ISABEL: Take off your clothes or I'll blow your head off!

TOM: *(Half laughing.)* I'm not going to—

ISABEL: *(Aiming the gun.)* I could bring down a bird at fifty yards.

(Tom hurriedly starts unbuttoning his shirt.)

TOM: Why do I have to—

ISABEL: *(Grimly.)* Do it!

(Tom gets his shirt off. Virginia comes hurriedly out from within, wrapping a bathrobe around herself.)

VIRGINIA: Gram!

ISABEL: *(Hardly noticing her; grimly, to Tom.)* Now your trousers, sir.

TOM: *(Pleadingly, to Virginia.)* She wants me to—

ISABEL: Take off your trousers!

VIRGINIA: Gram…

ISABEL: I said, your *trousers!*

(Tom hurriedly takes off his pants. He stands there in his shorts. To Virginia.)

ISABEL: Shall we leave him a fig leaf?

VIRGINIA: Oh yes, Gram!

ISABEL: *(To Tom.)* Would you have left *me* one?

TOM: *(Helplessly.)* I just wanted to see.

ISABEL: Well so do I!

(She gestures with her gun; Tom is about to remove his undershorts.)

VIRGINIA: *(Stepping between them.)* Oh, Gram, what are you doing?

ISABEL: I'm leaving you a picture. There it is. Portrait of a man. Do you want it? Is it worth it? Remember: he can steal your very soul!

(She lowers the gun. Tom grabs his clothes and rushes from the room. Isabel leans the gun somewhere and crosses to the table where he has left the manuscript. Virginia stands amazed. Isabel gathers up the manuscript and clutches it to her chest. She starts back for her room, then turns and looks at Virginia, swaying forward.)

ISABEL: Help me, Virginia.

(Virginia rushes to her as Isabel lurches forward. Virginia catches her in her arms as the papers scatter at her feet. Blackout. A moment. Then a radio announcer's voice is heard over the speakers.)

RADIO ANNOUNCER'S VOICE: …Also in the local news: America reached the end of an era last night when Mrs. Isabel Hastings Hoyt, a prominent figure in New York society during the period after World War I, died in her sleep at her home on East 81st Street. A recluse in recent years, Mrs. Hoyt is said to have been at one time the friend and confidante of many of the important artists and writers of her day. Her handsome brownstone house, with its rooms of fine furniture, will be purchased in its entirety by the National Historical Association. Mrs. Hoyt is survived by a single granddaughter, who served as her companion and was with her when she died.

(The lights come slowly up in the room. It looks just the same. From the window, once again, comes the sense of late afternoon. A suitcase is near the hall. The curtains are fully open now, and we can see partly into Isabel's room. We see the end of her bed, stripped of its covers. The doorbell rings. Virginia enters, from her grandmother's room, in a dark dress. The doorknocker is heard. She stands, does nothing. Then we hear a key working in a lock. Then Tom's voice is heard, off and below.)

TOM'S VOICE: Virginia!

(She hides the manuscript behind a pillow on the couch. After a moment, Tom comes in.)

TOM: *(Holding up a key.)* I still have a key.

VIRGINIA: Just put it on the table.

(He does. Pause.)

VIRGINIA: I've been nervous about the door. The lawyers said not even to answer it. The worst sort of people read the obituaries.

TOM: So I've heard.

VIRGINIA: There's even a security guard. Prowling around somewhere out there. To protect the loot.

TOM: I met him. I told him I was a friend of the family.

(Pause.)

VIRGINIA: Some friend. You weren't even here.

TOM: I just got your message.

VIRGINIA: I left messages all over.

TOM: I didn't know.

VIRGINIA: It was in the *Times*.

TOM: I was out of town.

VIRGINIA: There was even a picture.

TOM: I was away.

VIRGINIA: I gave them the one from the old Life. Waving goodbye. I thought at least that would bring you around.

TOM: I was in Saint Paul. For the whole month.

(Pause.)

VIRGINIA: Oh.

(Pause.)

TOM: But it didn't work. I came back to see you.

(Pause.)

VIRGINIA: You see, there was so much to do. You don't realize till it happens. I mean the medical certificate, and the funeral men, and the lawyers, and the bank, and the newspapers.

TOM: I'm very sorry.

VIRGINIA: Well I managed. Somehow. Amazingly enough. *(Pause.)* And of course Gram left a list.

(He steps toward her.)

VIRGINIA: I'm all right. I'm fine.

TOM: Look. Hey. I'm sorry about that night.

VIRGINIA: That was a terrible thing you did.

TOM: I got carried away.

VIRGINIA: You both did terrible things.

TOM: I didn't want it burned.

VIRGINIA: She did.

TOM: I know. I'm sorry. Really. I feel like hell.

(Pause.)

VIRGINIA: Would you like a drink?

TOM: No thanks.

VIRGINIA: It's right there. The brandy. I haven't touched it. I'm over that, too, I hope. Take it. Before the historians get into it.

TOM: No thanks.

(Pause.)

VIRGINIA: I have to be out of here today.

TOM: Where will you go?

VIRGINIA: I'm not sure. There's this hotel for women.

TOM: Oh Christ.

VIRGINIA: I know it.

(Pause.)

TOM: And then what?

VIRGINIA: Oh. Gram left another list. Want to hear?

TOM: Sure.

VIRGINIA: *(Takes a blue piece of paper out of her purse.)* There's no date so I don't know when she wrote it. *(Puts on glasses, reads.)* "Prospects for Virginia." *(Pause.)* "Make hors d'oeuvres for parties." *(Pause.)* "Take care of cats when people go away." *(Pause.)* "Find a girl's boarding school, and teach them to ride." *(She folds the list carefully, puts it back in her purse.)* You see? Lots of choices. *(Pause.)* Trouble is, I don't want to do any of them.

TOM: I'll help you find something.

VIRGINIA: Actually I…kept something.

TOM: Kept something?

VIRGINIA: I kept this. *(She produces the manuscript.)* I promised her I'd burn it. But I didn't. *(Pause.)* It was something to hold onto. *(She puts it down between them.)* There it is.

TOM: There it is.

VIRGINIA: Do you want it?

TOM: *(This is tough for him.)* No.

VIRGINIA: Are you sure?

TOM: I'm writing my own book now. Strangest thing: the minute I left here I started writing.

VIRGINIA: About Gram?

TOM: No, it's about—I'm not sure what it's about. I have these thoughts—no, I have these feelings, and I came back to work them out.
(Pause.)

VIRGINIA: Would you get a cab then, please?

TOM: O.K. You coming?

VIRGINIA: *(Not moving.)* I want to say goodbye.

TOM: All right.
(He goes off. She looks at her grandmother's chair. Then she takes the manuscript and quickly goes into Isabel's room. A moment. Then Tom comes back in. He stands at the doorway to the hall.)

TOM: Virginia?

VIRGINIA'S VOICE: *(From within.)* I'll be right there.

TOM: The security guy's getting the cab. He'll ring.

VIRGINIA'S VOICE: Thank you.

TOM: Hey lookit. You're golden now, you know that? You're free and clear. I'll take you around first thing in the morning. Introduce you to an editor at Scribner's. They'll give you a good deal. They used to publish Fitzgerald. *(Virginia comes out from Isabel's room. She is empty-handed.)*

TOM: All set?

VIRGINIA: I hope so.
(Pause.)

TOM: Where's the sacred tome?

VIRGINIA: In there.

TOM: In there?

VIRGINIA: In the fireplace.
(He looks at her, looks at the doorway where we see a flickering glow. He starts for the doorway, then reluctantly stops.)

TOM: Oh boy.

VIRGINIA: I know it.

TOM: Did you read it?

VIRGINIA: Cover to cover.

TOM: Was it Fitzgerald?

VIRGINIA: No.

TOM: It was, wasn't it?

VIRGINIA: No.

TOM: I'll bet it was.

VIRGINIA: It was just a play.

TOM: A play?

VIRGINIA: An old melodrama.

TOM: By Walter Babcock McCoy?

VIRGINIA: Exactly. Very old fashioned. Very old hat.

TOM: Was it called THE GOLDEN AGE?

VIRGINIA: Yes! And it ends right here in this room. There's this man and this woman.

TOM: He says he loves her. And wants her to live with him.

VIRGINIA: Ah, but she says she had this fabulous grandmother. And she hopes she's inherited some of her…spark, I think it was. And then she straightens her shoulders, which she learned to do in posture class at boarding school, and walks right up to the man and shakes hands. *(She speaks very softly.)* Goodbye.

TOM: *(Leaning forward to hear.)* What? What did you say?

(She gestures "nothing!" and walks away.)

TOM: Will I see you again?

VIRGINIA: You can bring me your book.

TOM: Not before I make a copy.

(The doorbell rings below.)

TOM: There's the cab. Can we share it?

VIRGINIA: Not today. But you could take down my bag. *(She starts out.)*

TOM: Can I at least keep the cat?

VIRGINIA: It got out.

TOM: Will it survive?

VIRGINIA: It did before.

TOM: That was a different cat.

VIRGINIA: So am I.

(She goes out. Tom goes to pick up her bag as the lights fade on the room.)

THE END

THE PERFECT PARTY

To André Bishop

INTRODUCTION

Here's a play which got, for the most part, excellent reviews when it opened at Playwrights Horizons in New York and moved smartly to off-Broadway for a commercial run. Despite the critical support, it didn't last terribly long, nor did it break any records when it did a summer tour and played at the Kennedy Center. Looking it over now, I still find it fairly funny, but I suspect its concerns are too limited to interest much of an audience beyond New York theatre-goers. It's no secret that New York can be a fairly parochial place when it comes to the theatre, and with *The Perfect Party*, I may have played into that trap. It hit the right buttons when it played in Manhattan, but went on to evoke only a bemused shrug elsewhere. In any case, I still find that I'm fond of how this play tries to work with elevated language and strives to achieve the kind of tongue-in-cheek satire that Oscar Wilde or Tom Stoppard do so easily. I suppose I have to admit that this particular tradition of English high comedy is not really the kind of humor that most Americans respond to, at least when a fellow American tries his hand at it.

ORIGINAL PRODUCTION

The Perfect Party was first produced in the Studio Theatre of Playwrights Horizons in New York City on April 2, 1986. It was directed by John Tillinger; the set was designed by Steven Rubin; the costumes were by Jane Greenwood; the lighting was by Dan Kotlowitz; and the production stage manager was Suzanne Fry. The cast was as follows:

Tony . . . . John Cunningham
Lois . . . . Charlotte Moore
Sally . . . . Debra Mooney
Wes . . . . David Margulies
Wilma . . . . Kate McGregor-Stewart

The Perfect Party moved to the Astor Place Theatre in New York City on June 24, 1986, under the auspices of Nicholas Benton, Stanley Flink, Norma and David Langworthy, Craig MacDonald, and Nathan Weiss. The cast was as follows:

Tony . . . . John Cunningham
Lois . . . . Charlotte Moore
Sally . . . . Debra Mooney
Wes . . . . Stephen Pearlman
Wilma . . . . June Gable

CHARACTERS

TONY: a middle-aged college professor
SALLY: his wife
LOIS: a reporter
WES: Tony's friend
WILMA: Wes's wife

SETTING

The play takes place in Tony's study, somewhat set apart from the rest of his house. It is a comfortable room, possibly wood paneled, with a desk, a couch, several chairs, plenty of books in bookcases, and good prints on the wall. Among these might be a picture of Monticello, a portrait of Hawthorne, a profile of Fitzgerald. There is also a television cabinet, possibly a stereo, and a VCR. One door upstage opens onto a hallway leading to the rest of the downstairs area.

ACT I

At rise: Tony and Lois enter from the hall. Tony is a good-looking, middle-aged man, dressed in a tuxedo. Lois is also good-looking and wears an elegant black dress.

LOIS: I understand you plan to make this a perfect party.

TONY: I certainly plan to try. *(He goes to a bar, which has been set up on top of his desk, and begins pouring her a Perrier.)*

LOIS: No, no. I'm serious. You announced it as such. You sent out invitations. I brought mine along. *(She produces an elegant invitation from her purse. It might be decorated with the logo from the program.)* "Come," you say here, "to a perfect party."

TONY: Did I write that?

LOIS: I believe you did. Unless someone is sending out invitations under your name.

TONY: No, no. I'll admit it. I wrote it. It's just that hearing it read aloud, on the eve of battle, so to speak, makes me a little nervous.

LOIS: I should imagine.

TONY: Washington before Yorktown.

LOIS: Yes.

TONY: Custer, before the Little Big Horn.

LOIS: Now, now.

TONY: Well, there are bound to be doubts.

LOIS: But you're still committed, aren't you? You still plan to give it a go?

TONY: Oh yes. Absolutely. All the way.

LOIS: Good. Otherwise I'm wasting my time. And possibly yours.
(He brings her her drink.)

TONY: Are you sure you won't have something stronger than Perrier?

LOIS: No, no. I have to keep a clear head. I have to decide whether to write you up.

TONY: I see.

LOIS: Besides, I happen to represent a major New York newspaper. It would be against the very grain of my profession if I drank on the job.

TONY: I understand.

LOIS: You, of course, should feel free to indulge.

TONY: I thought I might.

LOIS: After all, you must feel very much on the line. I mean, a perfect party.

TONY: At least I can start with a perfect martini. *(He returns to the bar to mix his own drink.)*

LOIS: A martini? That takes considerable courage.

TONY: I'm hoping it will give me considerably more.

LOIS: I notice you've made the party Black Tie.

TONY: Well I think people look and act their best in evening clothes.

LOIS: I tend to agree. Possibly because I'm a naturalist at heart—with a special fondness for the panda and the penguin.

TONY: Ah.

LOIS: *(Walking around.)* I want to know about this room.

TONY: This is my study.

LOIS: That tells me very little.

TONY: Ah well, then I'll tell you more. When my wife and I first bought this house, we called this room the den, possibly because we'd hibernate in here after dinner, like two contented bears, to engage in post-prandial love-play. Naturally, children arrived, and this became known as the family room. Our several cubs would barge in here at all times of the day or night, spilling food, tripping over toys, to gather around the cold, unblinking eye of what I call the Cyclops. *(He opens a cabinet, displays a television screen, closes it deftly.)* Finally, when my wife went to work, and my children left home, I moved my books in here, and turned it totally into my study.

LOIS: *(Sitting on the couch, taking notes from time to time.)* All that says a great deal about American marriage, and the diminishing role of the male within it.

TONY: I may be diminished, but I'm still indispensable. Here's where I pay a good part of the bills. And here's where I prepare courses on American history and literature, which I teach at a local university.

LOIS: Hence your earlier references to American battles.

TONY: Exactly. *(Indicates books in bookcase.)* And these are some of the authors I teach: Hawthorne, James, Fitzgerald, Cheever, Updike…

LOIS: Of course. I've already noticed some of their themes and rhythms, even in your casual discourse.

TONY: Yes, but I have other strings to my bow. Note over here I also have the complete works of Oscar Wilde, bound in leather.

LOIS: Oscar Wilde?

TONY: I inherited him from my grandmother.

LOIS: The source is immaterial. I'd be careful of Wilde. He's not American, and tends to undermine everything that is.

TONY: Nonetheless, here's where I keep him. And here's where we can talk, without being disturbed by the preparations for this evening's party which are taking place, as it were, offstage.

LOIS: And I suppose here's where you wrote the invitations.

TONY: That's right.

LOIS: Including the one which found its way to my newspaper.

TONY: Yes.

LOIS: Did you send it yourself, or did some public relations person slip it into the mail?

TONY: I sent it myself.

LOIS: May I ask why?

TONY: I thought it was news.

LOIS: That, of course, depends on what you tell me. For example, what gave you the idea for this party, and what do you hope to achieve by giving it? Remember while you're talking that I come from New York, which is a hectic, fast-paced city and makes us easily bored with unnecessary exposition.

TONY: A perfect party. Well. I think everyone in the world secretly wants to give one. It's at the heart of the social impulse. The caveman calling his fellow tribesman to the fire, the astrophysicist cupping his electronic ear to space—we all have this yearning to connect in some ultimate way with our fellow man.

LOIS: Or woman?

TONY: Of course. Sorry.

LOIS: Then would you define a perfect party?

TONY: A perfect party has a perfect shape. It starts, it builds, it crests, it explodes, and when it finally subsides, everyone involved—he who gives it, she who attends—is bathed in the pleasant afterglow of sweet remembrance.

LOIS: You make it sound vaguely sexual.

TONY: Do I? I hope I don't offend.

LOIS: No, no. I like sex, coming as I do from New York. But now I must ask you what we call colloquially the Passover question: namely, why now? Why is this night different from all other nights?

TONY: Well, I'm not getting any younger. I hear the clock ticking away. I've lived a complicated life in a complicated country, and I feel the compulsion to pull it all together in some sort of pattern, some sort of shape, just once, at least for an evening, before I die.

LOIS: Hmm. That's very touching…You're a persuasive man. Persuasive and charming…Much of what you say has a strange appeal. Sometimes I have the feeling that you're slightly naive, but that could simply come from the fact that you don't live in New York. Occasionally, also, you seem a little ornate, but I put that down to the unnecessary influence of Oscar Wilde.

TONY: So will you write me up?

LOIS: That now depends on your guest list.

TONY: Ah. Well. I happen to have one right here. *(He produces a lovely, elegantly tooled leather folder.)*

LOIS: *(Taking it.)* What a charming way to display your guests. I almost said perfect, but I didn't. *(She opens it.)* And what helpful headings. School chums. College pals. Navy buddies. Academic colleagues. *(To Tony.)* There's an awful lot of male bonding going on here, sir.

TONY: Read on. The women come in later with a vengeance.

LOIS: *(Reading.)* Old girls. Young students. Recreational companions. Sexual partners. Couldn't some of these categories be combined?

TONY: Good idea.

LOIS: *(Reading on.)* Family members...I'm glad to see you've squeezed your family in here somewhere.

TONY: They're an important part of my life.

LOIS: I always worry about those poor old mothers, sitting alone in the corner with their knees apart.

TONY: My mother keeps her knees together.

LOIS: I'm glad to hear it. *(She returns to the folder.)* Let's see what else. "Miscellaneous?" What's this "miscellaneous?"

TONY: Oh those are just people who don't fall into any particular category. People I've met and clicked with over the years. For example, there's a waiter from Buffalo, New York.

LOIS: How sweet. Which reminds me: did you get a chance to do any kind of ethnic or demographic breakdown on this guest list?

TONY: Well I avoided quotas. I don't believe in those. But I can say that I tried to include a full spectrum of racial and regional diversity. There are also several people coming whose sexual orientation is hardly conventional, and I've asked a smattering of mentally and physically handicapped. I've also taken the liberty of inviting two registered Republicans, just to leaven the lump.

LOIS: *(Closing the folder.)* I'm impressed.

TONY: Thank you.

LOIS: Extremely impressed.

TONY: Thank you very much.

LOIS: *(Patting the folder.)* What you've got here seems to be a kind of micro-cosm for America itself, in the waning years of the twentieth century.

TONY: Exactly.

LOIS: So if it works, if the party succeeds, it will mean that America itself, as a social and political experiment, will have succeeded.

TONY: That's it.

LOIS: So you and I are not just sitting around talking about a party, are we? There's a good deal more at stake tonight than that. What we're talking about, really, is whether this nation, or any other nation so constituted, can long endure.

TONY: Right!

LOIS: *(Getting up; enthusiastically.)* Goddammit, I'm going to put that in the paper, if I can improve the phrasing.

TONY: That must mean you've decided to write me up.

LOIS: I've decided more than that. I've decided to review you.

TONY: Review me? Do you mean that?

LOIS: Absolutely. Tomorrow morning, your party will receive a full-length review, possibly with a picture, in a major New York newspaper!

TONY: Fantastic! That's what I was hoping for.

LOIS: Well first, of course, I had to size you up.

TONY: I was terrified you might just settle for an announcement. Like a wedding. Or a funeral.

LOIS: No, no. We are running for the roses now. *(She folds up her notebook and tosses it down on the coffee table.)* I'm not even going to take any more notes. That might be distracting to you and to your guests. From here on in, I'm simply going to sit back and judge, coolly and dispassionately, with the interests of several million readers at heart.

(Pause.)

TONY: I wish you'd let me spike that Perrier with a little splash of white wine.

LOIS: I've already told you, sir: there are ethics in my profession which make that an immediate no-no.

TONY: At least call me Tony.

LOIS: I'm not even sure I should do that.

TONY: Oh come on. This is a party.

LOIS: All right, then. Tony.

TONY: And I may call you…what?

LOIS: Lois.

TONY: Lois. A lovely name, Lois.

LOIS: You may compliment my name, Tony, you may tempt me with alcohol, but I assure you right now I cannot be bought.

TONY: I see.

(Lois looks at her watch.)

LOIS: Now we've only a little more time before your guests arrive. I want to tell you something important. Something which probably no critic has ever before told the person about to be criticized.

TONY: Go on.

LOIS: When your invitation announcing a perfect party came across my desk at Arts and Leisure, something happened to me. I mean, *physically.* The hair on the back of my neck stood up, and my whole body began to shake violently.

TONY: Why, Lois?

LOIS: Because I suddenly thought: here might be the chance to write a perfect review!

TONY: Ah.

LOIS: Immediately, I ran into my editor's office. I pounded his desk, like some sob sister out of an old movie. I said, "Look, buster! Here's some guy out in the provinces planning a perfect party! Lemme at him!"

TONY: And he did.

LOIS: He did and he didn't. He said he'd print the review if it were any good. But I had to write it on spec. And I had to pay my own transportation here and back. For economic reasons, I took Peoples Express.

TONY: I appreciate the sacrifice.

LOIS: It was worth it. To get here. Because after I write this review, and see it printed, and hear it celebrated in the world at large, as God is my witness, I'll never fly Peoples again!

TONY: You're an ambitious woman, Lois.

LOIS: I am, Tony, but so are you. We are both onto something big tonight. Here you are, about to recreate the multiplicity of America under your own roof. And here I am, about to review that attempt for a major New York newspaper. Oh look, my friend, we were born to meet, you and I. We are dependent on each other. We are locked together in a profound embrace, like Ahab and the whale.

TONY: Couldn't you just relax and enjoy the evening?

LOIS: I could not. If I did, people would be giving parties from here to Hawaii, and calling them perfect, when they might not be at all.

TONY: But what's wrong with that?

LOIS: There have to be standards in this world, Tony, and naturally I'd like to be the one who sets them.

TONY: Oh God, that means we've got to be perfectly wonderful tonight, don't we?

LOIS: That, or perfectly terrible. Either way, it will make for a perfect review. *(There is a knocking on the door.)*

LOIS: Meanwhile, someone wants to come in, and frankly I'm rather glad, since our rhetoric was becoming a little inflated.

TONY: *(Calling toward door.)* Come in.
(The door opens. Sally enters in a lovely evening dress, carrying a tray of hors d'oeuvres.)

SALLY: I was getting bored hanging around in the hall, fussing with flowers, coping with caterers.

TONY: *(Going to greet her.)* Enter my wife Sally, powdered and perfumed from her bath! Gosh, Sally, you look just about as lovely as a woman of your age and general configuration can possibly look. *(He kisses her.)* Darling, this is Lois, who has come all the way from New York to check us out, and write us up.

SALLY: And possibly to put us down, am I right, Lois?

LOIS: Not unless you hurt, confuse, or bore me, Sally.
(They shake hands.)

SALLY: I'll try to do none of those things. I do hope, however, that somewhere along the line, I'll get a chance to express my true feelings.

TONY: Uh-oh.

LOIS: Your true *feelings?* Do you mean to say, Sally, that your true feelings are not in tune with this party, and you are actually, in this day and age, trying to cover them *up?*

SALLY: I'll say no more, though you'll notice how difficult it is for me to maintain eye contact.

TONY: Uh-oh.

LOIS: *(Looking from one to the other.)* It's against both my personal and professional ethics to intervene between a husband and wife. *(Pause.)* Unless I sense a story. I sense one now. How do you feel about this party, Sally. Be frank.

SALLY: *(Passing the hors d'oeuvres.)* I feel this is a perfect party, and we are perfectly in accord. Have some hors d'oeuvres.

LOIS: I still sense trouble at the top of the evening. It may well affect my review.

TONY: *(Quickly.)* The party wouldn't be perfect, Sally, if you didn't feel free to express an opinion.

SALLY: Then I don't like it very much.

TONY: Sally, my love—

SALLY: In fact I hate it. I hate the salmon mousse they're preparing in the kitchen. I hate the Chivas Regal being set up in the hall. I hate this goddamn dress which I bought on sale, at Lord and Taylors, out at that stupid, boring, fucking Mall!

TONY: It's a beautiful dress, Sally, and you look lovely in it.

SALLY: It stinks. It sucks. I hate it. You could feed a number of hungry people with what I paid for it. You could buy a respectable portion of a cat-scanner. You could reclaim several acres of wetlands with what I coughed up for this goddamn dress.

TONY: Civilization is expensive, Sally. I've told you that on a number of occasions.

SALLY: Then civilization is horseshit, if this is what it leads to.

TONY: Gosh, Sally. Wow. Gee whiz. I have to say I wasn't quite prepared for such strong feelings. Upstairs, in our bedroom, when you were putting on your earrings, I do remember hearing vague mutterings of discontent. But I didn't expect this explosion of distaste. It startles me, darling. And puzzles me as well.

LOIS: Perhaps I'm to blame here. I've known people to exaggerate their performances in front of critics. Maybe I'll go and review the mousse. *(She starts to leave.)*

TONY: No, no. Please.

SALLY: Yes. Please stay. You give me a vague sense of sisterhood at a time when I need it most.

TONY: It couldn't be a perfect party, Lois, if you only reviewed the food.

SALLY: Shit! There's that expression again. "A perfect party!" What if it isn't perfect, Tony? What if two of your buddy-pals get into a boring argument about batting averages? What if someone spills a drink, or loses his teeth, or puts a cigarette out in a dessert plate?

LOIS: What if someone even *smokes,* for that matter?

SALLY: *Exactly,* Lois. Or what if someone, totally accidentally, farts?

TONY: Good Lord.

SALLY: What if that happens? Does that mean the party is no longer perfect, Tony? Does Lois here go back to New York and tell the world we produced a disaster?

LOIS: Oh well let's cross that bridge when we come to it.

TONY: I'm sure that Lois will leave some margin for error.

LOIS: Not really. I might if I were from Boston or Saint Louis, but since I'm from New York, I'm compelled to be brutal.

SALLY: *(To Tony.)* You see? We're setting ourselves up here! I may not be a la-de-da college professor, but I know hubris when I see it. When people start wandering around the house talking about perfect parties, and inviting New York newspapers to write them up, then I get a primitive Sophoclean shudder. We are challenging the gods here tonight, Tony, and I don't like it one iota!

TONY: *(To Lois.)* Sally majored in Classy Civ at Vassar.

SALLY: Yes, but I got my Master's in Social Responsibility at a Community College.

TONY: Have a drink, Sally.

SALLY: I don't want a drink.

LOIS: He's always trying to persuade people to have drinks.

TONY: I'm simply trying to be a good host.

SALLY: Or else you're trying to drown a serious disagreement in a pool of alcohol.

TONY: I like to think

SALLY: All *right,* Tony! I will have a *drink.* I've decided to have… *(She thinks.)* …a Box Car.

TONY: A—Box Car?

SALLY: It's a drink which emerged during the Depression.

TONY: I'm not sure I know what's in a Box Car.

SALLY: You don't? And you're a perfect host?

TONY: I'm not sure I have the ingredients immediately available.

SALLY: *(Casually.)* Oh well, then, this isn't a perfect party.

TONY: *(Grimly.)* I'll make you a Box Car, Sally. There's a copy of the Joy of Cooking in the kitchen, and it has a complete section devoted to exotic beverages. I'll make you a Box Car, Sally, and you can be damn sure it will be a perfect one! *(He goes out, slamming the door.)*
(Pause.)

SALLY: *(To Lois.)* That was a ploy.

LOIS: I figured as much.

SALLY: To get him out of the room.

LOIS: Yes, I picked up on that.

SALLY: I don't really want a Box Car at all. *(Gets up and goes to the bar.)* What I really want is a tad of white wine, and I hope you'll join me, Lois.

LOIS: I shouldn't. But since you're a woman, I will.

SALLY: *(At bar.)* Then you agree with what I said about a sense of sisterhood, Lois.

LOIS: I certainly do. I resonated as soon as you walked in this room.

SALLY: I've simply got to talk to someone of the same sex about what I've been going through, recently, on this perfect party business.

LOIS: Feel free to talk. I'll consider it strictly off the record. If I write it up, I'll attribute it to unnamed sources.

SALLY: *(Bringing down the drinks.)* Well it's been hell, frankly. That man has become obsessed with parties, particularly perfect ones.

LOIS: He certainly seems to have an idée fixe, doesn't he?

SALLY: It's appalling. Ever since the children began leaving home, it's as if he were trying to reconstitute the family. On a large and general scale. With himself once again in control.

LOIS: How awful. You must feel as if you're living right in the middle of a bad translation of Molière.

SALLY: I do. It pervades our life. Whenever we go out, whenever we have people in, he has these huge expectations that the evening will click into place like some smooth, well-oiled machine. When it doesn't happen—and of course it doesn't—he is profoundly disappointed. He sits on the edge of the bed, in his pajamas, holding his head and groaning.

LOIS: When he should be making love to you.

SALLY: Exactly! Oh it's a mess, Lois. Our marriage is teetering on the brink.

LOIS: Now, now. Think positively.

SALLY: I'm trying to, Lois. But there's so much at stake here. Do you realize that he's quit his job because of this party.

LOIS: What?

SALLY: He has quit his job. He had a perfectly good job teaching American studies at a reputable university. The salary was insulting, but the fringe benefits made up for it.

LOIS: Did he have tenure?

SALLY: He most certainly did. And he was considered an excellent teacher. At least until recently.

LOIS: What happened recently?

SALLY: He tried to turn every class into a perfect class. The students rebelled, of course, and switched into Abnormal Psychology. That's when he quit, so he could turn his total attention to this party.

LOIS: But how does he expect to live, when the party's over?

SALLY: He expects to become a consultant.

LOIS: A consultant?

SALLY: On parties! That's why he brought you into the picture. He desperately wants a review. Because he desperately wants to become a celebrity.

LOIS: But that's what *I* want to be! And there's only room for a few of us at the top!

SALLY: I can't help it. That's what he wants. He says he comes from what was once the ruling class and if he can no longer lead this nation toward a more perfect union, he can at least show it how to entertain!

LOIS: Yes, but a consultant!

SALLY: I know. He sees himself traveling around the country giving lectures and seminars and workshops on parties in America, and how to give them. The other night he dreamed he was on the Merv Griffin Show.

LOIS: Oh no.

SALLY: That's what he dreamed.

LOIS: But that's outrageous! Merv is very choosy about his guests.

SALLY: You know that, I know that, Merv knows that, but Tony doesn't know it. He even thinks he might host a show of his own some day. On nation-wide TV.

LOIS: No.

SALLY: Or at least co-host.

LOIS: I'm stunned.

SALLY: I'm telling you, the man is obsessed. Did he show you his guest list?

LOIS: Yes he did, and I must say it was impressively democratic.

SALLY: I'm talking about his secret guest list.

LOIS: His *secret* guest list?

SALLY: He has a secret list of people whom he's asked to this party, and who he hopes will suddenly show up.

LOIS: Who's on it?

SALLY: Oh, God. Let me think. Abba Eban's on it.

LOIS: Abba Eban?

SALLY: Abba Eban is on that list. He thinks Abba Eban would be an addition to any party.

LOIS: Well, of course he would be, but...

SALLY: Ginger Rogers is also on the list.

LOIS: Ginger's on it?

SALLY: Absolutely. He's even bought a record of old dance tunes. If she shows up, he plans to roll back the rug, and spin her around the floor, to the tune of *Follow the Fleet*.

LOIS: That is sheer...

SALLY: Hubris is the word. I've already used it.

LOIS: You poor soul. Living with that.

SALLY: I'm all right. Think of him. Living constantly in the gap between how he wishes people would behave, and how they actually do. And trying to bridge that gap with this party, this evening.

LOIS: Sally: I can't tell you how much I appreciate your telling me these things. Women do connect in ways which are far beyond the world of men. I think we've proved that in the discussion we've had just now.

SALLY: Then I wonder if I might ask you a small favor.

LOIS: Name it.

SALLY: Give him a good review.

LOIS: What?

SALLY: Oh I'm not talking about a rave. You don't have to do that. Just compliment him on the basic idea. Mention a few good moments. Give him enough quotes so that he can show his clippings around.

LOIS: I can't do that, Sally.

SALLY: Of course you can.

LOIS: Sally, I can't. If I did that, if I let my affection for you influence my response, it would open the door to the most shoddy enterprises.

SALLY: But his future depends on what you say here.

LOIS: So does mine, dear heart. Don't think for one minute I'm not on the line here, too. My editor has his eye on this one. If I'm good, then he might promote me to White House functions and Hollywood galas. But if I fake it, if I strike one false note, then I might find myself a permanent stringer, doomed to cover church suppers and bowling tournaments in areas beyond even a commuting distance from New York.

SALLY: But think about Tony and me.

LOIS: Excuse me, Sally, but these days I find it hard to think about anyone but myself. We live in a narcissistic age, and it's foolish not to take advantage of it.

SALLY: But if you pan us, what will we do financially with Tony out of a job? We've got a kid still in college, and our VCR needs serious repairing.

LOIS: I can't help that, Sally. I've said all along that I must call this evening as I see it, and the Devil take the hindmost, even if the hindmost is your husband.

SALLY: *(Grimly.)* Then there's only one thing left for me to do.

LOIS: What's that?

SALLY: I'm not sure, but I'm hoping it will occur to me any minute.

(Tony enters, carrying a strange looking, dark brown drink, garnished with a limp radish, on a silver tray.)

TONY: One Box Car, coming up. *(He hands it to Sally.)*

SALLY: *(Eyeing it.)* What's in it?

TONY: I doubt if you'd want to know. Let me simply say that, like this evening, I hope the whole is greater than the sum of its parts.

(Sally looks at it, sips it.)

TONY: As for you, Lois, I'm delighted to see you with a wine glass in your hand. It indicates that you're taking a more participatory position.

LOIS: *(Wryly.)* Not at all. This happens to be a cool, dry, disengaged Chablis, with a slightly skeptical bouquet.

SALLY: *(Suddenly putting down her glass.)* Uh-oh.

TONY: What?

SALLY: This drink.

TONY: What about it?

SALLY: It doesn't agree with me at all. You'll have to call off the party.

TONY: Oh no.

SALLY: I'm serious. I feel perfectly awful. I've got a headache, and heartburn, and a mild case of psoriasis.

TONY: *(Going to her.)* Darling…

SALLY: *(Getting up.)* No, it's getting worse. Don't touch me. I've got to go right to bed. Here's what you better do. Post a sign on the door, saying that the party's canceled. Pay off the caterers, and get a reasonable rakeoff for what we didn't consume. Call Lois a cab. Tell the university you were just teasing when you quit. Then scramble some eggs, and bring them up to me on a tray, and maybe I'll feel well enough to sit up and have a nice game of Trivial Pursuit. Go on, honey. Get started. *(She is almost out the door.)*

TONY: Sally.

SALLY: What, for God's sake?

TONY: I don't believe you're sick at all.

SALLY: What do you mean? I'm about to upchuck all over the door.

TONY: I don't believe that, Sally. And I don't think Lois believes it.

LOIS: I most certainly do not.

SALLY: *(Whirling on Lois.)* Some sisterhood.

LOIS: I'm sorry, Sally. It's an implausible development, and I'd have to review it as such.

SALLY: Couldn't we all just go to the movies, or something?

LOIS: The movies are out of my bailiwick, Sally. Somebody else is assigned to review those.

SALLY: So I'm caught, aren't I?

TONY: I'm afraid you are, love.

SALLY: There's a moment in the *Iliad*...

TONY: *(Quickly; to Lois.)* Sally was Cum Laude at Vassar...

SALLY: There's a moment in the Iliad when Andromache joins Hector on the walls of Troy, right before he goes to his death at the hands of the Greeks. She says she hates what he's about to do, but she'll stand by him to the end while he does it. *(She takes Tony's arm and defiantly faces Lois.)* This reminds me of that moment.

LOIS: I appreciate your loyalty, though I question your analogy.

(A door bell rings, far offstage.)

LOIS: But that must be your first guests, thank God. Much as I like you both, I'm interested in seeing a few new faces.

TONY: *(Looking at his watch.)* It's still a little early for guests. Unless it's the Murchisons, who always arrive early and eat up all the Brie.

SALLY: I told the Murchisons to be late, for exactly that reason.

(The offstage door bell rings again.)

LOIS: Maybe you should answer the door.

TONY: Since I'm paying a catering company a great deal of money to do exactly that, I'm hoping I won't have to.

LOIS: I like the suspense. I find it charming. *(She sits down.)*

TONY: *(Quickly.)* I know who it is! It's our great friends, Wes and Wilma Wellman, who live down the street. They've realized the importance of the occasion, and have come over early to help us out.

SALLY: Exactly. Whenever we've been in a crisis situation—when my grand-mother died or the dishwasher broke down—the Wellmans rushed right over to be by our side.

(The door bell rings once again.)

TONY: *(Opening the study door.)* Yes. Now I hear their gentle voices murmur-ing in the front hall.

WILMA'S VOICE: *(From offstage, loudly.)* Yoo hoo!

TONY: *(Calling out.)* In the study, friends! *(To Lois.)* What is a party without true friends at your side? And what better friends could a man have than this stalwart and attractive couple? *(He looks out down the hall.)* Good gravy, it's Wes and Wilma, all right, but I'm not sure they're dressed for the occasion.

(Wes and Wilma enter awkwardly in old bathrobes. Wilma wears a bandanna around her hair.)

SALLY: You do look a little informal, dear friends.

WES: *(Anxiously.)* Tony, old pal, we had to rush over and tell you immediately.

TONY: Tell me what, old friends?

WILMA: We can't come to your party.

TONY: Can't come?

WES: Can't come.

TONY: But you answered affirmatively. I put your names in the yes column. I gave the count to the caterer.

WILMA: Things have come up, Tony.

WES: Personal things. Talk to you later. *(He grabs Wilma and starts out.)*

TONY: Wait, wait, wait! At least say hello to Lois.

WES: Hello, Lois.

WILMA: Hello, Lois.

LOIS: Hello, Wes and Wilma.

WILMA: *(Taking Wes's arm.)* Come on, Wes.

WES: *(Staring at Lois.)* Hold it. I know this woman from somewhere.

LOIS: I've slept with a number of men, but I don't think you were one of them.

WES: *(Moving toward her.)* No, this was prior to puberty… *(He thinks.)* Kindergarten, *(He remembers.)* P.S. 101. Brooklyn.

LOIS: You seem to have touched on my educational beginnings, though I like to think I've grown beyond them.

TONY: *(Hastily.)* I'm sure you have, Lois.

WES: You were a strange little girl. You sent out bitter, vindictive Valentines to the whole class. And when it came time for the school play—the Teddy Bear's Picnic, I think it was—you sat on the sidelines and loudly complained about the lighting.

TONY: Lois is a critic, Wes. How good to hear that her talents emerged at such an early age.

WILMA: I'm finding it difficult to contribute to the conversation, because I went to private school in the suburbs of Cleveland.

TONY: That's all right, Wilma. Lois is here from New York to write up the party.

LOIS: I am indeed. And I'm already impatient with these sentimental reminiscences. What we were, or did, when we were young is of interest only to our parents and our psychiatrists. What interests *me* is why you two have arrived embarrassingly early and strangely underdressed. This is the time when most people are still in the shower, or poking around in their clothes closets, deciding what to wear and who to be.

WES: That's exactly where we were, five minutes ago.

LOIS: In the shower? Or in the closet?

WILMA: *(Taking Wes's arm.)* In the shower, actually. Both of us. Celebrating the physical side of our marriage.

WES: That's not the point, honey. We have to go.

TONY: No, wait! Why can't you come to my party?

WILMA: It's a family obligation, Tony. Our daughter Debbie is giving a dance recital, and we feel we should be there.

TONY: Isn't that rather sudden?

WILMA: It is, Tony. But Debbie dances very much on impulse.

WES: And after Debbie dances, I have a political obligation.

TONY: Another one of those meetings on Israel?

WES: I like to think, Tony, that it's a meeting on the welfare of the entire free world.

TONY: Hey. *(With a side-glance at Lois.)* This is somewhat disappointing, friends.

WES: It's a question of priorities, Tony.

WILMA: Maybe we'll drop by for dessert.

(They are almost out the door.)

TONY: Wait!

(They stop.)

TONY: Wilma: I don't believe Debbie is dancing tonight. And I'll tell you why. Because tonight is the night she attends that top-secret weight-loss clinic in the cellar of the Congregational Church.

SALLY: That's true, Wilma. You told us that just yesterday.

WILMA: She could do her dancing there!

TONY: No, she couldn't, Wilma. It would disturb the class. And as for you, Wes, I don't think you have a meeting on Israel. This is Saturday night, after all, and there's a specific injunction in Leviticus which says, "Speak not of Zion on nights when the gentiles give parties."

WES: Is that true?

SALLY: He taught the Bible, Wes.

LOIS: It's a wonderful book.

TONY: Wes, Wilma, you obviously made up these inept excuses on the way over. There must be a far more profound reason why you feel you can't come.

(They look at each other.)

WES: *(Finally.)* There is, Tony.

WILMA: There really is.

TONY: Then out with it, friends.

WILMA: Well… *(She sits on the couch.)*

WES: It's too much for us, buddy. This perfect party. *(He sits beside her.)*

WILMA: The pressure…

WES: The sense of being so totally on the line…

WILMA: And now to be *judged*…

WES: By a New *Yorker*… *(He holds his head.)*

WILMA: Oh, Tony, it's tough enough going to any party these days, let alone a perfect one.

WES: So we thought we'd go to the movies instead.

SALLY: It's interesting how people keep turning toward the movies.

LOIS: They are looking like a rather attractive alternative.

WILMA: At least you don't have to make so much *effort* at the movies.

WES: Except with Meryl Streep.

WILMA: You can never tell what accent she's doing.

SALLY: If she ruins one more book for me.

WES: Is she in *The Color Purple?*

TONY: Now *wait!* Hold on! Wes! Wilma! What is this? You guys are supposed to be the mainstay of the evening.

WES: Maybe that's the trouble, Tony. Maybe you're putting too much on us.

WILMA: That's exactly it. You expect too much of your friends, Tony. I've sensed it for some time. Last week, when we were playing bridge, I heard this great groan of disappointment every time I lost a trick.

WES: And she wasn't even your partner.

WILMA: Or when we eat out together, and I order the chicken, I'm aware of your eyes on me, Tony. You make me think I should have ordered the veal.

SALLY: This has the ring of truth.

WES: We're just simple suburban people, Tony. All right, maybe I'm a urologist with a prestigious appointment at a major medical school…

WILMA: And maybe I'm a speech therapist in the local school system, with strong side interest in ceramics…

WES: But still, we're just an ordinary middle-class couple, Tony. And glad to be so.

TONY: No, goddammit! I don't accept that! You guys are easily capable of giving the suburbs a good name!

WES: Oh, hey…

TONY: I'm serious. In some ways, you stand for the full flowering of the American dream.

WILMA: Oh now…

TONY: *(Sitting on the arm of the couch.)* You do! Your rich ethnic roots, your pleasant home throbbing with the hum of working appliances, your weedless lawn with its well-placed shrubs, your over-educated children—well hell, you folks embody the best of that particular lifestyle, that's all.

WES: Go easy.

TONY: How can I go easy when I feel so strongly on the subject. Support me on this one, Sally.

SALLY: It's true, Wes and Wilma. He may sound fatuous, but he really admires you both.

LOIS: Yes, but do they belong at this party? They feel they don't, and I tend to agree with them.

TONY: No, no. They're fine people. You wait: They'll rise to the occasion as they always have. Won't you, Wes? Wilma?

WILMA: I'm not sure we can, Tony. We're too nervous.

WES: Tell him what we did this afternoon, we were so nervous.

WILMA: We went to our family therapist this afternoon.

WES: With the kids...

WILMA: Except for Debbie.

WES: And we shared with him our concerns about this party.

WILMA: And you know what he said, Tony? He said that our anxiety was based on the fact that, deep down, Wes and I are desperate to be a big hit.

WES: That's what he said. He said that Wilma and I have secret fantasies of being the life of this party.

WILMA: And the kids agreed!

TONY: But then here's your chance, guys! Make your move!

WILMA: No, Tony, no. The spotlight's too much on us.

WES: You don't throw a couple of amateurs onto the center court of Wimbledon, Tony.

WILMA: Our very eagerness to succeed has incapacitated us.

TONY: Then rise above it, folks. You've done it before. What about the DeVitas' Christmas party? That was straight hardball, and you came through then.

WES: That's true. We did. *(To Wilma.)* Particularly you, honey.

WILMA: Oh stop.

TONY: No, it's true. You guys were spectacular at the DeVitas'. I watched you working the crowd.

WILMA: Will the DeVitas be here? That might help. *(To Lois.)* I always do well around the DeVitas.

TONY: No, the DeVitas will not be here, Wilma, and I'll tell you why. Rose DeVita loses concentration on every subject she touches. She becomes difficult to follow, and when she's been drinking, well nigh impossible.

SALLY: Tony thought of inviting Monty DeVita without her.

TONY: Yes I did. I seriously thought of that. Because Monty can focus. The trouble is, lately he focuses too much. He seems to be only interested in the Dallas Cowboys, and who cares about them?

WES: I do.

TONY: Well I don't, Wes. So the DeVitas are out. *(Pause; with regret.)* Betty and Dick Washburn are out, too.

WILMA: I know. They called me. They're very upset.

TONY: I can't help that. Betty Washburn talks about nothing but Dick, and Dick doesn't talk at all. I told Betty on the phone—I called her specially—and said, "Broaden your range, Betty. Or at least broaden Dick." She said she'd try.

WILMA: Still, it's so cruel, cutting people out that way.

TONY: Well if it will make you feel any better, Wilma, I told both the Washburns and the DeVitas they could come to the party if they just stayed in the bedroom and watched TV and didn't try to participate in any of the dialogue.

SALLY: It's true. He did that.

TONY: But they all thought it over and decided to stay home.

WILMA: Everything you say just makes me feel the pressure all the more.

WES: She's sensitive on these things, Tony. So am I.

TONY: Which is another good reason why I want you guys here! You bring with you a sensitivity which comes from five thousand years of Jewish anxiety.

(A stunned moment.)

WILMA: Jewish? You invited us because we were Jewish?

WES: I have a problem with that, Tony.

LOIS: So do I!

SALLY: Yes, Tony! Honestly!

(They all begin to protest noisily.)

TONY: *(Shouting them down.)* All I meant was…

(They quiet down.)

TONY: All I meant was that Wes and Wilma are like the cellos in a Verdi ensemble. They provide a lovely, consistent, melancholy sound under the lighter, more eccentric melodies sung by some of our superficial guests. *(To Wes and Wilma.)* The very fact that you came over here just now, in obvious disarray, to express your concern, says something about your Jewish sense of social responsibility.

(The protesting begins again. All talk simultaneously.)

SALLY: Worse and worse.

WES: Now I'm feeling vaguely stereotyped.

WILMA: Yes, I'm still having trouble with that, Tony.

LOIS: I'm particularly sensitive, coming as I do from New York...

TONY: *(Shouting them down.)* All right, all right! Skip it! But can I count on you two tonight? Will you both go home, and change into what I'm sure are particularly fashionable clothes, since you must obviously have relatives in the garment industry.

(The loudest protests yet.)

TONY: Sorry! Really! I'm flailing around here simply because I don't want my cello section to walk out on me right before the opera begins! Now what say, folks? Are you with me or not?

WES: Excuse me, Tony. This calls for consultation.

(Wes takes Wilma upstage to consult. Tony, Sally and Lois watch them.)

TONY: *(To Lois.)* If they leave, I'm lost.

LOIS: I'm afraid that's true. The Jewish middle class is primarily responsible for keeping culture alive in this country.

TONY: I agree.

(Finally.)

WES: *(Coming downstage with Wilma.)* All right, Tony. We'll make a deal with you, because we're old and good friends.

TONY: Name your terms, Wes and Wilma.

WES: We'll come to the party if we don't feel we have to be perfect all the time.

WILMA: That's right, Tony. We want to be able to dare to fail.

WES: Our grandparents didn't come to this country from the shtetls of eastern Europe in order to feel pressured at a party, Tony. Now there it is. Take it or leave it.

TONY: I'll take it, of course!

WILMA: Oh good!

SALLY: Thank God.

(They all embrace.)

TONY: And I'll even up you one! Once the party gets going, you both should feel free to explore your own Jewishness even in front of our shallowest Protestant friends.

WES: That's great, Tony! I've always wanted to do that!

SALLY: It's getting close to that time, folks.

WILMA: Let's cut through by the Millworth's hot tub.

(They start out.)

TONY: Oh, but wait...

SALLY: *(Frustratedly.)* Let them get *dressed*, Tony!

TONY: I just have two quick points to add to our deal.

WES: Uh oh.

TONY: No, seriously. Wilma: when you get going out there, when the party is in full swing, try not to talk about your children.

WILMA: I love my children!

TONY: I know you do, Wilma, and so do I. But people who don't have any find it difficult to contribute to the conversation. And those who do, immediately want to talk about their own.

WILMA: I *hate* it when they do that. It's so boring.

TONY: Then don't give them the chance, Wilma. And, Wes…

WES: *(Suspiciously.)* Here it comes.

TONY: I have to ask you not to bring up Israel.

WES: *What?*

TONY: I'm asking you that as a favor, Wes.

WES: I feel strongly about Israel.

TONY: I know you do, Wes, and I'm impressed by your commitment. But I'm asking you not to talk about it tonight.

WES: You didn't invite any Palestinians, did you?

TONY: Yes I did, Wes!

(General uproar, once again.)

TONY: But they sent their regrets. Along with a very nice wedge of goat's milk cheese.

WES: O.K., I'll avoid Israel.

TONY: Good. Now get going. Both of you.

WILMA: Can we grab a shrimp or two on the way out?

TONY: You can, if you brush your teeth afterwards. Now so long.

SALLY: *(Joining them.)* I'll see you to the door. And then continue to fuss reluctantly with food and flowers.

(Sally, Wes, and Wilma go out. Pause.)

TONY: *(To Lois.)* That handles that.

LOIS: Yes…

TONY: *(Raising his glass.)* And the ship sails on.

LOIS: Yes.

TONY: I must say you stayed strangely in the background during that little confrontation, Lois.

LOIS: Did I?

TONY: I mean, you participated. But only occasionally. And your lines didn't have much energy or bite.

LOIS: *My* lines are not at issue here, Tony. I'm more concerned about yours.

TONY: Is something bothering you?

LOIS: Yes, Tony. There is.

TONY: Then let me have it. Now. We've only got a few minutes before the party begins, and I want to absorb it, integrate it, and act on it, if I can, before I greet my guests.

LOIS: Tony... *(Pause.)* Tony, I think I've already said how much I admire what you're trying to do here. A perfect party. There's something big about that, and, as we've said, something quintessentially American. Only in these United States could such a notion arise. It smacks of Whitman, and Gatsby, and Citizen Kane.

TONY: Thank you, Lois.

LOIS: No, I mean it. There's something huge and grandiose about it, yes, and tragic, too. To think that one man, in his own home, would try to crystallize the hopes and dreams of an entire nation...

TONY: *(Looking at her suspiciously.)* Somewhere in your thick syntax, Lois, I'm beginning to sense a "but," waiting to pounce... *(He passes her the hors d'oeuvres.)*

LOIS: But...*But*, Tony. *(She takes an hor d'oeuvre.)* Mmmm, this is good. But... Tony, I'm going to have to pass on this party.

TONY: Pass?

LOIS: It's an expression we use in New York. It means default. Withdraw. Walk.

TONY: Walk?

LOIS: After I finish my wine, Tony, and possibly one more of those delicious hors d'oeuvres...

(Tony passes her the tray. She takes it, holds it on her lap, and eats as she talks.)

LOIS: ...Thank you, my friend...I'm going to get up and walk out that door and not come back.

TONY: Now wait a minute.

LOIS: *(During mouthfuls of hors d'oeuvres.)* I don't intend to write up this party, Tony. I don't intend to mention it in a casual column, nor will I refer to it in subsequent reportage. I've had a pleasant half hour or so conferring with you and your lovely wife, and meeting your suburban friends, but I'm afraid that's as far as it goes.

TONY: But you decided to review us.

LOIS: I've changed my mind.

TONY: But if you don't, that would mean that this whole evening would pass unheralded, unjudged, and uncommemorated.

LOIS: Yes.

TONY: But then the world would little note, nor long remember, what we do here.

LOIS: That's right. Yes.

TONY: But don't you realize this is the first major cultural contribution a Protestant has made to this country since Cole Porter wrote *Kiss Me Kate?*

LOIS: I'm sorry, Tony.

TONY: But what's happened? Why leave us now?

LOIS: Let me try to explain it, to myself as well as to you. *(She thinks.)* For some time now, Tony, I've had the sense that there's something vital missing here tonight.

TONY: Something vital?

LOIS: *(She begins to circle around the room.)* Something…fundamental. At first, I thought it was simply a question of language. I mean we've all been very talky around here. Very literary, and all that. And what I thought I missed was the natural vulgarity and rich rhythms of the contemporary American vernacular.

TONY: I'm not going to wander around saying "fuck" and "shit" at my own party!

LOIS: Of course you're not, Tony, and I don't blame you. It's not our stilted language that's getting me down. The source of my unhappiness lies elsewhere. *(Pause.)* Now how do I put this? *(She sees the light.)* There's no sense of danger at this party.

TONY: Danger?

LOIS: Danger. Every good party has, underneath it, a fundamental sense of danger. And this party has none.

TONY: But I'll have to go back to teaching if it doesn't work.

LOIS: That's frightening, Tony, but it's not frightening enough. If you want this party reviewed, then it's got to be much scarier. Think, for example, of the great parties of history: the revels of Nero during the burning of Rome. The soirées at Versailles under the lengthening shadow of the guillotine. The last frantic dance on the deck of the Titanic. Those were dangerous parties, and I'm afraid this can't equal them.

TONY: You're asking for too much, Lois.

LOIS: Maybe I am, but so are you. Oh look, my friend, we're very much alike, you and I. We are born perfectionists. I have struggled out of the polyglot mire of a Brooklyn kindergarten toward the cool, clear vision of some social ideal. You, on the other hand, carry with you the memory of a civilized past gleaned from your corrupt and decadent ancestors. I am moving up. You are moving down. We have gravitated toward one another all our lives, like two lost planets in search of a sun. There's a tremendous magnetism between us, and if you weren't happily married, I think I'd initiate an affair with you immediately. But there's no danger here, Tony. None. Even a simple birthday party is infused with the sadness of passing time. A wedding is fraught with the perils of sex. A funeral throbs with the ache of last things. Behind the best human gathering is a sense of its own precariousness. We should dance on the edge of the abyss. And that's what I don't sense here, Tony. What is the threat? Where is the pain? It's all cozy and comfortable and polite. In fact, it's so polite, Tony, that you've let me make much too long a speech without interrupting me. It's symptomatic of the whole problem.

TONY: I'll interrupt you now!

LOIS: Yes, but you don't like doing it. You're a nice man with a pretty wife, and from all reports, several fine children. You were born with money, and you married more of it, and you've lived easily all your life. The gods have been good to you, Tony, and it shows. There's an aura of smug self-congratulation which pervades this house, coupled with the insidious influence of Oscar Wilde. But there's no danger here, so it isn't a perfect party, and I feel no need to review it. *(She holds out her hand.)* Thank you at least for a pleasant preliminary. I hope things go reasonably well, and everyone has a perfectly adequate time. *(She slaps him patronizingly on the back and starts for the door.)*

TONY: Wait! I could add danger.

LOIS: *(At the door.)* How?

TONY: Well I mean I could invite someone else at the last minute. Some Neo-Nazi. Some escaped convict.

LOIS: No, Tony…

TONY: I could have a small nuclear device ticking away in the cellar…

LOIS: Tony, please.

TONY: Why *not?*

LOIS: I would seem dragged in, and I'd have to say as much, when I reviewed it. *(She is almost out the door.)*

TONY: No, wait! Please! Really! *(He thinks quickly.)* What about my brother? *(Lois stops and turns.)*

LOIS: Your brother?

TONY: My twin brother. I've invited him.

LOIS: What's his name?

TONY: Tod.

LOIS: Tod?

TONY: Tod. Though his nickname is Toad.

LOIS: Either way, that's German for…

TONY: Death.

(Lois comes back into the room.)

LOIS: Is he…dangerous?

TONY: He's a killer.

LOIS: A murderer?

TONY: No. But he kills things.

LOIS: Cats? Hamsters? Things of that ilk?

TONY: No, he kills something else. He kills moments. He destroys moods. He annihilates atmospheres.

(Lois sits on the arm of the couch.)

LOIS: Tell me more.

TONY: I'll try. I'm the older, by half an hour. According to my mother, I was a perfect baby, and slid smilingly into the world. She was in the recovery room, celebrating my birthday with my father—raising a glass of champagne, sending a telegram to Yale, all that—when suddenly she gave a shriek and spilled her champagne. Out came Tod, who kicked and screamed and totally ruined the party.

LOIS: Your poor mother.

TONY: I know. It was as if, even then, even at his birth, Tod was a kind of afterthought, a kind of instinctive counterargument or contradiction, emerging from the same source.

LOIS: Do you look alike, you and Tod?

TONY: Almost exactly. He, of course, wears a mustache, while I, as you may have noticed, don't. After his birth, he struggled so much against his mother's embrace that she inadvertently dropped him. The infant broke his right leg, which was improperly reset, because he irritated the doctor. The result is that he has a pronounced limp, which gives him a certain Byronic appeal, but makes him a consistently disappointing tennis partner.

LOIS: How sad.

TONY: Yes. He was such an unhappy child that my mother sent him to Sunny Italy for Junior High School. He returned with a book on the Borgias and the permanent speech patterns of a Neapolitan pickpocket.

LOIS: Any other distinguishing characteristics?

TONY: Just one.

LOIS: And what is that?

TONY: He has— (He stops.) Never mind. It's not important. The point is that my brother is, or can be, an ultimately destructive human being. He is in constant competition with me, and everyone else. He has hacked his way through life's dark wood leaving a long, bloody spoor of victims behind him. He has been married at least four times, and divorced only twice. He was expelled from the Teamsters Union, and reprimanded by the C.I.A. His conversation is designed to make you thoroughly uncomfortable and even while he's doing it, you feel he's glancing over your shoulder, seeking out someone else to irritate even more. In short, he is probably the most dangerous person I have ever known, and already I'm having strong second thoughts about inviting him to this party.

LOIS: You said there was another characteristic which distinguished Tod from you.

TONY: Oh well. It's not important really.

LOIS: Tell me. It might prove to be helpful, later on.

TONY: I thought you were leaving.

LOIS: Frankly, now I'm on the fence. The notion of twins has always had a primitive appeal. It might just work at a party. I'm also intrigued by the mustache and the limp, and the Italian connection is unsettling. So tell me: What else does he have that you don't?

TONY: Well, to put it frankly, Lois, he has a considerably larger penis.

(Long pause.)

LOIS: I've decided to stay at this party.

TONY: You have?

LOIS: Yes. I've decided that the party may have some potential.

TONY: I'm delighted! I hope you won't be disappointed.

LOIS: That remains to be seen.

(The sound of a party begins to be heard offstage.)

TONY: People are beginning to arrive. I should go greet my guests.

LOIS: *(Taking his arm.)* I'll join you. To look them over. And to see if your brother Tod is among them.

TONY: He might not come.

LOIS: Why not?

TONY: Simply because I invited him.

LOIS: What if you called him and told him to stay away?

TONY: Then he'd show up immediately.

LOIS: Go make that call. I'm eager to meet this man.

(She goes out. He follows, after looking back into the room with an expression of both relief and dismay.)

END OF ACT I

ACT II

At rise: The study is empty. The door to the hall is open. Sounds of the party waft in. It doesn't seem to be going very well. Then Wes and Wilma enter. They are now dressed for the party: Wes wears a tuxedo, Wilma a long dress.

WES: What do you think you're doing out there?

WILMA: Me?

WES: Just what do you think you're doing?

WILMA: I am carrying on a series of decent conversations.

WES: Bullshit!

WILMA: I am keeping the party afloat!

WES: Double bullshit!

WILMA: I am partying like mad!

WES: That's not partying you're doing out there! That's crap! That's bullshit! You are shitting all over the floor out there! *(He goes to shut the door.)*

WILMA: Where? Name a time!

WES: When you were talking with that man by the bar.

WILMA: I was good with that man.

WES: You were lousy with that man, Wilma! You were totally irresponsible!

WILMA: He was telling me about his dog.

WES: And what did you tell him?

WILMA: I told him about our cat.

WES: Jesus, Wilma.

WILMA: Well, I had to say something.

WES: What we do with our cat is a private matter!

WILMA: Well I couldn't talk about our children.

WES: And then you shifted the subject to urban renewal.

WILMA: What's wrong with that?

WES: It was a lousy transition, Wilma, and you know it. It was fake, and false, and you could hear the gears grinding all over the room!

WILMA: Well I got bored with animals.

WES: That's not the point. You don't just suddenly slam a conversation into reverse! Jesus! It was pathetic. The poor guy practically dropped his drink. *(He gets a cube of ice from the bar, puts it in a towel, and holds it to his head.)*

WILMA: Well I don't see you lighting any fires out there tonight.

WES: I'm doing O.K.

WILMA: You are walking through it.

WES: I'm doing fine.

WILMA: You are a zombie. You are phoning it in. I saw you slouching on the couch with that man from Rhode Island.

WES: What's wrong with him?

WILMA: Nothing, except that he ravaged his own cleaning woman.

WES: He didn't ravage her, Wilma.

WILMA: He most certainly did. She's out there right now, by the vegetable dip, confirming the incident.

WES: Well he and I didn't discuss that.

WILMA: I'll bet you didn't.

WES: We didn't. I was advising him on his hernia.

WILMA: Bore me some more, Wes.

WES: Better me on the hernia, than you on the cat!

WILMA: Listen, I may have been crude out there. I may have forced a transition or two. But at least I was reaching out towards other people and other subjects. I didn't retreat, and commandeer the couch, and indulge in a lot of macho chest-thumping and groin-scratching with a ruptured rapist from Rhode Island!

(Wes grabs her and begins to twist her arm. Sally enters hurriedly, closing the door behind her.)

SALLY: You're fighting, aren't you?

(Wes and Wilma separate quickly.)

WILMA: Oh no, not really.

WES: We were just kind of sparring around, Sally.

SALLY: Oh God, this party. It doesn't seem to be gelling at all. Everywhere I go, middle-class married couples are bickering irritably over trivial issues. Our younger friends have gone upstairs slamming the door to the guest room, where they smoke dope and listen to loud, shrieking songs, with lyrics which are virtually incomprehensible. To avoid the din, the older folks have congealed in a gloomy corner, where they reminisce about Lawrence Welk and accuse each other of having Alzheimer's disease. Our Black and Hispanic friends, once so full of life, are huddled in sullen groups, discussing social inequities in a vaguely revolutionary tone. The gays and born-agains eye the goings-on with some contempt, depressed with our condition and their own. Even the caterers are losing interest. The bartender plies his trade with cynical abandon, confusing gin with vodka, spilling the bourbon, and stinting on the ice. The miserable maids prowl around the room, offering stale hors d'oeuvres and then snatching them away, before you've even had a chance to grab one. From off in the kitchen come sounds of an angry clatter, and unnecessary breakage, which, I am sure, we will be over charged for later. *(By now, she has collapsed on the couch in despair.)*

WES: It sounds like an image of America itself.

SALLY: Whatever it is, it is hardly a party, much less a perfect one. And to make things worse, I can't find Tony anywhere. I'm terrified he's doing something desperate.

WILMA: I think I saw him going into the bathroom.

WES: You're not supposed to notice things like that at a party.

WILMA: *(Furiously, to Wes.)* Well I *did!* *(Then to Sally.)* I also noticed that he had with him a small tin of black shoe polish.

SALLY: Black shoe polish? Then he *is* desperate. Tony hates to shine his shoes, particularly at a party.

WILMA: I wish Wes here would shine his occasionally.

WES: *(Threateningly.)* I don't know about my shoes, Wilma, but I know something of yours that needs a little blacking!

SALLY: Wes! Wilma! Please! You see what's happening? Now you're talking about wife abuse, which I've always felt was basically counterproductive.

WES: You're right, Sally. I apologize. For both of us.

WILMA: *(Indignantly.)* I can goddamn well apologize for myself!

SALLY: Now stop! We promised Tony we'd help make the evening a success, and here we are contributing to the disaster. Look at us, arguing in here, while that strange critic pokes around from room to room, like a dental hygienist in a ceaseless search for cavities. Oh I give up. I really do. The hell with it all. It just confirms what I've told Tony all along: there's no possibility for a civilized social life in America beyond the comforts of a few friends and the ghastly confines of the family.

WES: *(Joining her on the couch.)* Come on, Sally. We can do better.

WILMA: *(Sitting on her other side.)* Yes, Sally. Please. Let's try again.

WES: Don't be discouraged, Sally. Listen. Most parties hit a snag during the course of the evening. We learned about it in medical school. It's called hitting the wall. Or going into the tunnel. It happens even in Europe. The best thing we can do is drink plenty of liquids and ride out the pain.

SALLY: I wish I could believe that, Wes.

WILMA: No, it's good reliable advice, Sally. But perhaps I can add something, gleaned from my experience as a semi-professional potter. Let me say that a party is like a pot in process. It can't be pushed or prodded or poked. *(Sally blinks.)*

WES: You're spitting a little, Wilma.

WILMA: That's because I feel *passionate* on the subject.

(*Wes hands Sally a handkerchief. Sally wipes her face.*)

WILMA: What we've got to do now, Sally, is nurse this party. Caress it. Stroke it into shape. These are particularly feminine virtues, Wes, but you're welcome to watch.

SALLY: But what about Tony? This whole damn thing was his idea, and why should we bother, if he isn't even there?

WES: Maybe he is, and you just haven't seen him, Sally. It's a poor party indeed when husbands and wives hover around each other. For example, I plan to ditch Wilma as soon as I leave this room.

WILMA: It's true, Sally. He will. And I accept that. Men are like children at parties. They like to wander off, but they always scamper back for reassurance at the breast.

SALLY: (*Getting to her feet with a sigh.*) I'll try to believe that. Come on. Let's give it another go.

WES: Do you think we should all do a few stretch exercises first?

SALLY: (*Going to the door.*) No, no. Come on. There are times when you've simply got to go on faith in human nature.

(*She opens the door. Lois, who has been eavesdropping, tumbles in.*)

SALLY: Oh hi, Lois.

WILMA: Hi, Lois.

WES: Hi, Lois.

SALLY: Did you hear what we were saying, Lois?

LOIS: Of course not. Did you say anything important?

SALLY: Yes, actually. We were all just saying what a wonderful party this is.

WES: That's right. We were all just congratulating ourselves on how well things were going.

LOIS: Well none of that came through. I *did* happen to hear, however, someone compare a critic to a dental hygienist.

SALLY: Oh dear.

LOIS: I'd be careful of cracks like that, people. There will always be critics, and you're lucky enough to get a good one.

SALLY: Well all I know is I'm having a wonderful time!

WILMA: So am I. Aren't you, Lois? Aren't you having fun?

LOIS: I never comment till it's over. A responsible judge should always weigh all the evidence, good and bad, before imposing the death sentence.

SALLY: Oh dear. Maybe we'd better rejoin the party. Come, come, dear friends. Let's enjoy ourselves even more before the party ends.

(Sally herds Wes and Wilma out as the party sounds come up. Lois remains onstage. She takes a compact out of her purse, and begins to comb her hair, using the mirror to glance behind her. After a moment, Tod comes in. He wears a tuxedo, and looks just like Tony, except that he has a black mustache, slicked-back hair and a pronounced limp. Lois watches him in the mirror as he closes the study door behind him. The party sounds die out.)

TOD: *(Speaking throughout in a corny Italian accent.)* You Lois?

LOIS: I try to be, at least during daylight hours.

TOD: How about at night?

LOIS: Oh well, then I'm the Queen of Rumania.

> *(Tod comes farther into the room; he drags his foot behind him in an exaggerated limp. He might sing Italian words seductively "Spaghetti"… "Spumoni"…"Scongili"…etc. Finally.)*

TOD: Would you like to see my cock?

LOIS: I beg your pardon?

TOD: I said I've been drinking since seven o'clock.

LOIS: I hope you're still in control of all your faculties.

TOD: Goddamn right, you stupid mother.

LOIS: What?

TOD: I said I thought I might have another. *(He limps to the bar.)* May I mix you one?

LOIS: I don't think so, thank you.

TOD: It would do you good, you silly snatch.

LOIS: Excuse me?

TOD: I can easily mix you up a special batch.

LOIS: No thank you. No. Thank you.

TOD: *(Beginning to circle around her.)* Tell me about yourself, Lois.

LOIS: Where do I begin?

TOD: Do you like to fuck?

LOIS: Only when I laugh.

TOD: You're making it hard for me.

LOIS: Don't hold it against me.

TOD: You're turning me on. I have a weakness for repressed women.

LOIS: What makes you think I'm repressed?

TOD: I can tell. You're all bottled up.

LOIS: You think so?

TOD: Oh yes. Luckily, I like to open bottles. Particularly with my teeth.

LOIS: You're wasting your time.

TOD: Am I?

LOIS: Oh yes. I'm much more at home with the twist-off top.
  (*Tod sits down beside her on the couch.*)
TOD: You've got all the right answers, don't you, Lois?
LOIS: That's because I'm on to you. I know all about you.
TOD: What do you know? Be specific. Be concrete. (*He adjusts his stiff leg.*)
LOIS: I know, for example, that you've been out there wandering around from person to person, group to group, sowing seeds of dissension. I know you're here to systematically destroy your own brother's party.
TOD: Well you're wrong on that, Lois. I'm here to salvage it.
LOIS: Ha, ha. That's a good one. Ha, ha, ha. How, pray tell?
TOD: By giving you such a fucking good time in bed, Lois, that you'll stagger bowlegged back to your word processor and write an out-and-out rave!
LOIS: Ha, ha. And how do you propose to get me into that bed, Tod?
TOD: Well first, of course, I plan to give you a good, stiff drink. (*He gets up and goes to the bar again.*)
LOIS: I don't want a drink, Tod. I believe I've already indicated as much.
TOD: You'll want one, Lois, after you see what I'm making. (*He begins mixing a concoction in a silver cocktail shaker.*)
LOIS: Does it have a local habitation and a name?
TOD: I call it a Cardinal Sin.
LOIS: Then I won't like it. I have strong reservations about the Catholic hierarchy, coming as I do from New York.
TOD: I think you'll love this one, Lois. I think you'll lap it up. (*He works on the drink.*)
LOIS: Suppose I take a sip of this drink. Suppose I even chug-a-lug it. What happens next?
TOD: Well, of course, by then I'd be sitting beside you. And what I'd do is put my arm around you, and slowly caress your left breast until your nipple was firm and erect.
LOIS: But I wouldn't allow that, Tod. I'd take your hand and remove it with my own.
TOD: You wouldn't be able to, Lois. Both your hands would be thoroughly preoccupied.
LOIS: Preoccupied?
TOD: Yes. One would be holding the Cardinal Sin.
LOIS: All right. I'll grant that. But the other?
TOD: The other would be perched, like a frightened bird, on my throbbing loins.
LOIS: Hmmm.

TOD: You see. You get the picture? *(He continues to concoct the drink.)*

LOIS: I'm afraid I don't, Tod. I mean here we are in the middle of a party. People are bursting through that door every other minute.

TOD: That's why I'd maneuver you immediately to the master bedroom, under the pretext of showing you pictures of children and dogs.

LOIS: But still, people would come in and out. Visiting the bathroom. Combing their hair. Getting their coats, if the party continues to degenerate.

TOD: We'd solve that problem with Vaseline.

LOIS: Vaseline? Don't be foolish. Vaseline solves many problems, but not that one.

TOD: We'll put it on the doorknob, Lois, rendering it virtually unturnable. *(He moves toward her again.)*

LOIS: You have an answer for everything, don't you?

TOD: I believe I do. Yes.

LOIS: Well I'm still not sure I'd like such a situation, with people banging on the door and rattling the doorknob. I think I'd be distracted.

TOD: *(Sitting behind her, on the back of the couch.)* You wouldn't hear a thing, Lois. And I'll tell you why. Because by that time you would be writhing naked on the bed, among the furs and Burburys, emitting a series of wild exuberant love cries, ending in a veritable Vesuvian eruption of delight. People will be running for cover, Lois. You'll be scattering red hot lava over a relatively large area. And then, while you're still smoldering, maybe smoking occasionally but temporarily inactive, I'm going to take you into the bathroom, and give you a bath, and anoint your erogenous zones with Oil of Olay. And then dial your editor in New York, and hand you the telephone, and you're going to say into that phone, "Truly this was a perfect party, and I'm mighty glad I came."
(Pause.)

LOIS: You think I can be bought, don't you?

TOD: Yes I do.

LOIS: Know what I think, Tod?

TOD: No. What do you think, Lois?

LOIS: I think you've said those things hoping I'll be shocked. I think you want me to reject that drink, repulse your advances, and run from this room. I think you want me to pan this poor party in no uncertain terms.

TOD: You think that?

LOIS: Yes I do. But it won't happen, Tod. Bring me that drink immediately. *(He hobbles back to the bar to get the drink. He might sing a few more Italian words as he goes. He brings the drink; it is a weird, bubbling, bright red potion, emitting smoke. She takes it, looks at it, and smiles.)*

LOIS: A Cardinal Sin, eh?

TOD: That's what it's called in *The Story of O,* Lois.

LOIS: Down the hatch, with a one-two-three. *(She slugs it down, then slams the glass on the coffee table.)* There. I intend to take you on and top you, Tod, point by point, game by game. The bets aren't in yet, and the match isn't over. *(She stands up.)* So show me that master bedroom. Let's strip for action, and commence firing. And when everything's said and done, I want you to know that I still intend to assess this evening with a clear, unjaundiced eye!

(He grabs her and kisses her. Immediately, Sally opens the door and comes in.)

SALLY: Ah, Tony! Here you are!

(Tod breaks away from the kiss and looks at her.)

SALLY: Oh. Excuse me. I thought you were my husband, Tony.

TOD: No. I'm Tod. His twin brother.

SALLY: I see. I'm terribly sorry. *(She goes out.)*

TOD: *(To Lois.)* Goddammit, but you're a tough nut to crack, Lois.

LOIS: If there are any nuts to be cracked around here, Tod, let them be yours. *(She goes out grimly. Tony looks after her nervously, finishes the rest of the Cardinal Sin from the cocktail shaker. Then he starts off after her, remembers to limp, and almost catches his leg in the door as he leaves. A moment. Then Wes leads Wilma into the room. He closes the door behind him, looks at her, and then kisses her.)*

WILMA: What was that for?

WES: You know.

WILMA: I'm afraid I don't.

WES: You were fantastic out there!

WILMA: Really?

WES: You were terrific.

WILMA: Well thanks.

WES: You turned the whole thing around.

WILMA: Well I made an effort. I'll say that.

WES: Effort? You were flying out there! You went into orbit out there! What got into you?

WILMA: I don't know, Wes. The vibrations changed, or something. I just got on a roll.

WES: Roll? You were spinning! No one got *near* you.

WILMA: *You* got near me, Wes.

WES: Oh well…

WILMA: No, I'm serious. When that woman fell asleep in the corner? Who helped me slap her awake and get her going?

WES: Yeah well…

WILMA: I mean it. And when that older man tried to sneak out and go home, who threw a body-block on him in the front hall?

WES: Well it was fun. I'll say that.

WILMA: *(Hugging him.)* What a party! I can't wait to take this experience home and share it with our children.

WES: Sshh!

(They break apart and look toward the door.)

WILMA: *(Whispering.)* If we present it right, if we don't intrude on their private space or personal time, I think they might enjoy hearing about it.

WES: Yes, but I've got another idea.

WILMA: What?

WES: I want to sneak home and get our cat.

WILMA: Get our cat?

WES: Get it. Bring it here. And display it.

WILMA: Dis*play* it?

WES: To the group at large.

WILMA: You love that cat, don't you, Wes?

WES: Yes, I do.

WILMA: You're extremely attached to that animal.

WES: Yes, I am. Shall I get it?

WILMA: *(Holding him; gently.)* I'm going to say no on that, Wes. And I'll tell you why. It might serve as a conversation piece for two or three minutes. But then people will drift away. Or the cat will.

WES: I suppose you're right.

WILMA: After all, it can't talk.

WES: Thank God.

WILMA: Exactly.

(Both laugh. The door opens. Sally comes in. The party sounds come up. She closes the door quickly behind her and leans against it, breathlessly.)

SALLY: The party's beginning to crest!

WILMA: That's just what we were saying!

SALLY: It's amazing. Everything is suddenly coming together. It's as if somewhere someone had pulled a switch, and a huge gravitational force had come into play. It's like the beginning of civilization itself, if I remember my courses at Vassar correctly. First, there was this man, I don't even remember who he was, who sat down at the piano, and started idly fiddling with the keys. Then others began to gather around. A chord was sounded. A tune emerged. Someone began to sing. And then, as if out of nowhere, people produced other musical instruments. Harps...xylophones...Moog Synthesizers...And now!—Well, let's listen, and see how far they've come:

(She opens the door. From offstage we hear the huge sounds of the Mormon Tabernacle Choir—full orchestra and chorus—singing the "Battle Hymn of the Republic." A rich romantic light and an exotic fog spill into the study as the three stagger back, amazed.)

VOICES: ...His Truth is marching on!

Glory, Glory Halleluia!

Glory, Glory Halleluia!

Glory, Glory Halleluia!

His Truth is marching on!

(Sally, Wes and Wilma pick up glasses, trays, ice-buckets, as cymbals, triangles and drums. They march around the room, ending in a wild display of sympathetic enthusiasm. Finally, Sally closes the door and the sounds stop.)

SALLY: See?

WILMA: *(Wet-eyed, hugging her.)* It's a good party, Sally.

WES: A very good party indeed.

SALLY: Or rather we should say it *was* a good party.

WES: You mean it's over?

SALLY: It will be. I doubt if we can top that. I'd better go out and say goodbye.

WILMA: Did you ever find Tony?

SALLY: No, but I imagine he was in the chorus. He's got an excellent baritone if he stays with the main melody. *(She opens the door and heads out into the light, closing the door behind her.)*

WES: Should we leave, too? Shall I get our coats?

WILMA: I imagine Tony wants us to stick around for a postmortem.

WES: That's right. What's a party without a postmortem. It should be a gas. *(Leads her to couch.)* Come on. Let's relax.

(They sit down side by side.)

WES: There's nothing like a good party to bring you together.

(They settle back, romantically.)

WILMA: Mmm. This is lovely.

WES: Mmm hmmm. *(He thinks.)* Out there, when we were going strong, do you think we needed a little cutting?

WILMA: Cutting?

WES: Just a snip or two. Here and there. For example, when I was talking about the function of the urethra.

WILMA: You were lovely on the urethra. You were lyrical.

WES: Still, I might tighten it up for the next party.

WILMA: Well try. See how it floats. You can always go back.

WES: Actually, you might give a little thought to that joke about your mother.

WILMA: I'm not going to change a word of that, Wes.

WES: Just think about it.

WILMA: I'm not going to lose that laugh, Wes! I'm serious!

WES: O.K., O.K.

WILMA: Honestly. You can ruin something by tinkering with it.

WES: O.K., O.K.

(The door opens. Lois comes in, looking somewhat disheveled. Sounds of the party offstage indicate people are beginning to say goodbye. Lois closes the door behind her.)

WES: Oh. Hi Lois.

WILMA: Hi Lois.

(Lois has the visible traces of black mustache on her upper lip.)

LOIS: I'm looking for my purse.

WILMA: We thought you had left long ago.

LOIS: No. Actually, I've been…upstairs.

WES: Upstairs?

LOIS: Yes. The party took a strange turn in that direction, and I felt it was my duty as a critic to follow the thread. *(She sits down gingerly.)* Some of my colleagues, of course, have been known to leave in the middle, or rush rudely out at the end, without even saying goodbye. I don't do that, even if I have a deadline. I stick it out, to the bitter end. *(She powders her nose, sees the mustache, tries to figure it out, can't, powders over it.)*

WES: The bitter end? I hope that doesn't reflect your opinion of the party.

LOIS: Not necessarily. The bitter end may simply mean the end of a rope, or cable, that is wound around a bitt, or post.

WILMA: Yes, but it may also mean a painful, or disastrous, conclusion.

LOIS: *(Getting up, holding out her hand.)* Either way, goodnight. Nice to meet you both…You were interesting minor characters…Goodnight… Goodnight.

(She starts for the door. Tony comes in.)

TONY: You're leaving, Lois?

(Lois reels back with a little shriek.)

TONY: What's the matter?

LOIS: *(Regaining her composure.)* I thought for a moment you were someone else.

TONY: You may have momentarily confused me with my twin brother.

LOIS: That must be it.

TONY: Then you met him?

LOIS: Oh yes. We…met.

WILMA: I didn't know you had a twin, Tony.

TONY: I don't broadcast it. Nobody likes to be duplicated.

LOIS: Is he still here, by the way?

TONY: No, Lois, he's gone. I saw him skulking down the back stairs, and slinking off into the night, his tail between his legs.

LOIS: Let's hope that so-called tail remains there. Frankly, Tony, I don't want to meet him again. I feel that he and I exhausted every possible topic of conversation. *(She holds out her hand.)* And now I must say goodbye. As you know, I have a deadline to meet.

TONY: *(Shaking hands.)* I won't ask you to say ahead of time what you'll write about us.

LOIS: No. That would be a violation of some meaningless taboo.

TONY: I'll see you to the door, though.

LOIS: That won't be necessary. I'm sure Sally is out there, giving wet, warm kisses to the last of your guests. Goodbye, Tony. *(Grimly.)* And if you see that brother of yours, ask him to read my review. *(She goes out.)*
(Pause.)

WES: *(Looking after her.)* Something's gotten into that woman.
(Tony looks at him nervously.)

TONY: You're right, Wes, and I'm worried.

WILMA: Why? It was a spectacular party!

TONY: You know that, I know that. But does she?

WILMA: What makes you think she doesn't?

TONY: I don't know. There's something wrong. I can feel it in my bones.
(Sally comes in.)

SALLY: There. That's the last of our guests.

TONY: Did Lois say anything on the way out?

SALLY: Nothing. She just put her head down and went through the line like a fullback.

TONY: Could you tell anything from her expression?

SALLY: Nothing. She seemed particularly enigmatic. Her brow was furrowed…

TONY: Oh God!

SALLY: But on the other hand, playing about her lips was a Mona Lisa smile.

WILMA: See, Tony? You just can't tell!

SALLY: Oh. She did say one thing, though.

EVERYONE ELSE: WHAT?

SALLY: She said that she had been invited to give a capsule edition of her review over local television at eleven twenty-seven tonight.

WES: *(Looking at his watch.)* It's almost eleven twenty-seven now.

WILMA: Do you still have a TV in your study, Tony?

TONY: Actually, I do. I use it for watching *Masterpiece Theatre.*

SALLY: He uses it for watching Talk Shows, and wishing he could run one.

TONY: Used to, Sally. Yesterday. When I was young.

WILMA: Let's turn it *on! (She crosses to the TV cabinet, opens it, turns on TV.)*

TONY: Oh God! She'll say it was terrible! She'll say the food was bad, and the drinks were worse, and the company impossible!

SALLY: Ssshh.

(They all watch the screen intently.)

TV: *(Voiceover.)* …And now Lois Lumkin, our guest entertainment critic from New York, will tell us where she's been and what she thought of it.

(The lights come up on Lois's actual face, framed in the TV.)

LOIS: *(Brightly.)* Thanks, Bruce…Tonight's party causes me to feel emotions as mixed as its guest list. The basic idea—that someone would set out to give a perfect party—is farfetched but engaging.

(Everyone reacts enthusiastically.)

LOIS: The execution is something else again. It sputters where it should sparkle, and fizzles where it should dazzle.

(Everyone looks glum.)

LOIS: Perhaps I'll elaborate on these thoughts tomorrow in a major New York newspaper. Meanwhile, let me simply assign it a Seven…

SALLY: Seven's not bad…

LOIS: On a scale of Seventeen…

TONY: Oh Good Lord…

LOIS: And I had serious reservations about the lighting.

TONY: The *lighting?*

TV ANNOUNCER'S VOICE: Seen one party, seen 'em all, right, Lois?

(Lois laughs charmingly.)

SALLY: Turn that thing off.

(Tony slams shut the cabinet cutting off Lois in mid-laugh. Pause.)

TONY: Shit.

SALLY: I'm sorry, sweetie.

TONY: The lighting.

WES: What does she know, anyhow?

WILMA: Yes. What difference does it make?

TONY: *(Pacing around the room.)* Difference? What difference does it make? That woman is going to sit down and write an article which will appear in New York, and here, and in Upper Volta, for Chrissake, saying that I put on a lousy show!

SALLY: Not lousy, sweetheart. Just so-so.

TONY: That broad is going to go on National Public Radio, which is beamed by satellite into the farthest reaches of the Soviet Union, and announce that she's just been to one hell of a crumby party.

SALLY: Not crumby, love. Just disappointing.

TONY: That bitch is going to hang out in various two-star New York restaurants—

SALLY: Now stop it, Tony. You're exaggerating.

WILMA: Still, isn't it a shame that one woman should have such a far-reaching effect?

SALLY: She said, "Perhaps." She might not even review it.

TONY: Worse and worse! Love me, hate me, but don't ignore me! Fuck, piss, shit! *(He sinks into a chair.)*
(Pause.)

WILMA: I think we'd better go. I'm uncomfortable with such explicit language, even though I recognize its therapeutic value.

WES: Actually, I get a kick out of language like that. But I'll leave too, for the sake of our marriage. *(Embraces Tony.)* So long, Tony. If I could sum up the party in one word, I'd say it was interesting.

TONY: Thanks a bunch, Wes.

WILMA: *(Kissing Tony.)* No really. It was. We learned several things about parties we didn't know.

WES: And several things we didn't need to know.

TONY: Get out of here, guys!

SALLY: I'll show you to the door.

WES: Don't bother, Sally. You both should have deeply personal things to say to each other at a humiliating time like this.

WILMA: Yes, but don't say them. Just go to each other, look in each other's eyes, and hold each other, tightly, for a long, long time. And let the tears come, people. Let the—
(Everyone shouts her down with groans.)

TONY: Please *leave*, Wilma!

WES: *(At the door.)* Come to think of it, Tony, the lighting was bad. I meant to mention it myself.

TONY: *Scram!*

(Wes and Wilma go. Sally starts to clean up. Pause. Tony looks at her.)

TONY: My mother liked it.

(Sally says nothing.)

TONY: No kidding. She said it was a lot of fun.

(Still nothing from Sally.)

TONY: It's almost as if Lois had attended an entirely different party. Didn't she hear the singing? Jesus, what kind of a country do we live in, where one person calls the critical shots? It's cultural fascism, that's what it is! It's Nazi Germany! In Moscow, they have twenty critics, and nobody pays any attention to any of them.

(Nothing.)

TONY: Well. Back to the classroom. Probably at the high school level. If I'm lucky. Teaching nothing but courses on decline and decay. Spending the rest of my days searching the puffy, narcoticized eyes of my students for some faint, dim light of recognition. Knowing all along that all they know is that I couldn't even give a decent party.

(Still nothing from Sally as she cleans up. He glances at her again.)

TONY: It will affect you, too, of course. I imagine you'll lose your job at the hospital once they hear about this. You'll have to retool. Take up high tech state-of-the-art software. Sell chips and bits and disks and bytes in some vast suburban shopping center, where you're the only salesperson within an area of three square miles.

(Sally dumps the guest list into the wastebasket. He winces.)

TONY: Go on. Say it.

SALLY: Say what?

TONY: I'm a simple, shallow, smart-assed shit, and I deserve all this.

SALLY: I won't say that.

TONY: I'm a trivial-minded twit, and I had it coming.

SALLY: I won't even say that.

TONY: Then what are you going to say? Simply goodbye? Will you leave me?

SALLY: I might.

TONY: Knew it.

SALLY: It all depends on how you answer a question, Tony.

TONY: Don't tell me. Let me guess: why am I so fucking hung up on parties?

SALLY: That's not the question. My question is the oldest question in the world. It was first asked in the Bible, Genesis, Chapter Four, Verse Nine.

TONY: Wow, Sally. You've got almost total recall from Sunday School.

SALLY: My question is what God asks Cain. Namely, where is thy brother?

    (Pause.)

TONY: Would you repeat the question?

SALLY: I don't think I need to, Tony.

    (Pause.)

TONY: My brother, eh.

SALLY: Your brother.

TONY: Well, as I told the others, I believe he may have slinked—or slunk—anyway, I believe he has *sidled* off into the night.

SALLY: I don't believe that, Tony.

TONY: You don't believe it?

SALLY: I think he's still here.

TONY: *(Crossing to the door.)* Where? In the cellar? Cultivating toadstools?

SALLY: I think he's right in this room.

TONY: My twin brother? Tod? *(Looking around the room.)*

SALLY: I don't believe you have a twin brother, Tony.

TONY: But you saw him. You walked right into this room when he was kissing Lois!

SALLY: How do you know that, if you weren't there, Tony?

    (Pause.)

TONY: Uh oh.

SALLY: You made up this brother, Tony, in a desperate attempt to retrieve this party. You painted a cheezy mustache, with Kiwi shoe polish, on your upper lip. You cultivated a grotesque limp and a ludicrous accent. You didn't even bother to change your costume. You simply pretended to be this so-called twin brother.

    (Pause.)

TONY: How do you know I'm not my twin brother pretending to be me?

SALLY: That is a question only Pirandello could answer. Meanwhile, I'll ask another.

TONY: One is enough.

SALLY: This is simply a corollary to the first. Namely: did you or did you not copulate with that critic?

TONY: I…

SALLY: Yes or no.

TONY: I copulated.

SALLY: Thought so. You left your guests, you went upstairs, you put Vaseline on the doorknob, which was an old trick we used when the children were younger, and then you proceeded to have sexual relations with a woman who writes for the Arts and Leisure section of one of the finest newspapers in the entire free world.

TONY: That's all true.

SALLY: Jesus, Tony! How hungry you must have been for success!

TONY: I was. And I suppose it's no excuse to say that all Americans are.

SALLY: None at all.

TONY: I didn't think so.

SALLY: One final question.

TONY: Sally…

SALLY: Now this is a crucial question, and I have to put it carefully. When Lois, on television, implied that this party was disappointing, was she also referring to your sexual performance?

(Long pause.)

TONY: Yes.

SALLY: I thought so.

TONY: Are you going to leave me?

SALLY: I've got good reason to now, don't I?

TONY: Will you be taking the video cassette recorder?

SALLY: Don't jump the gun, Tony. That might have been one of your problems with Lois.

TONY: Sorry.

SALLY: You see, I'm thinking. I'm trying to put all of this together. So much has happened this evening that it takes all of my concentration just to keep these balls in the air.

(Tony winces.)

SALLY: Sorry, Darling. All right now, look, Tony. Let's be frank. I'm beginning to see a pattern here, and I think we should explore it before we make a final decision about our marriage.

TONY: O.K.

SALLY: Now bear with me, love. It seems to me that your attempt to achieve social perfection in the living room is echoed in your attempt to achieve sexual perfection in the bedroom.

TONY: Hmmm.

SALLY: But that's just the tip of the iceberg. This impulse to control, to shape, to achieve perfection permeates the fabric of this country. For example, I think it's indicative of what's wrong with American theatre.

TONY: American theatre?

SALLY: And American sports. And American foreign policy, where we are attempting to impose some ideal shape on the Middle East, Central America, and Southeast Asia.

TONY: Good God, that's true.

SALLY: I think it is. In other words, you could, in a sense, say that America itself, in its middle age, is trying to give a perfect party, at home and abroad.

TONY: I never looked at things that way before.

SALLY: Well look at them that way now. Because what we're really talking about is sexual, social, cultural, and political *imperialism,* on a large and general scale!

TONY: Good Lord.

SALLY: And it doesn't *work,* Tony. It doesn't work in the bedroom, and it doesn't work outside. That's why Lois walked out of here so bitterly disappointed. And why our embassies are being attacked all over the world. And why the Yankees can't seem to win the pennant.

TONY: So in other words, all I've done tonight is take American idealism, and reveal it for the dark, destructive dream it really is.

SALLY: I'm afraid that's the long and the short of it, darling.

TONY: What a grim vision, Sally. You've opened up an abyss. It seems that a party is just a power trip.

SALLY: At least your kind of party is, my love.

TONY: Oh God it's true! So what happens now? Will you leave me?

SALLY: I've thought of that.

TONY: Go off with some angry emissary from the Third World?

SALLY: I've thought of that, too.

TONY: Live in a newly-emerging democracy with a quasi-Marxist orientation? Experiment with alternative theatre and ambivalent sexuality? Give up partnering, and parenting, and hostessing, all the days of your life?

SALLY: I've thought of all these possibilities, and rejected them out of hand.

TONY: But then where do we go from here? What happens to *us?* What happens to *me?*

SALLY: Sweetheart—

TONY: *(Getting up, coming downstage.)* No, I'm serious now. What happens to me? I know what I am now. A fifty-year-old fool, all burdened down with eighteenth century ideals, nineteenth century impulses, and twentieth century despair. I've betrayed my wife, embarrassed my family, and irritated the critics! Oh I'm a hopeless case. If I were Lois, I'd pan me unmercifully. What do I do with the rest of my life? My children are gone, my teaching's behind me, my wife patronizes me unbearably.

SALLY: Tony…

TONY: No, really. I'm totally hung up. I'm a man without illusions, which means I'm no man at all. What happens to me now?

(A door bell rings offstage.)

SALLY: There's your answer.

TONY: A doorbell ringing late at night?

SALLY: That's it.

TONY: I doubt very much that it will dispel my current mood of despair. It's probably the children, all deciding to go to graduate school. Or else the I.R.S. disallowing me to deduct this party.

SALLY: Don't be cynical, Tony. It's just your friends, back for another try.

TONY: Another try?

SALLY: I told people, as they left, to take a short nap and then come back, after we'd had a chance to talk. This time, I said, it will be my party, and I'll be running it on totally different terms.

TONY: What terms?

SALLY: There will be no attempt to make this party perfect. There will be no shaping or judging or interrupting unless someone gets physically violent or is obviously misinformed. You will simply go among your friends and take them for what they are. There won't even be a caterer. Everyone is bringing over various ethnic dishes, and has promised to help clean up afterwards.

(Tony crosses to door, opens it, looks out. We hear the sounds of noisy chatter and rock music. "Burning Down the House" by the Talking Heads.)

TONY: It could turn into chaos, out there.

SALLY: That's the chance you'll have to take.

TONY: Do you mean to tell me that in that random and noisy disorder lies the future of America?

SALLY: I suppose you could say that.

(Tony closes the door and returns to her.)

TONY: I'm not sure I can live with that much ambiguity.

SALLY: You'll have to try.

TONY: But what about our personal life, Sally? Will you ever forgive me?

SALLY: Tony: you've done some terrible things tonight. You've compromised your marriage by fornicating with a first-string reviewer. You've compromised your aesthetic sensibilities by putting foul language into the mouth of a fake twin brother. Furthermore, by inventing this brother, you went against everyone's advice and imitated Oscar Wilde. There are many wives, I'm sure, who would be thoroughly fed up. But I'm not, Tony.

Through all your foolishness, I somehow sense a fundamental yearning to create a vital human community in this impossible land of ours. And so I forgive you.

TONY: Oh thanks, Sal.

(He kisses her. Wes and Wilma come in. Wes has his collar open and carries a beer. Wilma carries a casserole covered with tinfoil.)

WES: Come on in! The party's fine!

WILMA: And our children are here. And so are yours. And Lois has come back!

(Lois comes in, carrying a large container of Kentucky Fried Chicken.)

LOIS: Yes, and I realize that I, too, am an example of American idealism gone haywire. My standards are obviously too high.

(A lovely pink light shines on her.)

LOIS: I also notice an improvement in the lighting. I plan to go back in there now and re-review everything in sight from a much more generous perspective!

(Everyone cheers. They go off dancing merrily as the music and party sounds come up loud and clear.)

THE END

ANOTHER ANTIGONE

To John Tillinger

INTRODUCTION

This play, like several others of mine, has had a complicated and frustrating career. It is obviously rooted in Sophocles' great tragedy, but also has elements of a one-act called *The Old One-Two* which opened at Brandeis University in the early 70s while I was teaching at MIT. This one started off with some success at the Old Globe in San Diego, but ran into trouble when it moved to Playwrights Horizons in New York City. For reasons I've never been clear about, there was the implication in some of the reviews that the play was anti-Semitic. I emphatically believe that it's not, but it's difficult to prove a negative. Yes, the protagonist Judy Miller is Jewish, and yes, she is occasionally a pain in the neck, but so was Sophocles' Antigone whom Judy is supposed to be modeled after. Other people seemed to locate the anti-Semitism in Professor Harper, whose tendency to generalize on cultural differences I borrowed from the great Jewish scholar Eric Auerbach. Yet even if Harper was fundamentally prejudiced, his biases should hardly indict the whole play. In any event, New York critics and audiences seemed to have problems with *Another Antigone,* despite a first-rate production. The play hasn't had much of a professional life since, though it is done occasionally by colleges and community groups.

ORIGINAL PRODUCTION

Another Antigone was first produced in March, 1987, at The Old Globe Theatre in San Diego, California, with the following cast:

Henry.	George Grizzard
Judy.	Marissa Chibas
Diana.	Debra Mooney
Dave	Steven Flynn

It was directed by John Tillinger, designed by Steven Rubin, lit by Kent Dorsey. The stage manager was Dianne De Vita.

The play opened at Playwrights Horizons in New York City in January, 1988. The cast, director, and designers remained the same. The stage manager, in this case, was Neal Ann Stephens.

CHARACTERS

HENRY HARPER: Professor of Classics
JUDY MILLER: a student
DIANA EBERHART: Dean of Humane Studies
DAVID APPLETON: a student

SETTING

The play takes place in a university in Boston during the latter half of the spring term.

It is designed, as Sophocles' *Antigone* was, to be performed without an intermission. If one is deemed essential, however, it should occur after the third line on page 36.

The general effect of the set should evoke the Greek Revival architecture of a typical New England college. There should be columns and steps and benches. Somewhere in the center there should be a slightly abstracted desk and two chairs, indicating both Henry's and Diana's office. Near it is a bookcase, a filing cabinet, on which is an old hotplate, a possibly tin coffee pot, and a couple of cracked mugs. The general effect should be multi-scenic, fluid and shifting, indoors and out, and vaguely Greek.

At rise: Henry sits at his desk, perusing a typewritten paper. Judy sits in the other chair. She watches intently. He is middle-aged and conservatively dressed. She, in her early twenties, is casually dressed in whatever students are currently wearing.

HENRY: *(Finally, putting the document down neatly on the desk between them.)* Another Antigone.

JUDY: Did someone else write one?

HENRY: Sophocles wrote one.

JUDY: No, I mean someone in *class*.

HENRY: Aeschylus wrote one, which is lost. Euripides we think wrote one. Seneca tried to write one. Voltaire tried not to. Jean Anouilh wrote a rather peculiar one in 1944, during the Nazi occupation of Paris.

JUDY: But I'm the only one in *class* who wrote one.

HENRY: *(Weak smile.)* That's right. *(Pause.)* This year.

JUDY: You mean, other students wrote them in other years?

HENRY: Oh yes.

JUDY: Really?

HENRY: Of course. *(Henry goes to the filing cabinet. He pulls out a drawer.)* Let's see…Antigone…Antigone… *(He thumbs through a file of old folders and records.)* Here we are. *Antigone. (He takes out a particular folder.)* Now. I have a record of one in 1955, written during the McCarthy hearings. And another, by a student who I recall was black, about the Civil Rights movement in 1963. And of course there were two, no, three, which cropped up during the Vietnam war.

JUDY: Did anyone ever deal with the Nuclear Arms Race before?

HENRY: No. As far as I know, you are the first to apply the Antigone myth to that particular topic.

JUDY: The story really turned me on.

HENRY: I'm glad it did. It is one of the great works of Western literature. Antigone herself is the classic rebel, the ancestor to such figures as Saint Joan or Martin Luther.

JUDY: Oh yes. I see that.

HENRY: And Creon is the ultimate image of uncompromising political authority.

JUDY: I got that, too.

HENRY: Their clash is inevitable and tragic.

JUDY: I understand. *(Indicating her manuscript.)* I tried to make them like Jane Fonda and Ronald Reagan.

HENRY: I know what you tried to do, Miss…uh…Miss… *(He glances at her title page.)* Miller. I read all… *(He glances at the last page.)* twelve pages of it, in preparation for this conference.

(He slides the script across the desk to her. She takes it, looks at the title page, flips through it, looks at the last page, then looks at him.)

JUDY: You didn't mark it.

HENRY: I most certainly did. I underlined several run-on-sentences, and I circled a rather startling number of misspelled words.

JUDY: No, I mean you didn't *grade* it.

HENRY: No I didn't.

JUDY: Why not?

HENRY: Because this course is about Greek tragedy, and your paper isn't.

JUDY: Did you grade those other *Antigone's?*

HENRY: I most certainly did not. I simply keep a record of them on file, the way the Pope keeps a file on various heresies.

JUDY: Well mine isn't a heresy!

HENRY: It is, to me.

JUDY: Don't you believe in nuclear disarmament?

HENRY: Of course I do. I think the arms race is madness.

JUDY: Then don't you think these things should be said?

HENRY: Absolutely. And I believe I said them, back in February, when I was discussing the political background of Greek drama. Then, if you'll remember, I compared Athens and Sparta, and pointed out rather frightening analogies to the United States and the Soviet Union.

JUDY: I had mono in February.

HENRY: Mono?

JUDY: Nucleosis. I kept falling asleep at the Film Festival, even during *Psycho.*

HENRY: I'm sorry to hear that. You must get the notes, then, from a fellow student. You might need them when you write your term paper.

JUDY: But this *is* my term paper.

HENRY: It's not on an assigned topic.

JUDY: It's on *Antigone.*

HENRY: But it's not on Sophocles.

JUDY: But I spent two weeks working on it.

HENRY: Sophocles spent two years.

JUDY: But I'm taking other courses!

HENRY: And Sophocles didn't—I grant you.

JUDY: Yes, but…

HENRY: Miss Miller: At the beginning of the semester, I handed out a list of assigned topics. I stated specifically that any departures from these topics should be cleared through me. Now suddenly, long before the term is over, I discover this odd effort, stuffed under my door, with no previous permission whatsoever.

JUDY: I had to try it first. To see if it worked.

HENRY: Well, you did. And it didn't.

JUDY: So what do I do?

HENRY: You read the texts carefully. You attend class religiously. And in the middle of May, you hand in a fifteen-page, coherently organized, typewritten paper, with adequate margins and appropriate footnotes, on the main issues of this course.

JUDY: Couldn't you give me partial credit? For the idea?

HENRY: Miss Miller, how can I? It's misguided. It's wrong. You have taken one of the world's great plays, and reduced it to a juvenile polemic on current events.

JUDY: Juvenile?

HENRY: I'm sorry.

JUDY: Of course that's your opinion.

HENRY: I'm afraid my opinion is the one that counts.

JUDY: But what if I put it on?

HENRY: On?

JUDY: In front of the class—just reading it out loud.

HENRY: Miss Miller: we have only so much time before the end of the term. We have yet to absorb the very difficult concept of Greek tragedy. I doubt if there's time in class to play show-and-tell.

JUDY: Then I'll do it somewhere else.

HENRY: I'd spend my time on a paper.

JUDY: I'll do my play instead. You could come and see.

HENRY: I'm afraid I'd see a great gap in your education, Miss Miller. As well as in my list of grades.

JUDY: You mean I'd fail?

HENRY: You'd receive an incomplete.

JUDY: Which means, since I'm a senior, that I'd fail. I wouldn't graduate, Professor Harper.

HENRY: Which means you'd better not spend these last valuable days of your academic life on amateur theatrics. *(He gets up, begins organizing his books and notes.)* And now I have to teach a class. And I strongly suspect you have to go to one.

(Judy gets up, too.)

JUDY: Professor Harper, I don't want to sound conceited or anything, but you should know that after I graduate, I've been accepted for a special training program in investment banking at Morgan Guaranty Trust in New York City.

HENRY: My congratulations.

JUDY: Well, in my interview, they were particularly impressed by my leadership qualities, my creativity, and my personal sense of commitment. They wrote me that in a letter, Professor Harper.

HENRY: Congratulations again.

JUDY: I also heard, from someone who works there, that I'm only the second Jewish woman to be brought into that program at that level since its inception.

HENRY: I am virtually overwhelmed.

JUDY: Yes, well, I believe in my abilities, Professor Harper. I plan to apply them. I'm going to put this play *on*. I wrote it, and I like it, and I'm committed to what it says. And if it's no good now, I'll work to make it better. And I'll bet, by the end of the term, you'll be able to give me a straight A.

HENRY: *(Turning, as if at the door.)* Miss Miller: After such a magnificent display of American optimism and industry, I'm tempted to give you a straight A right now.

JUDY: Thank you.

HENRY: And I believe I would if this were a course on comedy. But alas, it is not. It's a course on tragedy. And you have just demonstrated that you have no conception of tragedy at all!
(He goes off, with his books and notes. Judy looks at him, and looks at her paper. She goes off, reading it aloud.)

JUDY: People of this land, we suffer under a yoke.
(She begins to realize a new pertinence.)
A tyrant rules our city, and unjust laws
Now squelch all forms of perfectly plausible protest…
(She goes off. As she goes off, Diana comes on to address the audience. She is a harassed, nervous, middle-aged woman, dressed efficiently. She speaks to the audience as if it were a group of concerned students. She might speak from note cards.)

DIANA: Good morning…I spoke to you as freshmen. I speak to you now as seniors and what we hope will be very generous alumni…The topic of today's meeting is "Preparing for the Future." I'll be brief, since I know all of you are waiting to hear from the Placement people about the world beyond these walls. I do want to make a quick comment on our curriculum, however. A number of you have recently complained about the traditional courses which are still required. Why, you ask, with tuitions so high and the search for jobs so increasingly competitive, are you forced to take such impractical courses? You may be sure, by the way, that the recruiting offices at I.B.M. and General Electric are asking the same question: Why must you take these things? After all, they are concerned only with some book, some poem, some old play. "Only some work," as my special favorite Jane Austen once said, "in which the best powers of the mind are displayed, in the best chosen language." Well, there you are. They're the best. And we need no reason beyond that to justify, for example, Professor Harper's course on Greek tragedy. It deals with the best. It exists. It is there. And will remain there, among several other valuable requirements, for what we hope is a very long time. *(She glances offstage.)* And now, Alice Zimmerman, from Placement, will talk to you about… *(She glances at her note card.)* "The Job Market Jungle versus the Graduate School Grind." Those of you who are tardy may now be seated.

(The late members of the audience may be seated here.)

DIANA: Have a good morning.

(She goes off as Dave comes on from another direction. He reads aloud from a typewritten script.)

DAVE: "No, Antigone, no. Please reconsider.

Do not take on this dangerous enterprise.

The risks are too great, the payoff insignificant."

(Judy comes on, as if down the steps of the library, carrying a stack of books.)

JUDY: *(Breathlessly.)* Look what I got. *(Reads off the titles.)* The Nuclear Insanity…A World Beyond War…Our Debt to the Future…I'm going to put all this in.

DAVE: You're racking up a lot of time on this thing.

JUDY: Well I want to make it good. Did you read the first scene?

DAVE: *(Reciting by heart.)* "No, Antigone, no. Please reconsider."

JUDY: What do you think?

(Pause.)

DAVE: You're in blank verse.

JUDY: I know that.

DAVE: Every line. *(Accentuates it.)* "Do *not* take *on* this *dang'*rous en*ter*prise."

JUDY: I know.

DAVE: How come?

JUDY: *(Accenting it.)* I *just* got *in*to *it* and *could*n't *stop.*

DAVE: *(Dramatically, as if it were Shakespeare.)* "The risks are too great, the pay-off insignificant."

JUDY: Want to do this?

DAVE: Me?

JUDY: Want to?

DAVE: *(Looking at script.)* This is a woman's part. This is her sister talking here.

JUDY: I've changed it. I've made it her lover.

DAVE: Get someone from Drama.

JUDY: I already did. Drama people are doing all the other roles. Please, Dave. Do it.

DAVE: *(Melodramatically.)* "No, Antigone, no. Please reconsider." *(Pause.)* I better not, Judy.

JUDY: I need company.

DAVE: No thanks.

JUDY: I thought you liked Greek stuff.

DAVE: I do.

JUDY: You even talked me into taking the course.

DAVE: I know, I know.

JUDY: You're always borrowing the books…

DAVE: Yeah, but I don't have time for anything anymore. I've got a double lab in my major this term. And a brutal schedule in track every weekend. And, as you know, I'm not doing too well in either.

JUDY: You're doing fine. You're just a slow starter. *(Slyly.)* Which is part of your charm.

DAVE: All I know is, you get straight A's, you've got a great job waiting for you on the outside, you can afford to fool around with drama. Me? I've only had one interview so far, and I blew it.

JUDY: You didn't *blow* it, Dave. You just overslept.

DAVE: Yeah well, how can we live together next year if I can't nail down a job in New York? I've got to get my grades up, Jude.

JUDY: All right, Dave. That's cool. I'll look for someone else. *(She takes her own copy of her script out of her backpack, looks at it, looks at him.)* Would you at least read it with me?

DAVE: Sure.

JUDY: From the top?

DAVE: Sure. Why not? *(Reading.)* "Hello, Antigone. And what brings you here, Worried and out of sorts on this spring morning?
You look like you've got something on—
(Pause.) —your mind."

JUDY: *(Reading.)* "My friend Lysander—"

DAVE: *(Looking at his script.)* Lysander? I have "Beloved sister."

JUDY: That's what I changed. I changed it to Lysander.

DAVE: Lysander? That's Shakespeare. It's from *Midsummer Night's Dream.*

JUDY: It's also Greek. I looked it up.

DAVE: But it primarily—

JUDY: *(Reads, with feeling.)* "My friend Lysander, will you join with me
 In picketing and protesting the bomb
 At several local military bases
 Where nuclear arms are stored? And would you be willing,
 O my loyal Lysander—"

DAVE: Lysander. Sounds like a disinfectant.

JUDY: *(Insistently.)* "Would you be willing, O my loyal Lysander
 Even to chain yourself to a chain-link fence
 Or lie down in the road in front of a gate
 And so prevent all types of vehicular access?"

DAVE: I do.

JUDY: "And if the state police or National Guard,
 Accompanied by snarling German shepherds,
 Attempted to dislodge us from our task,
 Would you be willing, my lover and my friend…
 To go to jail with me, and there remain
 At least till our parents post appropriate bail.
 (Pause.)

DAVE: Who'll you get for Lysander if I don't do it?

JUDY: Oh probably that blond fraternity type who lifts weights and played the
 lead in *Fool for Love.*

DAVE: Mark Shapiro?
 (Judy nods.)

DAVE: I'll do Lysander.

JUDY: Now don't if you don't want to.

DAVE: So I get another C in another course.

JUDY: Now think positively, Dave.

DAVE: So I mess up another interview.

JUDY: *(Handing him her script.)* I'll buy you a new alarm clock. Read from here.

DAVE: *(Looking at it.)* This is all new.

JUDY: I rewrote it last night. With you in mind.

DAVE: You knew I'd do it.

JUDY: I hoped you would.

(Henry reenters his office, settles into a chair to read a book.)

DAVE: *(Kissing her.)* "Antigone... *(Then reading.)*

Much as I've loved you, even since freshman year,
And lived with you since the second semester of sophomore,
Built you a loft for our bed in off-campus housing,
Prepared your pasta, shared your stereo,
Still I have fears about what you've just proposed.
The risks are too great, the payoff insignificant."

JUDY: What do you think?

DAVE: I love it.

JUDY: You do?

DAVE: I love you.

JUDY: *(Taking the script back.)* I don't like it.

DAVE: What's the matter?

JUDY: It sounds wrong. I'm going to rewrite it.

DAVE: Again?

JUDY: *(Gathering up her book and bag.)* I'll make it better.

DAVE: What if you cut Lysander?

JUDY: Why? You're good. I'm going to build up his part.

DAVE: *(Following her.)* "No, Antigone, no. Please reconsider."

(They go off as Diana appears in the doorway to Henry's office.)

DIANA: Henry?

HENRY: Yes? Come in. *(He sees her and jumps to his feet.)* Ah. Our Dean. Empress of all Humanities, including Remedial Reading. *(He gives her an elaborately courtly salute and bow.)*

DIANA: Knock if off, Henry.

HENRY: You look particularly lovely today, Diana. What is it? New hairdo? New blouse? New something.

DIANA: It's the same old me, Henry.

HENRY: No, no. There's something different. Maybe it's your eyes. They blaze like beacons 'cross The Hellespont.

DIANA: And it's the same old you, Henry. You've been saying things like that for twenty years.

HENRY: And meaning them, Diana.

DIANA: I used to think you meant them. Now I know different.

HENRY: Dear lady...

DIANA: Now I know that you just say these things by rote, Henry. You say them to the librarian in the reserve book room, and you say them to the Xerox woman, and you say them to the cashier in the cafeteria. You say them to keep us all at a distance, so you won't have to say anything else. If any of us did have a new blouse, you wouldn't notice it at all.

HENRY: Now, Diana…

DIANA: Let's change the channel, shall we, Henry? Something's come up.

HENRY: What dark words seek to escape through the gate of thy teeth?

DIANA: Judy Miller.

HENRY: Judy…?

DIANA: Miller.

(Pause.)

HENRY: Ah. Miss Miller. *(French accent.)* L'affaire Antigone.

DIANA: You know that's why I'm here, Henry.

HENRY: I swear I didn't. I have a number of students, a number of courses.

DIANA: You teach two courses, Henry. And you have relatively few students in each. Now let's focus, please, on the issue.

HENRY: Administration has made you cruel as Clytemnestra.

DIANA: Henry, *please.*

(Pause.)

HENRY: All right. Judy Miller.

DIANA: I understand—

HENRY: Would you like some coffee? *(He crosses to pour her some.)*

DIANA: Yes, please—I understand she brought in a rewritten version.

HENRY: She brought in *two* rewritten versions.

DIANA: Well she brought one to me, as well.

HENRY: The first? Or the second?

DIANA: A third.

HENRY: I said I wouldn't read that one.

DIANA: It's not bad, Henry. It's longer, it's getting better. It's now at least a play.

HENRY: It's hopeless.

DIANA: Give her a B for effort.

HENRY: A *B?* I won't give her any grade at all.

DIANA: A student takes our course, becomes inspired by an old play, writes a modern version…

HENRY: And demonstrates thereby that she knows nothing about Sophocles, nothing about the Greeks, nothing about tragedy.

DIANA: Henry, she tried.

HENRY: And failed. A B? A B means good. A B means very good. I am not so far lost in the current inflation of grades as to litter the campus with disposable Bs.

DIANA: Oh, Henry…

HENRY: I'm sorry. If I gave her a grade for that nonsense, Diana, it would make the whole course meaningless. *(Pause.)* It would make *me* meaningless. *(Pause. Diana lights a cigarette.)*

HENRY: Still smoking, I see.

DIANA: Sometimes.

HENRY: Don't.

DIANA: I smoke, Henry, when I find myself caught in the middle of something. Which seems to be the case a good deal lately with this job.

HENRY: Ah hah. Second thoughts from our Dean. You asked for that job, Diana. You agitated for it. All that chatter about the need for more women at the administrative level. Well, now you've sunk to that level and it's leveling you. Come back to the classroom where you belong.

DIANA: Sometimes I wish I could.

HENRY: *(Taking an ashtray out of a desk drawer, holding it out to her.)* At least put out that cigarette. Life is tragic enough without your contributing to it.

DIANA: Let me enjoy it, Henry.

HENRY: Your lungs or mine, Diana. *(He holds out the ashtray.)* Put it out.

DIANA: You win.

(She puts it out; he cleans out the ashtray, puts it away.)

DIANA: Now let me win one.

HENRY: No.

DIANA: How about partial credit?

HENRY: No.

DIANA: She's a senior. She needs to graduate.

HENRY: I'm sorry.

(Pause.)

DIANA: She's putting it on, you know.

HENRY: The play?

DIANA: She's putting it on.

HENRY: Reading it? In some dining hall?

DIANA: Staging it. She asked my permission to use Spingler Auditorium.

HENRY: You said No.

DIANA: I said Yes.

HENRY: You gave her permission?

DIANA: Of course I gave it to her. I had to give it to her. *(Pause.)* I wanted to give it to her.

HENRY: Traitor. Or is it, Traitress?

DIANA: Well, I'm sorry, Henry. But there seems to be a lot of interest cropping up for this thing. Several of the student anti-nuclear groups want to sponsor it. Bill Silverstein is writing some incidental music on the Moog Synthesizer. And someone over in Art has agreed to do simple neo-classic scenery. They plan to present it on the Friday night before graduation. For parents. And alumni. And friends.

HENRY: Poor Sophocles…

DIANA: Oh now.

HENRY: Set to the tune of a Moog Synthesizer.

DIANA: Yes well, it should create quite a stir.

HENRY: Quite a stir! That's it, exactly, Diana! Quite a stir! It will stir up a lot of cheap liberal guilt and a lot of fake liberal piety and a lot of easy liberal anger at the poor Creons of this world who are really working on this nuclear thing, and frantically trying to keep the world from blowing itself up!

DIANA: Oh, Henry…

HENRY: Do you know what tragedy is, Diana?

DIANA: I think I do, yes.

HENRY: I don't think you do, Diana. I don't think anyone in this happy-ending country really does. Tragedy means the universe is unjust and unfair, Diana. It means we are hedged about by darkness, doom, and death. It means the good, the just, and well-intentioned don't always *win*, Diana. That's what tragedy means. And if we can learn that, if I can teach that, if I can give these bright, beady-eyed students at least a glimmer of that, then perhaps some day we will be able to join hands with our enemies across the water, or our neighbors down below, or the outcasts in our own back*yard*, and create a common community against this darkness. That's what I believe, Diana. And that's what Sophocles believed in 443 B.C. when he wrote *Antigone*. That's what Shakespeare believed when he wrote *King Lear*. Tragedy keeps us honest, keeps us real, keeps us human. All great nations should have a tragic vision, Diana, and we have none. And that is why I cannot endorse what this woman, no, this *girl*, is doing when she puts on her strident little travesty for the passing parade in Spingler Auditorium on graduation weekend. That is not tragedy, Diana. That is just trouble-making. And I cannot give her credit for it.

(Pause.)

DIANA: May I have the ashtray back, please?

HENRY: No.

DIANA: I want it *back*, Henry. I don't want to tap ashes all over your floor.

HENRY: *(Handing it to her.)* Here. *(Gets up.)* I'll open the door.

DIANA: I'd leave the door closed, Henry. Open the window if you want. This is private. *(She smokes.)*

HENRY: *(Not opening anything.)* Private?

DIANA: Have you given any thoughts to your low enrollments, Henry?

HENRY: Thought? Of course I've given thought. In a world of television and Punk Rock, it's a little difficult to maintain—

DIANA: The Provost thinks there might be another reason, Henry.

HENRY: The Provost?

DIANA: He brought it up last fall, when he saw the registration figures.

HENRY: And what does the Provost think?

DIANA: Apparently...over the years...there've been complaints about you, Henry.

HENRY: Oh I'm sure. That I take attendance. That I take off for misspellings. That I actually *call* on people in class.

DIANA: No, it's something else, Henry. Some students...over the years...have complained that you're...biased.

HENRY: Biased?

DIANA: Prejudiced.

HENRY: *Prej*udiced?

DIANA: Anti-Semitic, Henry.
    (Pause.)

HENRY: Say that again.

DIANA: There's been a pattern of complaints.

HENRY: But on what *grounds?*

DIANA: Apparently the administration thinks you make certain remarks in the classroom. Which students pass on. And cause others to stay away.
    (Pause.)

HENRY: This is ridiculous.

DIANA: I agree.

HENRY: And outrageous.

DIANA: I think so, too.

HENRY: It's slander! I'm going to see the Provost right now!

DIANA: Hold on, Henry!

HENRY: I mean this is unconscionable. It's like the time five years ago when poor Bob Klein was accused of some late night unpleasantness in the lab by that little temptress in a T-shirt. He had to resign.

DIANA: He resigned because he was *guilty,* Henry.

HENRY: Well I'm not guilty of anti-Semitism. Or do you think I am?

DIANA: I think you...make remarks, Henry.

HENRY: Remarks?

DIANA: For example, in the curriculum meeting last fall…

HENRY: What did I say?

DIANA: You told that joke.

HENRY: It was a good joke. I got that joke from Jack Nathanson.

DIANA: Well no one laughed when *you* told it, Henry. And no one laughed when you delivered that diatribe against Israel last week at lunch.

HENRY: That wasn't supposed to be funny.

DIANA: Well it certainly wasn't.

HENRY: I mean, when you think how we let one small country so totally dominate our foreign policy…

DIANA: Henry!

HENRY: Well I mean it's insane! It's suicidal! Pericles warned us about it in 426 B.C.: "Beware of entanglements in Asia Minor," he said.

DIANA: Henry, Dick Livingston was sitting right across the *table* when you said those things!

HENRY: Is Dick Jewish?

DIANA: *I'm* Jewish, Henry.

HENRY: *You're* Jewish?

DIANA: Half Jewish. My mother was an Austrian Jew.

HENRY: I didn't know that.

DIANA: Well I am. And Judy Miller is Jewish.

(Pause.)

HENRY: Has she complained that I'm prejudiced?

DIANA: No. *She* hasn't…

HENRY: But you still think I'm some raving neo-Nazi who is pumping anti-Semitic propaganda into his courses three times a week?

DIANA: *(Quietly.)* No. I think you're a passionate teacher and scholar, whose lectures are loaded with extravagant analogies which are occasionally misinterpreted by sensitive Jewish students.

HENRY: And the Provost?

DIANA: The Provost thinks it's an issue which should never even arise. Seeing as how we're in the middle of a major fund drive. And more and more, it seems to be Jewish generosity that's keeping us all afloat.

HENRY: *(Thinking.)* I do the Auerbach thing at the beginning of the term.

DIANA: The Auerbach thing?

HENRY: A great scholar. Jewish, Diana. And superb! He sees two fundamental themes in Western culture. The Greek and the Hebraic. Odysseus versus Abraham. Public honor versus private conscience.

DIANA: Well maybe that starts you off on the wrong foot.

HENRY: No, no. It works marvelously. I carry it further. I build to the basic contrast between Athens and Jerusalem.

DIANA: Well maybe those generalizations could be taken the wrong way.

HENRY: Do you think so?

DIANA: Henry: This is a free country. And academic life is even more so. You may write four-letter words all over the blackboard. You may denounce the government, blaspheme God, take off your clothes…

HENRY: Good Heavens, Diana…

DIANA: You may do all of these things in here, and most of them out there. But there is one thing, here and there, you may not do. You may not be insensitive about the Jews. That is taboo. The twentieth century is still with us, Henry. We live in the shadow of the Holocaust. Remember that, please. And be warned.

(Pause.)

HENRY: I hear you, Diana.

DIANA: Thank you.

HENRY: I'll stay simply with the Greeks. I'll lash myself to the mast, and avoid the Bible. I'll even avoid the Book of Job.

DIANA: Thank you, Henry.

HENRY: I must say, Diana, I've never really understood the Old Testament anyway. All that brooding, internal self-laceration. And the sense of a special contract with God. The sense of being chosen. The sense of sure salvation somewhere on down the line. Have you ever felt that? I haven't. But the Jews must feel it. Even after Auschwitz, they feel it. Perhaps because of Auschwitz, they feel it all the more. I suppose that's why they put so much stock in their children. They spoil them, you know. Their children are generally spoiled. They bring them to dinner parties. They teach them to feel—what is that word?—"entitled." Perhaps that's why this girl, excuse me, this woman, this Miss Miller, feels so strongly she deserves special treatment.

DIANA: Henry.

HENRY: My children don't feel that way. I taught my children to tow the mark. To take their turn. To submit to authority. Of course, that hasn't worked out so well either. I mean, I don't hear from my children much anymore. The Jews hear from their children. Their children telephone them all the time. *(Turns to her.)* I'm painting myself into a corner, aren't I?

DIANA: Yes you are, Henry.

HENRY: Yes. Well. You're right. All this could be…misinterpreted. I'll try to be more careful.

DIANA: Yes, I would, Henry. Because the Provost is talking about cutting back.

HENRY: Cutting back?

DIANA: On courses that are—undersubscribed.

HENRY: My course on tragedy is required!

DIANA: Your course is on a list of *several* required courses. And the Provost can take it off that list any time.

HENRY: What? Tear from the Tree of Knowledge one of the last golden apples that still remain? A course that survived the ghastly chaos of the sixties? A course that—

DIANA: Henry, he can do it.

HENRY: I'll be more careful…"Whom the Gods would destroy, they first drive mad."

DIANA: Yes, well, and it might be a good idea, Henry—just to avoid any mis-understanding—to give Judy Miller a grade for what she's done.
(Pause.)

HENRY: You *think* so?

DIANA: Yes I do. Otherwise you might come out of this whole thing looking very much like Creon in that damn play.

HENRY: This is not a tragedy by Sophocles, Diana. It is a comedy by Aristophanes, at best. I am not Creon, and that little Jewish princess is not Antigone, Princess of Thebes.

DIANA: Cool it, Henry!

HENRY: *(With great reluctance.)* I'll give her a D. For Determination.

DIANA: Henry…

HENRY: *(Angrily.)* All right. A C, then. For Commitment.

DIANA: I don't think she'll accept a C.

HENRY: Won't *accept?*

DIANA: She feels she deserves a good grade.

HENRY: She'll get a good grade when she shows me some small awareness of what tragedy is. Lord knows she's shown me what it isn't.
(Judy comes out now. She sits on some steps or a bench downstage, takes a spiral notebook out of her backpack, and writes in it, concentratedly. Diana sighs and gets up.)

DIANA: If I were you, Henry, I'd head for the hills of New Hampshire after your last class. I wouldn't want to be around when the grades go in and that play goes on and that girl doesn't graduate. Go up to your cottage, chop wood, disconnect the telephone.

HENRY: I don't like to go up there alone.

DIANA: Oh dear. Trouble again?

HENRY: Elsa's moved out. Again.

DIANA: She'll be back.

HENRY: I don't think so. She says now the children have gone, I'm impossible to live with.

DIANA: Now where did she get an idea like that?

(She goes out. Henry exits, after a moment, another way. The lights come up more fully on Judy, hard at her writing on the steps in the sun. Dave comes on carrying a paperback book.)

DAVE: Hi.

JUDY: *(Looking up from her book.)* Hey, aren't you supposed to be in Chemistry?

DAVE: Missed it. Lost track of the time.

JUDY: But you flunked the last quiz.

DAVE: I got hung up reading one of your books.

JUDY: Which one?

DAVE: *(Showing her.)* Sophocles…*Antigone.*

JUDY: Oh.

(Pause.)

DAVE: It's good.

JUDY: It's fair.

DAVE: It's awesome.

JUDY: It's good.

DAVE: Maybe we should do that version.

JUDY: What about mine?

DAVE: Maybe you'd get your A if you did Sophocles.

JUDY: I've thought about that, Dave: In Sophocles, all she wants to do is bury one dead brother.

DAVE: True.

JUDY: In mine, she sees everyone in the *world* as her brother, and she's fighting to keep them all *alive.*

DAVE: O.K., Jude. *(He sits down beside her, takes out a banana.)* Want some?

JUDY: No thanks.

DAVE: *(As he eats.)* While I was reading, your dad called.

JUDY: Again?

DAVE: From the hospital. Between patients.

JUDY: What did he want?

DAVE: He wants you to graduate.

JUDY: I'll graduate.

DAVE: He wants to be sure.

JUDY: Did you tell him I'm appealing to the Grievance Committee? Did you say that the Dean herself is presenting my case?

DAVE: He said committees make him nervous.

JUDY: Well, parents make *me* nervous.

DAVE: He said he hasn't spent thirty years in the lower intestine just so his daughter could flunk college.

JUDY: Sounds familiar.

DAVE: He said write the paper. Get the degree. Argue with the professor after.

JUDY: That's my father.

DAVE: That's everyone's father.

JUDY: Actually, I got a letter from my mother today.

DAVE: Coordinated attack, huh.

JUDY: She wrote from her office. On her "Department of Mental Health" stationery. Saying I was just acting out my guilt for being so lucky in life.

DAVE: You are lucky.

JUDY: I know. and I know they've worked hard to keep it that way. Moving to Westport, so I could grow up in a "healthy suburban environment." Sending me to Andover, so I could frolic in preppy heaven. Europe last summer, so I could learn how to use a credit card. Hell, four years *here,* for God's sake. And now they're offering to pay a psychiatrist two hundred dollars a week so I can blame it all on them.

DAVE: You're kidding!

JUDY: My mother even enclosed a note from my grandmother saying that Jewish people should bend over backwards not to make waves.

DAVE: Got you surrounded, huh?

JUDY: Sure have.

DAVE: They all just want you to do well.

JUDY: I know that. I appreciate that.

DAVE: Look. Why not hedge your bets? Do the play *and* write the paper.

JUDY: I *can't,* Dave. I've tried and I can't. It all comes out fake and phony and not me.

DAVE: Then take the C. The Dean says Harper will give you that. Take it, and run.

JUDY: I can't do that either.

DAVE: Why *not?*

JUDY: I don't know, Dave. Here I am working with a bunch of really dedicated people…trying to reach out to the local community…on a subject which deals with the survival of the entire planet…don't you think that's worth a tad more than a C, Dave?

DAVE: Sure it is.

JUDY: Then let me go for it.

DAVE: O.K. Let's rehearse. *(He tosses the banana peel into a trash can with a basketball leap.)*

JUDY: Thanks, Dave. *(She hugs him.)* Listen to this new stuff. *(She reads what she has just written.)*

"Lately I'm feeling very much alone.
Even you, Lysander, seem to be backing off,
Advising caution, counseling compromise."

DAVE: *(Reading over her shoulder.)*

"I just don't want to see you get in trouble.
Just think what they could do to you, Antigone:
They could throw you in jail, there to be beaten up
By roving gangs of angry lesbians.
Or worse:
They could banish you, and send you off
With no degree to grace your resume
To fritter away essential earning years
In waitressing or joining a typing pool."

JUDY: *(Reading.)*

"Still, my conscience tells me I am right.
And if I am to suffer—" *(She stops; looks at him.)*

DAVE: What's the matter?

JUDY: Maybe I *am* just being a brat.

DAVE: No, no…

JUDY: A spoiled little JAP, playing sixties-type games as a last gasp before facing up to the real world…

DAVE: Naaa…

JUDY: Maybe I should just take a massive all-nighter in the library, and grunt out one of those boring, studenty papers with a title like "Tragic Irony in Sophocles" or some such thing.

DAVE: Sounds good to me. Want me to help?

JUDY: You don't have time. *(Looking at her notebook; reading.)*

"And yet this stupid arms race still goes on.
Oh it appalls me! God, it makes me mad!
(She begins to gather steam.)
It's as if the United States and Soviet Russia

Were two small boys comparing penises
With the fate of the world dependent on the outcome!"

DAVE: *(Covering his crotch.)* Right on, Antigone!

JUDY: *(Cranking up.)*

"Oh men, men, men!
Why are you all—with only a few exceptions—
(A glance at Dave.)
So miserably hung up on competition?
The Air Force General, the Corporation Executive,
The College Professor tyrannizing his students…"

DAVE: *(Looking over her shoulder.)* Hey! Where's that line? I don't see that.

JUDY: I'm improvising! I'm winging it!

"The College Professor tyrannizing his students,
It seems the entire world is under the thumb
Of self-important men. I fear, Lysander,
That one of these days, one of these little men
Will reach across his desk and push the button
Which will destroy us all!"

DAVE: Now that's pretty good.

JUDY: *(Gathering up her stuff.)* No it isn't. And you know it isn't. But I'll make it better. *(She starts off.)*

DAVE: *(Starting after her.)* I'll give you a hand.

JUDY: You better make up that chemistry. There's no reason for you to flunk out, even if I do. *(She goes.)*

DAVE: *(Calling after her.)* But I really want to— *(He looks at the Sophocles still in his hand, gets an idea, concludes quietly.)* Help.
(He goes off the opposite way as Henry enters to teach his class. He carries an old, worn leather book, stuffed with scraps of paper. He might use half-lens reading glasses, so that he can peer out at the audience as necessary.)

HENRY: It might be particularly appropriate at this point in the course to let Sophocles speak for himself. I will try to translate for you—directly from the Greek—portions of the great choral ode from the *Antigone*. I will attempt to make it speak as immediately as I can. And I hope, as you hear it, you will compare it to other local efforts on this subject that may have come to your attention in recent weeks. *(Opening his book, finding his place, translating with great feeling.)*
"There are many wondrous things in the world,
But nothing is more wondrous than Man." *(Looks up.)* Deinos…"wondrous"

…the other day I heard one of you use the word "awesome." All right. Let's try awesome. *(Returns to text.)*

"Nothing is more awesome than Man."

(Looks up; sighs.) Or yes. All right. Today: woman. The point is nothing is more awesome than the human being. Here I used to contrast this awesome view with the rather abject and quarrelsome vision of man emerging in the Old Testament. But I won't do that now. Rather, returning to the text… *(He does.)* I will simply call your attention to the series of magnificent images on the taming of nature: ships, plows, fishnets, ox-yokes… *(Looks up.)* Today planes, rockets, computers, laser beams… *(Returns to text.)* "which man has created through his uncanny technology."

(Looks up.) And then come our social inventions, those things we have invented to tame ourselves… *(Translates.)* "language which leads to thought"… "laws"…"medicine"…"religion"…"cities"… *(Looks up.)* There it is. The city. The *polis.* The human community. The result of all this creative activity. We'll come back to that. *(Translates.)*

"Man—or woman—is resourceful in everything, and proudly prepares for the future. But…"

(Looks up.) There is a big But here…*But…* *(Translates.)*

"There is one thing he can't tame, can't control: and that is Death."

(Looks up.) All right now, death was terrifying—the Greeks loved life—but Sophocles goes on to mention something *worse* than death. *(Looks at text.)* and here comes the crack of the whip: *(Translates grimly.)*

"Yet if, for the sake of pride, he…

(Looks up; is glad to use the feminine this time.) Or *she…* *(Returns to text.)*

"Goes too far, then he becomes an exile…"

(Looks up.) Which to the Greek was far, far worse than death. *(Translates.)*

"An exile without a country,

Lost and alone,

Homeless and outlawed forever."

You see? Sophocles joyfully celebrates the lawful human community, the Greek *polis,* but then threatens those who defy it with a death beyond death—exile, banishment, ostracism. *(Returns to the text.)*

"Lost and alone.

Homeless and outlawed forever."

(Looks up.) Last year, I compared these grim lines to the Hebrew's lamentations in the Psalms. This year, I will try to conjure up other images of profound alienation: *(He thinks.)* The haunted Orestes…Napoleon dying

his slow death on the desolate island of Saint Helena…some lost astronaut severed forever from the good, green earth… *(Returns to the text.)* "Homeless and outlawed forever."

(Pause.) Those words were written over two thousand years ago. I have read and taught them countless times. I get shivers up and down my spine every time I do.

(The bell rings. He closes his book.)

HENRY: I think even Sophocles would commend my theatrical timing. For the next session, read *The Trojan Women* by Euripides. Feminists will appreciate his sympathetic portrayal of women. Pacifists will admire his bitter attack on war. Classicists, however, prefer to reach beyond such limited responses. Thank you, and good afternoon.

(He gathers his books as Dave approaches him.)

DAVE: Professor Harper?

HENRY: *(Turning.)* Yes?

DAVE: I'm a friend of Judy's.

HENRY: Judy?

DAVE: Miss Miller.

HENRY: Ah.

DAVE: *(Holding out envelope.)* She asked me to give you this.

HENRY: "Has she sent poison or some other implement of dark death?"

DAVE: Excuse me?

HENRY: A line from *Medea*.

DAVE: It's just her term paper.

HENRY: She should be in class. She should hand it in herself.

DAVE: I think she's—a little mad at you, sir.

HENRY: Mad? At me? Because I want her to learn? Oh dear. Would you tell her, please, that the quest for truth and beauty is a slow and painful climb, and she shouldn't bite the hand that leads her. *(His little pun.)*

DAVE: I'll—tell her something.

HENRY: Good. Meanwhile, I'll take that paper, in hopes she soon will return to the fold.

DAVE: Thank you, sir.

HENRY: *(Opening the envelope, sliding the paper out far enough to read the title.)* "Tragic Irony in Sophocles' *Antigone*." A good, no nonsense title.

DAVE: I'll tell her, sir. *(He starts off.)*

HENRY: *(Pulling the paper out of the envelope.)* Lovely looking paper…Well typed.

DAVE: Mmm.

HENRY: Is this an electric typewriter?

DAVE: No actually, it's a word processor.

HENRY: She can't come to class, but she seems to have found time to form a relationship with a computer.

DAVE: Actually, I did the typing, sir.

HENRY: Well let's hope the contents are as attractive as the form. *(He starts to thumb through the papers.)*

DAVE: I'll be going, then. *(He starts off.)*

HENRY: *(As he reads; calling out.)* Oh, ah, Mr.—

DAVE: *(Stopping; turning.)* Dave.

HENRY: Do you have a moment?

DAVE: Well I—

HENRY: Would you be so kind as to accompany me to my office?

DAVE: Me?

HENRY: If you would.

DAVE: Now?

HENRY: If you'd be so kind.

(He turns and crosses slowly toward his office, still reading the paper. Dave hesitates a moment, and then follows. Henry enters his office, and sits at his desk, still reading. Dave stands in the doorway.)

HENRY: *(As he reads, gesturing vaguely.)* Please sit down, Mr....ah...

DAVE: Dave.

HENRY: Sit down, please.

DAVE: Thank you.

(He sits on the edge of the chair. Henry continues to read. Dave watches him.)

HENRY: *(As he reads.)* This...appears to be...an excellent paper.

DAVE: Is it?

HENRY: *(Thumbing through to the end.)* Even a cursory glance tells me it's first-rate.

DAVE: I'll tell her, sir.

HENRY: I've been around a long time. I've taught this course a good many years. I know a good paper when I see one, and I see one here.

DAVE: *(Almost at the door.)* That's great, sir.

HENRY: *(Quietly.)* Who wrote it?

DAVE: Huh?

HENRY: Who wrote this paper?

DAVE: Judy wrote it.

HENRY: No she didn't. I've also been around long enough to know that. She wrote a promising little essay for me at the start of the semester. She wrote a rather breathless hour exam. But she did not write this. She is not yet capable of the care and commitment I see emerging here.

DAVE: Maybe she's changed, sir.

HENRY: Ah. Then I would like to discuss this paper with her. Would you get her, please?

DAVE: I think she's rehearsing, sir.

HENRY: Then I must ask you to seek her out. Tell her I am passionate to engage in an intensive discussion with a kindred classicist.

DAVE: Sir...

HENRY: You might also tell her, *en passant,* that I think this is plagiarism, pure and simple. She has tried to pass off as her own the work of somebody else. This is an offense punishable, according to the rules, by... *(He has found the college rule book and is already thumbing through it. He finds his place.)* "Automatic failure of the course involved."

DAVE: Sir...

HENRY: *(Reading.)* "And, after due deliberation by the Discipline Committee, possible expulsion from the University." *(Pause. He looks at Dave.)*

DAVE: *(Quietly.)* Oh boy.

HENRY: You might also be interested in the fact that... *(He reads again from the book.)* "persons aiding or contributing to a plagiaristic act will similarly be charged and punished." *(Looks up.)* You personally might be interested in that, Mr.—?

DAVE: Appleton.

HENRY: Well I'm not going to press charges against you, Mr. Appleton.

DAVE: Sir—

HENRY: Nor am I going to press charges against Miss Miller. Believe it or not, I would hate to prevent her from graduating. I would simply ask you to tell her to make an appointment at her earliest convenience, so that I may explain to her why, in the world of scholarship and learning, plagiarism is a dark and bloody crime.

(Dave stands at the door.)

HENRY: That's all I have to say. You may go.

DAVE: She didn't write it.

HENRY: *(Infinitely patient.)* Yes I know. That's what I've been saying.

DAVE: No, I mean she doesn't even know about it.

HENRY: Doesn't know?

DAVE: She still wants her play to be her paper.

(Pause.)

HENRY: Then who wrote this?

DAVE: I did.

HENRY: Unbeknownst to her?

DAVE: Yes, sir.

HENRY: Hoping I'd give it a good grade, and she'd go along with it, and the problem would be solved?

DAVE: I don't know what I hoped.

(Pause.)

HENRY: *(Looking at paper again.)* And where did you get this paper? From some other student at some other college? From one of those companies who accept money and do your research?

DAVE: No! I wrote it myself.

HENRY: I don't believe that.

DAVE: Well I did.

HENRY: How could you? You're not in my course.

DAVE: I still wrote it.

(Pause. Henry looks at the paper, looks at Dave.)

HENRY: Sit down, please.

(Dave does. Henry is now all business.)

HENRY: Name three plays by Sophocles beside the *Antigone*.

DAVE: *Oedipus Rex, Oedipus at Colonnus…Ajax.*

HENRY: Describe Antigone's genealogy.

DAVE: Her father was Oedipus. Her mother, Jocasta. Her sister was Ismene. She had two brothers, Eteocles and Polynices. *(Pause.)* Who killed each other. *(Pause.)* Fighting. *(Pause.)* For the throne. *(Pause.)* Of Thebes. *(Pause.)*

HENRY: And what, briefly, do you think *is* the "Tragic Irony in Sophocles' *Antigone*"?

DAVE: I don't think it's Antigone's tragedy at all. I think it's Creon's.

HENRY: And why do you think that?

DAVE: Because she at least wins her point in the end.

HENRY: She dies.

DAVE: But she wins. He loses. Everything. The Gods are much more unfair to him.

(Pause.)

HENRY: You're very good.

DAVE: Thank you.

HENRY: Where did you learn all this?

DAVE: I read the play.

HENRY: *(Indicating paper.)* No. There's more here than just that.

DAVE: My grandfather liked the Greeks.

HENRY: Was he an academic?

DAVE: No. He just liked the classics. He spent most of his spare time in the library, reading the Greeks.

HENRY: And he taught you?

DAVE: Right. And I kept it up when I had time.

HENRY: I could never get my own son to read anything but science fiction.

DAVE: That's what my dad reads.

(They laugh together.)

HENRY: Why have you never taken a course from me?

DAVE: I couldn't fit it into my schedule.

HENRY: What's your major?

DAVE: Chemistry.

HENRY: Better worlds through chemistry, eh.

DAVE: Actually, my grades aren't too good.

HENRY: They'd be good in the classics.

DAVE: Not many jobs out there in that.

HENRY: Still, you should take my course.

DAVE: I wish I could.

HENRY: We could do a special seminar together. Study one play in depth. I'm fascinated with the *Antigone*. We could really dig in, you and I, next fall.

DAVE: I'm supposed to graduate this spring, sir.

HENRY: Oh dear…Then perhaps we might meet in the afternoon, from here on in. A small tutorial.

DAVE: I can't, sir. I'm on the track team.

HENRY: The track team? Splendid! The Greeks invented competitive sport!

DAVE: I know.

HENRY: *Hygies psyche meta somatos hygious.*

DAVE: Excuse me?

HENRY: We'll shift to Latin: *Mens sana in corpore sano.*

DAVE: *(Trying to translate.)* Sane mind…

HENRY: Sound mind in a sound body. The Tenth Satire by Juvenal.

DAVE: Juvenal…Tenth…

HENRY: You don't by any chance throw the discus, do you? No, that would be too much.

DAVE: I just run the Four Hundred.

HENRY: Ah. Fleet of foot. A true Greek. "Skilled in all ways of contending."

DAVE: Thank you, sir.

HENRY: Well, then, I wonder if I might keep this fine paper long enough for Mrs. Murphy to make a Xerox copy.

DAVE: Sure. *(He gets up to leave.)*

HENRY: Just to remind me occasionally of what a good student can do.

DAVE: Sure.

(He starts for the door. At this point, Judy enters at another part of the stage. She sits on a bench, and waits impatiently, as if in a waiting room.)

HENRY: You must be very fond of Miss Miller.

DAVE: I am.

HENRY: To have written this for her.

DAVE: I liked writing it.

HENRY: Will you be seeing her soon?

DAVE: I think so.

HENRY: Would you remind her that she and I have yet to resolve our difficulties?

DAVE: She's stubborn, sir.

HENRY: I give you permission to help her. Be her tutor. See that she gets some small awareness of Greek tragedy.

DAVE: She thinks she already has, sir.

HENRY: But she *hasn't!* She sees answers, solutions, revisions. Tell her there are things beyond the world of management which are profoundly unmanageable!

DAVE: She wouldn't listen, sir.

HENRY: Then she and I are on a collision course.

DAVE: I'm afraid so, sir. *(Dave starts for the door again.)*

HENRY: One more minute, please.

(Dave stops.)

HENRY: Appleton, you said your name was?

DAVE: That's right.

HENRY: English, I suppose.

DAVE: Originally.

HENRY: The English love the classics.

DAVE: Yes.

HENRY: And Miss Miller's Jewish.

DAVE: That's right.

HENRY: May I speak classicist to classicist?

DAVE: Yeah. Sure.

HENRY: What you are witnessing here, Mr. Appleton, is once again the age-old clash between Athens and Jerusalem.

DAVE: I don't get you, sir.

HENRY: Read Tertullian. Third century, A.D. "What is Athens to Jerusalem, or Jerusalem to Athens?" There it all is. The private conscience versus the communal obligation. Jew versus Greek. Miss Miller versus me.

DAVE: You think so?

HENRY: I do, but they tell me I shouldn't.

DAVE: It seems a little…exaggerated, sir.

HENRY: You're probably right. *(Henry gets up; takes his arm.)* Come, I'll walk with you down the hall. Plato and Aristotle, strolling through the colonnades of academe. We'll discuss simply Sophocles.

DAVE: O.K.

HENRY: *(As they go.)* And I hope Miss Miller appreciates this grand gesture you made on her behalf.

DAVE: God, I hope she never finds out about it.

(They go out as Diana comes on, carrying a folder. Judy gets up expectantly.)

JUDY: Well?

DIANA: The meeting's over.

JUDY: And?

DIANA: *(Deep breath.)* The Grievance Committee voted against you, Judy.

JUDY: *Against?*

DIANA: I'm sorry.

(They move into her office.)

JUDY: Did the students on the committee vote against me?

DIANA: I can't reveal the specific vote.

JUDY: How about you? How did you vote?

DIANA: I abstained, of course. Since I was presenting your case.

JUDY: How would you have voted? If you could have?

(Pause.)

DIANA: Against.

JUDY: What?!

DIANA: I put your case as fairly as I could, Judy. Really. But your argument simply didn't hold. The committee felt you were asking them to violate the integrity of the classroom. You want them to intrude on a principle that goes back to the Middle Ages.

JUDY: But other people do it all the time! There's a guy in Geology who got partial credit for skiing down Mount Washington!

DIANA: I know…

JUDY: And there's a girl who passed her Chemistry lab by cooking a crabmeat casserole.

DIANA: I know that, and I think it's disgraceful. But those are other instructors. We cannot dictate standards to *any* professor. You signed up for Greek tragedy. You bought the books. You read the syllabus. You agreed in effect to submit to the rules. There it is.

JUDY: There it is. Everyone seems to be backing off these days. You, my family, now the committee.

DIANA: Oh, Judy…

JUDY: *(Almost in tears.)* I guess I'm doomed to be alone.

DIANA: What about all those people working on your play?

JUDY: It's just extra curricular to them. I'm the one who's really on the line.

DIANA: Well what about that boy you go with?

JUDY: Oh, he just loves me, that's all.

DIANA: *(Lighting a cigarette.)* Well I'm sorry, Judy. I did what I could.

JUDY: Please don't smoke!

DIANA: I'm sorry.

JUDY: I think I'm allergic to it.

DIANA: All right, Judy.

JUDY: And it violates my air space.

DIANA: *(Putting cigarettes away.)* All right, all right.
    (Pause.)

JUDY: So what do I do?

DIANA: I told you: he's offered a C.

JUDY: I'm beyond a C.

DIANA: Beyond?

JUDY: I can't settle for a C.

DIANA: Then you won't graduate.

JUDY: Not in June. No.

DIANA: That's ridiculous!

JUDY: I'll make it up in summer school with that course on comedy where all they do is study *Annie Hall.* You can mail me my degree in September.

DIANA: That makes me a little angry, Judy. You told me you wanted to stand up with your class.

JUDY: I'm standing up, all right.

DIANA: But you'll lose your job! It depends on your graduating.

JUDY: I'll find another.

DIANA: That's not so easy these days.

JUDY: What's a job anyway? Is it the most important thing in the world? I suppose this is a hopelessly middle-class thing to say, but am I supposed to live and die over a job? Do you? You've been here a long time, worked your way up, now you're Dean of the whole department. Is that *it?* Are you in heaven now? Aren't there other things in your life beside your job?

DIANA: *(Taken aback.)* Of course there are, Judy…

JUDY: I mean, that's all I cared about, once upon a time. A *job.* I couldn't wait until I was scampering up and down Wall Street in my gray and white Adidas and a new suit from Saks, with my little leather briefcase swinging by my side. Meeting men for lunch and women for dinner, and both in the Health Club afterwards. A co-op on the East Side with a VCR and an answering machine with a funny message. Weekends at Sugarbush and Vineyard. Vacations in the Bahamas and France. Nailing down forty or fifty thou per annum within three years. Moving onward and upward through the corridors of power until I get an office with a corner view where I can look down on millions of women scampering up and down Wall Street in their gray and white Adidas.

DIANA: That's not the worst thing in the world!

JUDY: Isn't it? I'm not so sure. I'm beginning to think it's a con deal. All us women now killing ourselves to do those things that a lot of men decided not to do twenty years ago. I mean, here we are, the organization women, punching the clock, flashing the credit card, smoking our lungs out, while the really smart men are off making furniture or playing the clarinet or something. Look at you. Do you really want to be Dean, or are you just making some sort of feminist statement?

DIANA: Let's leave me out of this, please.

JUDY: Well all I know is I'm not so hung up on "The Job" anymore. It just seems like more of the same. More of what I did at Andover and at Westport Junior High before that. More of what I've done every summer, with my creative camps and Internships and my Special Summer Projects. Touching all the bases, following all the rules, ever since I can remember. And now here I am, about to graduate, or rather *not* graduate, because I've come up with the first vaguely unselfish idea I've ever had in my life, and this place, this institution—in which my family has invested at least seventy thousand dollars—won't give me credit for it.

DIANA: A C is a decent grade, Judy. We used to call it a gentleman's C.

JUDY: Well I'm no gentleman. *(She starts out.)*

DIANA: Judy…One more thing.

(Judy stops, turns.)

JUDY: What?

DIANA: The Provost sat in on the Grievance Committee meeting.

JUDY: And?

DIANA: After it was over, he took me aside. He asked me to ask you a question.

JUDY: Go ahead.

DIANA: …The Provost wondered if your difficulty with Professor Harper has anything to do with…ethnic issues.

JUDY: Say again?

DIANA: A student has recently complained that Professor Harper is anti-Semitic?

JUDY: Anti-Se*mitic*?

DIANA: That's the complaint.

JUDY: Anti-Semitic? It's probably that Talmudic type who sits in the front row and argues about everything. I bet he wears his yarmulke even in the shower.

DIANA: Ah, but you don't feel that way?

JUDY: No way.

DIANA: Oh, Judy, I'm so glad to hear it.

JUDY: I never even thought of it.

DIANA: Good. Then I'll tell the Provost.

JUDY: I mean should I worry about that? My grandmother says you have to watch out for that sort of thing at all times.

DIANA: Yes well, times change.

JUDY: Unless it's there, and I didn't see it.

DIANA: No, no…

JUDY: I mean, maybe I'm so assimilated into white-bread middle-class America that it passed me right by. Maybe I should reexamine this whole issue with that in mind. Thanks a lot, Dean! *(She goes out.)*

DIANA: *(Calling after her.)* Judy! Judy!…Oh God! *(She makes up her mind, opens a desk drawer, takes out a small tape recorder which she slams onto the desk. She pushes the buttons determinedly and then begins to dictate, pacing around her office as she smokes. Dictating.)* Monica, please type a letter to the Provost…Dear Walter…I herewith submit my resignation as Dean, to be effective at the end of this school year. I find I long to return to the clear lines and concrete issues of the classroom. I especially yearn to resume my studies of Jane Austen, and the subordinate role of women in the eighteenth century. I will miss, of course, the sense of bustle and activity I've found here in Administration. There's something to be said, after all, for the friendships which come from working closely with other people during regular hours—among which I count my friendship with the other Deans, and you, Walter, and Monica, my fine assistant…Indeed, in some-ways, I dread retreating to the hermetic world of bickering colleagues, sullen students, hopeless meetings, long hours of preparation… *(She slows down.)* …the loneliness of the library…the meals alone…the sense that something more important is going on everywhere else in the world… *(Long pause.)* Just type a rough draft of this, Monica. I'll look at it tomorrow.

(She clicks off the tape recorder, puts it back in her desk. Dave enters in a track suit, starts doing stretch exercises. Diana crosses to doorway, calls off.)

DIANA: Monica, see if you can locate Professor Harper…

(Then she takes some computer printout sheets out of her briefcase and begins to go over them at her desk as the lights dim on her. The lights come up more fully on Dave, doing stretch exercises. We hear the distant sounds of students cheering. Judy comes on. It is by now late enough in the spring so she doesn't wear a jacket.)

JUDY: Dave… *(She hugs him from behind.)*

DAVE: *(Through his stretches; pantingly.)* Hi…

JUDY: Am I bothering you?

DAVE: *(Grunting; stretching.)* Yes…But that's O.K.

JUDY: I just want to tell you something, David.

DAVE: *(Still exercising.)* Uh oh. When it's David, it's serious.

JUDY: I just want to tell you not to memorize any more of those speeches.

DAVE: Thank God.

JUDY: I'm changing everything.

DAVE: Again?

JUDY: I'm starting all over. From scratch.

DAVE: Why?

JUDY: I didn't like what we had. I can do better.

DAVE: Yeah?

JUDY: Now I'm on a totally different track. I mean, it's still *Antigone.* But I'm adding a whole new dimension.

DAVE: Are you throwing in acid rain?

JUDY: *(Laughing.)* No. I'm onto something much deeper.

(A whistle is heard offstage. Dave starts off.)

DAVE: There's the Four Hundred. I've got to go.

JUDY: So throw away the old stuff.

DAVE: Is there a lot new to learn?

JUDY: Mostly for me.

DAVE: Can you tell me where you're taking it?

JUDY: Well I'm striving for a more natural style.

DAVE: Way to go.

JUDY: And I'm connecting my attack on nuclear armaments with the issue of meaningful work.

DAVE: Excellent.

JUDY: And I'm making Antigone Jewish.

(She goes off. Another whistle from offstage. He looks after her, then runs off the opposite way as…the lights come up on Diana, who is still at her desk, working on printout sheets. After a moment, Henry appears in the doorway. He watches her affectionately for a moment.)

HENRY: *(Finally.)* Woman at her work. I am reminded of Penelope at her loom.

DIANA: *(Looking up; quickly putting away the sheets.)* Come in, Henry.

HENRY: *(Coming in.)* What a magnificent office, Diana! What corporate dimensions!

(As Diana puts her cigarette out.)

HENRY: Thank you…A view of the Charles! The spires of Harvard dimly seen up the river! How different it is from the monkish cells assigned to those of us who teach.

DIANA: You've been here before, Henry.

HENRY: Never. I've scrupulously avoided all official contact with the bureaucracy, except on my own turf. I wouldn't be here now, dear Diana, but for a series of rather frantic telephone messages left under my door. *(He takes a stack of pink slips out of his pocket, reads.)* Call the Dean…See the Dean…Please call or see the Dean.

DIANA: Sit down, Henry.

HENRY: *(Sitting.)* I will, but I must warn you I have very little time. We are now deep in the last plays of Euripides, particularly the *Bacchae,* which I continually find to be one of the more profoundly disturbing works of man. He has an even darker vision than Sophocles.

DIANA: Well maybe I've got some news that will cheer you up, Henry.

HENRY: Beware of Deans bearing gifts.

DIANA: Remember that grant you applied for two years ago?

HENRY: Ah yes. To go to Greece. To see the restorations at Epidaurus. *(Pause.)* And to restore a ruin or two in my own life.

DIANA: Well you've got that grant now, Henry.

HENRY: Now?

DIANA: I've been talking to the Provost. He's giving you next year off. All year. At full pay.

HENRY: Are you serious?

DIANA: I'm always serious, Henry. That's my problem, in case you ever notice. *(Pause.)*

HENRY: Why suddenly now?

DIANA: Ours not to reason why, Henry.

HENRY: I begged for that leave two years ago. I practically fell to my knees and supplicated the Provost like old Priam before Achilles. I thought if Elsa and I could just get away…

DIANA: Call her. Tell her you've lucked out, at long last.

HENRY: It's too late. She's…found someone. Apparently they sit and hold hands and watch television. Anyway, she wants a divorce.

DIANA: I am sorry.

HENRY: No, no, it's good. It's very good. The other shoe has dropped. Finally.

DIANA: Take one of your children then. Give them a trip.

HENRY: They wouldn't come. *(Pause.)* They have their own lives. *(Pause.)* Such as they are. *(Quietly.)* I'll go alone. *(Pause; he looks at her.)* Unless you'd come with me.

DIANA: Henry!

HENRY: Why not? Take a sabbatical. You're overdue.

DIANA: You mean, just—blip out into the blue Aegean?

HENRY: Exactly! Spend a naughty year abroad with an old satyr. Tell you what, I'd even let you smoke.

DIANA: I think I'd give it up if I went abroad.

HENRY: Then there we are!

DIANA: Oh gosh! To get away! To see something else besides these—walls! Just think, Henry… *(She stops.)* Just think. *(Pause. Sadly.)* It wouldn't work, Henry.

HENRY: It might.

DIANA: It already didn't, Henry. On that strange weekend in that gloomy hotel during the M.L.A. conference.

HENRY: That was a lovely weekend.

DIANA: It was not.

HENRY: Dido and Aeneas in their enchanted cave…

DIANA: Oh Henry, *please!*

HENRY: What's the matter?

DIANA: Dido, Penelope, Clytemnestra! I am not a *myth,* Henry! I am not a *met*aphor!

HENRY: My dear lady…

DIANA: No, no, I'm *me,* Henry! I live and breathe in my own right! Do you know anything about my *life?* Do you know where I live? Do you know I have a daughter in Junior High?

HENRY: Of course I know you have…

DIANA: What's her name, Henry? What's my daughter's *name?* It's not Electra and it's not Athena and it's not…

HENRY: Let me think…

DIANA: You don't *know,* Henry. And you don't know that my mother died last semester, and you don't know that I used to play the French horn. You don't *see* me, Henry. You don't see anyone. In your mind, everything is an example of something else! I suppose it's called stereotyping, but whatever it is, I don't like it, Henry! It makes me feel insignificant and unreal.

HENRY: Diana, dear friend… *(He moves toward her.)*

DIANA: No, now stay away from me, Henry. Don't touch me. Go to *Greece,* for God's sake! Find some young woman—excuse me, some sea nymph— who will throw herself into your arms on the topless shores of Mykenos. Really. Just go.
(Pause.)

HENRY: Tell the Provost I'll take a raincheck.

DIANA: A raincheck?

HENRY: Maybe in a year or two. When my life is more in order.

DIANA: It doesn't work that way, Henry. It's now or not at all.

HENRY: Then I'll have to forego it.

DIANA: Oh Henry…

HENRY: At this point in my life, I need my classes. Strange as that may seem. *(He starts out.)* And now, if you'll excuse me, the *Bacchae* call me to the dance.

DIANA: Henry!
(He stops.)

DIANA: Other things go on in this university at the end of the school year besides discussions of the *Bacchae.*

HENRY: *(Stopping, turning.)* Such as?

DIANA: *(Taking the computer printouts from her desk.)* Well, for example, Henry, there's something called preregistration, when students give an indication of what courses they'd like to take next fall.

HENRY: The annual body count.

DIANA: *(Indicating sheets.)* Exactly, Henry. And we in the Humanities are down.

HENRY: We are always down. We are doomed to be down. We live in an age where a book—a good book—is as obsolete as an Aeolian harp. All the more reason to keep standards *up.*

DIANA: You, particularly, are down, Henry.
(Pause.)

HENRY: How many did I get?

DIANA: Two.

HENRY: Two? Two next fall? Two students to take through the entire rise and fall of the Roman Empire.

DIANA: Two, Henry.

HENRY: How many for my elective on Plato?

DIANA: Four.

HENRY: Four. Two for Rome, four for Plato. Six students, next fall, out of over four thousand, have shown some interest in the classical tradition. This, in a country founded by Washington and Jefferson and Madison precisely to reestablish that tradition.

DIANA: Shakespeare, on the other hand, is up.

HENRY: I must say, Diana, I fail to understand why students choose what they do. They land on courses like starlings on a telephone wire. It seems totally random.

DIANA: The Provost is canceling all undergraduate courses with an enrollment of less than five, Henry.

HENRY: What?

DIANA: The Provost is canceling your courses.

HENRY: He has no right!

DIANA: He has every right. It's a budgetary thing. There are clear rules about it. Jack Edward's seminar on Racine goes. Sally Weiskopfs section on Keats. The history department lost the entire seventeenth century.

HENRY: I'll talk to him. These things can change. Students can sign up in the fall.

DIANA: He's laid down the law, Henry. Jack Edwards has already gone up and been refused.

(Pause.)

HENRY: Then I'll teach something else.

DIANA: Such as what, Henry?

HENRY: Dante. I'll teach Dante. I'm beginning to get a new understanding of Hell.

DIANA: Bill Brindisi's got Dante.

HENRY: Shakespeare, then. I'll do a section of Shakespeare.

DIANA: You don't like Shakespeare.

HENRY: Of course I like Shakespeare. He's just a bit…messy, that's all. And a bit over-picked. I refuse to spend an entire class focusing on the button image in *King Lear*. I'll do the Roman plays: *Julius Caesar, Coriolanus*…

DIANA: Jane Tillotson's got Shakespeare, Henry. All of him.

HENRY: All right then, what? Tolstoy? Joyce? I'm an educated man. I can do anything. Give me the freshman course—Introduction to Literature. I'll take it over. I'll muster that motley crew of junior instructors who teach it. We'll begin with the *Iliad,* and stride down the centuries, concluding with Conrad.

DIANA: I think they *start* with Conrad in that course, Henry.

HENRY: Oh really? Well, we'll change that. We'll—

DIANA: Henry. *(Pause.)* The Provost doesn't want you to teach. At all.

HENRY: Why not?

DIANA: He thinks your courses are becoming…problematic, Henry.

HENRY: The *Antigone* thing?

DIANA: And the anti-Semitic thing.

HENRY: I have scrupulously avoided anything controversial in my class.

DIANA: Apparently she hasn't, in her play. I hear it's more and more about being Jewish, and more and more about you.

HENRY: *(Quietly, with increasing anger.)* There is a law as old as Solon which allows a man to confront his accusers. I want to meet her, right now, in front of the Provost, and you, and Ariel Sharon, if he wants to be there!

DIANA: The Provost already met with her, Henry.

HENRY: And what did she say?

DIANA: Nothing! Everything! I don't know! He said it was all very general…He said you both deserve each other. He said if he didn't have the alumni breathing down his neck he'd turn you both loose in the ring, and the hell with it. But right now, all he wants to do is get her graduated and you out of the country, so that things can simmer *down.* Now go to *Greece,* Henry, and enjoy it!

HENRY: And when I come back he'll suggest early retirement.

DIANA: He might.

HENRY: He'll sweeten the pie. Buy me off with a few impressive benefits.

DIANA: You've been here a long time, Henry. I think they'd be very generous.

HENRY: I want to teach, Diana.

DIANA: I know.

HENRY: I need to teach.

DIANA: I know, I know…

HENRY: It's what I do.

DIANA: Henry, my old colleague…

HENRY: I am a classical scholar. I trained at Harvard. I have written three good books. I know a great deal, and I have to teach what I know, and I'm only good when I'm teaching it! My wife has left me, my children have scattered, I have nothing else but this! I have to teach, Diana. Have to. Or I'm dead.

DIANA: You need students, Henry.

HENRY: Then I'll have to get them, won't I?

(He goes off. Diana sits there for a moment, then opens her purse, takes out a pack of cigarettes. She shakes it, but it's empty. She gets up, and begins to walk toward the wings, calling out sweetly as she goes.)

DIANA: Monica?…Did you bring any cigarettes in today?…Because if you did, even though you're down to your last one, I intend to get it, Monica. I intend to wrestle you to the ground!

(She goes off as Judy comes on. She leans against a pillar in a rather theatrical pose and recites her lines, referring only occasionally to a script she carries, in her hand.)

JUDY: "So Creon has determined I go to jail. I wonder if this is happening because I'm Jewish. I don't mean simply that Creon's prejudiced—though he probably is. I mean more because of me. Maybe it's built into my Jewish blood to rise up against the Creons of this world. All I know is for the first time in my life I've felt in tune with something larger than myself. I've been to the library lately. I've studied my roots. And I've learned how often we Jews have stood our ground against injustice. Pharaoh and Philistine, Hittite and Herod have fallen before us. Roman generals and Spanish Inquisitors, Venetian businessmen and Russian Cossacks, Nazis, Arabs, McCarthyites—all the arrogant authorities of this world have tried to subdue us. And when we protest, they throw us into jail. Well, what's jail these days? Maybe this is a jail right here. This so-called ivory tower. This labyrinth of curricular obligations. This festering nest of overpaid administrators. This rotten pit of dry and exhausted pedants. This winter camp which capitalism creates to keep its children off the job market. What job market? Where are the jobs? Where is there decent work in an economy so devoted to nonessential goods and destructive weapons?"

(Dave comes on.)

DAVE: Judy—

JUDY: Wait. I'm almost done. *(She continues to recite.)* "Or maybe this whole damn country is a jail. Maybe we're all prisoners. Prisoners of these oppressive corporations, who capture us with their advertising, chain us to their products, and work us forever in meaningless jobs to pay for things we shouldn't even want."

DAVE: Judy. It's important.

JUDY: Hold it. *(She takes a deep breath.)* "And to protect this prison, this fortress

America, this so-called way of life, we arm ourselves with weapons which, if they're used, could ten times over destroy the world, blot out the past, and turn the future into a desolate blank. Are we so sure we're right? Is life in these United States so great? Would the homeless hordes on the streets of New York agree? Would the hungry blacks in the South? Would the migrant workers breaking their backs to feed us go along with it? Oh God, Lysander, this might be a terrible thing to say, but I don't think our country is worth dying for any more. The world at large is worth dying for, not just us."

DAVE: Wow! That's tremendous.

JUDY: Thank you.

(Pause.)

DAVE: *(Quietly.)* He wants to see you.

JUDY: The Provost? I know. I have a meeting with him in half an hour.

DAVE: No, *Harper! Harper* wants to see you.

JUDY: Harper?

DAVE: He called me at the lab.

JUDY: How come he called *you?*

DAVE: I don't know…I guess he knew I knew you. Anyway, he said he watched the rehearsal last night.

JUDY: *What?*

DAVE: He was there. And he wants to talk to you about it.

JUDY: Oh God. What did he think?

DAVE: Didn't say.

(The lights begin to come up on Henry's office, as Henry comes in, settles at his desk.)

JUDY: Oh Lord, he must have hated it. All that Creon stuff I put in. Well, maybe it'll do him good.

DAVE: He said he'd be in his office all afternoon. You better see him.

JUDY: *(Putting on lip gloss.)* I might. Then again I might not. First, of course, I have a major meeting with the Provost. *(She starts out.)*

DAVE: *(Calling after Judy.)* Hey, you're quite the Queen Bee around here these days.

JUDY: I'm another Antigone.

DAVE: Antigone dies in the end, remember.

JUDY: That's the old version. Mine ends happily ever after. *(She goes off.)*

DAVE: *(Calling after her.)* Ever hear of *hubris*, Judy? Know what that word means… *(He sees she's gone; speaks to himself.)* Pride. Overweening pride. For example, take a man whose father gives him a chemistry set when he's eight years old. This man takes Chemistry in high school, and majors in it in college. What makes this man think he can graduate if he doesn't study? What makes this man think he can find a job if he doesn't graduate? What makes this man stand around, talking to himself, when his final exam in Chemistry starts in five minutes, and he doesn't know the stuff at *all*? Pride, that's what. *Hubris.* Which leads to tragedy every time. *(He goes off grimly as the lights come up on Henry in his office. After a moment, Judy comes in.)*

JUDY: You wanted to see me, Professor Harper?

HENRY: *(Jumping up.)* Ah. Miss Miller. Yes. *(Indicates a chair.)* Please.
(Judy comes in.)

HENRY: How well you look.

JUDY: Thank you.

HENRY: I am reminded of a line from the *Andromache:* "I now wear different robes."

JUDY: I don't know that one.

HENRY: No matter. You look lovely. Life on the wicked stage becomes you.

JUDY: Thanks. *(She sits.)*

HENRY: Yes, well, now I have recently had the opportunity to watch you practice your play.

JUDY: You mean, re*hearse.*

HENRY: Yes. Rehearse. Last night, in fact. I happen to know old Bill, who's the custodian of the Spingler Auditorium, and he took me up to the back of the balcony and let me sit there unobtrusively and watch you rehearse your play.

JUDY: I heard.

HENRY: Oh yes? Well that's where I was. All evening. *(Pause.)* I found it… *(This is tough for him.)* Interesting. *(Pause.)* Quite interesting. *(Pause.)* The crude poetry, the naive theatricality…

JUDY: Thank you.

HENRY: Your work also demonstrated an earnestness and commitment which I found…refreshing, in a world which seems too often concerned only with the meaning of meaning.

JUDY: You mean, you *liked* it?
(Pause.)

HENRY: I…admired it.

JUDY: Well thank you very much! I appreciate that.

HENRY: I have decided it may substitute after all for your term paper.

JUDY: That's great!

HENRY: Miss Miller, you might be interested to know that Sophocles himself was a practical man of the theatre. Not only did he write his plays, but he directed most of them, and sometimes acted in them as well, just as you are doing.

JUDY: Really?

HENRY: Absolutely. And according to Aristotle—this might amuse you—he actually danced in a lost play of his called *Nausicaa*. He danced. He danced the part of a young woman playing ball.

JUDY: No kidding! That makes me feel very proud!

HENRY: Then I wonder if you would play ball with *me*, Miss Miller.

JUDY: What do you mean?

HENRY: Well now, last night, I noticed a number of people scurrying about, assisting with your production.

JUDY: Yes…

HENRY: Good, practical souls, hard at work. I mean, not only did I notice your personal and particular friend…

JUDY: Dave…

HENRY: Yes, Dave. A fine, stalwart young man. I noticed him. But I also noticed other actors, and that odd cluster of people pretending to be the chorus.

JUDY: Right…

HENRY: And then I hear there's to be an orchestra…

JUDY: A group. A combo, really…

HENRY: Well how many do you think are involved, in toto?

JUDY: In toto?

HENRY: Altogether.

JUDY: Oh…maybe…thirty-five.

HENRY: And of course not all of them will graduate this year, will they?

JUDY: No. Some. Not all.

HENRY: Miss Miller, I wonder if you would announce to everyone in your production that I'm planning to give a special seminar next fall.

JUDY: Special seminar?

HENRY: On the Greeks. And since these students have all been working on your *Antigone*, I'll give them the inside track. They *must*, however—you must tell them this—they *must* let the Dean's office know they're interested, so we'll have some indication of preenrollment.

JUDY: Professor Harper, I'm not sure they'd want to—

HENRY: Oh yes they would. Tell them this course will be—how shall I put it?—"project-oriented." They can put on plays. They can make models of the Parthenon. They can draw maps of the Peloponnesian Peninsula, I don't care!

JUDY: That doesn't sound like you, Professor Harper.

HENRY: Oh yes, yes. And tell them I'll grade it Pass/Fail, if they want. And I'll have very few papers. No papers at all, really, if that's what they want. Because the important thing is not papers, is it, it's the Greeks! We'll be studying the Greeks next year, that's the thing! We'll still be reading and discussing those fine old plays. We'll still be holding onto the heart of Western Civilization. That's what we'll be doing, Miss Miller, and you will have helped us do it!

(Pause.)

JUDY: You mean you want students next year.

HENRY: Yes, frankly, I do.

(Pause.)

JUDY: Wow!

HENRY: There it is.

JUDY: I always thought we had to go through you. I never thought you had to go through us.

HENRY: Well we do.

JUDY: You really *need* us, don't you? You have to have us.

HENRY: Without you, we'd die.

JUDY: I never knew that before.

HENRY: Now you do. *(Pause.)* So will you tell them about the course?

JUDY: Yes I will.

HENRY: And you'll encourage them to come?

JUDY: I'll tell them, Professor Harper. I'll let them choose.

HENRY: But you won't...undercut me?

JUDY: No, I won't do that.

HENRY: And you'll remind them to sign up immediately. So the administration will know.

JUDY: I'll do all that, sir. I mean, you have a right to live, too, after all.

HENRY: You're magnanimous in victory, Miss Miller.

JUDY: Thank you, sir.

HENRY: Now, before we turn to the crass topic or grades, suppose we celebrate the conclusion of these negotiations. *(Opens his drawer again, takes out a sherry bottle and two murky glasses.)* I keep this sherry around for those rare occasions when a fellow scholar stops by.

JUDY: Oh I don't—

HENRY: *(Pouring.)* Please. It's important. Old Odysseus and the nymph Calypso, in Book Five of the *Odyssey,* sharing a glass before they say goodbye. *(He hands her her glass, raises his in a toast.)* To peace and reconciliation. *(They click glasses and drink.)*

HENRY: Doesn't that hit the spot?

JUDY: Actually, it does.

HENRY: Have some more.

JUDY: Oh, well. No. I mean, all right.

(He pours her more, and a touch more for himself. Judy gets up.)

JUDY: You know, I was just thinking, Professor Harper…

HENRY: *(His little joke.)* That's always a good sign.

JUDY: No, seriously, I was thinking that you and I are basically very much alike.

HENRY: Ah? And how so?

JUDY: I mean we both see too big a picture.

HENRY: Elucidate, please.

JUDY: Sure. I mean, there you are, always talking about the Greeks versus the Jews, and here I am, talking about the Jews versus all authority.

HENRY: I see.

JUDY: Maybe we should both scale things down.

HENRY: Maybe we should. *(Settling back in his chair.)* In any case, I think you can count on receiving a B in my course, Miss Miller.

JUDY: A B.

HENRY: A strong B. A solid B. A B which leans longingly toward a B plus.

JUDY: I was kind of hoping I'd get an A.

HENRY: I don't think your work quite warrants an A, Miss Miller.

JUDY: You don't think so?

HENRY: Let's reserve the A's for Sophocles, shall we? It gives us something to go for.

(Pause.)

JUDY: That's cool.

HENRY: I take it you agree.

JUDY: I guess a B from you is like an A from anyone else.

HENRY: Well, thank you, Miss Miller.

JUDY: *(Getting up.)* Besides, I don't really believe in grades anymore.

HENRY: Good for you.

JUDY: I think I've grown beyond them.

HENRY: Unfortunately we live in a world which seems to require them. We have to toss them, like bones, to a ravenous administration.

JUDY: Oh God, I know. *They* even wanted me to take an A.

HENRY: And where did they propose you find that A?

JUDY: A professor in Drama saw a rehearsal, and offered to give me a straight A.

HENRY: Ah, but of course that wouldn't count.

JUDY: Oh sure. He said I could register it under Special Topics.

HENRY: Well then, I'm afraid I'd have to go to the Provost. To protest this blatant interference in my course.

JUDY: I just came from the Provost. It was his idea, actually.

   (Pause.)

HENRY: You mean you don't need a grade in my course to graduate.

JUDY: Not any more.

HENRY: You don't really need me at all.

JUDY: Technically, no.

HENRY: Why did you bother to come?

JUDY: I wanted your opinion of my *play!* I wanted to hear what you thought.

HENRY: And I told you: B.

JUDY: Right. Fine. And I'm accepting your B. I'll tell the Registrar. *(She starts out.)*

HENRY: Miss Miller.

   (She stops.)

HENRY: This professor who offered to intrude. Who was he?

JUDY: Who?

HENRY: Do I know him?

JUDY: He's new this year.

HENRY: What's his name?

JUDY: Bob Birnbaum.

HENRY: Bob—?

JUDY: Birnbaum.

   (Pause.)

HENRY: Of course.

JUDY: What do you mean?

HENRY: Once again Athens is forced to bow to Jerusalem.

JUDY: Explain that, please.

HENRY: I mean the Chosen People always choose to intrude.

JUDY: That's what I thought you meant. *(She strides for the door, then wheels on him.)* All bets are off, Professor Harper. I wouldn't recommend this course to a Nazi! And I'll take a good, solid, Jewish A from Birnbaum! *(She storms out.)*

HENRY: *(Quietly; to himself as he sits.)* Good God. What have I done?

   (The lights dim on him as he sits at his desk. Diana crosses the stage hurriedly, carrying a stack of folders. Dave is following her.)

DAVE: Dean…?

(She turns.)

DAVE: Could I speak to you for a minute, please?

DIANA: I'm sorry, but I'm late for an important meeting.

DAVE: The Committee on Academic Performance, right?

DIANA: That's the one.

DAVE: That's what I've got to speak to you about.

(She stops, looks at him.)

DIANA: Aren't you that friend of Judy Miller's?

DAVE: David Appleton. My name's coming up before the committee today. I flunked the Chemistry final. I'm not graduating.

DIANA: Chemistry will take care of you. There's infinite salvation: makeup exams, summer school, degrees given out in the fall…

DAVE: I don't want any of that. I want to switch to your department and be here all next year.

DIANA: Studying what?

DAVE: The Greeks.

DIANA: But we don't have a Classics Department anymore.

DAVE: You have Professor Harper.

DIANA: He may be on sabbatical next year.

DAVE: Oh. Then I'll make up my general requirements till he returns and take Ancient Greek on my own.

DIANA: (Starting out.) If you'd make an appointment with Monica, my assistant, we'll discuss all this.

DAVE: No, I've thought it through. I just need your approval.

DIANA: You're talking about another year's tuition.

DAVE: I know. And my dad's cutting me off. But I've gotten a double shift in the cafeteria. I'll get my degree next June, and apply for postgraduate studies with Professor Harper.

(Pause.)

DIANA: I'll tell the committee you're staying on.

DAVE: Thank you.

DIANA: I envy you.

DAVE: For studying with Harper?

DIANA: For being so sure.

(Judy enters.)

JUDY: What's going on, Dave?

DAVE: I'm changing my life.

DIANA: Make an appointment if you want to change it back! (She goes out.)

JUDY: We have a rehearsal, remember? I'm putting in the final rewrites.

DAVE: Can't make it. Got a class.

JUDY: At this hour? What class?

DAVE: Harper's actually.

JUDY: *Har*per's? *My* Harper?

DAVE: I've been auditing it for the past three weeks.

JUDY: Why?

DAVE: I like him. I like the subject. I like myself when I'm working on it.

JUDY: You never told me that.

DAVE: I knew it would freak you out.

JUDY: Damn right! He's a bigot, Dave.

DAVE: I don't think so.

JUDY: He's an anti-Semite.

DAVE: I don't think so, Judy.

JUDY: I *know* so! *Personally!* He made an anti-Semitic *slur!*

DAVE: He just generalizes, Judy. It's his tragic flaw.

JUDY: I don't buy that, Dave.

DAVE: All right, so he made a crack? So what? People make ethnic digs all the time in this country. We all get it in the neck—the Poles, the Italians, now the Wasps.

JUDY: The Jews are different! All though history—

DAVE: So I keep hearing. Still, seems to me you're people, like everyone else. I think this Jewish thing is getting out of hand. Suddenly nothing counts except you're Jewish!

JUDY: Dave...

DAVE: No, let me finish, for once in my life! I didn't fall in love with a Jewish Revolutionary, I fell in love with *you!* I fell in love with a particular person who liked Springsteen and Moo Sho Pork and staying in bed all day on Sunday. What happened to all that? What happens to us next *year?* These are the important things—not that you're Jewish, for God's sake!

JUDY: I think we're in a little hot water here.

DAVE: I guess we are.

(A bell rings.)

DAVE: Saved by the bell. *(He starts off.)*

JUDY: Dave.

(He stops.)

JUDY: We have rehearsal now.

DAVE: Work around me.

JUDY: It's too late for that.

DAVE: Look, it's his last class. The whole school knows about this. Everyone wants to see what he's going to say.

JUDY: Not if they're with *Antigone.*

DAVE: Give me an hour.

JUDY: No! It's him or me, Dave. You choose.

DAVE: Be serious.

JUDY: I am. I'll put in Mark Shapiro. I'll replace you. Totally.
(Pause.)

DAVE: Fair enough. *(He starts off again.)*

JUDY: *(Calling after him.)* Then it's true, what my grandmother said! You people always turn your backs when the chips are down!
(He turns, glares at her, then exits. She speaks softly, to herself.)

JUDY: Oh Lord. I'm as bad as Harper.
(She goes off slowly the opposite way. The lights come up on Henry as he comes downstage, addressing the audience once again as if it were his class. Dave enters, to sit on the side and listen, as if he were in class.)

HENRY: *(To audience.)* This has been a course on tragedy. That is what this course is supposed to be about *(Pause.)* First, let me remind you what tragedy is not. Tragedy has nothing to do with choice. If you can choose, it is not tragic. There are some people who think that our arms race with the Russians is tragic. It is not. It is not, because we have the choice, they have the choice, to say No, to stop, to disarm, to embrace each other in the name of peace at any time. So it is not tragic. It is stupid, yes. It is insane, it is suicidal, it is pathetic, but it is not—repeat Not—tragic, in the true Greek sense of the word. *(Pause.)* Tragedy occurs when you cannot choose, when you have no choice at all. This is hard for Americans to understand. Because most of us are free, or think we are. Nowhere else in the world, and never before in history, have so many people been so free to choose so many destinies. Perhaps, because of this freedom, it is impossible for us to sense what the Greeks called tragedy. We have no oracles, no gods, no real sense of ultimate authority to insist that if we do one thing, another will inevitably follow. We are free. *(Pause.)* On the other hand, there might come a time to some of us, to one or two, *(He glances at Dave.)* when we get an inkling, a glimmer, a faint shadow of a shadow of what it might have been like for the Greeks when they sat in a theatre and saw the universe close in on a man, or woman, because of some flaw, some excess, some overshooting of the mark... *(Pause.)* Then the net tightens, and as he struggles, tightens further, until he is crushed by forces total and absurd. *(Pause.)* Then we might be touching the outer borders of tragedy, as the Greeks once knew it. *(Pause. He takes up his book of* Antigone.*)* But I've just discovered something else about tragedy, or at least about Sophoclean tragedy. Something I thought I knew, but didn't understand till now. And that is what the tragic heroes do after the net has closed around them. What they do, even in the teeth of disaster, is accept responsibility, assert their own destiny, and mete out proudly their own punishments. This is what Oedipus does when he puts out his eyes. This is what Antigone does, when she hangs herself. And this is what Creon does, at the end of the same play. He has lost his wife, his children, all he holds dear. And he realizes why: that in his commitment to abstract and dehumanizing laws, he has neglected the very heart of life. And so he banishes himself from his own city. His Polis. He goes. He disappears. He leaves the stage, forever doomed now to wander far from the only community he knows, self-exiled and alone. *(Pause.)* I'll expect all papers under my door by five o'clock this evening. You may retrieve them, graded and with appropriate comments, from the Departmental office next Monday. Enjoy your summer. Read good books. Go to good plays. Think of the Greeks. Thank you and good bye.

(He sees Dave go, then crosses to his desk, where he leaves his book of Antigone. *Then he exits, as graduation music comes up loudly: an optimistic piece, played by a brass ensemble. Diana comes out in gown and colorful academic hood. She reads from a formal-looking document.)*

DIANA: Our final award is the Peabody Prize... *(Reads from card.)* "Offered annually to that student who best combines academic excellence with extracurricular commitment..." *(To audience.)* It is awarded this year to Judith Rachel Miller, of the graduating class, for her exceptional academic record as well as for her fascinating contemporary version of Sophocles' *Antigone.*

(Applause and cheers. Judy comes on, in academic robes. She accepts an envelope from Diana, who gives her a kiss.)

DIANA: Congratulations, Judy...And now refreshments will be—

JUDY: May I say something, please?

DIANA: *(Very reluctantly.)* All right.

JUDY: *(To audience.)* First, I want to thank everyone involved for making our play possible. *(Looks at envelope.)* And I want to thank the Peabody Foundation for making this prize possible. *(Looks out.)* And I want to thank my parents for making me possible.

(Diana tries to step in.)

JUDY: I'm not finished.

(Diana steps back.)

JUDY: *(To audience.)* Lately I've been doing some thinking, and as someone once told me, that's always a good sign. I've been thinking about this prize, for example. I guess it stands for everything I used to believe in: personal ambition…success… *(She peeks into the envelope.)* And sure, why not? money…I mean, these are the things they tell us make our country great… *(Diana looks worried.)*

JUDY: Trouble is, I'm beginning to think these things aren't so important. Maybe my play hasn't influenced anyone else, but it sure has influenced me. I don't feel good about my life anymore. I don't feel good about my country. I can't accept all this *stuff* that's going on these days. I can't accept it. No, I'm sorry, but I just can't accept it. *(She hands the envelope back to Diana and hurries off.)*

DIANA: Judy!

(She hurries off after Judy, as the lights come up on Henry's office. Dave enters, carrying a note. He finds Henry's book on the desk. He picks it up, looks at it, and starts deciphering the title.)

DAVE: Alpha…Nu…Tau…Iota…Gamma…Omicron…Nu…Eta…*Antigone.* *(Diana enters, no longer in her robes, but still carrying the prize envelope.)*

DIANA: Mr. Appleton? Monica told me you got a note from Professor Harper.

DAVE: *(Indicating the book.)* He said he was leaving me his book.

DIANA: But did he say where he'd *be?* We can't locate him anywhere.

DAVE: He just mentions the book.

DIANA: Oh dear.

DAVE: I'll find him. I'll track him down. Like Telemachus. In the *Odyssey.*

DIANA: You're beginning to sound a little like him.

DAVE: Maybe. In some ways.

DIANA: I suppose you heard about Judy.

DAVE: Saw it. From the sidelines.

DIANA: That girl seems to be interested in systematically hanging herself.

DAVE: She likes to go for broke.

DIANA: This prize is a sizable check. Do you know any cause she'd want to donate it to?

DAVE: Tell you what: I'll ask her. it'll give me an excuse to open diplomatic relations.

DIANA: I have a feeling we may have lost them both forever.

DAVE: Oh God, I hope not.

DIANA: So do I…Meanwhile, I have no idea how to summarize all this for the

Departmental report. What does Sophocles say at the end of that damn play?

DAVE: Well, he says that wisdom and reverence lead to happiness…

DIANA: Oh good. I'll go along with that! Thank you.

(Dave starts out, then stops, turns back.)

DAVE: But then he goes on to say that we only learn this when we're too old for it to make much difference.

DIANA: Then heaven help us all.

(They look at each other. Blackout.)

THE END

LOVE LETTERS

INTRODUCTION

Here's a play that sort of sneaked up behind me. When I wrote it, I didn't think it was a play at all, and sent it to *The New Yorker,* which promptly sent it back. I had written it almost as an exercise when I was shifting from the manual typewriter to a Radio Shack computer. Possibly the facility of the electronic keyboard and the ease with which you could adjust your mistakes reminded me of the scratch of the fountain pen and indelibly personal penmanship which were so much a part of the letter-writing culture in which I grew up. In any case, after some hesitation, I decided to try performing the work myself by reading it with Holland Taylor, an actress friend of mine, at the New York Public Library. One thing led to another—slowly at first, with a second stage production at the Long Wharf in New Haven, and then Monday night offerings of various teams during the New York run of *The Cocktail Hour.* Little by little various actors of various ages began to take a crack at it, and before long *Love Letters* was touring the country, being translated into many foreign languages, and becoming the centerpiece of countless benefits at home and abroad. Only the English seem to agree with my initial reservations. To them it's still not a play and never will be, and they try to drive a stake through its heart every time it shows up.

ORIGINAL PRODUCTION

Love Letters was initially presented by the Long Wharf Theater (Arvin Brown, Artistic Director; M. Edgar Rosenblum, Executive Director) in New Haven, Connecticut, on November 3, 1988. It was directed by John Tillinger; the lighting was by Judy Rasmuson; and the production stage manager was Beverly J. Andreozzi. The cast was as follows:

    Andrew Makepeace Ladd III . . . . John Rubinstein
    Melissa Gardner . . . . Joanna Gleason

CHARACTERS

ANDREW MAKEPEACE LADD III
MELISSA GARDNER

AUTHOR'S NOTE

This is a play, or rather a sort of a play, which needs no theatre, no lengthy rehearsal, no special set, no memorization of lines, and no commitment from its two actors beyond the night of performance. It is designed simply to be read aloud by an actor and an actress of roughly the same age, sitting side by side at a table, in front of a group of people of any size. The actor might wear a dark gray suit, the actress a simple, expensive-looking dress. In a more formal production, the table and chairs might be reasonably elegant English antiques, and the actors' area may be isolated against a dark background by bright, focused lights. In performance, the piece would seem to work best if the actors didn't look at each other until the end, when Melissa might watch Andy as he reads his final letter. They *listen* eagerly and actively to each other along the way, however, much as we might listen to an urgent voice on a one-way radio, coming from far, far away.

DO'S AND DON'TS
IN PRODUCING LOVE LETTERS

1. Don't use a curtain. Don't introduce music or singing or any other effects before the houselights dim or after the play is over.
2. The actors should enter and exit from the same side in a low light. The actor should pull out the actress's chair, she should sit, then he should sit, and then the lights come up and they do the play. In all entrances and exits, the woman should enter and leave the stage first, followed by the man. During the curtain call, they should take a bow on either side of the desk before meeting each other in front of it.
3. There should be no changing or adjusting of costumes between acts. The same outfit should be worn throughout.
4. No baby talk, please. When the actors read the earlier letters, they are still older people, looking back, reading what they wrote when they were younger.
5. No mugging, either. When the actors are receiving letters, they are simply recipients, reading letters in private, not people publicizing their reactions or making faces in front of a mirror.
6. If a decanter and water glasses are used, make sure that these do not become too much of a prop. If we see Melissa drinking all the time, she makes it simply a play about alcoholism.
7. Avoid crying. This applies particularly to Andy at the end. Let the audience do the crying, if it feels like it.
8. Don't mess around with the text. No embellishments, insertions, cuts, or silent mouthings, please. Trust what I wrote, perform it as written, and all will be well.

A.R. Gurney

PART I

ANDY: Andrew Makepeace Ladd, the Third, accepts with pleasure the kind invitation of Mr. and Mrs. Gilbert Channing Gardner for a birthday party in honor of their daughter Melissa on April 19th, 1937, at half past three o'clock...

MELISSA: Dear Andy: Thank you for the birthday present. I have a lot of Oz books, but not *The Lost Princess of Oz*. What made you give me that one? Sincerely yours, Melissa.

ANDY: I'm answering your letter about the book. When you came into second grade with that stuck-up nurse, you looked like a lost princess.

MELISSA: I don't believe what you wrote. I think my mother told your mother to get that book. I like the pictures more than the words. Now let's stop writing letters.

♦ ♦ ♦

ANDY: I will make my l's taller than my d's.

MELISSA: I will close up my a's and my o's.

ANDY: I will try to make longer p's. Pass it on.

MELISSA: You're funny.

♦ ♦ ♦

ANDY: Will you be my valentine?

MELISSA: Were you the one who sent me a valentine saying "Will you be my valentine?"

ANDY: Yes I sent it.

MELISSA: Then I will be. Unless I have to kiss you.

♦ ♦ ♦

ANDY: When it's warmer out, can I come over and swim in your pool?

MELISSA: No you can't. I have a new nurse named Miss Hawthorne who thinks you'll give me infantile paralysis.

ANDY: Will you help me go down and get the milk and cookies during recess?

MELISSA: I will if you don't ask me to marry you again.

BOTH: I will not write personal notes in class, I will not write personal notes in class, I will not...

ANDY: Merry Christmas and Happy New Year. Love, Andy Ladd.

MELISSA: I made this card myself. It's not Santa Claus. It's a kangaroo jumping over a glass of orange juice. Do you like it? I like YOU. Melissa.

ANDY: My mother says I have to apologize in writing. I apologize for sneaking into the girl's bath-house while you were changing into your bathing suit. Tell Miss Hawthorne I apologize to her, too.

MELISSA: Here is a picture I drew of you and me without our bathing suits on. Guess which one is you. Don't show this to ANYONE. I love you.

ANDY: Here is a picture of Miss Hawthorne without her bathing suit on.

MELISSA: You can't draw very well, can you?

＊ ＊ ＊

ANDY: Thank you for sending me the cactus plant stuck in the little donkey. I've gotten lots of presents here in the hospital and I have to write thank-you notes for every one. I hate it here. My throat is sore all the time from where they cut out my tonsils. They give me lots of ice cream, but they also take my temperature the wrong way.

＊ ＊ ＊

MELISSA: Merry Christmas and Happy New Year. Why did they send you to another school this year?

ANDY: Merry Christmas. They think I should be with all boys.

＊ ＊ ＊

MELISSA: You made me promise to send you a postcard. This is it.

ANDY: You're supposed to write personal notes on the backs of postcards. For example, here are some questions to help you think of things to say. Do you like Lake Saranac? Is it fun visiting your grandmother? Are your parents really getting divorced? Can you swim out into the deep part of that lake, or does Miss Hawthorne make you stay in the shallow part where it's all roped off? Is there anybody there my age? I mean boys. Please write answers to all these questions.

MELISSA: No. No. Yes. Yes. No.

ANDY: Dear Melissa. Remember me? Andy Ladd? They've sent me to camp so I can be with all boys again. This is quiet hour so we have to write home, but I've already done that, so I'm writing you. There's a real Indian here named Iron Crow who takes us on Nature walks and teaches us six new plants a day. This is O.K., except he forgot about poison ivy. I won the backstroke, which gives me two and a half gold stars. If I get over fifty gold stars by Parent's Day, then I win a Leadership Prize which is what my father expects of me. I'm making a napkin-ring in shop which is worth four stars and which is either for my mother or for you. I hope you'll write me back, because when the mail comes every morning, they shout out our names and it would be neat to walk up and get a letter from a girl.

MELISSA: Help! Eeeek! Yipes! I can't write LETTERS! It took me HOURS just to write "Dear Andy." I write my father because I miss him so much, but to write a BOY! Hell's Bells and Oriental Smells! I'm sending you this picture I drew of our cat instead. Don't you love his expression? It's not quite right, but I tried three times. I drew those jiggly lines around his tail because sometimes the tail behaves like a completely separate person. I love that tail. There's a part of me that feels like that tail. Oh, and here's some bad news. My mother's gotten married again to a man named Hooper McPhail. HELP! LEMME OUTA HERE!

ANDY: I liked the cat. Is that the cat you threw in the pool that time when we were playing over at your house in third grade?

MELISSA: No, that was a different cat entirely.

ANDY: This is a dumb Halloween card and wouldn't scare anyone, but I'm really writing about dancing school. My parents say I have to go this year, but I don't see why I have to. I can't figure out why they keep sending us away from girls and then telling us we have to be with them. Are you going to dancing school also? Just write Yes or No, since you hate writing.

MELISSA: Yes.

ANDY: Dear Mrs. McPhail. I want to apologize to you for my behavior in the back of your car coming home last night from dancing school. Charlie and I were just goofing around and I guess it just got out of hand. I'm sorry you had to pull over to the curb and I'm sorry we tore Melissa's dress. My father says you should send me the bill and I'll pay for it out of my allowance.

MELISSA: Dear Andy. Mummy brought your letter up here to Lake Placid. She thought it was cute. I thought it was dumb. I could tell your father made you write it. You and I both know that the fight in the car was really Charlie's fault. And Charlie never apologized, thank God. That's why I like him, actually. As for you, you shouldn't always do what your parents WANT, Andy. Even at dancing school you're always doing just the RIGHT THING all the time. You're a victim of your parents sometimes. That was why I picked Charlie to do the rumba with me that time. He at least hacks around occasionally. I'm enclosing a picture I drew of a dancing bear on a chain. That's you, Andy. Sometimes. I swear.

ANDY: I know it seems jerky, but I like writing, actually. I like writing compositions in English, I like writing letters, I like writing you. I wanted to write that letter to your mother because I knew you'd see it, so it was like talking to you when you weren't here. And when you couldn't *interrupt.* (Hint, hint.) My father says everyone should write letters as much as they can. It's a dying art. He says letters are a way of presenting yourself in the best possible light to another person. I think that, too.

MELISSA: I think you sound too much like your father. But I'm not going to argue by MAIL and anyway the skiing's too good.

ANDY: Get well soon. I'm sorry you broke your leg.

MELISSA: Mummy says I broke it purposely because I'm a self-destructive person and went down Whiteface Mountain without asking permission. All I know is I wish I had broken my arm instead so I'd have a good excuse not to write LETTERS. I'm enclosing a picture I drew of the bed pan. I'm SERIOUS! Don't you love its shape?

❧ ❧ ❧

ANDY: Andrew M. Ladd, III, accepts with pleasure the kind invitation of Mrs. R. Ferguson Brown for a dinner in honor of her granddaughter Melissa Gardner before the Children's Charity Ball.

MELISSA: I'm writing this letter because I'm scared if I called you up, I'd start crying, right on the telephone. I'm really MAD at you, Andy. Don't you know that when you're invited to a dinner before a dance, you're supposed to dance with the person giving it at least TWICE. And I don't mean my grandmother either. That's why they *give* dinner parties. So people get *danced* with. I notice you danced with Ginny Waters, but you never danced with me once. I just think it's rude, that's all. Straighten up and fly right, Andy. How do you expect to get anywhere in life if you're rude to women? Nuts to you, Andy, and that goes double on Sunday!

ANDY: I didn't dance with you because I've got a stretched groin. If you don't know what that means, look it up some time. I was going to tell you in person but I got embarrassed. I stretched it playing hockey last week. The only reason I danced with Ginny Waters is she takes tiny steps, but you always make me do those big spins and we could have gotten into serious trouble. I tried it out at home with my mother first, and it hurt like hell. That's why I didn't dance with you. I'm using a heating pad now and maybe we can dance next week at the junior assemblies.

MELISSA: I don't believe that hockey stuff. I think Ginny Waters stretched your groin. And next time you cut in, I'm going to stretch the other one.

ANDY: Huh? You obviously don't know what a groin is.

MELISSA: You obviously don't know what a joke is.

◆ ◆ ◆

MELISSA: Merry Christmas and Happy New Year. Guess what? I'm going to a psychiatrist now. My mother says it will do me a world of good. Don't tell anyone, though. It's supposed to be a big secret.

ANDY: Merry Christmas and Happy New Year. I have a question and would you please write the answer *by mail,* because sometimes when you call, my mother listens on the telephone, and when she doesn't my little brother does. Here's the question: do you talk about sex with the psychiatrist?

MELISSA: I talk about sex all the time. It's terribly expensive, but I think it's worth it.

ANDY: If I went to a psychiatrist, I'd talk about you. Seriously. I would. I think about you quite often.

MELISSA: Sometimes I think you just like me because I'm richer than you are. Sometimes I really have that feeling. I think you like the pool, and the elevator in my grandmother's house, and Simpson in his butler's coat coming in with gingerale and cookies on a silver tray. I think you like all that stuff just as much as you like me.

ANDY: All I know is my mother keeps saying you'd make a good match. She says if I ever married you, I'd be set up for life. But I think it's really just physical attraction. That's why I liked going into the elevator with you at your grandmother's that time. Want to try it again?

✦ ✦ ✦

MELISSA: HELP! LEMME OUTA HERE! They shipped me off to this nunnery! It's the end of the absolute WORLD! We have to wear these sappy middy-blouses, and learn POSTURE in gym, and speak French out LOUD in class. "Aide-moi, mon chevalier!" Oh God, it's crappy here. All the girls squeal and shriek, and you can hear them barfing in the bathroom after the evening meal. We can only go to Hartford one day a week IF we can find a chaperone, and there are only two dances with boys a year, and if we're caught drinking, even *beer*, it's wham, bam, onto the next train and home, which is WORSE! Can you come visit me some Sunday afternoon? We can invite boys to tea from four to six. There are all these biddies sitting around keeping watch, but if the weather's good, we could walk up and down the driveway before we have to sign in for evening prayers. They've made me room with this fat, spoiled Cuban bitch who has nine pairs of shoes, and all she does is lie on her bed and listen to *Finian's Rainbow.* "How are Things in Glocca Morra?" Who gives a shit how things are *there?* It's here where they're miserable. The walls of this cell are puke-green, and you can't pin anything up except school banners and pictures of your stupid family. What family? Am I supposed to sit and look at a picture of Hooper McPhail? Come save me, Andy. Or at least WRITE! Just so I hear a boy's voice, even on paper.

ANDY: Just got your letter. They shipped me off too. Last-minute decision. Your mother told my mother it would do me good. She said I was a diamond in the rough. I'll write as soon as I'm smoother.

MELISSA: Dear Diamond. You, too? Oh, I give up. Why do they keep pushing us together and then pulling us apart? I think we're all being brought up by a bunch of foolish farts. Now we'll *have* to write letters which I hate. But don't let them smooth you out, Andy. I like the rough parts. In fact, sometimes I think you ought to be a little rougher. Love. Me.

ANDY: I'm very sorry to be so late in replying but I haven't had much time. I also have a lot of obligations. I have to write my parents once a week, and three out of four grandparents, *separately,* once a month, and Minnie, our cook, who sent me a box of fudge. Plus I have all my schoolwork to do, including a composition once a week for English and another for history. My grandmother gave me a new Parker 51 and some writing paper with my name on it as a going-away present, but still, that's a lot of writing I have to do. Last week I was so tied up I skipped my weekly letter to my parents, and my father called the school long-distance about it. I had to go up on the carpet in front of the Rector and say I wasn't sick or anything, I was just working, and so I had to write my parents three pages to make up for the week I missed. So that's why I haven't written till now. (Whew!) School is going well, I guess. In English, we're now finishing up Milton's *Paradise Lost.* In history, we're studying the causes and results of the Thirty Years War. I think the Catholics caused it. In Latin, we're translating Cicero's orations against Catiline. "How long, O Catiline, will you abuse our patience?" When I get home, I'm going to try that on my little brother. In French, we have to sit and listen to Mr. Thatcher read out loud all the parts in *Andromache,* by Jean Racine. It's supposed to be a great masterpiece, but the class comes right after football practice, so it's a little hard to stay awake. In Sacred Studies, we have to compare and contrast all four gospels. It's hard to believe they're all talking about the same guy. In Math, we're trying to factor with two unknowns. Sometimes I let X be me and Y be you, and you'd be amazed how it comes out.

My grades are pretty good. They post your weekly average outside study hall and last week I got 91.7 overall average. Not bad, eh? I got a letter from my grandfather telling me not to be first in my class because only the Jews are first. I wrote him and told him I wasn't first, but even if I was, there are no Jews here. We have a few Catholics, but they're not too smart, actually. I don't think you can be smart and Catholic at the same time.

I was elected to the Student Council and I'm arguing for three things: one, I think we should have outside sports, rather than keeping them all intramural. I think it would be better to play with Exeter than just play with ourselves. Two, I think we should have more than one dance a year. I think female companionship can be healthy occasionally, even for younger boys. And three, I think we should only have to go to chapel *once* on Sunday. I think it's important to pray to be a better guy, and all that, but if you have to do it all day long, you can get quite boring. And if you get boring to yourself, think how boring you must be to God.

I'm playing left tackle on the third team, and I'll be playing hockey, *of course,* this winter, and I think I'll try rowing this spring since I always stank at baseball.

Now I have to memorize the last five lines of *Paradise Lost.* Hold it…Back in a little while…There. That wasn't so hard, maybe because it reminds me of you and me, sent away from home. I'll write it down for you:

Some natural tears they dropp'd, but wip'd them soon;
The World was all before them, where to choose
Their place of rest, and providence their guide:
They hand in hand with wand'ring steps and slow,
Through Eden took their solitary way.

There you are. I wrote that without looking at the book, and it's right, too, because I just checked it, word by word. It's not so bad, is it? In fact, it sounds great if you recite it in the bathroom, when no one is in the shower or taking a dump. Love, Andy.

MELISSA: Thanks for your letter which was a little too long. I guess you have a lot of interesting things to say, Andy, but some of them are not terribly interesting to me. I want to hear more about your FEELINGS. For instance, here are MY feelings. This place STINKS, but I don't want to go back home because Hooper McPhail stinks, and I haven't heard of another boarding school that DOESN'T stink, which means that LIFE stinks in general. Those are my feelings for this week. Write soon. Love, me.

ANDY: One feeling I have almost all the time is that I miss my dog, Porgy. Remember him? Our black cocker who peed in the vestibule when you patted him when you came back to our house after the skating party. I miss him all the time. Some of the masters up here have dogs, and when I pat them I miss Porgy even more. I dream about him. I wrote a composition about him for English called "Will He Remember?" and got a 96 on it. It was about how I remember him, but will he remember me? I have a picture of him on my bureau right next to my parents. By the way, could I have your picture, too?

MELISSA: Here's a picture of me taken at the Hartford bus station. I was all set to run away and then decided not to. This is all you get until I get my braces off Christmas vacation. Don't look at my hair. I'm changing it. By the way, do you know a boy there named Spencer Willis? There's a girl here, Annie Abbott, who met him in Edgartown last summer and thinks he's cute. Would you ask him what he thinks of her?

ANDY: Spencer Willis says Annie Abbott is a potential nympho. I'm sorry to tell you this, but it's true.

MELISSA: Annie says to tell Spencer he's a total turkey. Tell him she'd write and say so herself but she's scared of barfing all over the page.

ANDY: Do you get out for Thanksgiving? We don't, because of the war.

MELISSA: We do, but I don't. I've been grounded just for smoking one lousy

Chesterfield out behind the art studio. So now I have to stay here and eat stale turkey with Cubans and Californians. That's all right. I was supposed to meet Mummy in New York, but it looks like she can't be there anyway because she's going to Reno to divorce Hooper McPhail. Yippee! Yay! He was a jerk and a pill, and he used to bother me in bed, if you must know.

❧ ❧ ❧

ANDY: I liked seeing you Christmas vacation, particularly with your braces off. I really liked necking with you in the Watson's rumpus room. Will you go steady with me?

MELISSA: I don't believe in going steady. It's against my religion. I hated that stuff with all those pairs of pimply people in the Watson's basement, leaning on each other, swaying to that dumb music with all the lights off. If that's going steady, I say screw it. My mother says you should meet as many boys as you can before you have to settle down and marry one of them. That way you'll make less of a mistake. It didn't work for her but maybe it will work for me.

ANDY: Can we at least go to the movies together during spring vacation?

MELISSA: I don't know, Andy. I like seeing you, but I don't want to go home much any more. My mother gets drunk a lot, if you must know, and comes into my room all the time, and talks endlessly about I don't know what because she slurs her words. The only really good time I had was when I came over to your house Christmas Eve. That was fun. Singing around the piano, hanging up the stockings, playing Chinese Checkers with your brother, helping your mother with the gravy. I liked all that. You may not have as much money as we have, but you've got a better family. So spring vacation I'm going to visit my grandmother in Palm Beach. Ho hum. At least I'll get a tan. P.S. Enclosed is a picture I drew of your dog Porgy who I remember from Christmas Eve. The nose is wrong, but don't you think the eyes are good?

ANDY: I'm stroking the 4th crew now. Yesterday, I rowed number 2 on the 3rd. Tomorrow I may row number 6 on the 2nd or number 4 on the 5th. Who knows? You get out there and work your butt off, and the launch comes alongside and looks you over, and the next day they post a list on the bulletin board saying who will row what. They never tell you what you did right or wrong, whether you're shooting your slide or bending your back or what. They just post the latest results for all to see.

Some days I think I'm doing really well, and I get sent down two crews. One day I was obviously hacking around, and they moved me UP. There's no rhyme or reason. I went to Mr. Clark who is the head of rowing and I said, "Look, Mr. Clark. There's something wrong about this system. People are constantly moving up and down and no one knows why. It doesn't seem to have anything to do with whether you're good or bad, strong or weak, coordinated or uncoordinated. It all seems random, *sir.*" And Mr. Clark said "That's life, Andy." And walked away. Well maybe that's life, but it doesn't *have* to be life. You could easily make rules which made sense, so the good ones moved up and the bad ones moved down, and people *knew* what was going on. I'm serious. I'm thinking about going to law school later on.

MELISSA: Your last letter was too much about rowing. Do you know a boy there named Steve Scully. I met him down in Florida, and he said he went to your school, and was on the first crew. He said he was the fastest rower in the boat. Is that true, or was he lying? I think he may have been lying.

ANDY: Steve Scully was lying. He doesn't even row. And if he did, and rowed faster than everyone else in the same boat, he'd mess the whole thing up. He said he got to second base with you. Is that true?

MELISSA: Steve Scully is a lying son of a bitch, and you can tell him I said so.

❧ ❧ ❧

ANDY: Will you be around this summer? I think I've got a summer job caddying, so no more camp, Thank God.

MELISSA: I'll be visiting my father in California. I haven't seen him in four years. He has a new wife, and I have two half-sisters now. It's like going to find a whole new family. Oh I hope, I hope...

ANDY: Do you like California?

❧ ❧ ❧

ANDY: Write me about California. How's your second family?

❧ ❧ ❧

ANDY: Did you get my letters? I checked with your mother, and I had the correct address. How come you haven't answered me all summer?

ANDY: Back at school now. Hope everything's O.K. with you. Did you get my letters out in California, or did you have a wicked step-mother who confiscated them?

MELISSA: I don't want to talk about California. Ever. For a while I thought I had two families, but now I know I really don't have any. You're very lucky, Andy. You don't know it, but you are. But maybe I'm lucky, too. In another way. I was talking to Mrs. Wadsworth who comes in from Hartford to teach us art. She says I have a real talent both in drawing and in painting, and she's going to try me out in pottery as well. She says some afternoon she's going to take me just by myself to her studio in Hartford, and we'll do life drawings of her lover in just a jock-strap! Don't laugh. She says art and sex are sort of the same thing.

◆ ◆ ◆

ANDY: Dear Melissa. I have four questions, so please concentrate. One: will you come up to the mid-winter dance? Two, If so, can you arrive on the eleven-twenty-two Friday night train? Three, Does the Rector's wife have to write your Headmistress telling her where you will be staying? Four. Does the Rector's wife also have to write your mother?

MELISSA: The answer is yes, except for my mother, who won't care.

◆ ◆ ◆

ANDY: I have to tell you this, right off the bat. I'm really goddamn mad at you. I invite you up here for the only dance my class has been able to go to since we got here, I meet you at the train and buy you a vanilla milkshake and bring you out to school in a taxi, I score two goals for you during the hockey game the next afternoon, I buy you the eight dollar gardenia corsage, I make sure your dance card is filled with the most regular guys in the school, and then what happens? I now hear that you sneaked off with Bob Bartram during the Vienna Waltz, and necked with him in the coatroom. I heard that from two guys! And then Bob himself brought it up yesterday at breakfast. He says he French-kissed you and touched BOTH your breasts. I tried to punch him but Mr. Enbody restrained me. I'm really sore, Melissa. I consider this a betrayal of everything I hold near and dear. Particularly since you would hardly even let me kiss you goodnight after we had cocoa at the Rector's. And you know what I'm talking about, too! So don't expect any more letters from me, or any telephone calls either during spring vacation. Sincerely yours.

MELISSA: Sorry, sorry, sorry. I AM! I HATE that Bob Bartram. I hated him even when I necked with him. I know you won't believe that, but it's true. You can be attracted to someone you hate. Well, maybe *you* can't, but I can. So all right, I necked with him, but he never touched my chest, and if he says he did, he should be strung up by his testicles. You tell him that, for me, at breakfast! Anyway, I got carried away, Andy, and I'm a stupid bitch, and I'm sorry. I felt so guilty about it that I didn't want to kiss you after the cocoa.

And besides, Andy. Gulp. Er. Ah. Um. How do I say this? With you it's different. You're like a friend to me. You're like a brother. I've never had a brother, and I don't have too many friends, so you're both, Andy. You're it. My mother says you must never say that to a man, but I'm saying it anyway and it's true. Maybe if I didn't know you so well, maybe if I hadn't grown up with you, maybe if we hadn't written all these goddamn LETTERS all the time, I could have kissed you the way I kissed Bob Bartram.

Oh, but PLEASE let's see each other spring vacation. Please. I count on you, Andy. I NEED you. I think sometimes I'd go stark raving mad if I didn't have you to hold onto. I really think that sometimes. Much love.

❦ ❦ ❦

MELISSA: Happy Easter! I know no one sends Easter cards except maids, but here's mine anyway, drawn with my own hot little hands. I drew those tears on that corny bunny on the left because it misses you so much, but maybe I've just made it all the cornier.

❦ ❦ ❦

MELISSA: Greetings from Palm Beach. Decided to visit my grandmother. Yawn, yawn. I'm a whiz at backgammon and gin-rummy. Hear you took Gretchen Lascelles to see *Quo Vadis* and sat in the *loges* and put your arm around her and smoked! Naughty, naughty!

❦ ❦ ❦

MELISSA: Back at school, but not for long, that's for sure. Caught nipping gin in the woods with Bubbles Harriman. Have to pack my trunk by tonight and be out tomorrow. Mummy's frantically pulling strings all over the Eastern Seaboard for another school. Mrs. Wadsworth, my art teacher, thinks I should chuck it all and go to Italy and study art. What do you think? Oh, please write, Andy, PLEASE. I need your advice, or are you too busy thinking about Gretchen Lascelles?

❦ ❦ ❦

ANDY: To answer your question about Italy, I think you're too young to go. My Mother said she had a roommate once who went to Italy in the summer, and the Italians pinched her all the time on the rear end. Mother says she became thoroughly over-stimulated. So I think you should go to another school, graduate, go to college, and maybe after that, when you're more *mature,* you could go to Italy. That's my advice, for what it's worth, which is probably not much, the way things are going between you and me.

❦ ❦ ❦

MELISSA: Here I am at Emma Willard's Academy for Young Lesbians. Help! Lemme outa here! "Plus ca change, plus c'est le same shit." Are you coming straight home this June because I am. I want to see you. Or are you still in love with Gretchen Lascelles?

ANDY: For your information, I'm not taking Gretchen Lascelles out any more. I brought her home after the Penneys' party, and my father caught us on the couch. He told me that he didn't care what kind of girls I took out, as long as I didn't bring them around my mother. Even though my mother was up in bed. Still, I guess Gretchen can be embarrassing to older people.

MELISSA: I hope to see you in June, then.

ANDY: Can't come home in June. Sorry. I have to go and be a counselor at the school camp for poor kids from the urban slums. I'm Vice President of my class now, and I'm supposed to set an example of social responsibility all through July. I'll be writing you letters, though, and I hope you'll write me.

MELISSA: I don't want to write letters all the time. I really don't. I want to see you.

ANDY: You just need more confidence in your letter-writing ability. Sometimes you manage to attain a very vivid style.

MELISSA: Won't you please just stop writing about writing, and come home and go to the Campbells' sports party before you go up to that stupid camp? PLEASE! I behave better when you're around. In PERSON! PLEASE!

❧ ❧ ❧

ANDY: Greetings from New Hampshire. This card shows the town we're near, where we sneak in and buy beer. We're cleaning the place up now, and putting out the boat docks, and caulking the canoes, because the kids arrive tomorrow. Gotta go. Write soon.

MELISSA: I miss you. I really wish you had come to the Campbells' sports party.

ANDY: Dear Melissa. Sandy McCarthy arrived from home for the second shift here at camp, and he told me all about the Campbells' sports party. He said you wore a two piece bathing suit and ran around goosing girls and pushing boys into the pool. Do you enjoy that sort of crap? He said the other girls were furious at you. Don't you want the respect of other women? Sandy also said you let Bucky Zeller put a tennis ball into your cleavage. Are you a nympho or what? Don't you ever like just sitting down somewhere and making conversation? Sandy says you're turning into a hot box. Do you like having that reputation? Hell, I thought there was a difference between you and Gretchen Lascelles. Maybe I was wrong. Don't you care about anything in this world except hacking around? Don't you feel any obligation to help the poor people, for example? Sometimes I think your big problem is you're so rich you don't have enough to do, and so you start playing grab-ass with people. I'm sorry to say these things, but what Sandy told me made me slightly disgusted, frankly.

❧ ❧ ❧

ANDY: I wrote you a letter from New Hampshire. Did you receive it?

❧ ❧ ❧

ANDY: Are you there, or are you visiting your grandmother, or what?

❧ ❧ ❧

ANDY: Are you sore at me? I'll bet you're sore at me.

ANDY: I'm sorry. I apologize. I'm a stuffy bastard sometimes, aren't I?

ANDY: The hell with you, then.
MELISSA: Oooh. Big, tough Andy using four-letter words like hell.
ANDY: Screw you!
MELISSA: Don't you wish you could!
ANDY: Everyone else seems to be.
MELISSA: Don't believe everything you read in the papers.

MELISSA: Dear Andrew Makepeace Ladd, the Turd: I just want you to know you hurt me very much. I just want you to know that. Now let's just leave each other ALONE for a while. All right? All right.

ANDY: Dear Melissa: My mother wrote me that your grandmother had died. Please accept my deepest sympathies.
MELISSA: Thank you for your note about my grandmother. I loved her a lot even though she could be a little boring.
ANDY: Congratulations on getting into Briarcliff. I hear it's great.
MELISSA: Thank you for your note about Briarcliff. It's not great and you know it. In fact, it's a total pit. But it's close to New York and I can take the train in and take drawing at the Institute three days a week. And in two years, if I stick it out, Mummy's promised that I can go live in Florence. I hope you like Yale.
ANDY: Would you consider coming to the Yale-Dartmouth game, Saturday, Oct. 28th?
MELISSA: I'll be there.
ANDY: Uh-oh. Damn! I'm sorry, Melissa. I have to cancel. My parents have decided to visit that weekend, and they come first, according to them. My mother says she'd love to have you with us, but my father thinks you can be somewhat distracting.

MELISSA: You and your parents. Let me know when you decide to grow up.

ANDY: How about the Harvard game, November 16th?

MELISSA: Do you plan to grow up at the Harvard game?

ANDY: Give me a chance. I might surprise you.

MELISSA: O.K. Let's give it a try. You should know that I'm even richer now than when you said I was rich, thanks to poor Granny. I plan to drive up to the front gate of Calhoun College in my new red Chrysler convertible, and sit there stark naked, honking my horn and drinking champagne and flashing at all the Freshmen.

ANDY: Here's the schedule. We'll have lunch at Calhoun around noon. Then drive out to the game. Then there's a Sea-Breeze party at the Fence Club afterwards, and an Egg Nog brunch at Saint Anthony's the next day. I'll reserve a room for you at the Taft or the Duncan, probably the Taft, since the Duncan is a pretty seedy joint.

MELISSA: Make it the Duncan. I hear the Taft is loaded with parents, all milling around the lobby, keeping tabs on who goes up in the elevators. Can't WAIT till the 16th.

ANDY: The Duncan it is. Hubba hubba, Goodyear rubba!

❧ ❧ ❧

MELISSA: Dear Andy. This is supposed to be a thank-you note for the Yale-Harvard weekend, but I don't feel like writing one, and I think you know why. Love, Melissa.

ANDY: Dear Melissa. I keep thinking about the weekend. I can't get it out of my mind. It wasn't much good, was it? I don't mean just the Duncan, I mean the whole thing. We didn't really click, did we? I always had the sense that you were looking over my shoulder, looking for someone else, and ditto with me. Both of us seemed to be expecting something different from what was there.

As for the Hotel Duncan, I don't know. Maybe I had too many Sea-Breezes. Maybe you did. But what I really think is that there were too many people in that hotel room. Besides you and me, it seemed my mother was there, egging us on, and my father, shaking his head, and *your* mother zonked out on the couch, and Miss Hawthorne and your *grand*mother, sitting on the sidelines, watching us like hawks. Anyway, I was a dud. I admit it. I'm sorry. I went to the Infirmary on Monday and talked to the Doctor about it, and he said these things happen all the time. Particularly when there's a lot of pressure involved. The woman doesn't have to worry about it so much, but the man does. Anyway, it didn't happen with Gretchen Lascelles. You can write her and ask her if you want.

MELISSA: You know what I think is wrong? These letters. These goddamn letters. That's what's wrong with us, in my humble opinion. I know you more from your LETTERS than I do in person. Maybe that's why I was looking over your shoulder. I was looking for the person who's been in these letters all these years. Or for the person who's NOT in these letters. I don't know. All I know is you're not quite the same when I see you, Andy. You're really not. I'm not saying you're a jerk in person. I'm not saying that at all. I'm just saying that all this letter-writing has messed us up. It's a bad habit. It's made us seem like people we're not. So maybe what was wrong was that there were two people *missing* in the Hotel Duncan that night: namely, the real you and the real me.

ANDY: Whatever the matter is, we're in real trouble, you and I. That I realize. So now, what do we do about it? Maybe we should just concentrate on dancing together. Then we can still hold each other and move together and get very subtly sexy with each other, and not have to deliver the goods all the time, if you know what I mean. Come to think of it, maybe that's why they sent us to dancing school in the first place. Maybe that's why dancing was invented.

MELISSA: At least we should stop writing LETTERS for a while. You could start telephoning me, actually. Here is our dorm number: WILSON 1-2486.

ANDY: I hate talking to you on the telephone. Yours is in the hall and ours is right by the college dining room. People are always coming and going and making cracks. Telephoning is not letter-writing at all.

MELISSA: I called the telephone company and they've put a private phone in my room. ROGERS 2-2403. It's sort of expensive, but at least we can TALK!

❧   ❧   ❧

ANDY: The reason I'm writing is because your phone's always busy. Or else ours is. And I can't afford a private one. Maybe we should just start writing letters again.

MELISSA: No letters! Please! Now order that telephone! I'll lend you the dough. Just think about it. You can talk back and forth, and hear someone's real voice, and get to know someone in LIFE, rather than on WRITING PAPER, for God's sake! Now get that phone! Please!

ANDY: I'm writing because when I telephoned, you just hung up on me. One thing about letters: you can't hang up on them.

MELISSA: You can tear up letters, though. Enclosed are the pieces. Send them to Angela Atkinson at Sarah Lawrence.

ANDY: What the hell is the matter?

MELISSA: I hear you're now writing long letters twice a week to Angela Atkinson, that's what's the matter.

ANDY: O.K. Here goes. The reason I'm writing Angie Atkinson is because I just don't think I can stop writing letters, particularly to girls. As I told you before, in some ways I feel most alive when I'm holed up in some corner, writing things down. I pick up a pen, and almost immediately everything seems to take shape around me. I love to write. I love writing my parents because then I become the ideal son. I love writing essays for English, because then I am for a short while a true scholar. I love writing letters to the newspaper, notes to my friends, Christmas cards, anything where I have to put down words. I love writing you. You most of all. I always have. I feel like a true lover when I'm writing you. This letter, which I'm writing with my own hand, with my own pen, in my own penmanship, comes from me and no one else, and is a present of myself to you. It's not typewritten, though I've learned how to type. There's no copy of it, though I suppose I could use a carbon. And it's not a telephone call, which is dead as soon as it is over. No, this is just me, me the way I write, the way my writing is, the way I want to be to you, giving myself to you across a distance, not keeping or retaining any part of it for myself, giving this piece of myself to you totally, and you can tear me up and throw me out, or keep me, and read me today, tomorrow, any time you want until you die.

MELISSA: Oh boy, Andy!...Love, Melissa.

ANDY: No, I meant what I wrote in my last letter. I've thought about it. I've thought about all those dumb things which were done to us when we were young. We had absent parents, slapping nurses, stupid rules, obsolete schooling, empty rituals, hopelessly confusing sexual customs...oh my God, when I think about it now, it's almost unbelievable, it's a fantasy, it's like back in the Oz books, the way we grew up. But they gave us an out in the Land of Oz. They made us write. They didn't make us write particularly well. And they didn't always give us important things to write about. But they did make us sit down, and organize our thoughts, and convey those thoughts on paper as clearly as we could to another person. Thank God for that. That saved us. Or at least saved me. So I have to keep writing letters. If I can't write them to you, I have to write them to someone else. I don't think I could ever stop writing completely. Now can I come up and see you next weekend, or better yet won't you please escape from that suburban Sing-Sing and come down here and see me? I wrote my way into this problem, and goddamn it, I'm writing my way out. I'll make another reservation at the Hotel Duncan and I promise I'll put down my pen and give you a better time.

MELISSA: Dear Andy: Guess what? Right while I was in the middle of reading your letter, Jack Duffield telephoned from Amherst and asked me for a weekend up there. So I said yes before I got to where you asked me. Sorry, sweetie, but it looks like the telephone wins in the end.

ANDY: Dear Melissa: Somehow I don't think this is the end. It could be, but I don't really think it is. At least I hope it isn't. Love, Andy.

END OF PART I

(The event works best if everyone takes a short break at this point.)

PART II

MELISSA: Hey! Yoo-hoo! Look where I am! Florence, Ooops, I mean Firenze! I LOVE it!

ANDY: What are you doing in Florence?

MELISSA: What am I doing? I'm painting, among other things.

ANDY: Good luck on the painting. Go slow on the other things.

❦ ❦ ❦

ANDY: Merry Christmas.

MELISSA: Buon Natale…

ANDY: Happy Birthday…Mother wrote you won an art prize in Perugia. She said it was a big deal. Congratulations…

MELISSA: Congratulations on making Scroll and Key, whatever that is…

ANDY: Merry Christmas from the Land of Oz…

MELISSA: Felice Navidad from the Costa del Sol…

ANDY: Happy Birthday from the Sterling Library…

MELISSA: Hear you graduated Summa Cum Laude and with all sorts of prizes. Sounds disgusting…

ANDY: Anchors Aweigh! Here I am, looking like Henry Fonda in *Mister Roberts,* writing this during the midwatch on the bridge of a giant attack aircraft carrier, churning through the Mediterranean, in the wake of Odysseus and Lord Nelson and Richard Halliburton. You'll be pleased to know our guns are loaded, our planes in position, and our radar is constantly scanning the skies, all designed simply and solely to protect you against Communism. The next time you see me, I want you to salute.

MELISSA: I should have known you'd join the Navy. Now you can once again be with all boys.

ANDY: We come into La Spezia in January. Could we meet?

MELISSA: Sorry. I'll be in Zermatt in January.

ANDY: Ship will be in Mediterranean all spring. We'll come into Naples, March 3, 4, or 5? How about standing on the pier and waving us in?

MELISSA: As the French say, "Je suis desolée." Am meeting Mother in Paris in March. Why don't you sail up the Seine?

ANDY: Merry Christmas from Manila. I've been transferred to an Admiral's staff…

MELISSA: Happy New Year from Aspen…

ANDY: What are you doing in Aspen?

MELISSA: Going steadily down hill.

ANDY: Hello from Hong Kong…

MELISSA: Goodbye to San Francisco…

ANDY: Konichiwa. Ohayo Gozaimas. Shore duty in Japan

MELISSA: Hey, you! Rumor hath it you're hooked up with some little Jap bar-girl out there. Say it isn't so…

❦ ❦ ❦

MELISSA: Mother wrote that you're living with some Japanese geisha girl and your family's all upset. Is that TRUE?

❦ ❦ ❦

MELISSA: Did you get my letter? You're so far away, and your Navy address is so peculiar that I'm not sure I'm reaching you. I hear you're seriously involved with a lovely Japanese lady. Would you write me about her?

ANDY: Merry Christmas and Happy New Year. I thought you might appreci-ate this card. It's a print by the Nineteenth Century artist Hiroshige. It's called "Two Lovers Meeting on a Bridge in the Rain." Love, Andy.

MELISSA: Hey, you sly dog! Are you getting subtle in your old age? Are you trying to TELL me something? If so, tell me MORE!

❦ ❦ ❦

MELISSA: I told my psychiatrist about the great love affair you're having in Japan. I said I felt suddenly terribly jealous. He said that most American men have to get involved with a dark-skinned woman before they can con-nect with the gorgeous blonde goddesses they really love. He brought up James Fennimore Cooper and Faulkner and John Ford movies and went on and on. Is that TRUE? Write me what you think. I'm dying to hear from you.

❦ ❦ ❦

MELISSA: Did you get my last letter? I hope I didn't sound flip. Actually I've just become involved with someone, too. His first name is Darwin and he works on Wall Street where he believes in the survival of the fittest. I'd love to hear from you.

❧ ❧ ❧

MELISSA: Your mother told my mother that you've decided to marry your Japanese friend and bring her home. Oh no! Gasp, Sob, Sigh. Say it isn't so.

❧ ❧ ❧

MELISSA: I've decided to marry Darwin. He doesn't know it yet, but he will. Won't you at least wish me luck?

❧ ❧ ❧

ANDY: Lieutenant Junior Grade Andrew M. Ladd, III, regrets that he is unable to accept the kind invitation of...

MELISSA: Dear Andy. Thank you for the lovely Japanese bowl. I'll put flowers in it when you come to visit us. *If* you come to visit us. And *if* you bring flowers. Maybe you'll just bring your Japanese war bride, and we can all sit around and discuss *Rashomon*. I know you'll like Darwin. When he laughs, it's like Pinocchio turning into a donkey. We're living in a carriage house in New Canaan close to the train station, and I've got a studio all of my own. P.S. Won't you PLEASE write me about your big romance? Mother says your parents won't even talk about it any more.

ANDY: Dear Melissa: I'm writing to tell you this. Outside of you, and I *mean* outside of you, this was probably the most important thing that ever happened to me. And I mean *was*. Because it's over, it's gone, and I'm coming home, and that's all I ever want to say about it, ever again.

❧ ❧ ❧

MELISSA: Mr. and Mrs. Darwin H. Cobb announce the birth of their daughter Francesca...

ANDY: Many congratulations on the baby.

MELISSA: Harvard Law School yet! Are you getting all stuffy and self-important?

ANDY: As you know, I've always liked to write letters. I decided I might do better trying to write laws, which, after all, are the letters that civilization writes to itself.

MELISSA: Yes you ARE getting all stuffy and self-important. Come and have a drink with us some time. We're right on the way to New York. And sooner or later everyone comes to New York.

ANDY: Read the New York Times account of your show in Stamford. Sounds like you are causing a series of seismic shocks up and down the Merritt Parkway

MELISSA: Don't joke about my work. There's more there than what they said in your goddamn BIBLE, the New York Times. Enclosed see what OTHER critics said. Notice they think I'm GOOD! I AM, too! Or could be. If I can only FOCUS...

ANDY: Sorry, sorry, sorry. I know you're good. I've always known it.

❧ ❧ ❧

MELISSA: Hear you made Law Review, whatever that means. I assume you review laws. I wish you'd review some of the marriage laws...

ANDY: Just a quick note. Are you in any trouble?

MELISSA: I don't understand your last note. We're fine. All fine. Everyone's fine.

❧ ❧ ❧

ANDY: Congratulations on baby number two...

MELISSA: Number two is a perfect way to describe this particular baby...

ANDY: Greetings from Washington. Here clerking for a Supreme Court Justice which isn't quite as fancy as it sounds...

❧ ❧ ❧

MELISSA: Dear Andy: I was very sorry to hear about the death of your father. I know he was a great influence on you, and I know you loved him very much. I also know he didn't like *me*. I'm sure he thought I was bad for you, and I probably was. Still, he was a good, decent man, and I always knew where I stood with him when you'd bring me home to your family, back in the old days, back in the Land of Oz. I wish I'd had a father like that. Please accept my deepest sympathies. Love. Melissa.

ANDY: Dear Melissa. Thank you for your note on my father. I did love him. He was a classy guy, the best of his breed. Even now he's gone, I can still hear him reminding me of my obligations to my family, my country, and myself, in roughly that order. All my life, he taught me that those born to privilege have special responsibilities, which is I suppose why I came home alone from Japan, why I chose the law, and why I'll probably enter politics at some level, some time on down the line. Thanks for writing. Love. Andy.

◆ ◆ ◆

MELISSA: Merry Christmas. I'm enclosing a snapshot mother took of me and the girls. Don't I look domestic? Stop looking at my hair! By the way, you'll notice you-know-who is not in the picture.

ANDY: Thanks for the Christmas card. Are you in trouble?

MELISSA: Greetings from Reno. Could I stop by Washington on the way back East?

ANDY: Let me know when you're coming. You can meet Jane.

MELISSA: Jane?

ANDY: I'm going out with a great girl named Jane.

◆ ◆ ◆

MELISSA: Melissa Gardner Cobb regrets that she will be unable to accept the kind invitation of...

ANDY: Dear Melissa: Had to add my two-cents worth to Jane's thank-you note for the wedding present. (Guess who is jealously peeking over my shoulder to make sure this isn't a love letter.) First of all, thanks for the present, whatever it was. Ah, a tray! I am now told it was a tray. A *hand-painted* tray. Hand-painted by you, I'll bet. Anyway, thank you. I hope all goes well with you, as it does with us. We'll be moving to New York in the fall. I've got a job with one of those high-powered law firms. It will probably be stuffy as hell for a while, but I'll learn the ropes. Besides, it's in my home state and might be a good jumping-off place for something political a little way down the line. We BOTH want you to come to dinner once we're settled in. And don't say you never come to New York. Sooner or later everyone comes to New York, as someone once wrote me, long, long ago.

◆ ◆ ◆

ANDY: Merry Christmas from us to you. Where are you these days?

❧ ❧ ❧

ANDY: Happy Birthday. See? Even a married man never forgets.

❧ ❧ ❧

ANDY: Get well soon. Mother wrote that you had had some difficulty. I hope it's not serious, and by now you're feeling fine.

❧ ❧ ❧

ANDY: I can't remember exactly what one dozen red roses are supposed to say, but here they are, and I hope they say, "cheer up."

❧ ❧ ❧

ANDY: Hey! I sent you some flowers a while back. Did you receive them? Are you all right?

❧ ❧ ❧

MELISSA: Dear Andy. Yes, I'm all right. Yes, I got your flowers. Yes, I'm fine. No, actually, I'm not fine, and they tell me I've got to stop running around saying I am. I'm here at this posh joint outside Boston, drying out for one hundred and fifty-five dollars a day. One of my problems is that I got slightly too dependent on the Kickapoo joy juice, a habit which they tell me I picked up during the party days back in Our Town. Another is that I slide into these terrible lows. Mummy says I drag everybody down, and I guess she's right. Aaaanyway, the result is that my Ex has taken over custody of the girls, and I'm holed up here, popping tranquilizers, talking my head off in single and group psychiatric sessions, and turning into probably the biggest bore in the greater Boston area.

ANDY: Have you thought about doing some painting again? That might help.

❧ ❧ ❧

ANDY: Did you get my note about taking up art? You were good, and you know it. You should keep it up.

MELISSA: I *did* get your note, I *have* taken it up, and it *helps*. Really. Thank you. I'm channeling my rage, enlarging my vision, all that. I hope all goes well with you and—wait, hold it, I'm looking it up in my little black book...ah hah! Jane! It's Jane. Hmmmm. I hope all's well with you and Jane.

ANDY: Merry Christmas from Andy and Jane Ladd. And Andrew the Fourth! Guess the name of the dog.

MELISSA: Porgy.

ANDY: You got it.

❧ ❧ ❧

MELISSA: Merry Christmas from San Antonio. Am trying the Southwest. I can see the most incredible shapes from my bedroom window. And there's also a pretty incredible shape now sleeping in my bed.

ANDY: Seasons Greetings from the Ladd family. (Mother wrote you were planning to get married again.)

MELISSA: I was. I did. I'm not now.

ANDY: Donner, Rhodes and McAlister announce the appointment to partnership of Mr. Andrew M. Ladd, III...

MELISSA: Dear Andy: Now you're such a hot-shot lawyer, could you help me get my children back? Darwin hardly lets me near them, and when he does, they behave as if I had some contagious disease. I wasn't much of a mother, but maybe I could improve, if I just had the legal responsibility

ANDY: Better stay out of this one...Our past connections...conflict of interest...

MELISSA: Hello from Egypt. I'm trying to start again in the cradle of civilization.

❧ ❧ ❧

ANDY: Christmas Greetings from the Ladds: Andy, Jane, Drew, Nicholas, and Ted. And of course Porgy.

MELISSA: Am thinking of moving to Los Angeles. Do you know anyone in Los Angeles? Does anyone know anyone in Los Angeles?

ANDY: Joy to the World from all the Ladds. Note our new address.

MELISSA: Merry Christmas. Hey you! What's going on? Just when I decide to move to New York, I see you've scampered off to the suburbs.

ANDY: I find the suburbs generally safer.

MELISSA: Chicken.

❖ ❖ ❖

MELISSA: Mother wrote that you won some important election for the Republicans. I'm terribly disappointed. I love all politicians, but I find Democrats better in bed…

ANDY: I'm a liberal Republican with a strong commitment to women's rights. Doesn't that count?

MELISSA: Depends on your position.

❖ ❖ ❖

MELISSA: Paintings and drawings by Melissa Gardner. The Hastings Gallery. 422 Broadway. March 18 through April 30. Opening reception March 20, 6 to 8 P.M. Note I've gone back to my *maiden* name. That's a laugh.

ANDY: Got your announcement for your new show. Good luck. P.S. I'd love to have one of your paintings. We could use a little excitement on our living room walls. Seriously. What would one cost?

MELISSA: Come to the show and find out.

ANDY: Never made your show. Sorry. Things came up.

MELISSA: Chicken again.

ANDY: You're right.

MELISSA: Actually, it's just as well. I'm going through what the critics call an "anarchistic phase." They say I'm dancing on the edge of an abyss. You'd better stay away. I might take you with me when I fall.

❖ ❖ ❖

ANDY: Dear Friends: Jane tells me that it's about time I took a crack at the annual Christmas letter, so here goes. Let's start at the top, with our quarterback, Jane herself, who never ceases to amaze us all. Not only has she continued to be a superb mother to our three sons, but she has also managed to commute into the city and hold down a part-time job in the gift shop at the Metropolitan Museum of Art. Furthermore, she is now well on her way to completing a full-fledged master's degree in Arts Administration at SUNY Purchase. More power to Jane, so say we all.

We are also proud of all three boys. Young Drew was soccer captain at Exeter last fall, and hopes to go on to Yale. Nicholas, our rebel in residence, has become a computer genius in high school, and has already received several tantalizing offers for summer jobs from local electronics firms. We all know that it's tougher to place our youngsters in meaningful summer employment than to get them into Harvard, so we're very proud of how far Nick has come. Ted, our last but in no way our least, now plays the clarinet in the school band at Dickinson Country Day. Since Jane and I are barely capable of singing "You Are My Sunshine" without going disastrously flat, when we hear him produce his dulcet sounds, we look at each other "in a wild surmise."

We recently bought the family summer place from my brother and sister, and hope to spend as much time as we can there, gardening, relaxing, and as the boys say, "generally veging out." Jane and I have become killers on the tennis court, and hereby challenge all comers. If any of our friends are in the Adirondack area this summer, we expect telephone calls, we expect visits, we expect elaborate house presents.

I've enjoyed very much serving on the State Legislature. We've proposed and written a number of bills, and we've won some and lost some. All my life I've had the wish to do something in the way of public service, and it has been a great pleasure to put that wish into practice. For those of my friends who have urged me to seek higher office, let me simply say that I have more than enough challenges right here where I am.

Jane and the boys join me in wishing each and all of you a Happy Holiday Season.

MELISSA: Dear Andy. If I ever get another one of those drippy Xeroxed Christmas letters from you, I think I'll invite myself out to your ducky little house for dinner, and when you're all sitting there eating terribly healthy food and discussing terribly important things and generally congratulating yourselves on all your accomplishments, I think I'll stand up on my chair, and turn around, and moon the whole fucking family!

ANDY: You're right. It was a smug dumb letter and I apologize for it. Jane normally writes it, and it sounds better when she does. I always felt better writing to just one person at a time, such as to you. I guess what I was really saying is that as far as my family is concerned, we're all managing to hold our heads above water in this tricky world. Jane and I have had our problems, but we're comfortable with each other now, and the boys, for the moment, are out of trouble. Nicky seems to be off drugs now, and Ted is getting help on his stammer. Porgy, Jr., my old cocker, died, and I miss him too much to get a replacement. I'm thinking of running for the Senate next fall if O'Hara retires. What do you think? I'd really like your opinion. If you decide to answer this, you might write care of my office address. Jane has a slight tendency toward melodrama, particularly after she got ahold of your last little note.

MELISSA: The Senate yet! I should have known. Oh Andy, just think! Once again, you can be with all boys. Oh hell, go for it, if you want. You'll be an image of righteousness and rectitude in our god-forsaken land. Or maybe it's just me that's godforsaken these days.

ANDY: The Honorable Andrew M. Ladd III wishes to express his thanks for your generous donation to his senatorial campaign...You sent too MUCH, Melissa! You didn't need to.

❧ ❧ ❧

MELISSA: Greetings from Silver Hill. Slight regression in the liquor department. They say it's in the genes. Lord knows, my mother has the problem, and my father, too, in the end. Anyway, I'm working on it. Darwin is being a real shit about the girls. He's cut down on my visitation rights, so when you get to Washington, I want you to write a special law about vindictive ex-husbands, banishing them to Lower Slobbovia, forever and ever. Amen.

❧ ❧ ❧

ANDY: Seasons Greetings from Senator and Mrs. Andrew M. Ladd and family.

MELISSA: Season's Greetings indeed! Is that all you can say to me after forty years? I'm warning you, Andy. Keep that shit up, and I swear I'll come down and moon the whole Senate.

ANDY: Sorry. My staff sent that out. Merry Christmas, old friend. How are you? Where are you these days?

MELISSA: Living in New York—alone, for a change—but the big question is, WHO am I these days? That's the toughie. I keep thinking about that strange old world we grew up in. How did it manage to produce both you and me? A stalwart upright servant of the people, and a boozed out, cynical, lascivious old broad. The best and the worst, that's us.

ANDY: Don't be so tough on yourself. Get back to your art.

MELISSA: I'll try.

♦ ♦ ♦

ANDY: Merry Christmas, Happy New Year, and much love.

MELISSA: Much LOVE? MUCH love? God, Andy, how sexy! Remember how much that meant in our preppy days? If it was just "love" you were out in the cold, and if it was "all my love," you were hemmed in for life—but "Much Love" meant that things could go either way. Remember?

♦ ♦ ♦

ANDY: Merry Christmas and love from us all.

MELISSA: Saw you on *Sixty Minutes*. You looked fabulous. And that was a great little pep talk in the Senate on "our responsibilities" to Latin America. But don't forget to keep your eye on the ball.

ANDY: Thanks for your card. What ball?

MELISSA: The ball is that money doesn't solve everything. It helps, but not as much as people think. Take it from one who knows. That's the ball.

ANDY: Merry Christmas and love. What are you up to these days?

MELISSA: I'm trying to work with clay. Remember that kind of clay we used in Mrs. Mickler's art class in fourth grade? That old gray stuff? We called it plasticene. I'm trying to work with that. I'm making cats, dogs...I even made a kangaroo jumping over a glass of orange juice. Remember that? I'm trying to get back to some of those old, old feelings I had back in the Homeland. I have to find feelings, any feelings, otherwise I'm dead. Come down and help me search. I have a studio down in Soho and we could...um, er, uh, well we could at least have DINNER and talk about old times, couldn't we, Senator Ladd? P.S. Did you know that my mother got married again? At the age of eighty-two? To my father's BROTHER yet! So now you have to call her Mrs. Gardner again, just like the old days. The wheel seems to be coming around full circle. Hint, hint.

ANDY: A quick note on the way to the airport. When you write, put "attention Mrs. Walpole" on the envelope. She's my private secretary, I've alerted her, and she'll pass your letters directly on to me. Otherwise, the whole office staff seems to get a peek. In haste...

MELISSA: I'm having a show opening January 28 through Feb. 25. Won't you come? I'd love to have you see what I've been up to. Maybe it will ring a few old bells.

ANDY: Can't make it. I'll be on an official visit to the Philippines most of February, then a week's spring skiing at Stowe with the boys. Good luck.

✦ ✦ ✦

ANDY: How did the show go?

✦ ✦ ✦

ANDY: Haven't heard from you. Tell me about the show.

✦ ✦ ✦

ANDY: I want to hear from you. Please.

MELISSA: The show stank. The crowd hated it, the critics hated it, I hated it. It was nostalgic shit. You can't go home again, and you can quote me on that. I'm turning to photography now. Realism! That's my bag. The present tense. Look at the modern world squarely in the face, and don't blink…Oh Andy, couldn't I see you? You're all I have left.

ANDY: I'll be in New York next Tuesday the 19th. Have to make a fund-raising speech at a dinner. I could stop by your place afterwards.

MELISSA: I'll be there all evening.

✦ ✦ ✦

ANDY: Red roses. This time I think I know what they mean.

MELISSA: All I know is that after last night I want to see you again.

✦ ✦ ✦

MELISSA: Any chance of any other fund-raisers coming up in the near future?

✦ ✦ ✦

MELISSA: Mrs. Walpole, are you there? Are you delivering the mail?

ANDY: I'm sorry I've taken so long to reply. I've been upstate mending a few fences, and then to Zurich for a three-day economic conference, and then a weekend with Jane, mending a few fences *there*...Darling, I'll have to ask you not to telephone the office. Every call has to be logged in, and most of them get screened by these over-eager college interns who like to rush back to Cambridge and New Haven and announce to their class-mates in political science that Senator Ladd is shacking up on the side. The phones simply aren't secure. At long last, the letter beats out the tele-phone, my love! And guess what? I'm writing this with the old Parker 51 my grandmother gave me when I went away to school. I found it in the back of my bureau drawer with my Scroll and Key pin, and my Lieutenant J.G. bars from the Navy, and the Zippo lighter you gave me at some dance. The pen didn't even work at first. I had to clean it out, and then traipse all over Washington looking for a store which still sells a bottle of ink. Anyway, it feels good holding this thing again. It feels good writing to you again. Longhand. Forming my d's and t's the way Miss Emerson taught us so long ago. I know you've never liked writing letters, but now you HAVE to! Ha, ha. As for business: I plan to come through New York next Wednesday, and I'll call you from the airport if there's time to stop by.

MELISSA: Sweetheart, I LOVED seeing you. Come again...

ANDY: ...will be stopping through a week from next...

MELISSA: ...Did you ever *dream* we'd be so good at sex?

ANDY: ...Two up-tight old Wasps going at it like a sale at Brooks Brothers...

MELISSA: ...I figure fifty years went into last night...

ANDY: ...Let's go for a hundred...

MELISSA: ...Oh my God, come again soon, or sooner...

ANDY: ...I'm already making plans...

(The letters begin to overlap)

MELISSA: ...have to go to San Francisco to visit the girls. Couldn't we meet somewhere on the way?

ANDY: ...I don't see how we can possibly go public...

MELISSA: ...some country inn, some deliciously seedy motel...

ANDY: ...I don't see how...

MELISSA: ...see you more than for just a few hours...

ANDY: ...price we have to pay...

MELISSA: ...I'm getting so I think about nothing but how we can...

ANDY: ...I'm not sure I can change my whole life so radically...

MELISSA: ...other politicians have gotten divorced...Rockefeller, Reagan...

ANDY: ...Jane...the children...my particular constituency...

MELISSA: ...you've become the center of my life. If you left, I don't think I could...

ANDY: ...because of the coming election, I don't see how we can...

❧ ❧ ❧

MELISSA: Dear Andy: A reporter called up from the Daily News. What do I do about it?

ANDY: Nothing.

MELISSA: I suppose you know all this, but there's a crack about us in Newsweek. And Mother heard some radio talk show where they actually named names. What should I do? Go away? What?

ANDY: Nothing.

MELISSA: They called Darwin, you know. They tracked him down. The son of a bitch told them this has been going on for years.

ANDY: Wish it had been.

MELISSA: Now they're telephoning. What do I say?

ANDY: Say we're good old friends.

MELISSA: Friends, I like. Good, I like. Old, I'm beginning to have problems with.

ANDY: Then don't say anything. Hang up. This, too, shall pass.

MELISSA: Will I be seeing you again?

ANDY: Better not, for a while.

MELISSA: I meant, after the election...

ANDY: Better lie low for a while.

MELISSA: I miss you terribly...

ANDY: Better lie low.

MELISSA: I NEED you, Andy. You're my anchor man these days. Without you, I'm not sure I can...

(The letters begin to overlap again)

ANDY: Hold on now. Just hold on...

MELISSA: ...where were you? I waited three hours hoping that you'd at least call...

ANDY: ...please don't telephone...Mrs. Walpole was sick that day and...

MELISSA: ...I haven't seen you in over a month now...

ANDY: ...the coming election...

MELISSA: ...surely you could at least take time out to...

ANDY: ...if I want to be reelected...

MELISSA: ...I need you. I need to be with you. I don't know if I can...

ANDY: ...the election...the election...the election

❖ ❖ ❖

MELISSA: I haven't heard from you in six weeks, Andy.

❖ ❖ ❖

MELISSA: Are you trying to tell me something, Andy?

❖ ❖ ❖

MELISSA: Is this it, Andy?

❖ ❖ ❖

MELISSA: Congratulations on landslide victory. Love. Melissa.

ANDY: Could we meet at your place next Sunday night?

MELISSA: Oh thank God...

ANDY: I meant that we have to talk, Melissa...

MELISSA: Uh oh. Talk. I'm scared of talk. In fact, I dread it...

❖ ❖ ❖

ANDY: Dearest Melissa: Are you all right? That was a heavy scene last Sunday, but I know I'm right. We've got to go one way or the other, and the other leads nowhere. I know I sound like a stuffy prick, but I do feel I have a responsibility to Jane, and the boys, and now, after the election, to my constituency, which had enough faith and trust in me to vote me back in despite all that crap in the newspapers. And it wouldn't work with us anyway, in the long run, sweetheart. We're too old. We're carrying too much old baggage on our backs. We'd last about a week if we got married. But we can still write letters, darling. We can always do that. Letters are still our strength and our salvation. Mrs. Walpole is still with us, and there's no reason why we can't continue to keep in touch with each other in this wonderful old way. I count on your letters, darling. I always have. And I hope you will count on mine...

♦ ♦ ♦

ANDY: Are you there? I keep putting "please forward" on the envelopes but who knows...

♦ ♦ ♦

ANDY: Now I've even resorted to the telephone, but all I get is your damn machine...Please. I need to hear from you...

♦ ♦ ♦

ANDY: Senator and Mrs. Andrew M. Ladd, III, and family send you warm Holiday greetings and every good wish for the New Year.

MELISSA: Andy Ladd, is that YOU? Blow dried and custom-tailored and jogging trim at fifty-five. Hiding behind that lovely wife with her heels together and her hands folded discreetly over her snatch? And is that your new DOG, Andy? I see you've graduated to a Golden Retriever. And are those your sons and heirs? And—Help!—is that a *grand*child nestled in someone's arms? God, Andy, you look like the Holy Family! Season's Greetings and Happy Holidays and even Merry Christmas, Senator Ladd. We who are about to die salute you...

ANDY: Just reread your last note. What's this "we who are about to die" stuff?

♦ ♦ ♦

ANDY: May I see you again?

♦ ♦ ♦

ANDY: I want to see you again, if I may.

♦ ♦ ♦

ANDY: Dear Mrs. Gardner. I seem to have lost touch with Melissa again. I wonder if you might send me her latest address.

＋　＋　＋

ANDY: Dear Melissa. Your mother wrote that you'd returned to the Land of Oz. I'm flying up next Thursday to see you.

MELISSA: No! Please! Don't! Please stay away! I've let myself go. I'm fat, I'm ugly, my hair is horrible! I'm locked in at the funny farm all week, and then Mother gets me weekends if I'm good. They've put me on all sorts of new drugs, and half the time I don't make sense at all! I can't even do finger-painting now without fucking it up. My girls won't even *talk* to me on the telephone now. They say I upset them too much. Oh, I've made a mess of things, Andy. I've made a total, ghastly mess. I don't like life any more. I hate it. Sometimes I think that if you and I had just…if we had just…oh but just stay away, Andy. Please.

ANDY: Arriving Saturday morning. Will meet you at your mother's.

MELISSA: DON'T! I don't want to see you! I won't be there! I'll be GONE, Andy! I swear. I'll be gone.

＋　＋　＋

ANDY: Dear Mrs. Gardner: I think the first letter I ever wrote was to you, accepting an invitation for Melissa's birthday party. Now I'm writing you again about her death. I want to say a few things on paper I couldn't say at her funeral, both when I spoke, and when you and I talked afterward. As you may know, Melissa and I managed to keep in touch with each other most of our lives, primarily through letters. Even now, as I write this letter to you, I feel I'm writing it also to her.

MELISSA: Ah, you're in your element now, Andy…

ANDY: We had a complicated relationship, she and I, all our lives. We went in very different directions. But somehow over all those years, I think we managed to give something to each other. Melissa expressed all the dangerous and rebellious feelings I never dared admit to…

MELISSA: *Now* he tells me…

ANDY: And I like to think I gave her some sense of balance…

MELISSA: BALANCE? Oh Hell, I give up. Have it your way, Andy: balance.

ANDY: Most of the things I did in life I did with her partly in mind. And if I said or did an inauthentic thing, I could almost hear her groaning over my shoulder. But now she's gone I really don't know how I'll get along without her.

MELISSA: *(Looking at him for the first time.)* You'll survive, Andy…

ANDY: I have a wonderful wife, fine children, and a place in the world I feel proud of, but the death of Melissa suddenly leaves a huge gap in my life…

MELISSA: Oh now, Andy…

ANDY: The thought of never again being able to write to her, to connect to her, to get some signal back from her, fills me with an emptiness which is hard to describe.

MELISSA: Now Andy, stop…

ANDY: I don't think there are many men in this world who have had the benefit of such a friendship with such a woman. But it was more than friendship, too. I know now that I loved her. I loved her even from the day I met her, when she walked into second grade, looking like the lost princess of Oz.

MELISSA: Oh, Andy, PLEASE. I can't bear it.

ANDY: I don't think I've ever loved anyone the way I loved her, and I know I never will again. She was at the heart of my life, and already I miss her desperately. I just wanted to say this to you and to her. Sincerely, Andy Ladd.

MELISSA: Thank you, Andy.

THE END

THE OLD BOY

To John Rubinstein and Paul Benedict,
who helped me immeasurably in trying to get it right

INTRODUCTION

I have mixed feelings about *The Old Boy*, and most of the critics did, too. I think it has a good story, along with a good "back story" as the TV people would say. It also has some strong scenes, especially between the two boys. But the mother seems to run away with the play in a way she shouldn't, and the character of Alison seems to have less weight on stage than she does on the page. (I knew I was in trouble with her when the costume designer and I couldn't agree on what she might wear at the end of Act One.) Another problem is that the play drives toward the climax of a Big Speech, which, when it finally arrives, is articulate, well-meaning, and something of a bore. The movies could make it work by cutting away to reaction shots, but on stage, we all simply have to sit there. If I had a second chance with this play, I'd find a better way of doing that speech—possibly by indirection. I do like the final scene of the play, when we get there, though it may be too late. In any case, *The Old Boy* is one of those plays which almost makes it, and in the theatre, almost is not enough.

ORIGINAL PRODUCTION

The Old Boy was first produced at Playwrights Horizons (André Bishop, Artistic Director) in New York City, on May 6, 1991. It was directed by John Rubinstein; set design was by Nancy Winters; the costume design was by Jane Greenwood; the lighting design was by Nancy Schertler; the sound design was by Bruce Ellman and the production stage manager was Michael Pule. The cast was as follows:

Dexter	Richard Woods
Bud	Clark Gregg
Sam	Stephen Collins
Harriet	Nan Martin
Perry	Matt McGrath
Alison	Lizbeth MacKay

The Old Boy was revised and opened at the Old Globe Theater in San Diego, California, on January 18, 1992. It was directed by Paul Benedict; the set and lighting designs were by Kent Dorsey; the costume design was by Christine Dougherty; the sound design was by Jeff Ladman and the production stage manager was Peter Van Dyke. The cast was as follows:

Dexter	Franklin Cover
Bud	Rob Neukirch

Sam. . . . . John Getz
Harriet. . . . . Rosemary Murphy
Perry . . . . Christopher Collet
Alison . . . . Harriet Hall

CHARACTERS

SAM: middle-aged; Under Secretary of State for Political Affairs
BUD: younger; Sam's aide
DEXTER: older; Vice-Rector of a distinguished private boarding school
HARRIET: older; Perry's mother
ALISON: middle-aged; Harriet's daughter-in-law
PERRY: young; Harriet's son

SETTING

The play takes place primarily at a distinguished Episcopal boarding school in a small New England town during graduation weekend in early June, now and in the past.

An open set, designed to accommodate a number of different playing areas, indoors and out. Centrally located is the sitting area of the best room in one of those old New England inns which service the private schools near which they are located: a few pieces of good, simple Early American furniture, particularly a bench, which will serve as a couch, a student's bed, and ultimately the front seat of a car. Pictures of the school, or of student teams, may be in evidence. There is also an unobtrusive bar with liquor bottles, and a telephone somewhere else. Scene shifts are indicated by changes in lighting and music.

ACT I

In darkness: the sound of a boy's choir singing:
  "Brightest and best of the sons of the morning,
  Dawn on our darkness, and lend us thine aid…"

The hymn fades into the sound of church bells chiming the hour—four p.m.—
as Dexter enters the sitting area, followed by Bud. Dexter is in his sixties, dressed
in a seersucker suit, wearing a clerical collar. Bud is in his thirties, wears a
summer suit, and carries an attaché case.

DEXTER: *(Proudly.)* …And lo and behold! Our Celebrity Suite!

BUD: *(Looking around.)* Uh huh.

DEXTER: We keep it specially reserved for guests of the school. There is a bar…two televisions…*three* telephones—including one in the bathroom, which always struck me as slightly excessive…Do you think this will content your lord and master?

BUD: It's O.K.

DEXTER: *(Peering within.)* Ah ha! I spy! His bags are already in the bedroom. I had them brought up during the press conference.

BUD: How come the press conference?

DEXTER: There seemed to be some demand.

BUD: I thought we agreed no publicity.

DEXTER: Oh well. Our school paper…The local weeklies…

BUD: I thought we agreed.

DEXTER: Surely he can't steal in and out like a thief in the night.

BUD: I wrote you a letter. I spelled it out. This was to be a totally private visit. Then the minute we arrive, you set up mikes on the front lawn!

DEXTER: But he was proud and pleased. *(Going to a window.)* Look at him, still surrounded by students. He's enjoying himself tremendously.

BUD: What about tomorrow?

DEXTER: Tomorrow?

BUD: When he makes the Commencement Address. Do you plan any PR?

DEXTER: I thought possibly our local station…

BUD: Radio?

DEXTER: Well actually it's a television station…

BUD: You're putting him on *TV?*

DEXTER: Oh just for local consumption…

BUD: The answer is No.

DEXTER: No?

BUD: No TV, under any circumstances.

DEXTER: May I take the liberty of asking why?

BUD: Because he's got a good chance to be nominated governor. We don't want to broadcast the fact that he's a closet preppy, sneaking on the old school tie.

DEXTER: Oh now really...

BUD: Private schools are political poison, Reverend. Take it from one who graduated from South Boston High.

DEXTER: Nonsense. Politicians are always trotting out Yale and Harvard.

BUD: Colleges are fine. You can earn your way there. But prep schools—forget it. They speak pull, they speak privilege. They go against the democratic grain.

DEXTER: Oh yes? Well I dare say that this school, because of its large endowment and generous scholarship program, is as democratic as any high school in the country. More so, in fact, because we draw students from all over the country—indeed, all over the world! It might be time for someone to stand up and publicly point that out.

BUD: Fine. But not him. And not tomorrow. And not on TV. Are we clear on that?

(Sam enters.)

SAM: What's the trouble? *(Sam is good-looking, well-groomed, middle-aged.)*

DEXTER: I am being asked to hide your light under a bushel.

SAM: Bud is being political again?

BUD: Bud is being practical again.

SAM: Relax, Buddy. Loosen up. *(Looking around.)* And hey! What a pleasant room.

DEXTER: Henry Kissinger spent a weekend here. And Helen Hayes.

SAM: Good Lord. Together?

DEXTER: Heavens no!

BUD: That's a preppy joke.

DEXTER: Oh. Ha ha. I see...

SAM: Actually, I think my father stayed in this room, the weekend I graduated.

DEXTER: He may well have. Wasn't he a Trustee?

SAM: He sure was. And I remember, after the ceremony, he brought me back here, sat me down in this chair, and offered me a dry martini. He said if I planned to drink, it was best I do it in front of him.

DEXTER: Ah yes. That was the standard approach to alcohol.

SAM: I'm glad it wasn't applied to fornication.

DEXTER: What?

BUD: Another joke.

DEXTER: Oh. Ha ha. Yes. I see.

SAM: Actually, the old man was a little late, as far as liquor was concerned. Little did he know that for three years, I'd already been sneaking out with the gang after the Saturday night movie, trying to get smashed on Wildroot Cream Oil Hair Tonic.

DEXTER: You, Sam? Winner of the Leadership Prize?

SAM: Oh, sometimes I led in the wrong direction.

DEXTER: I shouldn't know that. Now I'll have to suspend you immediately.

SAM: Good. That gets me out of my speech tomorrow.

DEXTER: You don't want to speak? To your old *alma mater?*

BUD: He jumped at the chance.

SAM: That's true…But now I'm here, I feel as if I'm suddenly back on the debating team, knees shaking, stomach in knots, about to represent the school in a crucial contest against Andover. God, does anyone ever let go of this place?

DEXTER: Some of us feel it's important to hold on to.

SAM: Right. Of course. I'm sorry.

BUD: I need to phone.

(Dexter indicates onstage phone.)

BUD: I'll go in there. *(He goes off to the bedroom.)*

SAM: *(Looking towards the bedroom.)* What a big bed! A man could get lost in it.

DEXTER: How sad your lovely wife couldn't be here to share it with you. Wasn't her father in the class of '32?

SAM: That was my first wife.

DEXTER: Ah. Then I should have liked to meet her replacement.

SAM: She has her own agenda. You know wives these days.

DEXTER: Not well, I'm afraid.

SAM: You never married?

DEXTER: You might say I married the school. We've been together thirty-four years.

SAM: You've done better than I have… *(Looking toward the bedroom.)* Now Bud there has a nice, stay-at-home wife, whom he's probably telephoning right now. And three sweet kids who call me "sir" when he brings them to the office.

DEXTER: Speaking of that, what do *we* call you, when we introduce you tomorrow? Mr. Ambassador? Mr. Congressman? What?

SAM: Oh I'll just settle for your Majesty.

DEXTER: How about Mr. Governor?

SAM: That might be jumping the gun.

DEXTER: Oh now. Your young friend has high hopes.

SAM: We'll see…I suppose, when you have to be official, you could say Mr. Secretary. *Under* Secretary, way under, low man on the totem pole, but Secretary nonetheless. Otherwise I hope you'll just call me Sam. As you used to. When I was a boy here.

DEXTER: All right, Sam. And you should call me Dexter.

SAM: Not "Sir?" Not "Friar Tuck," which we called you behind your back?

DEXTER: Nowadays there's more alliteration involved.

SAM: I'll settle for Dexter.

DEXTER: Fine. And I'll ask the boys and girls to call you Mister.

SAM: Girls! I keep forgetting you have girls here now!

DEXTER: We have lots of things here now. We have a complete program in Asian studies. We have an active Hillel society. And we have compulsory sex education for all entering students.

SAM: Compulsory sex? Sounds better than compulsory Latin.

DEXTER: No, I meant…

SAM: I know what you meant, Dexter, and I'm sorry. I apologize for all my asinine remarks. Ever since I came back, I've been systematically regressing into some adolescent wise guy. You should sting me with six demerits and confine me to study hall.

DEXTER: Now, now. Just as long as you give a good speech tomorrow.

SAM: Uh-oh. What if the trumpet giveth an uncertain sound?

DEXTER: Ah hah! You remember your Sacred Studies. "If the trumpet giveth an uncertain sound, who shall prepare himself for battle?"…Paul. First Corinthians.

SAM: Which I just read the other night.

DEXTER: Good heavens! Since when do politicians read the Epistles of Saint Paul?

SAM: When they're staying in some hotel. And can't sleep. And are tired of reading everything else. "Sounding brass and tinkling cymbal." That's me these days.

DEXTER: Oh now.

SAM: I'm serious. I guess that's really why I came back, Dexter. I have this uncontrollable need to return to the well.

DEXTER: I'm sure we can refresh you. Remember the words of our founding Rector: "No boy leaves this school unimproved."

(Bud comes out of the bedroom.)

BUD: I talked to the office. They say the Indonesian thing is heating up again. The White House wants you to call Jakarta and straighten things out.

SAM: Why do the Indonesians always wait till the weekend? *(He starts for the telephone.)* If you'll excuse me, Dexter…

DEXTER: May I just raise one other small point, before you take up scepter and crown?

SAM: *(Stopping.)* Shoot.

DEXTER: Do you remember a boy in your class named Perry Pell?

SAM: Of course! I was his Old Boy.

BUD: His what?

DEXTER: Old Boy. It's a system we have. A student who's been here—an Old Boy—or Old Girl, these days—is assigned to a New Boy, or New Girl, and guides him, or her, through the dark wood of the first year. Sam was an Old Boy to Perry Pell… *(Turning to Sam.)* Who is dead, I'm afraid.

SAM: Dead?

DEXTER: He died last winter. Some accident, apparently.

SAM: I didn't know that.

DEXTER: Neither did the Alumni Office. His mother just told us.

SAM: I remember his mother.

DEXTER: And she remembers you. In fact, that's why she's here.

SAM: Here?

DEXTER: She heard you were delivering the Commencement Address, and up she came. I think she wants you to say a few words in memory of Perry.

SAM: Glad to.

DEXTER: I told her you had a very tight schedule, but perhaps she could stop by for a drink around five thirty, before we submit to the evening's festivities. I'll officiate, of course.

SAM: Fine with me.

DEXTER: Frankly, if I may speak briefly of treasures laid up on earth, she has proposed a major gift to the school in Perry's name.

SAM: Big bucks?

DEXTER: An indoor tennis facility. Two courts, a viewer's gallery, locker facilities—for both sexes, of course. She hopes you'll announce it tomorrow as well.

SAM: Of course…Did Perry's wife come along, by any chance?

DEXTER: Actually, yes. You knew her?

SAM: She was my date for the senior dance. That's how he met her.

DEXTER: What a small world!

SAM: It was then…

DEXTER: Well now I'll leave you to render unto Caesar the things that are Caesar's. *(He goes.)*

SAM: *(Broodingly.)* Perry Pell…

BUD: Sam.

SAM: Mmmm? Oh. All right. The Indonesian thing… *(Starts again for the phone.)*

BUD: This stinks, Sam.

SAM: Now, now.

BUD: This sucks, Man. I'm serious. I don't like this gig.

SAM: Something wrong with your room, Bud?

BUD: Sure. Per usual, they put me over the parking lot.

SAM: I'll tell them to change it.

BUD: They're using you, Sam.

SAM: Oh come on…

BUD: They're taking advantage! I make the deal, in and out, a quiet weekend in New England. And now suddenly you're giving cocktail parties, and announcing indoor tennis courts, and doing preppy press conferences on the front lawn!

SAM: That's the first press conference I ever enjoyed.

BUD: And you got so chuckly and nostalgic I almost puked.

SAM: Easy, Bud.

BUD: Sam, we're running for the roses here! You have a clear track, all the way to November! There's only one little hitch in the whole picture, Sam.

SAM: And what is that, Bud, as if I didn't know.

BUD: The preppy thing.

SAM: *(Making it grimly portentous.)* "The Preppy Thing."

BUD: No one likes Wasps any more, Sam.

SAM: The Irish adore us.

BUD: Not always, Man. It's a love-hate thing.

SAM: You're Irish, Bud, and you love me.

BUD: I do love you—I mean, not *love* you, like you…No, all right, love you. Don't tell Katie, but I do. I think you're the most decent guy I ever met. I'm betting on you, Sam. Which is why I quit my law firm, and took a salary cut of twenty grand, and am holed up here all weekend, overlooking a parking lot, rather than home with Katie and the kids. I mean, it bugs me, Sam! You were all signed up! Keynote speech at the National Conference of Mayors. Network coverage, hot issues, strong party support. Then Dexter calls, and you opt for this. People are pissed, Sam.

SAM: I know that.

BUD: Maybe you *don't* know how much I had to cover your ass, Sam. I piled story on top of story.

SAM: I appreciate it, Bud. Really.

BUD: Yeah, well, then what's the *real* story? Any thoughts? Now you're here?

SAM: I don't know. Maybe I'm like an Atlantic salmon. I got a whiff of those old headwaters, and just had to head upstream.

BUD: Don't salmon die when they do that?

SAM: *(Laughing.) Pacific* salmon do, Bud. The Atlantic salmon tends to survive…Oh hell, all I know is that there's something here. Something I missed, or lost, or need. Something I had to look for.

BUD: Then look for it *quietly,* O.K.?

SAM: Which means?

BUD: Which means don't stand up tomorrow, after you've reneged on a great speech on the problems of urban America, and in your best George Plimpton accent focus on a fancy tennis facility dedicated to some geek named Perry Pell. Please, Sam. That, don't do.

SAM: I—intend to pay my respects to a good friend.

BUD: Sometimes I think you don't want to win, Sam.

SAM: Sometimes I don't.

BUD: You'd better call the Indonesians.

SAM: *(Stretching out on the couch.)* Suppose you take over the Pacific Rim this weekend.

BUD: What'll I say?

SAM: Say we deeply deplore whatever it is they're doing.

BUD: That won't wash.

SAM: Then tell them to do it our way.

BUD: They don't want to.

SAM: Then say the check is in the mail.

BUD: *(Taking his attaché case.)* That'll fly. I'll be in my room. *(Starts out; stops; turns.)* Don't get caught in this shit, Sam. Really. You've got too much to lose.

SAM: The past has a way of sneaking up on you, Bud.

BUD: So does the future…

(He goes off, as music comes up: a boys' choir singing: "Oh Paradise, Oh Paradise…" Sam gets up, takes off his jacket, looks out. Greenery and bird sounds.)

SAM: *(Now younger; calling out.)* Come on, you guys! Many hands make light work!…Keep going!…Rake 'em into three main piles!

(Harriet Pell appears in autumn light. She is a classy woman, with neat hair, wearing conventional, expensive clothes in the style of the early sixties. She calls to Sam.)

HARRIET: You there! Young man ! May I speak to you, please?

SAM: Excuse me?

HARRIET: I'm looking for the young man in charge of the work program.

SAM: That's me.

HARRIET: Then you're our Old Boy! *(Calling off to Perry.)* I've found Sam, Perry! I've found our Old Boy! *(To Sam.)* I'm already impressed. Making all those boys do all that work.

SAM: We all have to pitch in. It creates a sense of community.

HARRIET: Well I want to create a sense of Perry Pell. *(Calls off again.)* Perry! We're waiting!

(Perry comes on reluctantly; he is young, dressed in jacket and tie.)

HARRIET: Perry, this is Sam. Shake hands, Perry. Good, firm grip. Look him right in the eye.

(The boys shake hands. Perry moves away.)

HARRIET: That's Perry, Sam. And I'm his mother. *(She holds out her hand.)*

SAM: *(Shaking hands with her.)* I figured.

HARRIET: I was very particular about selecting Perry's Old Boy. I asked for someone of the same age, in the same class, but who's been here a year. I want
someone who plays sports WELL, and has recognizable leadership qualities. You obviously fill the bill.

SAM: Thanks.

HARRIET: I understand your father went here.

SAM: He's a trustee, actually. And my grandfather went here. And two uncles.

HARRIET: Mercy! You *are* an Old Boy! See, Perry? Sam knows the ropes, up
and down the line. He'll help you fit in.

SAM: I'll sure try.

HARRIET: Now Sam, you should know that Perry is an only child.

PERRY: *(Quietly.)* Mother...

HARRIET: No, Darling. Sam should know that. He should also know that your
father is totally out of the picture. *(To Sam.)* I've had to take over from
scratch in that department.

PERRY: Come on, Mother...

HARRIET: Sam should know these things, Dear. So he can whip you into shape.

PERRY: You forgot to tell him I'm toilet trained. *(He exits again.)*

HARRIET: *(Laughing nervously.)* He has an unusual sense of humor. *(Looks off.)*
But he retreats. He withdraws. He backs away. He goes to Washington

with his school to visit the major monuments, ends up alone at the movies. He gets invited to his first formal dance last Christmas, winds up in a corner, reading a book. He reaches the semi-finals of our local tennis tournament, and what? Defaults, so he can go to New York and visit his father.

SAM: Would he have won the tennis tournament?

HARRIET: No, Sam. No. I do not think he would have won. I think he would have lost. Because he refuses to go to the net.

SAM: No net game, huh?

HARRIET: No net game, Sam. Neither in tennis, nor in life. I'll bet you have a net game.

(They might sit together on the bench.)

SAM: Don't have much else.

HARRIET: Well Sam, you and I know, in our deep heart's core, that sooner or later people have to run to the net, and put the ball away. Otherwise, they lose. I hope your parents tell you the same thing.

SAM: My mother's given up tennis. She's not too well actually.

HARRIET: Oh dear. Nothing serious, I hope.

SAM: I hope…

HARRIET: *(Looks off.)* Look at Perry, standing by that lake. Watch. Soon he'll start skipping stones.

(They watch.)

HARRIET: See? That sort of thing can go on for hours! I'm all for marching to a different drummer, but this one won't march at all!

(Chapel chimes are heard. She gets up.)

HARRIET: Well. I suppose it's time to go. *(Calls off.)* I'm leaving, Darling! Time for the changing of the guard. *(To Sam.)* Look how he walks. Just like his father. Who now slouches around Greenwich Village, calling himself an artist.

(Perry comes on again.)

HARRIET: Shoulders back, Darling. And goodbye. *(Kisses him.)* Be strong, write lots of letters, and pay attention to your Old Boy. *(Shakes hands with Sam.)* Goodbye, Sam. I'm counting on you.

(She kisses Perry again, and goes. Pause. The boys look at each other.)

SAM: Where's your stuff? *(No answer.)* Where's your stuff, Perry?

PERRY: *(Very quietly.)* Over at the dorm.

SAM: What?

PERRY: *(Louder.)* Over at the dorm.

SAM: Met your roommate?

PERRY: Yeah.

SAM: Like him?

PERRY: He's O.K.

SAM: What about your bed?

PERRY: What about it?

SAM: Made your bed yet?

PERRY: No.

SAM: Come on. We'll go down to the dorm and make your bed.

PERRY: I don't want to make my bed.

SAM: You've got to make your bed, Perry. They have inspections. You get demer-its.

PERRY: *(Almost inaudibly.)* I don't think I'm right for this place.

SAM: Huh?

PERRY: *(Shouting.)* I DON'T THINK I'M RIGHT FOR THIS PLACE!

SAM: Sssh. Hey. Go easy.

PERRY: I think I've made a serious mistake.

SAM: New boys always say that.

PERRY: No, it's not right for me. I can tell. Guys are playing hockey with Coke cans in the halls. I got stuck with the upper bunk. My roommate treats records like shit...

SAM: The first day always feels that way.

PERRY: No, I can tell when I'm not right for things. I wasn't right for boxing lessons. I wasn't right for Wilderness Camp.

SAM: I hear you're a great tennis player, though.

PERRY: I'm O.K....Do guys ever run away from this place?

SAM: Not really.

PERRY: I might do it.

SAM: Run *away?*

PERRY: I might.

SAM: Where to?

PERRY: New York.

SAM: New YORK?

PERRY: Where my Dad lives.

SAM: You'd live with your Dad?

PERRY: I'll get my own place.

SAM: In New YORK? It's hugely expensive.

PERRY: I've got money. And I'll get a job.

SAM: Hey wow! You mean you'd just... *(Pause.)* Well you can't.

PERRY: Why not?

SAM: You need an education, Perry.

PERRY: My grandfather quit school after seventh grade, and made sixty million dollars. Where do you get a taxi around here? *(Starts off.)*

SAM: If you try to shove off, Perry, I'd have to turn you right in.

PERRY: Why?

SAM: Because... *(Pause.)* Because I'm your Old Boy. I'm responsible for you.

PERRY: Just say you didn't know.

SAM: Nope. Can't. I promised your mother.

PERRY: Then I'll wait for another time.

SAM: Let's sit down for a minute. *(He indicates the bench.)*

PERRY: I don't want to sit down.

SAM: Just sit. It doesn't hurt to sit—unless you have hemorrhoids.
   (Perry doesn't sit.)

SAM: At least look out at the Lower School pond.
   (More bird sounds.)

PERRY: I'm looking.

SAM: I noticed earlier you were skipping stones on that pond.

PERRY: And?

SAM: Didn't it kind of calm you down? Doing that?

PERRY: Maybe.

SAM: Know why?

PERRY: Why?

SAM: You were connecting with Nature.

PERRY: Get serious.

SAM: I *am* serious, Perry. Consider what you can do with that pond. You can skinny-dip in it, up by the dam. You can play hockey on it in the winter, you can build a raft on it in the spring. You can connect with it all during the school year. And whenever you do, you're connecting with Nature, Perry. And when you connect with Nature, it makes you a better guy.

PERRY: Save it for Sunday, O.K.?

SAM: No, it's true. I'm going to tell you something personal now. When I was a kid, I dreaded going here. I mean, my father entered me at BIRTH, for God's sake. I had no choice, even for another boarding school. My mom wanted me to stay at country day, but he vetoed the proposition. This was it. And when it came time to come, he just put me on the bus. My mom wasn't allowed to drive me up, because *his* mom didn't. "Throw him in the water, and he'll swim," my Dad said. And the day I left, my mom and I were both crying, but he wouldn't even let us do *that*. I mean, your mom at least came WITH you.

PERRY: Don't remind me.

SAM: Anyway, here I was, stuck here, and at first I felt really low. So I took it out on people. I took it out on fat guys, for example. I'd tease them and grab their tits and all that. I mean, I was a real shit. But then I took a good long walk around the Lower School pond, and connected with nature, and now I honestly feel I'm a better guy.

PERRY: I don't mind fat guys.

SAM: Neither do I. Now. I *like* them, in fact. That's my point. And that's just an example of what happens here. What also happens is you get the finest education in the United States. You read Cicero in Latin in your Fourth Form year. You study European History, right on up to World War One. You read Shakespeare and Chaucer with the dirty parts left in.

PERRY: What dirty parts?

SAM: "The hand of time is on the prick of noon." How about that?

PERRY: *(Sarcastically.)* Oh, I'm shocked! I'm disgusted!

SAM: O.K., so it doesn't hit you. So we'll shift to sports. Consider the athletic program.

PERRY: I read the catalogue, Sam.

SAM: All I'm saying, this is one great school. Guys all over the country are knocking themselves out to come here. The sons of two United States senators go here. The head of General Motors has his grandson right here. Katharine Hepburn's nephew goes here, and a kid whose mother was married to Ty Cobb. There are Jewish guys here now, and they raise the level of discourse, and Negroes on scholarship, who are a credit to their race. There are foreigners here, too—Japanese, and South Americans, and a kid from Hungary who took on Communist *tanks!* Oh, I'm telling you, Perry, if the Russians dropped a bomb on this place, it would cripple the entire free world!

PERRY: Aren't you slightly overdoing it?

SAM: O.K., but everyone here is a privileged person. And we have a responsibility to stay. We have a responsibility to take the courses, and go to chapel, and improve our bodies and our minds. That way, we become leading citizens. So if you ran away, you'd be turning your back on society and yourself.

PERRY: All you're saying is go make your bed. Right?

(Pause.)

SAM: Right. *(He laughs.)* I'm full of shit sometimes, aren't I?

PERRY: Yeah well who isn't?

SAM: No, but I sometimes get carried away. I'm glad you brought it to my attention, Perry. You'll be good for me. Just as I'll be good for you. Now. What about that bed?

PERRY: I guess I'll make it.

SAM: And I'll help you, Perry. And then we'll stir up a game of frisbee.

PERRY: I stink at frisbee.

SAM: We'll deal with that, Perry. We'll work on that. Meanwhile, do you know how to make hospital corners?

PERRY: No, frankly.

SAM: I'll show you how to make hospital corners.

(They run out. Another hymn: "Rise up, Oh Men of God..." Dexter enters, carrying a tray of glasses, an ice bucket, and some potato chips.)

DEXTER: Room service, room service, courtesy of the school!

SAM'S VOICE: *(From within.)* Be right out!

DEXTER: *(Crossing to the bar.)* No tipping, please! *(He sets the tray down, calls off the other way.)* Ladies! I believe the governor is ready to convene the legislature.

(Harriet and Alison come in. Harriet now looks older and wears contemporary clothes. Alison is attractive and also well dressed.)

HARRIET: *(Looking around.)* What a lovely room! Somewhat larger than those cubicles we've been assigned to!

(Sam enters, pulling on his jacket and tie.)

SAM: Welcome, welcome.

HARRIET: *(Going to him.)* Oh Sam! Dear boy! How good to see you again! *(She embraces him warmly.)*

SAM: I'm so sorry about Perry, Mrs. Pell.

HARRIET: He adored you, Sam. He kept clippings from your whole career.

ALISON: Hello, Sam.

SAM: Alison.

(They kiss on the cheek.)

DEXTER: *(Officiating with the drinks.)* Now who'll have what? Mrs. Pell?

HARRIET: Oh let's see. It's June, isn't it? I think I might be talked into a gin and tonic.

DEXTER: Gin and tonic it is.

HARRIET: *(Leading Sam to the bench.)* Now sit here, Sam. Next to me.

DEXTER: *(To Alison.)* Mrs. Pell, Junior?

ALISON: Just club soda, please. *(She sits off to one side.)*

DEXTER: A little wine, for thy stomach's sake?

ALISON: No thank you. No.

DEXTER: Sam?

SAM: Light scotch, please, Dexter.

HARRIET: "Light scotch, please." I remember that very well. When you stopped by Grosse Pointe on your way west with Perry. Always light scotch.

SAM: Sometimes it wasn't so light.

HARRIET: Oh Sam, you've never gone overboard in your life.

ALISON: Oh yes he has.

(Sam, Harriet and Dexter look at her.)

ALISON: Long ago and far away.

HARRIET: Oh well, we all lose our grip occasionally. I did when I got married. But I came to my senses fast, let me tell you.

DEXTER: Sam, where's your ubiquitous amanuensis?

SAM: Who? Oh, you mean Bud.

DEXTER: Won't he join the dance?

SAM: Bud's in his room, proving that most of the important work in government is done by junior members of the staff.

ALISON: Isn't your wife here?

SAM: Couldn't make it.

HARRIET: Oh dear. And I hear she's perfectly lovely. She was a Thayer, wasn't she? From Philadelphia.

SAM: That was my first wife.

HARRIET: You traded her in?

SAM: Three years ago.

ALISON: The new one's name is Carol, and she has two children by her first marriage, just as you have two by yours, and you live in an old brick row house in Georgetown, where she runs a real estate office, and you serve the country at home and abroad.

SAM: Good for you.

ALISON: Oh I keep up.

SAM: You know more about me than I know about you.

ALISON: What's to know?

HARRIET: I'll tell you what's to know: Alison and Perry lived a lovely life together. They produced a sweet boy—my dear grandson… *(To Dexter.)* Who I hope will be admitted to this school the year after next.

ALISON: He's certainly been admitted to enough others.

HARRIET: *(To Dexter.)* He has minor behavior problems.

ALISON: Which are threatening to become major.

HARRIET: He's in military school at the moment.

ALISON: Which he hates.

HARRIET: Which is ironing out a few wrinkles.

ALISON: If not burning a few holes.

DEXTER: I'm sure we can find a place for him, Mrs. Pell.

ALISON: If he wants to come.

HARRIET: How do they know what they want at that age? They must be pointed, they must be pushed.

ALISON: He might do better if he chose.

DEXTER: *(Passing a plate.)* Potato chips, anyone? They're all I could drum up.

SAM: You look like you're serving Holy Communion, Dexter.

DEXTER: What? Oh dear. Ha ha. That's two demerits, for blasphemy.

HARRIET: Sam, I want to tell you about Perry. *(Pause.)* It was a ghastly mistake. He misread his prescription, and took all the wrong pills.

ALISON: Oh…

HARRIET: Alison, of course, has a different opinion.

ALISON: The doctor has a different opinion.

HARRIET: Doctors don't know! I know Perry. I know that he'd never intentionally leave us without even saying goodbye. No. I'm sorry. No.

SAM: I'm sorry, too, Mrs. Pell.

HARRIET: I wish you'd been there, Sam. To keep him up to the mark.

SAM: We kind of lost touch after school.

HARRIET: He loved you, Sam. He loved this school. It was a turning point in his life.

DEXTER: That's why your gift will be so appropriate, Mrs. Pell.

HARRIET: He loved tennis, Sam.

ALISON: Well he didn't *love* it.

HARRIET: He won the Tennis Trophy!

ALISON: He liked other things more.

HARRIET: He won the Tennis Trophy here at school! He played on the Varsity at college!

ALISON: But he gave it up.

HARRIET: He loved the game, Alison. We watched Wimbledon together. Now stop contradicting.

ALISON: I wish…oh well.

SAM: What, Alison?

ALISON: I wish, instead of this tennis thing, it could be something to do with music.

HARRIET: As a me*mo*rial? For *Perry?*

ALISON: He loved music.

HARRIET: Couldn't play a note.

ALISON: He loved listening to it.

HARRIET: Music lessons for six years. Down the drain.

ALISON: But he listened to music all the time. What if there were some sort of place, with comfortable chairs, and good books all around, and a music collection, where people could put on earphones and listen to music, or read, or even sleep, if they wanted to.

HARRIET: That sounds very much like retreating to me.

ALISON: But Perry'd love a place like that.

HARRIET: That sounds like unconditional surrender.

ALISON: But—

HARRIET: I say tennis, Alison. And I happen to be paying the bill.

ALISON: *(To Sam.)* You can see how my mother-in-law and I get along.

HARRIET: Ah, but we always understand each other in the end, don't we, dear?

ALISON: I'm afraid we do.

HARRIET: *(Looking around.)* I suppose you all think I'm a superficial woman simply interested in a snobby game.

DEXTER: Oh no. Heavens, no. Mercy, not at all.

HARRIET: Well, let me tell you something about tennis. When I was a girl, I was taught the game, and one of the things I learned was that every set, every game, every point is a new chance. As opposed to golf. There you are doomed from the start. Do badly on the first hole, you carry your mistakes on your back forever.

DEXTER: I see! What you're saying is that there is infinite salvation in tennis! Like Catholicism. Whereas golf is Protestant and predestined.

HARRIET: I don't know about that. I do know that when I was young, I made a mistake. I married the wrong man. But because I played *tennis,* I didn't feel I had to live with him for the rest of my life. I said "All right, I've lost the first set. Time to change courts and start again." That's what I learned from tennis. And that's what Perry learned. And that's what I want the boys and girls at this school to learn, by playing tennis all year round. *(With a glance at Alison.)* Rather than slinking off into some corner to listen to what? *La Forza del Destino?* Am I right or am I right, Sam?

SAM: Perhaps we shouldn't decide tonight.

ALISON: And the former Ambassador to Iceland once again exercises diplomatic immunity.

DEXTER: We DO have to decide whether or not to have our second drink here, or at Hargate, where the Rector and his Lady are waiting to greet us.

SAM: Let's go.

DEXTER: And then we'll proceed to the main dining room, where we will sup at the head table. Then, following our repast, and after the ladies have had a chance to powder their noses, we will attend the spring production of *All's Well That Ends Well.*

HARRIET: *(Taking Sam's arm as they go.)* Poor Sam. You're stuck with us all evening.

SAM: All the more chance to hear about Perry.

DEXTER: *(To Alison.)* After you, Mrs. Pell.

ALISON: *(Who has been staring off.)* What? Who? Oh right, I keep forgetting that's me. Thank you.

(She goes out, followed by Dexter, as the music comes up: the overture to La Forza del Destino. Perry enters, in sweater and slacks, reciting, occasionally referring to a paperback playbook. He is very good.)

PERRY: "My father had a daughter lov'd a man

As it might be perhaps, were I woman,

I should your lordship…She never told her love,

But let concealment like a worm i'th'bud

Feed on her damask cheek…

We men may say more, swear more; but indeed

Our shows are more than will; for still we prove

Much in our vows, but little in our love."

(Sam enters, now wearing a sweater, hockey skates slung over his shoulder.)

SAM: *(Gesturing toward "the record player.")* Turn down the Farts of Destiny, will ya?

PERRY: *(Going to turn it off.)* The Force of Destiny, Sam. *La Forza del Destino.* Jesus. You and that joke. We've heard it too many times.

SAM: We've heard the Farts of Destiny too many times. Bruiser MacLane says you're driving him batty with that record.

PERRY: He plays *Moon River* night and day.

SAM: That's different. Yours is an opera.

PERRY: What's wrong with opera?

SAM: Bruiser says it's fifty percent fag.

PERRY: Oh come on…

SAM: He *knows*, Perry. He's from San Francisco!

PERRY: Stop playing Old Boy, Sam. That was last year, O.K.?

(Sam throws himself on the "bed.")

SAM: O.K. Fine. Play what you want. Who gives a shit?

PERRY: What's eating you?

SAM: Nothing. *(Pause.)* Except I just got a call from the old man.

PERRY: And?

SAM: He can't take me skiing at Stowe spring vacation.

PERRY: Why not?

SAM: Too expensive. He SAYS. But I think he's got a girl.

PERRY: Well that happens. I mean, your mom's been gone almost a year.

SAM: I know it happens, Perry. I'm not dumb. *(Pause.)* I also know he doesn't love me.

PERRY: Oh come on...

SAM: He *likes* me. But he doesn't love me. I used to think if I did well, if I won prizes and stuff, maybe he'd love me. But now I wonder.

PERRY: At least he leaves you alone.

SAM: Look, your mother wants the best for you because she thinks you deserve it. My dad thinks I'll never really measure up. That's the difference. *(Pause.)* Anyway. Spring vacation. Maybe I'll come south and hook up with you.

PERRY: Actually, I'll be in New York spring vacation.

SAM: I thought the tennis team planned to practice in South Carolina.

PERRY: I'm not playing tennis this year.

SAM: WHAT?

PERRY: I decided to be in the spring show.

SAM: Do both, for God's sake.

PERRY: Can't. I got a lead role, and the tennis team has too many games away.

SAM: But you're due to play second on the varsity this year!

PERRY: That's the way the ball bounces.

SAM: All I can say is it better be one hell of a good play.

PERRY: It's Shakespeare.

SAM: Oh God, not again. What play?

PERRY: *Twelfth Night,* actually.

SAM: That's not such a great play, Perry. I got a C minus on that one.

PERRY: I like it. A lot.

SAM: You playing that duke?

PERRY: No actually, not.

SAM: Then who? One of those clowns who think they're so funny?

PERRY: Actually, I'm playing Viola.

SAM: Viola? You mean the *girl?*

PERRY: She's a boy all during the play.

SAM: But she's really a girl.

PERRY: She wears pants all the way through.

SAM: But she is definitely a *girl,* Perry.

PERRY: O.K. she's a girl.

SAM: You played a girl last year.

PERRY: I played Mercutio last year.

SAM: You also played a girl.

PERRY: In the musical. Because they asked me too. I won the prize for Mercutio.

SAM: Perry, let me say something here. Now how do I put this? You and I are good friends now, right?

PERRY: Right.

SAM: I mean, we're way beyond last year's Old Boy shit. I mean, when my mother died, and I wanted to bug out, *you* were the Old Boy, actually. You got me to stay.

PERRY: Misery loves company.

SAM: Yeah, well we're even. This is just friends talking. Friend to friend. And I'm not saying this just for an excuse to go south spring vacation, either. What I'm saying is I really don't think you should take that part in that play, Perry.

PERRY: Here beginneth today's bullshit.

SAM: No, but remember last year? That Fairy Perry stuff?

PERRY: That's over now.

SAM: Because of your *tennis* it's over! I'm telling you, you play another girl, and keep up this opera crap, it'll start up again! It's a bird, it's a plane, it's Fairy Perry!

PERRY: Knock it off, O.K.

SAM: They even called me a fairy for hanging out with you. That's how I got in that fight that time. I was defending *both* of us.

PERRY: I can defend myself, Sam.

SAM: You'll have to, if you take that part.

PERRY: Fat Pig Hathaway gets those pig jokes all the time. Piggy-piggy. Sooey. Oink oink. He lives through it.

SAM: What you don't know is, Perry, Fat Pig had to see a psychiatrist last summer. He had to cancel a canoe trip.

PERRY: Alas and alack.

SAM: I'm *serious,* for Chrissake. The choices you make in school are extremely significant, Perry. They can have a important effect on your later life.

PERRY: O.K. Now apply the bullshit quotient: divide that by two point five…

SAM: Oh hell. I give up.

(Pause.)

PERRY: In Shakespeare's time, boys played all the girls' parts.

SAM: I know that.

PERRY: Same with the Greeks. Same on up to the Seventeenth Century. Guys played girls all the time.

SAM: Who doesn't know that?

PERRY: Yeah well, no one ran around calling them fairies, Sam. They were considered first-rate guys. Actors from Athens served as ambassadors to Sparta.

SAM: No wonder Athens lost the war.

PERRY: Ha ha. Big joke. Remind me to laugh some time.

SAM: I just can't believe you like acting better than tennis.

PERRY: I like—being someone else.

SAM: It's kind of weird, when you think about it, Perry.

PERRY: Maybe I'm weird then.

SAM: Well people who are weird work on the problem. They try *NOT* to be weird.

PERRY: Maybe I like being weird. Ever think of that?

SAM: Didn't you like it when you beat that guy from Exeter in the JV match last year? Three great sets, the last one ten-eight. Didn't you like that?

PERRY: I loved that!

SAM: Yeah, but it's not weird enough, huh. So you're going to give up a major slot on the Varsity Tennis Team, which could make you captain next year. Which could get you into Columbia, which is in New York City, your favorite place. Which won't happen if your grades go down because you spend too much time rehearsing plays, playing a girl. *(Pause. Sam looks at his watch.)* Well, I'm late for the debating society. Maybe I'll do better over there. *(Starts out.)*

PERRY: Sam.

(Sam stops.)

PERRY: You did O.K.

SAM: *(Coming back in.)* If you played tennis, we could end up in Florida. We could check out the Yanks in spring training! Your favorite team, man!

PERRY: Get going, Sam.

(Sam starts out again, then stops again.)

SAM: I just wish you'd talk to Bruiser MacLane, that's all. He'll tell you about *real* fairies. Guys who look at you in the men's room. Guys who—

PERRY: Get out of here, Sam!

SAM: O.K., but think tennis, Man!

(Sam runs off, as Perry stands looking after him. He gets his Shakespeare book, ponders it, then goes slowly off as a hymn comes up: "Creations, Lord…" It becomes dark on stage. Bud, in his shirtsleeves, comes in, holding a FAX sheet.)

BUD: *(Toward bedroom.)* Sam? *(He turns on a light, goes to the telephone, dials quickly.)* Hi. It's me…Give me Bill again…Bill, I just picked up your FAX down at the desk. Now listen: you checked this out, right? I don't want to go out on a limb here, Man…You're sure then?

(Sam comes in from the hall.)

BUD: Uh huh…uh huh…Thanks. I'll return the favor, Bill. *(Hangs up.)*

SAM: Still burning the midnight oil, Bud? I thought we were all to make a conscious effort to conserve energy.

BUD: How was *All's Well That Ends Well?*

SAM: Fine, except for the ending.

BUD: This FAX just came in from Washington.

SAM: About Indonesia?

BUD: About your friend…How he died.

SAM: *(Taking it.)* Thinking of transferring to the F.B.I., Bud?

BUD: You asked.

SAM: I didn't ask *you.*

BUD: I happened to have a call in to Treasury. The guy on night security ran a quick check.

SAM: I know how he died, Bud.

BUD: I don't think you do.

SAM: *(Reads, looks up.)* AIDS?

BUD: Suicide. Because of AIDS. Made it look like an accident. To make it easy on his family.

SAM: You sure?

BUD: I double-checked.

(Pause.)

SAM: Go to bed, Bud.

BUD: Still plan to make a speech about this guy?

SAM: Of course.

BUD: You still plan to make a speech, at a posh prep school, with the primary right down the road, at a time when people who are HIV positive can no longer get into the country, about a close friend who died of AIDS?

SAM: I said I would.

BUD: If our friends on the Right get wind of this…

SAM: I'll deal with that.

BUD: Let me write it, then.

SAM: You didn't know him.

BUD: All the better.

SAM: Bud…

BUD: This is a minefield, Sam.

(Knocking from off.)

BUD: Christ. Who's that. Jesse Helms?

SAM: *(Calling.)* Come in.

(Alison comes in.)

ALISON: Am I interrupting something?

BUD: Looks like I am.

SAM: Bud's going to bed.

BUD: Bud's going to work. *(He leaves.)*

ALISON: I'm sure he thought I was here to seduce you.

SAM: Why would he think that?

ALISON: Because that's what I plan to do.

SAM: Damn! I planned to seduce *you*.

ALISON: We can take turns.

SAM: I take it you got my little note.

ALISON: Found it under my door.

SAM: I figured the bar downstairs was about to close, and since I have this sitting room…

ALISON: Absolutely. And I got Harriet to go straight to bed. I heard her snoring like a soldier when I tip-toed past her door.

SAM: May she dream of Swedish tennis stars, all running to the net.

ALISON: Amen.

SAM: So. Here we are.

ALISON: The Old Boy and his Old Girl…Do you ever think about those days?

SAM: I'm thinking about them now.

ALISON: That summer on Martha's Vineyard…

SAM: Ah. The Vineyard…

ALISON: No cracks, please. It was home to me. My father ran the hardware store, remember?

SAM: What I remember is the sail locker of the Edgartown Yacht Club.

ALISON: Don't rush things.

SAM: You're right. If I'm going to re-seduce you, I should ply you with alcohol.

ALISON: The way you did then? With scotch? Stolen from the Yacht Club bar?

SAM: What'll you have this time?

ALISON: Nothing, thanks.

SAM: Given it up?

ALISON: Trying to.

SAM: You and everyone else in the post-Industrial World. Makes it tougher to seduce people. *(Makes himself a drink.)* You look terrific, by the way.

ALISON: Do I look to the manner born?

SAM: You sure do.

ALISON: Good. I've been working on it since the day we met.

SAM: Do you remember that day?

ALISON: Totally. I was waitressing at the Clamshell, earning money for college.

SAM: And I was visiting Kip Farraday, from school.

ALISON: Whoever. I never knew your names. All I knew was you moved in a flock. The annual migration, the June arrival of the summer boys, with your white teeth, and old sneakers, and no socks, and great wads of money stuffed in your Bermuda shorts.

SAM: Not much in mine.

ALISON: No. You were different. The flock blew into the Clamshell, and blew out, but you stayed. And ordered another cheeseburger. And introduced yourself.

SAM: And asked you to the movies…

ALISON: And to the beach the next day. But I'll have you know it took you a week to get me into that sail locker.

SAM: Do you remember I rigged up a bed for us with someone's silk spinnaker?

ALISON: I remember everything. That was my first time.

SAM: Mine, too.

ALISON: I know. *(Pause.)* It was a lot of firsts. It was the first time I began to wonder where you came from, you summer boys. Suddenly all I wanted in the world was to get off that island, and see where you went after Labor Day.

SAM: And so you did.

ALISON: Yes I did. Thanks to you. What a gentleman you were! Inviting me up here for that dance. That was another thing summer boys didn't do.

SAM: I hope you had a good time.

ALISON: Oh I did! *(Pause.)* No, I didn't. *(Pause.)* My shoes were wrong. *(Pause. She looks at her feet.)* Well, they're right now, goddammit.

SAM: *(Getting close to her.)* I like the shoes.

ALISON: Thank you.

SAM: *(Nuzzling her.)* I like what's in them.

ALISON: Still the same old line, I see.

SAM: Sure you won't have a drink?

ALISON: No thanks. I'm not an alcoholic, I don't think, but liquor gets me going.

SAM: All the more reason.

ALISON: I think we should talk about Perry.

SAM: I know about Perry.

ALISON: The whole story?

SAM: Enough. Bud did some homework. Are you all right?

ALISON: Me? Oh you mean, my health? Sure. Fine. I had myself thoroughly tested. It was unlikely, anyway. We hadn't slept together for years. So you see it's perfectly safe for you to be seduced.

SAM: Poor Alison.

ALISON: No, actually, *not* poor Alison. Rich Alison, which was what I wanted. They say if you marry money, you end up earning every cent of it.

SAM: Was it grim?

ALISON: Not for a while. We had one hell of a good time at first. Perry was lavishly affectionate. And we had great fun. We bought this gorgeous house outside of town, had horses, dogs, even a baby. Money does a lot, Sam. It kept us going for quite a while. Until he announced he was gay.

SAM: Announced?

ALISON: Sat me down one day, and told me point blank. And I said, "Oh, don't be silly, just because our sex life is a little dicey lately," so then he said he'd just made love with the man who cleaned the pool. I remember hearing that goddamn *Forza del Destino* blaring away in the background.

SAM: Oh boy.

ALISON: So I said get out. Darken our pool-house no more. Something like that. *(Pause.)* Do you think I would have said that if it had been a woman? *(Pause.)* I know he never said it when I'd been with men. *(Pause.)* Maybe I will have a drink after all.

SAM: You're sure, now?

(Chapel chimes are heard.)

ALISON: I am sure. How about rye and ginger, for old times sake?

SAM: There's neither one.

ALISON: Then vodka. Straight. Thanks.

(Sam pours it.)

ALISON: Aaanyway, off he went, into outer darkness. And then came the explosion. He must have been building up steam all along. Lover after lover after...But did I get divorced? Not this cookie! Oh no. I bided my time. Why? Money. Harriet paid the hush money, or whatever you want to call it. And I was free to continue a few discreet relationships of my own. Then, when he got sick, I couldn't...I mean, I couldn't just...I mean, he was *dying.*

SAM: Were you...hey, do you mind these questions?

ALISON: I like them. You're the first person who's had the guts to ask.

SAM: Were you with him when he died?

ALISON: No. By then, he had found his one true love. In his precious New York. A dear man who runs a travel agency. And who took care of him. And helped with the pills. And came to the funeral. And cried. Well, we all cried.

SAM: Poor guy. Not even saying goodbye…

ALISON: I know. That sweet man. We loved each other, in a way. In a good way. Of course, it wasn't…the way he felt about his final friend. Or the way I felt about you.

SAM: Uh oh.

ALISON: Oh no. Don't worry. We played that scene out years ago. Remember? The old Whaler Bar, on Madison Avenue, the day after Labor Day? Me tossing down rye and gingers and spilling my guts all over the table. You sipping your goddamn scotch. And spurning me.

SAM: I didn't "spurn" you, Alison.

ALISON: You said you didn't love me.

SAM: I said I didn't love you enough.

ALISON: Enough for what, for God's sake?

SAM: Enough to stay faithful, at different colleges, all the next year. Enough to get married after we graduated. Which is what you wanted.

ALISON: Your father didn't like me.

SAM: He didn't know you.

ALISON: He didn't want to know me.

SAM: He didn't think I was ready to get involved.

ALISON: But Perry was.

SAM: Seems so.

ALISON: You told me he was.

SAM: Did I?

ALISON: But you didn't tell me Perry was gay.

SAM: I didn't know Perry was gay.

ALISON: Oh Sam.

SAM: I didn't believe it.

ALISON: Oh Sam.

SAM: I thought he could change.

ALISON: You thought I could change him.

SAM: Maybe.

ALISON: The Old Boy passes the ball to the Old Girl.

SAM: Oh come on.

ALISON: Yes, well, I tried. I tried very hard.

SAM: Oh Alison.

ALISON: And if I ultimately didn't succeed, at least I ended up in that golden land where the summer boys came from.

SAM: Otherwise known as Grosse Point.

ALISON: Exactly. Sometimes it's very gross, and sometimes there's no point, but I got what I wanted in the end.

(Sam goes for another drink; Alison holds out her glass.)

ALISON: Where are your manners?

SAM: Already?

ALISON: Why not?

(Sam makes her another.)

ALISON: Gosh. I suppose this is what makes you such a good politician. You have a drink with people, and before long they're spilling the beans, and you've got them in your pocket.

SAM: *(Bringing her drink.)* Pocket, hell. I'm trying to get you in my bed. *(He touches her hair.)*

ALISON: Hey! No fair! I've stripped down, I'm sitting here stark naked, and you're still buttoned to the nines! *(She kicks off her shoes.)*

SAM: What do you want to know?

ALISON: I'm not even sure. I've read so much about you. You were even in the magazine on the airplane, coming east. Harriet pointed it out to everyone in First Class.

SAM: Oh well, it's been mostly luck and pull.

ALISON: Don't be modest.

SAM: I'm serious. Mostly appointments, mostly through the Old Boy network. Kip Farraday, the guy from the Vineyard, got me my first job in the State Department, and I've been shunting around ever since.

ALISON: Aren't you running for governor in the fall?

SAM: If I'm nominated.

ALISON: Big step.

SAM: So they tell me. I'm trying to get cranked up for it.

ALISON: You don't want it?

SAM: I *want* to want it. That's about as far as it goes. Frankly, Alison, I have to say…I've been feeling a little…bankrupt lately. About what I do. I mean, I'm still writing the checks, but I'm not sure the money is there any more.

ALISON: Sounds like you'll make a good governor.

SAM: *(Laughing.)* Thanks.

(They kiss.)

ALISON: *(Finally breaking it off.)* Hey! What about the lovely second wife, who sells condos in Washington and looked so trendy in *Vanity Fair?*

SAM: Ah. *(Pause.)* We're getting divorced. She's shoving off as soon as the political dust settles.

ALISON: Well, well.

SAM: It's tough being a politician's wife. I'm not always there, and when I am…

ALISON: You're not always there.

SAM: Exactly.

ALISON: Some rag I read in the supermarket called you a womanizer.

SAM: Whatever that means…

ALISON: It means you run around screwing women.

SAM: Hmmm.

ALISON: Do you?

SAM: Yes. Sometimes. Yes. Recently, too much so.

ALISON: Why?

SAM: Wish I knew.

ALISON: Sounds like you're going through your own explosion.

SAM: Maybe so.

ALISON: You and Perry. And me. All trying to make up for lost time.
    (Pause.)

SAM: Let's make up for it right now. Come on. I'll rig the bedroom up like a sail locker.

ALISON: I think we're beyond the sail locker now.

SAM: I suppose we are.

ALISON: I think we've arrived at the Biltmore Hotel. Remember the Biltmore? The plan was to spend a fantastic night there before we went off to our colleges.

SAM: O.K. Let's pick up where we left off.

ALISON: God, you were the perfect gentleman. You took my arm and walked me there, after our big scene at the Whaler Bar. You checked me in. You stayed with me while I simmered down. You even lent me your handkerchief, which I still have. But like many gentlemen, you neglected to pay the bill.

SAM: Your bill was paid, Alison.

ALISON: Not by you, it wasn't.

SAM: Perry paid the bill.

ALISON: How do you know that?

SAM: And drove you up to college afterwards.

ALISON: How do you know that, Sam?

SAM: I asked him to.

ALISON: You ASKED him to?

SAM: I suggested it.

ALISON: I never knew that before.

SAM: You think I'd leave you stranded in some strange hotel?

ALISON: I always thought it was just luck, coming down in the morning, seeing Perry waiting in the lobby, under the clock. He never told me it was prearranged.

SAM: Because he was a gentleman, too.

ALISON: Of course! Dumb! Dumb me! I should have known! Both of you, gentlemen, all the way. You didn't want to dance with me any more, so you got your friend to cut in.

SAM: I thought I was doing the right thing.

ALISON: Fuck the right thing!

SAM: Hey! Go easy.

ALISON: I'm suddenly feeling a little set up, Sam!

SAM: I think that is rather a bald way of…

ALISON: I'm beginning to feel you set up my whole damn LIFE!

SAM: Oh now hey, Alison.

ALISON: And never a call, to either of us, after you did it. Just a wedding present, card enclosed.

SAM: I thought it best not to interfere.

ALISON: Oh sure. The Under Secretary of State sets up a puppet regime and then walks away from it. *(She goes to the bar.)*

SAM: Maybe you've had enough.

ALISON: Maybe I haven't…Do you still think it was the Right Thing, knowing what you know now?

SAM: I think…I think we should terminate this little brush up course in ancient history. We're not getting anywhere.

ALISON: I'm getting somewhere.

SAM: Oh yes?

ALISON: You know why I came up here this weekend? I wanted to show you how well I've survived after all these years.

SAM: As indeed you have…

ALISON: I also wanted to go to bed with you and show you that little old Alison Shaeffer from the Clamshell still knows how to do it!

SAM: You might keep your voice down.

ALISON: But now I know I don't want that at all. All I want to hear is you say something along the lines of "I'm sorry."

SAM: I'm perfectly willing to say…

ALISON: No! You'll never say it! Not really! Not you! Not you and all the other old, old BOYS in your fucking CLUB, moving your same dead old ideas around the backgammon board down in Washington!

SAM: I think you may have had too much to…

ALISON: Moving PEOPLE around, too! Moving kids off to Viet Nam and the Middle East and Lord knows where it'll be next! Moving ME around, goddammit! Moving Perry! Oh Christ, I thought I came to show you my shoes, but now I'd like to use them to brain you, you goddamn son of a bitch! *(She throws a shoe at him.)*

SAM: *(Backing off.)* Hey, come on, please…

ALISON: Oh hell. Don't worry. That wouldn't do any good, either. I'd never be able to bash my way through that thick shell you guys have built around yourselves all these years, no, wrong, all these GENERATIONS! *(She finds her shoe, puts it back on.)* No wonder your wives give up, trying to break in! No wonder you fool around, trying to break out! Well let me tell you something, Mr. Old Boy! *I'm* sorry! ME! I'm saying it to you. Know why? Because I don't think you've ever loved anyone. Love? You don't know the meaning of the word! You wouldn't know it if it stared you in the face!

(She storms out. Sam stands, staring after her. A hymn comes up: "Ten Thousand Times, Ten Thousand…" Fade to black.)

END OF ACT I

ACT II

The ringing of church bells. Sam, looking disheveled, with rumpled hair, in his shirtsleeves, sits writing on a note pad, sipping coffee. After a moment, the sound of knocking.

SAM: *(Calling out.)* It's open!
  (Bud comes in, dressed as before. He carries his briefcase.)
BUD: You look awful.
SAM: Thanks.
BUD: No, you do.
SAM: I didn't get much sleep last night.
BUD: Who does around here? Christ, between drunken parents arguing in the parking lot, and those fucking bells!…Goddammit, ding-dong!
SAM: The Call to Worship, Bud. In about a half an hour, we're going to stride manfully to the Chapel, where for a rather long hour, we will thank thee, Lord, Our God, with hearts, and hands, and voices. *(He returns to his work.)*
BUD: *(Glancing toward the bedroom.)* All clear, by the way?
SAM: Of course it's all clear.
BUD: She left?
SAM: She didn't stay.
BUD: That's something new.
SAM: No comment. *(Again he returns to his work.)*
BUD: You really do look kind of beat, Sam.
SAM: I'll get fixed up.
BUD: I brought along some of that pancake they gave you on McNeil-Lehrer. Want me to get it?
SAM: Nope. *(He crumples up a paper.)*
BUD: What the hell are you doing?
SAM: Trying to figure out what to *say.*
BUD: *(Opens his folder.)* I've said it. Right here. I'm quite proud of it, actually. After some passionate remarks about the need for new standards in American education, I modulate neatly into a discussion of public health, and wind up with a tender plea for human compassion.
SAM: You're a cynical bastard, Bud.
BUD: I like to win, Sam.
SAM: Think I'll do this one on my own, actually.

BUD: Yes? It doesn't look like you're getting very far.

SAM: I haven't, yet.

BUD: You've got twenty minutes before the schedule kicks in. *(Reading from his folder.)* Services in the chapel at ten. Coffee for special guests in the vestry at eleven-fifteen. Commencement exercises begin promptly at noon.

SAM: Then I'll wing it.

BUD: *Wing* it? You?

SAM: I've done it before.

BUD: Oh sure. With the League of Women Voters?

SAM: That was O.K. *(He starts off to get dressed.)*

BUD: *(Calling after him.)* What? The Q. and A. was a ritual castration.

SAM: What about the Gridiron Club?

BUD: Oh right. When you tried to be funny.

SAM: I was funny. I got a huge laugh.

BUD: That was a groan, Sam. A universal groan.

SAM: Anyway, this will be different. I know my audience better.

BUD: That's what scares me. You'll get all preppy and in-group, the way you were at that press conference.

SAM: *(As he gets dressed.)* You think so, Bud? Why? All I plan to do is open with a couple of sly, demeaning jokes about Blacks and women. Then, after some comments about Trust Funds and Deb parties, I'll slip into the main body of my speech, pleading passionately for lower Capital Gains taxes and higher caliber handguns. I'll try to season these thoughts, of course, with vigorous, contemporary language: "Gosh," I'll say, and "What the Dickens!" and even "Darn it all!" Toward the end, I'll toss in a few subtle anti-Semitisms, but gee whiz, Bud, most of those will be directed strictly against Israel. Finally, I'll refer to my old friend Perry, but I'll be so tight-assed and tongue-tied that it will only show that I'm totally out of touch with my own feelings.

BUD: You're kind of hyper today, aren't you?

SAM: Oh yes I am, Bud. Yes I am. So hyper that when the ceremony is over, I plan to dash back here and change into my pink polo shirt and lime-green pants with little whales on them. Then, after too many martinis, and too few chicken sandwiches—on white bread—with the crusts cut off—I'll just drive recklessly off into the sunset in my green Volvo station wagon for an adulterous affair with the waitress at the local cocktail bar.

BUD: That last little detail has the ring of truth.

SAM: Oh hell, Bud. Lighten up.

BUD: I'm thinking of your career, Sam.

SAM: And your own.

BUD: Sure my own. Katie called last night.

SAM: What else is new?

BUD: I'll tell you what's new. What's new is a new offer from my old law firm. Six figures. With a guaranteed partnership in three years. That's what's new.

SAM: What does Katie think?

BUD: She wants me home. The kids want me home. The dog wants me home.

SAM: What about the cat?

BUD: The cat can't make up its mind…And neither can I, Sam. I said I'd decide today.

SAM: You mean you'd quit on me? Even before the convention?

BUD: I want to stay, Sam. Really! I want to go all the way to the top right by your side. There are some guys, they walk into a room, and you like them, you trust them, you could work for them easily all the days of your life! You're one of those guys, Sam. I sensed it when I met you, and the voters will sense it, too. You're our best shot in this weird world, and if you'll just keep your eye on the goddamn ball, you could be president one of these days!

SAM: And you think I'd mess that up if I said a few words about a dear, dead friend.

BUD: I think you might. Yes.

SAM: Well I'm sorry. I have certain loyalties…

BUD: Maybe it's time to stop playing Old Boy, Sam.

SAM: Maybe you're getting a little big for your britches, Bud.

BUD: Which is an Old Boy expression if I ever heard one.

SAM: Bug off, Bud.

BUD: Fuck you, Sam!

SAM: Watch the language, please!

BUD: Fuck? Fuck's bad? We don't say it, we just do it, huh?

(Dexter comes in, now in Sunday clericals.)

DEXTER: Behold, the Bridegroom cometh!

SAM: Good morning, Dexter.

DEXTER: I'm here to conduct you to chapel.

SAM: You must think we need it.

DEXTER: Oh, I've walked in on worse in my thirty-odd years at the school.

BUD: I'll bet you have.

DEXTER: *(To Sam.)* I'm doing the sermon today. The Rector has awarded me that privilege.

SAM: *(As he ties his tie.)* You obviously run the joint, Dexter. You should be Rector yourself.

DEXTER: I put myself up for it, you know. During the last search. I proposed myself as an in-house candidate.

SAM: How'd you come out?

DEXTER: Fine, for a while. I was a finalist in the selection process. I had high hopes.

SAM: What happened? Why'd they pick that fatuous gladhander over you?

DEXTER: Oh well. You see, he was married. I wasn't. It came down to that.

SAM: Ah.

(Pause.)

BUD: *(Who has been looking out.)* I notice a TV van out there.

DEXTER: Oh yes. I meant to say.

BUD: You meant to say what?

DEXTER: Mrs. Pell wants some sense of the occasion.

BUD: I thought we agreed.

DEXTER: It's strictly local news. And the cameras will remain unobtrusively in the rear.

BUD: Which means they'll commandeer the front row. And go national if they can.

DEXTER: Oh now. Let's be more charitable with our brethren of the press.

SAM: Let's at least go to church…You coming, Bud?

BUD: I already hit early Mass in town.

SAM: Go for the Double Feature.

BUD: No thanks.

SAM: Come on. It's a gorgeous service. The rich, compelling language of the Book of Common Prayer…"We have left undone those things which we ought to have done. And we have done those things which we ought not to have done. And there is no health in us."

DEXTER: Good for you, Sam. Letter-perfect.

BUD: It's a great sound-bite, Sam. You could base your campaign on it.

SAM: Go back to bed, Bud.

BUD: I'm awake, Man! You're the one who's asleep. *(He goes out.)*

DEXTER: What an insistent young man.

SAM: He'll go far.

DEXTER: I envy the Catholics. They see things so clearly. Martin Luther made it all much more difficult when he put us in charge of our own salvation.

(More church bells.)

DEXTER: Well. We should go.

SAM: Lead, kindly light. *(He goes into the bedroom for his jacket.)*

DEXTER: You might be interested to know that I'm speaking today on Saint Paul.

SAM: *(From bedroom.)* Hey! My buddy!

DEXTER: Yes. I dug up the sermon I gave the year you graduated. I explore how Paul moves beyond the erotic to a larger kind of love.

SAM: Sounds like just my meat.

(They go off, as Harriet comes on, followed by Perry. She is dressed for graduation, He wears a senior blazer and slacks, and carries a sports trophy with a tennis player mounted on top.)

HARRIET: There he goes! Cut him loose from the herd!

PERRY: *(Calling out.)* Sam! Hey, Sam!

(Sam comes on, now in his graduation blazer.)

PERRY: Mother wants to see you.

SAM: *(Hugging him; indicating the trophy.)* Congratulations, Man! The tennis trophy! What did I tell ya?

PERRY: Where's your Leadership Cup?

SAM: I left it with my father. He wants it for mixing martinis.

HARRIET: Hail to the chief who in triumph advances. *(She shakes Sam's hand.)* I simply want to congratulate you, Sam, for walking off with every prize in the school.

PERRY: Except the tennis trophy, Mother.

HARRIET: Oh well, that was a foregone conclusion.

PERRY: I wish I'd won the Drama Cup.

HARRIET: I'm delighted you didn't, darling. *(To Sam.)* Now, Sam: what new worlds will you conquer next?

SAM: Princeton, I hope.

HARRIET: You hope? Aren't you sure?

SAM: My father's had some setbacks lately. We had to apply for a scholarship. If I don't get it, I'll end up at State.

HARRIET: Surely it's time to pull a few strings.

SAM: Those strings are getting a little frayed these days.

HARRIET: I wish you could join Perry at Middlebury.

PERRY: I wish I'd gotten into Columbia.

HARRIET: Nonsense. Middlebury is the perfect solution. They have skiing, they have square dancing…

SAM: They have girls.

HARRIET: Exactly, Sam. They are co-educational. Which means hundreds of lovely girls, all there waiting to be kissed…

PERRY: Maybe they're there for other reasons, Mother.

HARRIET: Maybe they are…Now Perry, dear, I wonder if you'd go stand in that line, and get us one of those delicious-looking fruit punches on this hot June day?

SAM: I'll do it.

HARRIET: No, I want Perry to do it. Would you, dear? For your mother and your Old Boy?

PERRY: *(Saluting.)* Aye, aye, sir. *(Goes off.)*

HARRIET: *(Watching him go.)* That, Sam, is your doing.

SAM: What?

HARRIET: That. The whole thing. The tennis prize, Middlebury, the confident way he walks. I put it all down to you, Sam. You've been a marvelous Old Boy.

SAM: That was just the first year, Mrs. Pell. Now he's one of my best friends.

HARRIET: There are friends and there are friends, Sam.

SAM: No. I'm serious. We would've roomed together this year, except I can't stand the *Forza del Destino.*

HARRIET: It's that *Forza* thing we've still got to fight, Sam. All the way to the finish.

SAM: Excuse me?

HARRIET: Tell me. What are your plans for the summer, Sam?

SAM: Teaching sailing, actually.

HARRIET: Teaching *sailing!*

SAM: On the Vineyard.

HARRIET: On Martha's Vineyard! What fun.

SAM: I visited there last summer, and this summer I got the sailing job at the Yacht Club.

HARRIET: How enterprising, Sam.

SAM: It's a job, anyway. And I like it there.

HARRIET: Perry wants to spend his summer in New York.

SAM: So he said.

HARRIET: He says if he can't go to Columbia, he can still do that.

SAM: Sounds fair to me.

HARRIET: Taking some stupid course on Medieval music.

SAM: He loves music.

HARRIET: It does not seem like a terribly healthy summer to me, sitting around that hot, dirty city, listening to monks sing madrigals.

SAM: It's what he wants.

HARRIET: Of course, his father's there. Who now claims to be a photographer. And lives with an Italian woman half his age. And hardly gives Perry the time of day.

SAM: Perry likes him, though.

HARRIET: I know. *(Pause.)* It's hard not to. *(Pause.)* Sam, have you ever been out west?

SAM: No.

HARRIET: Would you like to go?

SAM: Of course.

HARRIET: All right now, Sam. Here's the thing. I would like it very much if you took Perry on a good, long trip out west this summer.

SAM: Oh I couldn't—

HARRIET: No, now wait. I will give you the Buick station wagon, and *carte blanche* financially. My Aunt Esther has a ranch in Montana and you can stop there for as long as you want. You can fish, you can ride, you can even work if you feel like it. Or you can move on. You can go to Nevada and gamble. You can go to Wyoming and visit the brothels. You can end up in Hollywood, I don't care, just as long as you go. I think it will be good for you, I know it will be good for Perry.

SAM: Wow!

HARRIET: There you are.

SAM: Except I've already got this job.

HARRIET: I should imagine, Sam, that there are twenty other boys who would give their eye-teeth to teach sailing on Martha's Vineyard.

SAM: There's another thing, though.

HARRIET: What other thing?

SAM: I've got this girl, Mrs. Pell.

HARRIET: Ah. The Girl.

SAM: We're kind of going together.

HARRIET: Yes. Perry told me about The Girl.

SAM: She's the real reason I got the job down there.

HARRIET: Ah yes. Now let's see if I've got the facts straight. You met her there last summer, and her father owns a hardware store, and she came up to some dance.

SAM: Right.

HARRIET: Perry said he treated you both to dinner at the Inn. He said she was very attractive.

SAM: She thought Perry was terrific.

HARRIET: And I'm sure she thinks you're *more* than terrific.

SAM: We get along.

HARRIET: Well then she'll keep.

SAM: Keep?

HARRIET: While you go west.

SAM: Could I bring her along?

HARRIET: No, Sam. That might be a little tricky.

SAM: Then I don't know…

HARRIET: I'll tell you something else, Sam. There need be no more difficulty about Princeton. I know a man on the Board of Trustees, and I'll sing him your praises.

SAM: What if Perry doesn't want to go west?

HARRIET: He'll go, if you go.

(*Pause. Sam thinks.*)

SAM: This is a tough one, Mrs. Pell.

HARRIET: It's the tough ones that are worth winning, Sam.

SAM: O.K. I'll do it.

HARRIET: Would you, Sam? That is princely of you. Princely. Of a Princeton man…Now I want to meet your parents. I want to tell them they've produced a prince among men.

SAM: Just my father's here. My step-mother couldn't make it.

HARRIET: Oh dear. Not ill, I hope.

SAM: Oh no. She's down south, marching for Civil Rights.

HARRIET: What fun. Well, then I'll tell your *father* he's produced a prince among men.

SAM: He won't agree.

HARRIET: What? Doesn't he appreciate you?

SAM: He thinks I could stand some improvement.

HARRIET: (*Taking his arm.*) Oh well, all parents think that about their children.

(*They go off, as Perry comes out in khakis and a flannel shirt. He shouts for Sam a number of times, as if they were in great open space. Then he goes to the bench and honks the "horn" as if it were a car.*)

PERRY: (*Calling off.*) Come on! We haven't got all day!

(*He honks again. Other car sounds are heard passing, as if he were parked along a highway. Finally Sam enters, now in a pullover shirt.*)

PERRY: Where the hell have you been?

SAM: I was talking to those babes we met on the trail.

PERRY: I've been waiting for half an hour.

SAM: They want to party.

PERRY: Can't.

SAM: They have beer.

PERRY: Can't, Sam. Have to make Sacramento by four tomorrow.

SAM: They have beer, they have burgers.

PERRY: We've got to sell the car and make a four o'clock plane. Now get the hell IN.

SAM: *(Looking over his shoulder.)* We could catch another plane. There are plenty of planes. You think there's just one plane?

PERRY: I've got to make Freshman week.

SAM: What's Freshman week? That's for high school guys. You're beyond that shit, Perry. You're a big boy now.

PERRY: In, Sam. Please.

(Sam reluctantly gets in the car; Perry starts to turn the key. Sam grabs his hand.)

SAM: The dark-haired one thought you were cute, Perry.

PERRY: She did not.

SAM: She did. She said, "Where's your cute friend?"

PERRY: She didn't say that.

SAM: She said, "Where's your cute friend? I want to open my throbbing loins to him, tonight, under the Western stars."

PERRY: *(Starting the car; they jerk forward.)* Bullshit.

(They drive.)

SAM: So where will we camp tonight then?

PERRY: On the way somewhere.

SAM: What'll we do? Toast marshmallows? Tell ghost stories?

PERRY: Jesus, Sam. There's such a thing as making conversation.

SAM: *(Looking back.)* O.K. I'll begin. Seen any good-looking girls lately?

PERRY: Very funny.

(They drive.)

PERRY: I keep thinking about next year.

SAM: I keep thinking about back there.

PERRY: I'll bet we don't connect much next year. Different colleges, different friends. I'll bet we don't see each other much any more.

SAM: *(Mock sentimental.)* "I'll be seeing you, in all the old familiar places…"

(He turns on the "radio." We hear classical music. He finds a ball game. At an exciting moment, Perry turns it off.)

SAM: Hey! Come on!

PERRY: You really piss me off sometimes, Sam. You know that?

SAM: Yeah well don't get so corny, then.

PERRY: Just because I have feelings, I'm corny. Just because I value our friendship, I'm now corny.

SAM: Change the channel, Perry.

PERRY: Sometimes I think you're a cold son of a bitch, Sam. You really are a cold, thoughtless guy sometimes.

SAM: Oooh. Ouch. What brought that on?

PERRY: You leave me standing there while you shoot the breeze with a couple of babes. You always have to listen to the fucking Red Socks, but when an opera comes on, we have to turn it right off...

SAM: Oh for Chrissake.

PERRY: And when we were at the ranch, you kept going after that waitress...

SAM: What's wrong with that?

PERRY: You didn't even *like* her. You *said* you didn't like her. And yet you screwed her, you son of a bitch.

SAM: So what if I did?

PERRY: You never even told her goodbye.

SAM: That was an oversight.

PERRY: That was shitty, Sam. That was shitty behavior.

SAM: Just because you...

PERRY: Because I what?

SAM: Don't care about girls.

PERRY: I care about girls. I cared about that girl. I cared about her more than you did.

SAM: Then why don't you care about those girls back THERE? Why, during this whole trip, whenever there's a chance to go out with girls, you're always backing off, for Chrissake?

PERRY: Bullshit, Sam. Apply the bullshit quotient, please.

SAM: You're always backing off. I mean, when we were in Reno, and had that chance to go to that cat house, you wanted to go to *Lawrence of Arabia!* I mean, what are you? A fag, or what?

(Perry jams on the brakes; both lurch forward.)

PERRY: I'm not a fag, Sam.

SAM: Those girls are just SITTING there, waiting for us to make our MOVE!

PERRY: I'm not a fag.

SAM: Well I mean, you've got your problems, Perry.

PERRY: *(Hitting him on the arm.)* I'm not a fag.

SAM: *(Hitting him back.)* Hey! Knock it off!

PERRY: Get out of the car!

SAM: Says who?

PERRY: Me! Get out of my goddamn car, Sam!

SAM: *(Getting out.)* O.K. Fine. I'll go back and see those girls! *(Through the "window.")* So long, fag.

PERRY: *(Jumping out of the car.)* Don't call me that.

SAM: *(Going off.)* Fag! Fag! Fairy Perry!

PERRY: *(Leaping on him.)* Go fuck yourself, Sam! Go fuck yourself!

(They fight. Sam is stronger. He ultimately gets on top.)

SAM: Or should I fuck YOU, Perry? Want your Old Boy to fuck you? Huh? Huh? *(He plants a big kiss on Perry's lips.)* How's that? Is that what you want?

(Perry rolls free. They both get up, separate. Sounds of traffic going by are heard periodically.)

PERRY: I'm not a fag, Sam!

SAM: O.K., O.K. I'm sorry.

PERRY: I don't know what I am. But I'm not that.

SAM: O.K., O.K. *(Pause.)* I think the trouble with us, the trouble with both of us, is we just need more sex. Men don't get sex, they get frustrated, and fight among themselves. It happens with rats. *(Pause.)* Now here we are out west the summer before we go to college, and you're constantly bringing me down as far as girls are concerned, and so naturally, I just blew up.

PERRY: Just leave it, Sam. O.K.

SAM: I mean, that's why I thought you should see those babes. Our last chance out here, and I thought you should have a sexual experience. That's all I thought, and I'll bet your mother would agree with me.

PERRY: I've had a sexual experience.

SAM: Yeah, yeah.

PERRY: O.K. Don't believe me then.

SAM: When?

PERRY: That's my business.

SAM: Not this summer, that's for sure.

PERRY: Last summer, if you must know. While you were having yours.

SAM: When you went to New York?

PERRY: Right.

SAM: Do I know her?

PERRY: No.

SAM: Did you get in?

PERRY: No.

SAM: But you came close?

PERRY: Maybe.

SAM: Where'd you meet her?

PERRY: At a friend's.

SAM: What friend?

PERRY: We met at my father's.

SAM: She was a friend of your father's?

PERRY: Right.

SAM: Oh my God! An older woman! Did she show you the ropes? Remember *Room at the Top?*

PERRY: Yes.

SAM: Jesus. Sneaky Pete here. Last summer he's learning the ropes from Simone Signoret! How come you didn't tell me?

PERRY: I don't have to tell you everything.

SAM: Thought I'd tease you about it?

PERRY: Maybe.

SAM: You like her, don't you? That's why you turned down those babes. You like her. I can tell.

PERRY: It's not a her, Sam.

SAM: Not a her?

PERRY: I was sleeping on the couch over at my father's, and this friend of his got in bed with me.

SAM: Jesus! Did you kick him out?

PERRY: Sure. Oh sure. That's what I did. Immediately.

SAM: You told your dad, I hope.

PERRY: No.

SAM: My dad would've gone through the ROOF!

PERRY: My dad's kind of loose about things, actually.

SAM: But God! It must've been GROSS! Did he touch your dong?

PERRY: No. Of course not. No.

SAM: So. Ho hum. Big deal. What are you? Scarred for life? That make you scarred for life?

PERRY: No.

SAM: O.K. Then it's water over the dam.

PERRY: It's not over the dam yet.

SAM: What? He's still bothering you?

PERRY: Not bothering me.

SAM: Whatever you call it, there are laws against it, Perry.

PERRY: Are there laws against going to plays?

SAM: What are you talking about?

PERRY: Remember when I got special permission from school to see the Royal Shakespeare? This guy got the tickets.

SAM: Jesus. And you went!

PERRY: I wanted to see the play.

SAM: You are grossing me out here, Perry. You are definitely grossing me out. Did you have a sexual encounter?

PERRY: I don't want to talk about it.

SAM: You did, didn't you? You had a sexual encounter with this guy.

PERRY: All right. I did.

SAM: Oh my God! This is total gross-out time!

PERRY: Well you might as well know I'm meeting him in New York tomorrow night!

SAM: Is that why you wanted to get back?

PERRY: Yes!

SAM: Oh my God.

PERRY: I like him, Sam. I like him more than you ever liked that waitress at the ranch.

SAM: I can't believe I'm hearing this.

PERRY: Yeah, well, he wants me to come down from Middlebury and see him this fall, and stay at his place, and go to the opera with him, too, if I want to!

SAM: And you want to?

PERRY: I don't know what I want.

SAM: Get in the car. Get in the CAR, Perry! My turn to drive.
(They get back in the car; Sam drives.)

SAM: You were right, what you said back there, Perry. About maybe not seeing each other much after this…Because I have to tell you, Perry, if you start hanging out with guys like that, and going to the opera all the time, if that's what you want, then count me out.

PERRY: I'm not sure I want that.

SAM: Well, I know what I want. I want to walk into a room with a pretty girl on my arm, and know that she's mine for the evening. I want to get married some day, and have great sex three times a night, and even during the day. I want to have kids, and dogs, and play sports on weekends, and be a respected leader in my community. I want to move on up and contribute something positive to my country and the world. Maybe you think that's bullshit, but that's what I want.

PERRY: I want that, too. You think I don't want that? I want that every minute of the day. I see a guy getting cozy with a girl, I envy him. I see a baby carriage, I think that's never for me. I see a house, just some dumb *house* for shit's sake, and I wonder if I'll ever live in one, and who would ever live there with me.

SAM: Oh come on.

PERRY: It's true, Sam…And at night, I have these feelings…these other feelings…these strong feelings…about guys…sometimes even about you, Sam…

SAM: Me? Jesus, Perry…What—do you have us doing?

PERRY: We—make love.

SAM: Am I any good?

PERRY: I'm serious, Sam!

SAM: I know. Go on.

PERRY: I have these feelings. And I pray, I PRAY—I don't believe in any of that horseshit—but I pray to God that He will take…that He will BURN these feelings out of me for ever and ever, and send me some GIRL, and we'll fall in love, and live happily ever after.

SAM: I know a girl who likes you a lot.

PERRY: Yeah? Who?

SAM: Alison.

PERRY: Alison?

SAM: She likes you a lot. *(Pause.)* Do you like her?

PERRY: Of course.

SAM: You sure said you did when I brought her up to school.

PERRY: I like her a lot.

SAM: Take her out if you want.

PERRY: Take Alison out?

SAM: You'd be a great pair.

PERRY: I thought you liked her.

SAM: My father wants me to cool it.

PERRY: But she likes *you.*

SAM: She thinks you're a fascinating guy.

PERRY: She thinks I'm a big spender.

SAM: "A fascinating guy." Those were her exact words.

PERRY: She said that?

SAM: I swear. Now think positively. Take your sexual desires and refocus them on Alison.

PERRY: I thought she was your girl.

SAM: I'm not ready for a steady relationship.

PERRY: That's for sure.

SAM: Actually, you'd be getting me off the hook.

PERRY: We got along, didn't we? Alison and me. That time.

SAM: I couldn't get a word in edgewise.

PERRY: I told her we were kindred spirits.

SAM: There you are. Kindred spirits. Hey, suppose I fix you up with her. I'm seeing her in New York next week. I'll work something out. Meanwhile, you tell your faggy friend to bug off...

PERRY: I'll say I've got a previous engagement.

SAM: O.K. Say that. And hey! Alison's going to the University of Vermont this fall. You could drive over from Middlebury in that new Corvette your mother promised you. She loves Corvettes. She told me. You'll snow the pants off her. So see? It's perfect! Your prayers are answered, Buddy!

PERRY: Right.

SAM: So. We are no longer dooooomed to hang around bars with creeps in New York, and listen to the Farts of Destiny. We're rejoining the human race. Is it a deal?

PERRY: It's a deal, Sam. It's a real deal.

SAM: *(Pulling over.)* Fine. Now let's pull over and take a good manly pee. Those beers with those babes have caught up with me.

(Sam stops the car. They exit. Traffic sounds are heard, then drowned out by: A hymn: "For the Beauty of the Earth..." Alison comes on, holding a cup of coffee; she looks around. The hymn fades as Harriet enters.)

HARRIET: What are you doing out here?

ALISON: Getting a little fresh air.

HARRIET: Alison, dear, I'm not sure it's a good idea to be stalking around, in front of all these students, with a cup of coffee in your hand. You look a little...disconnected. Come back into the vestry.

ALISON: No thanks.

HARRIET: Then I wonder if you might tell me what in heaven's name is the matter. You've contradicted me all weekend. I thought we were a solid front, you and I. Do you think our dear Perry would be happy if he knew his mother and his wife had suddenly started bickering in public?

ALISON: I'm not sure.

HARRIET: Well, *I'm* sure of several things, Alison. I'm sure that life will be much pleasanter for both of us if we don't argue. I'm sure that those handsome checks which land on your doorstep every Christmas are not based on your being disagreeable. I'm sure that my grandson's future is at least some-what dependent on you and I pulling together.

(She sees Sam, who enters, now dressed in his suit.)

HARRIET: Ah, dear Sam! Come inside before the graduation march. We're having coffee and rolls.

ALISON: The coffee's weak, the rolls are repulsive.

HARRIET: Alison—I think you and I should probably continue our own conversation on the trip back down to the real world. *(She takes Alison's cup and goes.)*

ALISON: *(To Sam.)* I've been waiting to waylay you.

SAM: Uh-oh. Do you plan to keep your shoes on?

ALISON: I'll try…Are you all right, by the way?

SAM: I think so.

ALISON: I was watching you all during chapel. You just sat and stared. And then disappeared.

SAM: I took a walk around the pond.

ALISON: Thinking about your speech?

SAM: Thinking about lots of things. I was a manipulative bastard, wasn't I?

ALISON: Oh hell, I made my own bed, too. Though I didn't get much sleep in it last night.

SAM: I wish I could make things up to you.

ALISON: You can, actually. That's why I'm waylaying you. I wonder if you could get me a job.

SAM: A job?

ALISON: Through your Old Boy network. I can't live this way any longer. I want to earn my own keep. Which means a job. I suppose I could slink back to the Clamshell, but I like to think I've grown beyond it.

SAM: Let's see…Who do I know in the shoe business?

ALISON: No, I'm serious. I can't type, or work a computer, or do any of those things. But I'm smart. And still ambitious.

SAM: I'll check around.

ALISON: I'd be wonderful in the State Department. After all, I've maintained a diplomatic front for over half my life.

SAM: Until last night.

ALISON: Lookit, I've been in analysis long enough to know that you don't get that mad at people unless you feel pretty strongly about them.

SAM: I'll buy that.

ALISON: So. Suppose we work it this way. You find me a job, any job, anywhere, and we'll forgive and forget. Or rather remember—the good things. There's something between us, Sam. There was on the Vineyard, and there was in your room last night. We might even see each other occasionally…

(Pause.) I mean, if I worked in Washington… *(Pause.)* Or even if I didn't. *(Pause.)* Oh Lord. Now I feel I'm back at the Whaler Bar, pleading for your attention.

SAM: I'll try to find you a job, Alison.

ALISON: Thank you.

SAM: But I can't see you again.

ALISON: Why not?

SAM: Perry.

ALISON: Perry's dead now.

SAM: So am I.

(Harriet, Dexter and Bud join them. Dexter wears an academic robe, and carries another, along with a purple hood. They all talk almost at once.)

DEXTER: All rightee! Time to gird up our loins! *(He begins to drape Sam with an academic robe.)*

BUD: *(To Sam.)* What did I tell you? That TV crowd has moved right in.

HARRIET: Sam, dear, when you mention the tennis court, say I'm thinking of a clay surface. It gives a truer bounce. Be sure you mention clay.

DEXTER: *(Fussing with the robes.)* Hath not the potter power over the clay? Paul. Romans. Nine, Twenty-one.

ALISON: *(Low to Sam.)* Are you sure you're all right?

DEXTER: *(Adjusting a purple hood.)* We couldn't decide which of your honorary degrees to reflect in your hood. The purple from Williams, or the blue from Yale.

BUD: *(Handing Sam a stack of note cards.)* You can fall back on these if you get into trouble.

DEXTER: *(Adjusting the hood.)* We finally chose Williams. The imperial purple seemed particularly appropriate.

SAM: Dexter, did Paul say the truth shall set thee free?

DEXTER: *(As he fusses with the robes.)* No, that was Christ. In the Fourth Gospel. Why?

SAM: I can't get it out of my head.

(A trumpet fanfare is heard.)

DEXTER: Ah, the trumpet soundeth…Mrs. Pell, if you would stand over there, behind the Class Marshall…

HARRIET: Absolutely. *(Harriet goes off.)*

DEXTER: And Mrs. Pell, Junior, if you would stand beside her…

ALISON: All right.

(Alison goes off. Dexter turns to Bud.)

DEXTER: And you, Sir, have a reserved seat out in front.

BUD: Right. I see it. Out by the parking lot.

(Bud goes off the opposite side. The lights focus in on Sam and Dexter, now center.)

DEXTER: And now Sam, what will happen is that we'll march over to the dais, and then we'll have the prayers, and the hymn, and the handing out of diplomas, and then the awarding of the prizes, and then the Rector will make the introduction, and you'll speak. It's as simple as that.

(Dexter is out by now. Sam is alone on stage, as if on the speaker's platform.)

SAM: Thank you, Doctor Fayerweather… *(Carefully.)* Members of the faculty… members of the graduating class…students…parents…distinguished guests… babies…golden retrievers…and squirrels. *(Pause. He glances at Bud's notes, then rejects them, tucking them away in his jacket.)* When I was a boy here, we were always looking for the right answers. Sometimes they were in the back of the algebra book. "If A works twice as hard as B," and so forth, and the answer would always be some neat, round number, like four, and it was our job to show how we arrived at it. And at the end of the school year, we'd take exams, and neatly circle all our answers, fold our blue books, and sign the pledge on the outside: "I pledge my honor, as a gentleman, that I have neither given nor received help." *(Pause.)* We also found answers at home, when we returned for vacation. "If I go out on a date, what time do I have to be home?" The answer was twelve. "What's wrong with Communism?" It's evil. "What must I do to earn your love and respect?" Work twice as hard as B. Always there were answers. And if neither the school nor our family could provide them, we still assumed they were there, somewhere on down the line, at Harvard, in Washington, or in Heaven. *(Pause.)* Today we're lucky if we find the right questions. Maybe that's all a good school can do these days—teach us good questions.

At least, since I've been back, it's taught me to ask a few. And maybe now it's time for me to take an exam on them. After all, as Mr. MacDonald over there used to say in Classy Civ, "the unexamined life is not worth living." O.K.? So here's my final exam. *(Pause.)* First question. Big question. Huge subject. Love in the Western World. What in God's name is our problem? Why do we worry so much about unconventional forms of love? Are we afraid of love? Are we threatened by it when it stands out from the crowd? Here at school, we studied those long, bloody wars fought over religion. This country was founded as a haven from these wars. If we so cherish religious tolerance, why not sexual tolerance as well? Will there be a time when people's sexual natures are considered matters for their own soul, like their religion? Answer: let's hope. *(Pause.)* Next question. What about the AIDS epidemic? Is this the result of sexual freedom, or sexual repression? By maligning gay people, any group of people, have we caused them to turn in on themselves in self-destructive ways? And by doing this, by creating these ghettoes, have we ghettoized ourselves, cutting ourselves off from the rich diversity which constitutes American life? I can see Mr. Burnham writing in the margin: "Interesting, if true." *(Pause.)* Main question. Is there something in my own life which relates to all this? Yes. Oh yes. I can answer this one. When I was a boy here, I had a friend—a good friend—a gay friend—whom I persuaded to conform to a conventional life. Why? Was it natural? No. It was unnatural, to him. Was it right? No. It was wrong for him. Why did I do it, then? Was it something in me—some attempt to deny some passion in my own soul? Mr. Montgomery might add this comment: "Try to avoid clichés." *(Pause.)* Final question. What happened to this boy? He died. Why did he die? From a desperate attempt to make up for lost time. Who is responsible for that? Me. I am responsible. I was his Old Boy. I had a special obligation. *(Pause.)* "Bullshit," Perry might say. "Apply the bullshit quotient immediately." But I don't think I'm bullshitting now… *(Pause.)* Optional question. Extra credit. What can I do about this? Nothing. Can I bring him back? No. Can I apologize to him? No. Too late, too late, too late. What then?…Oh Perry, why do I discover this now, only now, when there's nothing to do, nothing to be done…when I can never tell you…never say…never even… *(Stops, looks around.)* I pledge my honor as a gentleman that I have neither given nor received…Oh God. *(He covers his face with his hands. Then Dexter appears solicitously, speaks to the audience.)*

DEXTER: Perhaps we might conclude the ceremonies with another hymn. *(Calling off.)* Would you start us off, Mr. Benbow? *(Starts singing, leading.)* "Faith of our fathers, Holy Faith…"
(He puts an arm around Sam and helps him from the stage as the music and singing come up. Bud enters, dials the telephone.)

BUD: Hi. Looks like I'll be home for dinner…Oh sure. We'll be out of here fast…Because he booted the ball, Baby. I'll tell you when I get there… *(Knocking is heard off.)*

BUD: Someone's at the door…We'll talk when I get home…Hey. Keep the kids up, will you? Haven't seen them in centuries…Love you, too… *(Hangs up; calls out.)* Yo! It's open.
(Harriet comes in.)

HARRIET: I'd like to speak to your lord and master.

BUD: He's taking a shower.

HARRIET: Well, I'm leaving. I wonder if you'd give him a message.

BUD: Shoot.

HARRIET: Tell him, if you would, that I have fought all my life against what is soft and sick and self-indulgent.

BUD: O.K.

HARRIET: Tell him that I left my husband, and raised my son, and hope to raise my grandson in the belief that there are such things as traditional values, decent behavior, and basic self-control.

BUD: O.K.

HARRIET: *(Starts out, then turns.)* You might also tell him that he's broken my heart.

(She goes, as we hear the sound of a shower and Sam singing.)

SAM'S VOICE: "Fling out the banner! Let it ride,

Skyward and seaward, high and wide!"

(Dexter comes out from within.)

BUD: How's he doing?

DEXTER: Him that hath ears, let him hear…Perhaps you'd like to stay while I investigate the extent of the damage.

BUD: Sure.

(Dexter goes off. Sam comes out in a terry cloth robe, toweling his hair. He crosses to get the Bible by the telephone.)

SAM: Where've you been?

BUD: Right here. Calling Katie.

SAM: Told her you'll take the new job, right?

BUD: Not yet.

SAM: Ah. *(Crossing back, he flashes at Bud, and exits.)*

BUD: You O.K.?

SAM: *(Reentering.)* Never better. It's weird. *(Exits again.)*

BUD: Feel like talking shop?

SAM: *(Now off.)* Sure. While I get dressed.

BUD: *(Speaking towards off.)* O.K., here goes. I'm not worried about the local news. That won't matter much. Tomorrow, when it goes nationwide, that's when the trouble starts…"Well-bred"—Or will they say "White-bread—Gubernatorial candidate delivers bizarre, highly emotional diatribe on gay rights at posh New England prep school." Not to mention the visual thing. *(Sam comes out in khakis and an informal shirt, carrying a Val-Pac and a windbreaker.)*

SAM: The visual thing?

BUD: That moment at the end when you pulled your Muskie…

SAM: I never touched my muskie.

BUD: *Senator* Muskie, Sam. New Hampshire, '72. He cried. It cost him the primary. They called it "womanish behavior."

SAM: *(Putting on his shoes.)* Maybe it got me the women's vote.

BUD: It got you the Gay vote, Sam. If that…The President will be very kind, of course. He'll give you a sad smile, and ask you to transfer to the Department of Health and Human Services.

SAM: I'll quit before he gets around to it.

BUD: O.K. So I'll call party headquarters, and say you're withdrawing. For personal reasons.

SAM: Withdrawing?

BUD: You don't still plan to go for it.

SAM: Sure. What's the problem?

BUD: Here's the problem, Sam. The media will say…carefully, of course, to avoid a libel suit…that you're gay as a goose.

SAM: They said that about Saint Paul.

BUD: Christ, Sam.

SAM: And about him, too.

BUD: Watch it, Pal.

SAM: You wait, Bud. They'll say it about you.

BUD: Fuck you, Sam.

SAM: Fuck you, Bud.

(Dexter comes in.)

DEXTER: I keep walking in on the same scintillating exchange.

SAM: I've just discovered the pleasure of saying four-letter words.

DEXTER: It's a limited pleasure, and soon will pale. I've come to say a more significant word. Namely, goodbye.

SAM: *(Shaking hands.)* So long, Dexter. I hope my speech didn't thoroughly disappoint you.

DEXTER: Well, I have to say that Mrs. Pell is giving her tennis court to Andover. And the Rector is thinking of removing your name from the list of distinguished Alumni.

SAM: Yippee! That makes it official! I'm no longer an Old Boy!

DEXTER: As for me…if you want my opinion… *(Pause.)* I was very moved by what you said. *(Pause.)* It made me wonder if once upon a time, I should have… *(Pause.)* But no. This is a good school, and I hope I've helped make it a better one.

SAM: *(Embracing him.)* You have, Dexter. You have indeed.

(Alison enters.)

ALISON: Well, what d'ya know?

SAM: What?

ALISON: What. The man says what. *(To Dexter and Bud.)* Here is a man I thought was buttoned up for life. I told him so, last night, right here in this room. And now, today, he's suddenly turning himself inside out and upside down in front of all America. *(To Sam.)* That's what. You were great, Sir.

SAM: You might have a slight disagreement about that with your mother-in-law.

ALISON: Already did. She wanted me to deny everything you said, or she'd cut me off without a cent.

SAM: What did you say?

ALISON: Never mind, but she left without me.

SAM: Then you need a ride.

ALISON: I've already found one. I ran into some folks who have room in their back seat of their green Volvo station wagon. They're headed in the general direction of my son's school. I'll stop there. Or rather start there... *(She starts out.)*

SAM: Alison. I don't know how much clout I'll have now, but I owe you a job.

ALISON: I'll remember that. I'll also remember your speech for a long, long time. Thank you.

(She goes; Dexter gets himself a glass of wine.)

SAM: Well, come on, Bud. Let's go.

BUD: What makes you think I'm going with you, Sam?

SAM: Because you love me. You admitted it yesterday.

BUD: I also admitted yesterday I work for winners. I see a loser here.

SAM: You need a ride back down, Man.

BUD: I imagine, knowing this school, there's a chartered bus headed straight for Grand Central.

DEXTER: I'm afraid there is.

SAM: That's dumb, Bud.

BUD: Ten minutes in a car with you, you'd con me out of that new job and back onto your staff.

SAM: I'd sure try.

(A hymn is heard softly: "I Heard the Sound of Voices.")

SAM: Well, I'm off, then. *(Hugs Bud.)* I'll miss you, Buddy. *(He starts out.)*

BUD: Sam! You could at least tell me what your plans are.

SAM: I thought I'd stick my thumb up my ass and go on faith.

BUD: That's a compelling agenda for the '90s, Sam.

DEXTER: And a rather lonely notion, besides.

SAM: I got it from Paul. *(He goes.)*

DEXTER: *(To Bud.)* That's not Paul. And he shouldn't say that it is.

BUD: He was kidding. *(Looks after Sam.)* I think.

(He goes. Dexter salutes them with his wine, as the music comes up and the lights dim.)

THE END

SWEET SUE

For Nikos Psacharopoulos

INTRODUCTION

This is the only play I ever wrote that made it to Broadway. (*The Golden Age* and *Love Letters* had brief runs in quirky theatres that were technically listed as Broadway, but nobody was fooling anybody.) *Sweet Sue* came to Broadway because it had Mary Tyler Moore and Lynn Redgrave playing the double leads, and their star power enabled it to run six months. They both were terrific, and good sports as well, because the reviews, at least for the play, were not good at all. I thought I was being very daring and innovative when I wrote it, telling the same story from two different angles. I told myself I was a theatrical Picasso, opening up the dramatic form, breaking the realistic mode, illuminating character in a new way—all that stuff. The trouble was that the story I had to tell wasn't strong enough to support what I was trying to do... Audiences and critics, struggling to find a reason for such a strange device being superimposed on a light comedy, tried to reduce the two Sues into various categories, such as the id and the ego, or the dark side and the light, and so forth, and what should have been a liberating lark became an intellectual exercise. I had the secret hope that *Sweet Sue* might find a life outside of New York, since it was so easy to produce and its issues so accessible, but it never did. The Japanese and the Italians, apparently, have had some success with it, but that's about it. Having said all that, I also have to say that I had a wonderful time working on it, in Williamstown where we started, in Boston where we tuned it, and in New York, when we brought it in. The play was fun to write, the rehearsal process was invigorating, and everyone connected with the produciton had a good time—or at least I hope so. I look back on the experience with great fondness, and remind myself that the pleasures of congenial collaboration are what made me want to be a playwright in the first place.

ORIGINAL PRODUCTION

Sweet Sue was presented by Arthur Whitelaw, Dick Button, and Byron Goldman, by arrangement with the Williamstown Theatre Festival (Nikos Psacharopoulos, Artistic Director) at the Music Box Theatre in New York City on January 8, 1987. It was directed by John Tillinger; the scenery was by Santo Loquasto; the costumes were by Jess Goldstein; the lighting was by Ken Billington; the casting was by Donna Isaacson and John Lyons; the production stage manager was Ed Aldridge; the stage manager was Noel Stern; the general management was Kingwill and Goossen, Inc.; and the associate producers were Norma and David Langworthy. The cast, in order of appearance, was as follows:

Susan	Mary Tyler Moore
Susan Too.	Lynn Redgrave
Jake.	John K. Linton
Jake Too	Barry Tubb

CHARACTERS

SUSAN WEATHERILL: a woman in her late forties, to be played by two actresses: Susan and Susan Too

JAKE: a man in his early twenties, to be played by two actors: Jake and Jake Too

SETTING

The play takes place primarily in the third floor studio of Susan's house in a suburb outside New York during the course of a recent summer.

AUTHOR'S NOTES

On the casting: This is a two-character play to be performed by four actors. The lines and scenes are distributed so that no actor or actress dominates the play. It would be a mistake to break the parts down into different psychological aspects or alter-egos of the characters. Rather we should see two different but complete approaches to each role, as if we were attempting to sketch the human figure from two different perspectives.

On the set: Similarly, the set should reflect this sense of sketching. Upstage, there should be shelves containing many of the props used in the play. Behind them, the suggestion of a window and a vision of suburban greenery. Clothes-trees may also hold costumes and accessories. Chairs, stools, and a cot are distributed informally around, and are introduced into a scene by the actors as they are needed. There is a love seat downstage right. Downstage left is a large table which can be converted into a drawing table, a kitchen counter or a dinner table as necessary. The overall effect is that of an artist's studio, within which other spaces can emerge.

On the staging: Scenes should overlap when possible, even as an artist's sketches might present several perspectives or positions simultaneously. It is as if we were leafing through a sketchbook, retaining an image of one drawing even as we move onto the next.

ACT I

At rise: The lights come up on Susan, sketching Jake, who sits naked, his back to the audience, downstage on a stool. Upstage, Susan Too stands by the daybed, watching Jake Too stuff clothes into a backpack. Both Susans wear jeans with shirts or smocks.

SUSAN: *(As she sketches.)* This is the way it should have ended, Jake.

JAKE: You think so?

SUSAN: Absolutely. It would have solved everything.

JAKE: Maybe you're right, Mrs. Weatherill.

SUSAN: And you would have called me Susan.

JAKE: Susan…

SUSAN: See how easy that is? Because now we have a professional relationship, Jake.

JAKE: Right, Susan.

SUSAN: I'll draw a beautiful picture, and then you'll put on your pants, and go home.
    (Susan Too turns from the window.)

SUSAN TOO: You're dreaming again.

SUSAN: I know…

SUSAN TOO: The same dumb old dream…

SUSAN: Got a better one?

SUSAN TOO: How about a short, sweet, civilized goodbye? *(She turns to Jake Too.)* It's better this way, Jake.

JAKE TOO: *(Packing.)* You think so?

SUSAN TOO: Oh yes. I think it's definitely for the best.

JAKE TOO: Maybe you're right, Mrs. Weatherill.

SUSAN TOO: At least you could call me Susan as you go.

JAKE TOO: Susan…

SUSAN TOO: I mean, we've known each other since June.

JAKE TOO: Right. *(He hoists his backpack to his shoulder.)*

SUSAN TOO: Well then, goodbye, Jake. *(She holds out her hand.)*

JAKE TOO: Goodbye, Susan.
    (They shake hands.)

SUSAN: *(From her stool; watching.)* Is that it?

SUSAN TOO: I thought so. Yes.

SUSAN: Just shaking *hands*?

SUSAN TOO: *(Quickly.)* I think I could survive a goodbye kiss, Jake.

JAKE TOO: *(Kissing her affectionately.)* Goodbye, Mrs. Weatherill—I mean, good-bye, Susan. *(Jake Too starts off.)*

SUSAN: And you'd let him go? Just like that?

SUSAN TOO: Certainly.

SUSAN: I don't believe it.

SUSAN TOO: *(Quickly.)* Jake!

    (Jake Too stops.)

SUSAN: Knew it.

SUSAN TOO: *(To Jake Too.)* How about a beer before you go?

JAKE TOO: O.K.

SUSAN TOO: We'll sit down, you and I, and have a beer.

JAKE TOO: O.K. *(He takes off his backpack.)*

SUSAN: *(To Susan Too.)* You don't like beer.

SUSAN TOO: I do. I love it. Occasionally. *(Takes Jake Too's arm.)* Come on. We'll see if we can find a good, cold beer.

    (They start off.)

SUSAN: *(Calling after Susan Too.)* You hate beer, and you know it.

SUSAN TOO: Why don't you stick to your professional relationship?

    (Susan Too and Jake Too go off upstage right. Susan returns to sketching Jake.)

SUSAN: Getting bored? Just sitting there?

JAKE: Actually, I'm psyched.

SUSAN: Well all I know, Jake, is that for twenty-five years, ever since art school, I've had to work from photographs—copying, illustrating, regurgitating, until I thought I'd totally lost track of the human form.

JAKE: And then you discovered mine.

SUSAN: Exactly! What a pleasure this is! To work from nature. To look at life directly.

JAKE: It's a pleasure for me, too.

SUSAN: Really? You mean that?

JAKE: Sure. How many guys in the world get paid twenty-five bucks an hour to sit around naked in front of a great looking woman?

SUSAN: Thank you, Jake.

JAKE: You're welcome, Mrs. Weatherill.

SUSAN: *Who,* for God's sake?

JAKE: I mean, Susan.

    (Susan Too returns with a can of beer, followed by Jake Too, also with a beer.)

SUSAN TOO: He'd never do that.

SUSAN: Why not?

SUSAN TOO: Because he kept saying he wouldn't. You'd be lucky to get him in a towel.

(Jake now covers himself with a towel.)

JAKE: Actually, this feels a little easier, Mrs. Weatherill.

SUSAN TOO: See?

SUSAN: *(To Susan Too.)* Thanks a bunch. *(She returns to her sketching.)*

SUSAN TOO: *(To Jake Too.)* I thought we'd sit here.

JAKE TOO: O.K. *(He sits on the loveseat.)*

SUSAN TOO: We'll make this a Jewish goodbye, Jake. Do you know what that is?

JAKE TOO: Not really.

SUSAN TOO: Well, you see, the Wasps leave without saying goodbye. The Jews say goodbye without leaving.

JAKE TOO: That's a good one, Susan.

SUSAN: *(Looking up from her sketching.)* That's an old one, Susan.

SUSAN TOO: *(Joining Jake Too on the love seat.)* Let's talk about music, Jake.

JAKE TOO: Music?

SUSAN TOO: The great equalizer.

JAKE TOO: Oh I don't know. I took a course this spring at Dartmouth, and the Professor said that never before in history has there been such a tragic gap between the generations.

SUSAN TOO: Tragic gap?

JAKE TOO: And this gap is demonstrated by our different tastes in music.

SUSAN TOO: Oh but surely there's music to bridge that gap.

JAKE TOO: He didn't mention any.

SUSAN TOO: How about Mozart? How about Puccini? *(Ironically.)* What about a song named "Sweet Sue?"

JAKE TOO: It must have slipped his mind.

SUSAN TOO: What? He forgot my theme song? I'll have to send him one of my greeting cards: "Lovingly designed by Sweet Sue."

SUSAN: *(Singing as she sketches.)* "Every star above…Knows the one I love…"

SUSAN TOO: *(Singing.)* "Sweet Sue…Just you…" Didn't you ever hear that song before this summer?

JAKE TOO: I might have.

SUSAN TOO: You must have.

JAKE TOO: I think maybe they play it in airports and bus stations.

SUSAN: *(Still sketching.)* So much for music.

SUSAN TOO: Well I don't see you accomplishing very much in the art department.

SUSAN: I've never been very good at drawing towels.

JAKE: *(Starting to get up.)* Maybe I'd better go.

SUSAN: No, please! No.

SUSAN TOO: *(Coming down to Jake.)* At least finish my beer. *(She hands him her beer.)*

JAKE: Hey, thanks.

SUSAN TOO: *(To Susan.)* You can put it in the drawing. Call it "Boy with Beer."

SUSAN: Or how about "Man with Can?"

JAKE: I like that better, Mrs. Weatherill.

BOTH SUSANS: Who?

JAKE: *(Toasting them with his beer.)* I like that better, Susan.

    (Jake Too picks up his backpack.)

JAKE TOO: I'll be going then.

SUSAN: *(Getting up.)* Wait! I never finished my drawing.

JAKE TOO: Maybe it's just as well.

SUSAN: I don't even have a snapshot I can copy.

JAKE TOO: I'll send you one this fall.

SUSAN: You won't.

SUSAN TOO: You never will.

SUSAN: After you've gone, I'll have nothing.

SUSAN TOO: At least I have this. *(Susan Too takes the drawing pad and pencil from her.)*

SUSAN: *(To Jake Too.)* I'll drive you to the bus then.

JAKE TOO: That's O.K.

SUSAN: I want to drive you.

JAKE TOO: I don't want you to.

SUSAN: Have you got another ride?

JAKE TOO: Maybe.

SUSAN: With that girl?

JAKE TOO: Maybe. *(He is almost out.)*

SUSAN: *(Anguished.)* Jake!

    (He stops and turns.)

SUSAN: I have my pills, Jake. Remember my pills. *(She takes them from her skirt pocket.)* I might take them. I might take the whole bottle!

JAKE TOO: Not you, Mrs. Weatherill. You're too big for that.

    (He goes out. Susan stands looking after him, holding the pills.)

JAKE: *(Finishing the beer, getting up from the stool.)* I'll be going then.

SUSAN TOO: Wait! I never finished my drawing.

JAKE: Maybe it's just as well.

SUSAN TOO: I don't even have a snapshot I can copy.

JAKE: I'll send you one this fall.

SUSAN: *(At window; looking out.)* He's gone.

SUSAN TOO: *(To Jake.)* At least listen to some music first.

JAKE: What kind?

SUSAN TOO: I'll find something. *(To Susan.)* Give me a hand here!

SUSAN: *(Turning to her.)* He's gone forever.

SUSAN TOO: Not yet. Quickly. Take over while I find some music. *(Hands her the drawing pad.)*

SUSAN: I can't.

SUSAN TOO: Please. Help me hold him.

> *(Susan takes the drawing pad and sits downstage center. Susan Too crosses to a stack of records on one of the shelves.)*

SUSAN TOO: I've got some great operas here, Jake.

JAKE: Operas?

SUSAN: He likes the Talking Heads, not Tosca.

SUSAN TOO: *(Shuffling through records.)* You like *Tosca,* don't you, Jake? Everyone likes *Tosca.*

JAKE: I don't know *Tosca.*

SUSAN: *(Trying to sketch him as he stands.)* Don't move…Hold still.

SUSAN TOO: How about this? *(She puts a record on.)* I was listening to this the day you arrived.

> *(The music comes up: The aria "Visi d'arte" from Tosca.)*

SUSAN: This brought you in, Jake. This landed you on my doorstep, with that dumb backpack and those flowers sticking out.

> *(Jake Too enters upstage, as described.)*

SUSAN TOO: Listen: She's singing about how she lives for art, lives for love…

JAKE: Sorry, Mrs. Weatherill. *(He starts to leave again.)*

SUSAN: Oh, just listen, Jake, please. Let's go back, let's start again from square one.

JAKE: 'Bye, Mrs. Weatherill.

> *(He goes out as Jake Too comes downstage.)*

JAKE TOO: *(Simultaneously with Jake's exit line.)* Hi, Mrs. Weatherill.

> *(Both Susans jump, turn to look at him.)*

JAKE TOO: Jesus. Did I scare you? I kept calling. First at the door, then all the way up the stairs.

SUSAN TOO: The music might be a little loud.

JAKE TOO: I thought I'd follow it to its source.

SUSAN: I'll turn it off. *(Susan goes to turn the music off.)*

JAKE TOO: I'm Jake.

SUSAN TOO: Who? *(She looks at Susan.)*

SUSAN: Ted's roommate.

SUSAN TOO: Ah.

JAKE TOO: We met up at Dartmouth last fall? Parents' weekend?

SUSAN TOO: Of course!

JAKE TOO: You took Ted and me out to dinner at the Surf and Turf.

SUSAN: It all comes back.

SUSAN TOO: I remember very well, Jake.

JAKE TOO: Good to see you again, Mrs. Weatherill.

SUSAN: Good to see you too, Jake.

JAKE TOO: *(Awkwardly handing her the flowers.)* Oh. These are for you. I got them at the bus station.

SUSAN: Why thank you. *(She takes them.)*

JAKE TOO: It's a pretty trivial house-present from someone who'll be staying all summer.

SUSAN TOO: All summer?

SUSAN: All summer *long?*

JAKE TOO: Didn't Ted tell you?

SUSAN: No, actually.

JAKE TOO: Jesus! He said it was O.K. He said he'd lined up two houses to paint, and I could stay right here while we were doing it.

SUSAN TOO: Well he forgot to tell me.

SUSAN: Let's take care of these. *(She takes the flowers across to the drawing table, gets a vase from the shelf.)*

SUSAN TOO: They're lovely, by the way. I love them.

JAKE TOO: God, maybe I should turn around, and grab the next bus back to Ohio.

BOTH SUSANS: No!

SUSAN: Of course you can stay, Jake.

SUSAN TOO: *(Low, to Susan.)* But not all summer.

SUSAN: *(Low, to Susan Too.)* But Ted said he could.

SUSAN TOO: *(Low, to Susan.)* I mean, what are we? A hotel? A summer *camp?*

SUSAN: *(Low, to Susan Too.)* Oh come on.

SUSAN TOO: Where will he sleep? What does he eat?

SUSAN: *(To Susan Too.)* We'll work out something. *(To Jake Too.)* We'll work out something. *(Taking flower vase.)* I'll get some water *(Goes off left.)*

JAKE TOO: I called Ted two days ago. To check it out. I made a point of calling.

SUSAN TOO: *(Snipping stems of flowers.)* You'll have to excuse Ted. He's been a little distracted lately. He's in love.

JAKE TOO: You mean with Nancy?

SUSAN TOO: *I'll* say with Nancy. You know Nancy?

JAKE TOO: She came up to Dartmouth every weekend this spring.

SUSAN TOO: Well then you know. You know what love can do.

JAKE TOO: He's been kind of spacey, all right.

SUSAN TOO: There you are.

> (*Susan returns with flower vase, takes flowers, crosses to put them on table behind love seat.*)

SUSAN: Maybe he told me, and it slipped my mind. Who knows? I've been a little spacey myself lately.

SUSAN TOO: For various reasons.

SUSAN: Which have nothing to do with love.

SUSAN TOO: I seem to be of two minds about almost everything.

JAKE TOO: I know the feeling.

SUSAN TOO: You too?

JAKE TOO: Especially when it comes to girls.

SUSAN TOO: With me, it's because I'm trying desperately to do something different in my work.

SUSAN: But that's *my* problem. *Your* problem is, where are you going to sleep.

SUSAN TOO: There's only one bed in Ted's room, so I'll have to put you in the girl's room.

SUSAN: They've left the nest, so it's all yours.

SUSAN TOO: If you can clear a path through the debris.

SUSAN: Maybe you should stay up here.

JAKE TOO: Here?

SUSAN TOO: (*Aside to Susan.*) Here?

SUSAN: Why not? (*To Jake Too.*) That daybed is perfectly comfortable, and you'll have your own bathroom. With a working shower.

SUSAN TOO: (*Aside to Susan.*) But I might want to work here.

JAKE TOO: But, hey, this is your studio.

SUSAN: That's all right. You'll be out painting houses during the day, and I don't work here at night.

SUSAN TOO: (*To Jake Too.*) I'll get you a blanket.

SUSAN: There you go.

> (*Susan Too goes off left.*)

JAKE TOO: (*Looking around.*) It's great up here, I'll say that...Light...Plenty of space...

SUSAN: It used to be the maid's room. Two maid's rooms, actually. Ted's father had it all done over to keep me happy while he commuted to Philadelphia.

JAKE TOO: So you could work, huh?

SUSAN: Oh yes. And it turned out I *had* to when he joined a commune in Vermont.

JAKE TOO: Ted says you've made it all on your own.

SUSAN: Well, here I was, stranded in the suburbs, with three small children...

JAKE TOO: *(Indicating her bulletin board.)* And a talent to draw, huh?

SUSAN: A small talent.

JAKE TOO: Ted says you were the one who designed that little face that says "Have a Good Day."

SUSAN: Ted exaggerates.

JAKE TOO: He says you have a major contract with Hallmark greeting cards.

SUSAN: I have a minor understanding with Hallmark greeting cards.

JAKE TOO: He says you're a major artist.

SUSAN: That's Ted.

(Susan Too returns with a blanket.)

SUSAN TOO: Ted has been my personal cheering section during some pretty tough times. *(She begins to make up the bed.)*

JAKE TOO: Well that's what he says, anyway.

SUSAN TOO: Well I'm not an artist.

SUSAN: Though I wish I were.

SUSAN TOO: I'm an illustrator. I copy other people's ideas. Repeat them. Pretty them up.

SUSAN: An artist looks at the world directly, and tells us the truth.

SUSAN TOO: I don't do that. I look away.

SUSAN: I lie.

JAKE TOO: Oh come on.

SUSAN: *(Flipping through a stack of greeting cards.)* I do. Look, come here: fat little Santa Clauses. Coy little Easter bunnies. Hearts and flowers. That's me. Hearts and flowers for cocktail napkins and thank you notes.

JAKE TOO: *(Picking up a card.)* This one's cool.

SUSAN: No, it's no good. You see, no shadows, no darkness. It's all bright and light and easy...

SUSAN TOO: *(To Susan, coming downstage from the bed.)* Where did I put that pillow?

SUSAN: I'll get it. *(She goes off upstage right.)*

SUSAN TOO: A friend once told me, a professor friend...how did he put it? I've devoted my career to cheering myself up. Well, in the process, I've tried to cheer up the American middle class. And pay the bills. And put three kids through college.

JAKE TOO: Way to go.

SUSAN TOO: Oh yes. I'm very proud of Sweet Sue. She's worked very hard. I don't know where I'd be without her.

(Susan returns with a pillow, putting it in a pillowcase.)

SUSAN: But this summer I intend to give her a break.

JAKE TOO: A break?

SUSAN: Yep. I intend to send her off on a good, long vacation.

SUSAN TOO: If I can.

SUSAN: Yep. Because this summer, while she's gone, I hope and pray I can do one thing…

SUSAN TOO: One small thing…A drawing, a sketch even.

SUSAN: A flower…a tree.

SUSAN TOO: Yes, a tree…I'd love to draw a tree, which is totally, totally…

SUSAN: True.

SUSAN TOO: If I can do that…

JAKE TOO: How will you know when you've done it? Will it be printed in The New York Times or something?

SUSAN TOO: Oh sure!

SUSAN: You bet!

SUSAN TOO: No, I'll be able to tell, all by myself.

SUSAN: I'll just have a gut feeling. But I'll know. If it happens, I'll know I'm good. *(She returns to the drawing table.)*

JAKE TOO: I've got a project for this summer, too.

SUSAN TOO: Yes, and I think you boys are wonderful, painting houses, earning money for college…

JAKE TOO: No, no, no, I didn't come here just to earn money, Mrs. Weatherill.

SUSAN TOO: What, then?

JAKE TOO: I came here because— *(He stops.)* Forget it. I'll tell you when I know you better.

(Meanwhile Susan has picked up the telephone on the drawing table and started dialing.)

SUSAN TOO: Well then it's a crucial summer for both of us, isn't it? All the more reason to make yourself at home. Here. *(She gives him a towel.)* Take a shower. Take two showers, like everyone else your age, and I'll see if I can locate Ted.

(Susan Too goes out upstage right. Jake Too goes out tossing the towel to Jake who comes on from upstage right. He uses the towel to dry his hair. Meanwhile, Susan is putting down the telephone.)

SUSAN: *(Slamming down the telephone.)* Well he won't answer.

JAKE: Ted?

SUSAN: He won't answer the *phone.* Here his roommate suddenly arrives from out of town and he's totally incommunicado.

JAKE: That's O.K.

SUSAN: You see, he's over at Nancy's, and both her parents work in the city. So Ted and Nancy spend the entire day…Well, I suppose you know this, you're his roommate…But they spend the entire day in bed together. *(Dials again.)* Well I'll just keep at it.

JAKE: Like Ted, huh?

SUSAN: What? Oh. Yes. *(Weak laugh, then listens. On telephone.) Now* they've put on that stupid answering machine: *(She mimics the machine.)* "We are unable to come to the phone right now…" *I'll* say they're unable. *(Into the phone.)* A message for Ted: please call your mother. *(She hangs up irritatedly.)*

JAKE: It's O.K., Mrs. Weatherill.

SUSAN: Honestly, those two.

JAKE: They get along better than any couple I know.

SUSAN: Too well, in my humble opinion.

JAKE: I envy them.

SUSAN: You do?

JAKE: I really do. To get along that well with another person…To connect that way all the time…

SUSAN: Oh they connect, all right…

JAKE: A lot of people don't, though. A lot of people never do. Ever. In their entire lives.

SUSAN: A lot of people don't need to. Some people create a working partnership just with themselves.

JAKE: Yeah I know. I read this book called *How to Be Your Own Best Friend.* That's OK, I can live with that. But Ted and Nancy have it ten times better. I'd give my left…arm for a relationship like that. *(He crosses to the love seat to put on his shoes.)*

SUSAN: I suppose when she came up to Dartmouth, they kicked you out of your room.

JAKE: Ah, well, you know…

SUSAN: I mean, there you are paying perfectly good tuition, and not being able to sleep in your own bed.

JAKE: We worked it out. Really. *(He changes into a clean shirt at the bed.)*

SUSAN: Yes well, I think there should be some restraints on these things. I'm all for sex, I think sex is a wonderful thing, but I don't think it has to consume *(She notices his bare back, avoids looking, and continues.)* …our every waking moment. We have rules in this house, Jake. I'll tell you that right now. We have very specific rules. I told the girls, I tell Ted constantly, this is not a hotel. He keeps wanting to have Nancy spend the night, and the answer is no. What we do outside, out there in the wayward world, is our own business. But this house is sacrosanct, as far as I'm concerned. I like to think I've kept it an oasis of decency in a world gone absolutely haywire on the subject of sex.

(The telephone rings. She answers it immediately.)

SUSAN: Hello, darling. Am I interrupting something? Well, guess who's here? Your best friend from Dartmouth…Yes, right here, and we've been having a lovely chat…So do you think you could possibly drag yourself over to join us?…Good. I'm so glad. Thank you, sweetheart. *(She hangs up, turns to Jake.)* He'll be right over.

JAKE: Oh yeah?

SUSAN: With Nancy.

JAKE: Great.

SUSAN: And I imagine they're very hungry.

(She goes quickly off upstage right. Jake starts out downstage right. as Susan Too comes on in an apron, carrying a tray of ingredients for preparing dinner.)

SUSAN TOO: Did you have a good day at work today?

JAKE: Same as usual.

SUSAN TOO: What color paint did you use?

JAKE: White. What else?

SUSAN TOO: Just wondered. Silly question.

SUSAN TOO: *(She gets a bowl from a nearby shelf. He starts out again.)* Where're you going?

JAKE: Out.

SUSAN TOO: Out?

JAKE: I thought I'd go to a movie.

SUSAN TOO: How will you get there? Didn't Ted take his car?

JAKE: I'll walk.

SUSAN TOO: Walk? In this town? You'll be violating the leash law.

JAKE: I'll take my chances.

SUSAN TOO: I suppose you could have my car.

JAKE: Nah…

SUSAN TOO: What'll you do about food?

JAKE: There's a pizza joint downtown.

SUSAN TOO: Don't you want to have a bite with me?

JAKE: Again?

SUSAN TOO: Why not?

JAKE: My mother said I should stay out of your hair.

SUSAN TOO: Don't be silly. Who likes to eat alone?

JAKE: *(Coming to the table.)* I don't, that's for sure.

SUSAN TOO: Well then…

(She begins to grate cheese. He sets the plates.)

SUSAN TOO: You'll have to put up with zucchini again tonight. Everyone grows it around here. And nobody likes it.

JAKE: I like it.

SUSAN TOO: Good.

JAKE: I like the way you cook it, anyhow. *(He takes a bite.)*

SUSAN TOO: Ted hates it.

JAKE: That's his problem.

SUSAN TOO: Not that it makes much difference. Seeing as how he eats over at Nancy's every night.

JAKE: Not every night.

SUSAN TOO: This is the second night in a row. He drops you off after work, then makes a beeline over to Nancy's.

JAKE: That's O.K.

SUSAN TOO: Still, you'd think he could at least wait to see Nancy until after desert.

JAKE: Maybe Nancy *is* the dessert.

(Both laugh.)

JAKE: Actually, Ted and I made a deal this summer not to be a drag on each other.

SUSAN TOO: So you end up wandering off to the movies alone.

JAKE: I end up lucking out.

SUSAN TOO: Pasta and zucchini with your roommate's mother?

JAKE: Homemade chow with a great looking woman.

(A moment: She looks at him.)

SUSAN TOO: Get yourself a beer, by the way.

JAKE: O.K. *(He goes upstage to get it from a shelf upstage right.)* And the usual white wine for you?

SUSAN TOO: On the rocks this time, please. I got a slight buzz on last night.

JAKE: Come off it.

SUSAN TOO: No, I did. You might not have noticed but I had three glasses. I probably bored you silly. Nattering on, like an old crone.

JAKE: *(Bringing the beer and wine.)* I had a ball. Really. I did.

(They toast, glass to can.)

SUSAN TOO: I suppose we'll have to do something about finding you a girl.

JAKE: I'll buy that.

SUSAN TOO: There's this sweet girl Jennifer Blum who's supposed to be around this summer.

JAKE: I met her.

SUSAN TOO: You met Jennifer?

JAKE: Does she teach swimming at the high school pool?

SUSAN TOO: I think she might.

JAKE: Goes to Hamilton? Kind of fat?

SUSAN TOO: Chubby?

JAKE: Chunky? Ted calls her thunder-thighs?

SUSAN TOO: That's cruel. *(Pause.)* But that's the one.

JAKE: I met her.

SUSAN TOO: And?

JAKE: No go.

SUSAN TOO: Didn't take?

JAKE: Mrs. Weatherill, I've got my problems with women.

SUSAN TOO: Oh well. Jennifer Blum is not God's only answer to mankind.

JAKE: No, but still. I've got my problems. I have great trouble establishing a meaningful relationship with them. I mean, I try to talk to them, I try to initiate a conversation, but to be honest with you, I give off these signals that I'm only interested in their bodies.

SUSAN TOO: Oh now.

JAKE: No, it's true. It's an old story with me, actually. My parents are serious Presbyterians, and ever since Sunday school, maybe I've been trying to make up for lost time. Women pick up on it, Mrs. Weatherill. They all think I just want to jump their bones.

SUSAN TOO: Really?

JAKE: Sure. And the terrible thing about it is...it's true! But I'm fighting it, I swear. I'm really working on it. In fact, remember I told you I had a summer project? That's it. That's my project. That's why I'm here. To make myself establish a meaningful relationship with a woman. To see if I can learn to maintain eye contact with one for at least five minutes without glancing at her, well, breasts.

(Susan Too discreetly covers her chest.)

JAKE: *(Getting up, throwing down his napkin.)* See? Now I've even made *you* nervous.

SUSAN TOO: No, no.

JAKE: Sure I have. Oh God. You know, I was planning to go to medical school up at Dartmouth. My dad's a pharmacist, and he always wanted me to go one better, and be a doctor. I was doing fine, too, I was passing organic chemistry and everything. But I gave it up, Mrs. Weatherill.

SUSAN TOO: Why?

JAKE: Because I can't get my head together about *women!* They could come in with an earache, and I'd end up giving them a complete physical.

SUSAN TOO: I doubt that.

JAKE: Yeah, I'm exaggerating. My dad says I've just got normal human instincts. But wouldn't it be fantastic if you could take these instincts, and commit them to one person all the time, all your life! I mean, my dad did that. I'd like to do it, too. *(He sits down at the table again.)*

SUSAN TOO: You'll find someone.

JAKE: You sound like my mom.

SUSAN TOO: Well, you will, and she'll be very lucky.

JAKE: Thanks.

(They eat.)

JAKE: I'll bet there are a lot of guys hanging around you.

SUSAN TOO: Not many.

JAKE: Come on. I'm always hearing the phone ring...

SUSAN TOO: Mostly business.

JAKE: It rang tonight.

SUSAN TOO: You heard that?

JAKE: You were on for a long time.

SUSAN TOO: Bud Wainwright.

JAKE: Is he a big deal?

SUSAN TOO: Not so much anymore.

JAKE: But you like him.

SUSAN TOO: In occasional doses.

JAKE: And he likes you, obviously.

SUSAN TOO: He likes baseball.

JAKE: So do I.

SUSAN TOO: Not like Bud. He *lives* the game. He has season tickets to Yankee Stadium, and he's always dragging me along.

JAKE: Hey wait a minute.

SUSAN TOO: What.

JAKE: He wanted to take you to the Yankee-Red Sox game tonight? And you turned him *down?*

SUSAN TOO: Yes.

JAKE: Jesus, Mrs. Weatherill! *Why?*

SUSAN TOO: I didn't want to go.

JAKE: Because of me?

SUSAN TOO: No.

JAKE: To keep me company?

SUSAN TOO: No!

JAKE: I'd feel terrible if you turned down a good seat at a major game because of me!

SUSAN TOO: Well I didn't, Jake. I just wanted to stay home. Unlike you, I'm not quite so dependent on the opposite sex. *(Pause.)* Oh I was once, I suppose. Too dependent. The result was, I was married much too young, and before I knew it, I had three small children.

JAKE: And then you found out what was causing it, right?

SUSAN TOO: *(Laughing.)* I suppose you could say that… *(More seriously.)* Well, I'm not young now. And I like very much being my own boss. Now. How about some ice cream? We have…Heavenly Hash or Cookie Crunch. Which?

JAKE: Both, please.

(Jake Too enters in his undershorts with Playboy magazine, gets into the daybed. Susan Too brings Jake his ice cream.)

SUSAN TOO: Next time I'll ask Bud Wainwright to take you to the game instead.

JAKE: I dunno. Can't get ice cream like this at a ballpark.

(Jake eats as Susan Too cleans up. Jake Too rolls over and falls asleep.)

JAKE: Actually, Mrs. Weatherill, I gotta tell you this: The reason I didn't eat over at Nancy's was I was hoping I could eat here again with you.

SUSAN TOO: I see.

JAKE: Sure. The movies were just a fall-back position. I didn't even know what was playing.

SUSAN TOO: Well, I'm glad you stayed.

JAKE: I mean, I'm torn. I'm into movies, I'm a movie freak sometimes, but I also like hanging out with you.

SUSAN TOO: Thank you, Jake.

JAKE: Want to go to the movies with me?

SUSAN TOO: Me? Tonight?

JAKE: So I can earn my keep around here?

SUSAN TOO: I don't like the movies much these days, Jake.

(Susan enters eagerly.)

SUSAN: Unless it's something good.

SUSAN TOO: Which it never is.

JAKE: Where's the paper? Let's see what's playing. *(He gets a newspaper from a shelf thumbs through it.)* We'll find something, Mrs. Weatherill.

SUSAN: Well if we're going out on a date, we'll make it Dutch treat. And you can at least call me Susan.

JAKE: Better not.

SUSAN: What's the matter?

JAKE: Ted doesn't want me to.

SUSAN: Ted?

JAKE: I asked him if I could call you by your first name and he said no.

SUSAN: Why not?

JAKE: He said he preferred the formalities.

SUSAN TOO: *(Who is finishing cleaning up.)* Maybe it's just as well.

SUSAN: *(To Susan Too.)* Why?

JAKE: *(Reading newspaper.)* This one's supposed to be great. It's about a teenage vampire ravaging a retirement home. All *right!*

SUSAN TOO: Think I'll skip that one, thanks.

JAKE: Just kidding. There's a French one down in the Village.

SUSAN: That's supposed to be marvelous!

JAKE: I'll get my jacket. *(He goes out right.)*

SUSAN TOO: I can't go.

SUSAN: *(Undoing Susan Too's apron.)* Of course you can.

SUSAN TOO: What? Isn't that the one about this older woman who falls in love with an Algerian beach boy?

SUSAN: *(Fixing Susan Too's hair, as if they were standing together, facing a mirror.)* You got it.

SUSAN TOO: You mean I should just show *up?* At the Fine Arts? With my son's roommate? Standing in line for tickets? Meeting the Wilsons and the Perlmutters head *on?*

SUSAN: Why not?

SUSAN TOO: What happens when we get inside? Do I behave like his date? Do I order one of those huge Cokes, and suck noisily on a straw?...
(Susan takes off her own scarf, gags Susan Too with it, and then adjusts it around her neck.)

SUSAN TOO: ...Do we put our feet upon the seats in front of us, and talk all during the show?

SUSAN: *(Standing back; looking at her.)* There. You look gorgeous.

SUSAN TOO: What do I say to Bud Wainwright if he gets wind of this? Which he will. Knowing Bud.

SUSAN: I don't know. Tell him you're checking out the Little League.

SUSAN TOO: Oh I can't! I just can't!

(Jake comes back on in a jacket.)

JAKE: All set?

SUSAN: Absolutely. Can't wait. *(Hands him the keys.)* You do the driving, sir. *(Their hands touch. There is a brief moment of slow motion. Then Susan gives Susan Too a gentle push. Susan Too exits hesitantly, looking back, followed by Jake. Susan remains onstage, watching them go. For a moment, she looks longingly at Jake Too, who lies on the cot, asleep. Then she crosses to a shelf and brings her drawing equipment back onto the table.)*

SUSAN: It's raining, it's pouring, the old man is snoring.

JAKE TOO: *(Rolling over; half awake.)* Wumph.

SUSAN: It's raining. You can't paint houses today.

JAKE TOO: *(Sitting up suddenly.)* What time is it?

SUSAN: Late. Almost eleven. Ted's off buying turpentine or something.

JAKE TOO: How come he didn't wake me up?

SUSAN: I told him to let you sleep.

JAKE TOO: Guess you want to work here, huh?

SUSAN: Guess I have to.

JAKE TOO: I'll get dressed in the john then.

(He exits right covering himself with the bedclothes. Susan begins to work at the drawing table.)

SUSAN: *(Calling off.)* Did you hear the little argument downstairs this morning?

JAKE TOO: What?

SUSAN: There was a small argument at the breakfast table.

JAKE TOO: *(Offstage.)* What about?

SUSAN: I'm not sure. Ted was in a terrible mood. That's why I wouldn't let him wake you.

JAKE TOO: *(Offstage.)* Maybe he had a fight with Nancy.

SUSAN: No, I don't think it was Nancy. *(She organizes her work as she talks.)* I think it was you. I think he's jealous of you. I really do. He's been cock of the walk around here for the past few years, and now suddenly there's this other man, sitting at the table, taking his mother to the movies, all that. I suppose Freud has something to tell us here. But it made for quite a little scene at the breakfast table, I can tell you that. Not that your name ever came up. Oh no. Never. It was all about why were the cornflakes soggy. And why couldn't we get a VCR. And why couldn't Nancy spend the night in his room. But you were the hidden agenda. I'm sure of that. *(Pause.)* Did you hear me?

(Jake Too comes partly out from offstage, hair wet, a towel around his waist.)

JAKE TOO: You were saying something, Mrs. Weatherill?

SUSAN: Just chattering on.

JAKE TOO: I was in the shower.

SUSAN: Probably just as well.

(He goes back off.)

SUSAN: Though I do want to bring up a little plan I've been hatching. Can you hear me now?

JAKE TOO: *(Offstage.)* I can hear.

SUSAN: I was going to ask you if you wanted to earn a little extra money in your spare time.

JAKE TOO: *(Offstage.)* There's not much spare time, actually.

SUSAN: Oh sure there is. Late afternoons…Sundays…Rainy days like today.

(Jake Too comes out still in his towel, partially covered with shaving cream, holding a razor.)

SUSAN: I thought you might want to earn a little extra cash, that's all.

JAKE TOO: Doing what?

SUSAN: Modeling. *(Pause.)* For me. *(Pause.)* For my work. *(Pause.)* When I'm not drawing trees.

JAKE TOO: You mean…posing?

SUSAN: Exactly.

JAKE TOO: No thanks, Mrs. Weatherill.

SUSAN: No?

JAKE TOO: No. *(He starts off.)*

SUSAN: Probably just as well. The way Ted's behaving these days, he'd go through the roof.

JAKE TOO: I'd never do it anyway, so there's no problem.

SUSAN: Fair enough.

(He is almost off.)

SUSAN: May I ask why not?

JAKE TOO: I'd be embarrassed, Mrs. Weatherill.

SUSAN: Why?

JAKE TOO: You mean naked, don't you?

SUSAN: Not necessarily.

JAKE TOO: I'd still be embarrassed.

SUSAN: That's silly.

JAKE TOO: Yeah well I would be. *(He goes off.)*

SUSAN: *(Leaving her work, crossing right toward "the bathroom.")* Now that is what I call the Sweet Sue Syndrome. I'm serious. I'm beginning to think we're all a little too prudish… *(She inadvertently looks off right at Jake Too in the bathroom, then quickly moves downstage.)* …around here. Me included. I told Ted, I told him just this morning, that I intend to stop making cracks about him and Nancy. That's his business, and it's fine. I also insist on a little reciprocity. If everyone else is going through some rite of passage this summer, why can't I? *(She furtively takes a pill, with water.)* I mean, this is an important summer for me too, you know. My last child is leaving fast. My work is lately a little the worse for wear. My sense of personal well-being… *(She puts the pills away.)* …leaves something to be desired. And what do I want to do about it? I want to stretch, that's what. I want to draw the human form occasionally. I want to develop my craft somewhat beyond the level of Porky Pig! And why the hell *can't* I? I don't see why Ted has to be the secret police around here.

(Jake Too comes out, buttoning his shirt.)

JAKE TOO: Since Ted is out every night, maybe I'd better get into some good summer reading.

SUSAN: Maybe you'd better.

JAKE TOO: *(Tossing Playboy into the wastebasket.)* Get rid of this Playboy. *(He kisses it goodbye.)*

SUSAN: Good for you.

JAKE TOO: What's your favorite book? I'll read that.

SUSAN: My favorite? Oh it's much too long for you.

JAKE TOO: Tell me what it is and I'll read it.

SUSAN: Tolstoy's *Anna Karenina*. Try that on for size.

JAKE TOO: I read it already.

SUSAN: You did not.

JAKE TOO: I did so. Comp Lit. Sophomore year.

SUSAN: And did you like it?

JAKE TOO: I loved it.

SUSAN: You did not.

JAKE TOO: It's one of my favorite books, I swear.

SUSAN: *(Looking at him.)* I'm amazed.

JAKE TOO: We should talk about it some time.

SUSAN: I'd love to do that. Anytime.

JAKE: Actually, I'm better after I've eaten.

SUSAN: Go, go, go, go.

(Jake Too exits upstage right. Susan calls after him.)

SUSAN: I'm absolutely amazed! Ted couldn't get past the second chapter!

(Jake enters from right with bedclothes. They make the bed together.)

JAKE: Ted and I had a big fight two days ago.

SUSAN: A fight?

JAKE: A big one. We were painting the Kaplan's screen porch, and he threw a whole can of primer at me.

SUSAN: Good Lord. What was the issue?

JAKE: He thinks I suck up to you.

SUSAN: He thinks you what?

JAKE: Suck up. It means—

SUSAN: I know what it means.

JAKE: He's still mad about that extra brownie you gave me.

SUSAN: But you're the guest!

JAKE: He's still mad.

SUSAN: Good lord. I'll buy a whole stack of brownies this afternoon.

JAKE: Yeah, well I doubt if that will do it, Mrs. Weatherill.

(He sits on the cot and puts on his shoes. Jake Too comes on from upstage right carrying a carton of orange juice. The two Jakes surround her.)

JAKE TOO: Maybe I do suck up to you.

SUSAN: That's ridiculous.

JAKE TOO: No kidding. Maybe I do. Do you think I hang around you too much?

SUSAN: No. Not at all. No.

JAKE TOO: Because I have such a great time whenever I'm with you. I think you're the greatest...

JAKE: I mean, of all my friends' mothers...

JAKE TOO: I think you're the best.

SUSAN: Thank you, Jake.

JAKE TOO: And I'll tell you something else...

JAKE: Maybe I'd better not...

JAKE TOO: No, I want to tell you. You were a big factor in my decision to come here this summer.

JAKE: Of course I wanted to earn money, meet a girl...

JAKE TOO: But I also wanted to see you again, after that dinner we had up at Dartmouth.

JAKE: It was a great dinner...sirloin steak...strawberry shortcake...

JAKE TOO: But we had such a good conversation, remember?

JAKE: Of course maybe I drank too much beer...

(Susan waves him down.)

JAKE TOO: But I remember thinking, hell, here's quite a lady.

JAKE: I mean for someone's mom...

SUSAN: *(Wheeling on Jake impatiently.)* Ah leave it alone, will you? *(To Jake Too sweetly.)* Go on.

JAKE TOO: Oh I don't know. All I know is if it hadn't been for you I'd have ended up working in my dad's drugstore this summer. I'd be handing out poison ivy lotion and suppositories all summer long. And now look at me: having an intense conversation with a terrific woman even before breakfast. I feel lucky as hell, Mrs. Weatherill.

SUSAN: Why, thank you, Jake. *(She goes to her drawing table.)*

JAKE: *(Grabbing Jake Too's arm, taking him aside.)* Hey, man, cool it! What're you doing? Making the moves on Ted's mom?

JAKE TOO: Just talking, that's all. Just saying things.

JAKE: Yeah well you make it sound like you want to get it on with her.

JAKE TOO: Oh Jesus. Did it come out that way?

JAKE: It sure did, man. I thought that's what we're trying to get away from this summer!

(He cuffs him and goes out indignantly, as Susan Too comes on in a bathrobe, carrying "Anna Karenina." She settles on the love seat downstage right and begins to read.)

SUSAN: *(Who has been clearing off the drawing table; to Jake Too.)* I keep thinking about that evening.

JAKE TOO: At the Surf and Turf?

SUSAN: Do you remember what we talked about?

JAKE TOO: Sure. Don't you?

SUSAN: Music.

JAKE TOO: You told me all about opera.

SUSAN: *(Getting an album from a shelf.)* And you told me all about the Talking Heads. I bought their album when I got back. I studied it religiously.

JAKE TOO: Did you like it?

SUSAN: A little. I'm beginning to like "Little Creatures."

JAKE TOO: Did you ever try dancing to it alone?

SUSAN: No. Should I?

JAKE TOO: Sure. If you want.

SUSAN: Maybe I will. Some night. Late. After a glass of wine. With the door locked.

JAKE TOO: Well I went and took a music course second semester.

SUSAN: Did you learn about Puccini?

JAKE TOO: I learned about the tragic gap.

SUSAN: Well, we got along anyway. At the old Surf and Turf.

JAKE TOO: Still do, don't we? I'll bet we connect on a lot of things. Take that album cover. I'll bet you like that.

SUSAN: *(Looking at it.)* Not much, actually.

JAKE TOO: What's wrong with it?

SUSAN: Let me show you something. *(Takes an old drawing from a low shelf and puts it on the table.)* I did this in Art School.

JAKE TOO: *(Looking at it.)* Hey!

SUSAN: It's just an apple with a bite in it.

JAKE TOO: I like that bite!

SUSAN: It's my bite. Nobody else did a bite. But it helped me shade it…see?… darken it, thicken the whole thing.

JAKE TOO: Christ, you even drew teeth marks.

SUSAN: Sure. Otherwise it would just be another easy apple for the Hallmark printing presses.

JAKE TOO: I couldn't have this, could I?

SUSAN: Nope. Sorry. I need it. It's the last thing I did before I left school and got married. I look at it now and then to remind myself that I am capable of doing things which have…well, bite.

JAKE TOO: Maybe you'll do something else this summer.

SUSAN: Maybe. Maybe something different. Maybe something better. *(She puts the drawing away.)*

JAKE TOO: You'll do it.

SUSAN: You're very nice. Of all Ted's friends, I think you're one of the…Of course, I like all of Ted's friends…But I really think you're one of the nicest.

JAKE TOO: Even if I don't like opera?

SUSAN: Even if you won't model for me.

JAKE TOO: Know why I won't do that?

SUSAN: Why?

JAKE TOO: I'm scared it would turn me on.

SUSAN: *(Embarrassed.)* Oh honestly.

JAKE TOO: It's true. Now you know.

SUSAN: Thank you, Jake.

JAKE TOO: Oh Christ, I've got to get myself a GIRL!

(Jake Too goes out quickly. Susan puts away her materials as the lights begin to shift tonight. Susan Too, on the loveseat, looks up from her book and calls out to her.)

SUSAN TOO: Hey.

SUSAN: Who, me?

SUSAN TOO: What's going on here?

SUSAN: I don't know what you mean.

SUSAN TOO: Are you falling in love with him?

SUSAN: No! *(Pause.)* I suppose you could say I'm a little...infatuated.

SUSAN TOO: I'll buy that.

SUSAN: Think it shows?

SUSAN TOO: I think it's beginning to.

SUSAN: Well it's fresh. It's fun. It's romantic.

SUSAN TOO: It's dangerous.

SUSAN: Yes! I suppose you could say it's the courtship I never had.

SUSAN TOO: Courtships are supposed to *lead* somewhere.

SUSAN: I know... *(She sits beside Susan Too on the loveseat.)* Maybe I should get away for a few days.

SUSAN TOO: Good idea.

SUSAN: Visit Harvey Satterfield on the Vineyard.

SUSAN TOO: Now we're talking.

SUSAN: I'll call him in the morning. Tell him I want to play with someone my own age.

SUSAN TOO: That's the ticket.

SUSAN: Or am I running away from the situation?

SUSAN TOO: No.

SUSAN: I could be.

SUSAN TOO: Yes.

SUSAN: Well what if I am? Is that the worst thing in the world? I'm sorry, but I'm not of the school which says as soon as you feel a spark of something, you immediately have to start fanning the flame! What's wrong with putting a damper on things?

SUSAN TOO: Nothing's wrong at all.

SUSAN: So I'll go to the Vineyard.

SUSAN TOO: Yes.

SUSAN: Throw a little salt water on the situation.

SUSAN TOO: Yes!

SUSAN: And then come back and continue my work.

SUSAN TOO: Work.

SUSAN: My summer project. My tree. My series of trees.

SUSAN TOO: Right.

SUSAN: I'll do a whole damn forest if I have to.

SUSAN TOO: Good for you.

SUSAN: Three cheers for the Protestant ethic.

SUSAN TOO: Two cheers anyway.

SUSAN: And I'll accomplish something good this summer, rather than fritter it all away on a hopeless flirtation with a kid half my age! *(Susan puts a suitcase on the drawing table.)*

SUSAN TOO: *(As a cheer.)* Go Susan!!

SUSAN: Right on!

SUSAN TOO: Where is he, by the way?

SUSAN: Out.

(Jake enters upstage left tiptoeing, carrying his shoes as if he were coming down a hall, late at night.)

SUSAN TOO: At this hour?

SUSAN: It's late, isn't it?

SUSAN TOO: It's too late.

SUSAN: I couldn't agree more.

(She goes off; as Jake comes into the light.)

SUSAN TOO: That you, Jake?

JAKE: Just me, Mrs. Weatherill.

SUSAN TOO: Well, well. Home is the hunter.

JAKE: Huh?

SUSAN TOO: Not only are we painting houses this summer, but now we are painting the town.

JAKE: Checking the scene a little.

SUSAN TOO: I thought you were just going to play miniature golf.

JAKE: We stopped at a bar afterwards.

SUSAN TOO: So Ted told me.

JAKE: Hoisted a few.

SUSAN TOO: So Ted said. When he got home. Two hours ago.

JAKE: Yeah well. Good night, Mrs. Weatherill. *(Starts off.)*

SUSAN TOO: I hear you met a girl.

JAKE: Right.

SUSAN TOO: At this bar.

JAKE: Right.

SUSAN TOO: What fun.

JAKE: It was, actually.

SUSAN TOO: Did she give you a ride home?

JAKE: Yep.

SUSAN TOO: That was thoughtful. I mean, it's a long walk from the Red Devil Bar and Grill.

JAKE: Yeah well. Good night, Mrs. Weatherill. *(He starts off again.)*

SUSAN TOO: I must say I am a tad concerned, Jake.

JAKE: About what?

SUSAN TOO: Going to bars.

JAKE: Oh come on.

SUSAN TOO: Drinking beer until all hours of the night. Riding around in cars with strangers.

JAKE: Nancy knew her.

SUSAN TOO: I wonder if Nancy knew her very well. I wonder if Nancy is particularly friendly with women who pick up strange men in bars.

JAKE: Mrs. Weatherill...

SUSAN TOO: I don't like it, Jake. Frankly I was quite worried. You should realize that I am in loco parentis here.

JAKE: My parents would be asleep.

SUSAN TOO: Well I'm not, Jake. I'm very much awake. I had another big argument with Ted about it. I told him he had no business leaving you there.

JAKE: I *asked* him to. I made him go without me.

SUSAN TOO: Why?

JAKE: So I could get to know this girl.

SUSAN TOO: And did you?

JAKE: A little.

SUSAN TOO: I still don't like it. You'll be exhausted tomorrow. You could fall off a ladder, and kill yourself.

JAKE: I won't, Mrs. Weatherill. Good night.
(Once again, he starts off. Susan enters in a bathrobe, carrying a similar volume of "Anna Karenina.")

SUSAN: I thought you and I had a little date tonight.

JAKE: What?

SUSAN: I thought after you'd played miniature golf, you were going to rush back here for our long-awaited talk on *Anna Karenina*.

SUSAN TOO: *(From couch.)* I thought that was the deal. *(She holds up the identical book.)*

JAKE: Sorry. I forgot.

SUSAN: I've started it again. I'm almost halfway through.

JAKE: I'm sorry. We were having so much fun at the bar, I forgot. Can we talk about it tomorrow?

SUSAN: *(Overlapping.)* Well, I guess if having fun in the bar takes precedence over your commitments...Well that is typical of your generation, isn't it. Boy, talk about a tragic gap. It's a tragic gulf, as far as I'm concerned. It's a tragic chasm... *(Pronouncing the "ch.")* or chasm... *(Pronouncing the "k.")* or ravine, or whatever the hell it is.

(She goes out angrily. Susan Too, still on the couch, has taken a sip from a glass of white wine hidden on the table behind her.)

SUSAN TOO: I must say, Jake, that I hope I won't have to spend the rest of the summer waiting up.

JAKE: No way, Mrs. Weatherill.

SUSAN TOO: It seems to me I've spent most of my life waiting. Waiting for my parents to finish cocktails so we could eat. Waiting for my husband to come back from work. Waiting for my husband to come back. Waiting for my children after school. Waiting for a telephone call from Hallmark. Wait, everyone said. Be patient be polite, be good and decent and true, and it will all fall into place.

JAKE: Mrs. Weatherill...

SUSAN TOO: I wonder how many women in the world have spent their lives waiting. *(She indicates her book.)* Anna does. Even after she runs off with Vronsky, she spends most of her time waiting.

JAKE: That's true.

SUSAN TOO: Maybe she shouldn't have bothered.

JAKE: She had nothing to keep her at home.

SUSAN TOO: That's right. Nothing. Except her son.

JAKE: I dunno, Mrs. Weatherill. You can get carried away. To be honest with you, that's what happened to me tonight. I got carried away with this girl. And that's what happened to Anna Karenina. Sometimes you just gotta go with it. Or you're dead.

SUSAN TOO: Seems to me she's dead either way.

JAKE: Yeah, but at least she lived before she died.

SUSAN TOO: And you want to live too, don't you?

JAKE: Absolutely.

SUSAN TOO: So, you met a girl.

JAKE: Right.

SUSAN TOO: Is she attractive?

JAKE: Sort of.

SUSAN TOO: And you like her?

JAKE: Sort of.

SUSAN TOO: And she likes you?

JAKE: I guess.

SUSAN TOO: And she has a car.

JAKE: It's her dad's.

SUSAN TOO: *(Getting up.)* Cars are wonderful things, aren't they?

JAKE: Sure.

SUSAN TOO: They have wheels, they have radios, they have back seats.

JAKE: Hey…

SUSAN TOO: No, no. I understand these things. I'm not that old. I didn't grow up B.C.—Before Cars.

JAKE: I know you didn't, Mrs.—

SUSAN TOO: Of course, then, we were all probably much too choosy about whose car we got into.

JAKE: Yeah well.

SUSAN TOO: Sounds like you've found your meaningful relationship this summer.

JAKE: I don't know about that.

SUSAN TOO: Sounds to me like you have.

JAKE: I don't know.

SUSAN TOO: I suppose she'll be coming around the rest of the summer. *(Susan enters from left with a stack of clothes which she slams onto the table.)*

JAKE: Who knows?

SUSAN TOO: Coming around. Honking her horn. Eager to take you off for some hot and heavy times in the back seat of Daddy's car.

JAKE: Go easy, Mrs. Weatherill.

SUSAN TOO: Yes well, I think you'd better get some sleep, Jake. You'll need it. *(She goes off, upstage left.)*

JAKE: *(Calling after her.)* Good night, Mrs. Weatherill.

(She doesn't answer. He goes off the opposite way. Susan packs her suitcase briskly.)

SUSAN: *(Singing.)* "Every star above

Knows the one I love"

(Jake Too appears from right. He is eating a messy-looking sandwich.)

JAKE TOO: Going places?

SUSAN: Yes. Exactly. I'm taking a long weekend. Didn't Ted tell you?

JAKE TOO: Guess he forgot. Want some peanut butter and banana? *(He offers her a bite of his sandwich.)*

SUSAN: No thanks…Anyway, you'll have to fare for yourselves this weekend. I'll be leaving in half an hour. And I doubt if I'll be back until late Sunday night.

JAKE TOO: Have a good time, Mrs. Weatherill. *(He starts out, right.)*

SUSAN: I will definitely try to…um, Jake…

(He stops.)

SUSAN: I suppose all sorts of things will go on in this house while I'm gone.

JAKE TOO: Huh?

SUSAN: What was that movie you told me about?

JAKE TOO: *Risky Business?*

SUSAN: I suppose all sorts of risky business will go on in this house.

JAKE TOO: Oh no.

SUSAN: Oh yes. But I don't want to know about it.

JAKE TOO: O.K. *(He starts off again.)*

SUSAN: Jake—

(He stops.)

SUSAN: I do have a couple of no-no's, however.

JAKE TOO: Shoot.

SUSAN: I don't want anyone sleeping in my bed, thank you very much. I know it's the only double bed in the house, and consequently very tempting, but I don't want anyone in it, is that clear?

JAKE TOO: Yes, Mrs. Weatherill.

SUSAN: Nor do I want to come home and find the liquor supply totally depleted.

JAKE TOO: O.K.

SUSAN: If you do have to drink liquor, I'd like to think you'll supply your own.

JAKE TOO: O.K.

SUSAN: I'm willing to provide the beer for you and Ted when I'm around, but I'm not going to actively contribute to the delinquency of every strange type who shows up here the minute I turn my back.

JAKE TOO: Gotcha, Mrs. Weatherill.

SUSAN: As for drugs, I believe you've heard my opinion on that subject many times.

JAKE TOO: Right. Gotcha. Noted, Mrs. Weatherill. *(Jake Too starts out as Jake enters.)*

JAKE: Where're you going, by the way?

JAKE TOO: *(Returning.)* Where *are* you going?

SUSAN: Just a weekend away.

JAKE TOO: Won't tell, huh?

SUSAN: A friend of mine just bought a house on the Vineyard.

JAKE TOO: The Vineyard?

JAKE: You mean, *Martha's* Vineyard?

SUSAN: The same. *(She continues to pack.)*

JAKE TOO: Whoa!

JAKE: Oh my God, you'll have a ball!

SUSAN: I hope so. We'll see.

JAKE TOO: Does she live near the beach?

SUSAN: Who?

JAKE TOO: Your friend.

SUSAN: It's a he, actually.

JAKE TOO: Oh yeah?

JAKE: It's a guy, huh?

SUSAN: It's an old friend. *(She packs.)*

JAKE: *(Teasingly.)* Well well, Mrs. Weatherill. Going to get a little action.

SUSAN: Don't get fresh, Jake.

JAKE TOO: A little action.

SUSAN: I mean it, Jake! Don't get smart, please!

JAKE: Just kidding. Sorry.

SUSAN: *(Continuing to pack.)* To answer your question, yes, he *does* live near the beach.

JAKE TOO: Oh boy.

SUSAN: It sounds like a lovely location. And I'm very much looking forward to a little sun and sea.

JAKE TOO: You'll get plenty of sun all right.

SUSAN: Well at least the weather forecast is good. *(She is packing a bathing suit.)*

JAKE TOO: I mean, you won't need that. *(He indicates the bathing suit.)*

SUSAN: What are you talking about?

JAKE TOO: I hear nobody wears a bathing suit on Martha's Vineyard.

SUSAN: Don't be silly.

JAKE TOO: It's true.

JAKE: This guy from Massachusetts told me at school.

JAKE TOO: They all go in nude up there.

JAKE: Then they roll around in these mud-baths.

JAKE TOO: It's a very sexy place, Mrs. W.

JAKE: James Taylor, Carly Simon, Jackie O': They all spend their time up there rolling in the mud, skinny-dipping, and getting it on.

SUSAN: I am visiting a Professor of Moral Philosophy, Jake.

JAKE TOO: Bet you wish he taught Biology.

SUSAN: I wish no such thing. He's an old friend. He got his divorce about the same time I got mine. We've seen each other off and on ever since.

JAKE TOO: You mean clothes off or clothes on?

SUSAN: Now *stop* that! That's very fresh, Jake. Really.

JAKE: Sorry.

(Susan packs.)

SUSAN: He's a very nice man. Ask Ted. Ted knows him. Knows him and likes him. Everyone likes him, as a matter of fact. He's a very likable man.

JAKE: And he likes you, huh?

SUSAN: I think so, Jake. I hope so.

JAKE TOO: Likes you enough to invite you for a sexy weekend on Martha's Vineyard.

SUSAN: All right, Jake. Have it your way. Yes.

(Susan Too comes on, carrying a beach bag and other items of clothing. She helps pack.)

SUSAN TOO: Actually, I invited myself.

JAKE: No kidding.

SUSAN TOO: He's an academic. He likes to read, look at birds, grow tomatoes. He doesn't always…

SUSAN: Make his move.

SUSAN TOO: Sometimes he has to be…

SUSAN: Prodded a little.

SUSAN TOO: Which, of course, is part of his charm.

SUSAN: Actually, it's a very different sort of thing, really.

SUSAN TOO: Very different.

SUSAN: I mean, we're older. We don't have to…We don't want to…

SUSAN TOO: We have other interests.

SUSAN: Exactly.

SUSAN TOO: Besides sex.

SUSAN: It's a generational thing, actually. Your generation is tyrannized by sex. You're bombarded with it day and night. Your music, your TV ads…

SUSAN TOO: You're obsessed by it. You think it's the be-all and the end-all. But it isn't.

SUSAN: I mean, I know sex…

SUSAN TOO: I'm no stranger to sex… *(She rubs her arms with suntan lotion.)*

SUSAN: Bud Wainwright and I had what you might call a…

SUSAN TOO: A sexual relationship.

SUSAN: After the baseball, we'd always go back to his condo, and…

(Pause.)

SUSAN TOO: The point is that there are other ways to connect to another human being…

SUSAN: Many other ways…

SUSAN TOO: You can read the same books, enjoy the same music.

SUSAN: Now this Vineyard gentleman and I have built up a very warm, very congenial relationship over the years…

SUSAN TOO: Very warm, very congenial…

SUSAN: He introduced me to opera, for example.

SUSAN TOO: Yes, we listen to opera together.

SUSAN: And there's very little sex involved at all.

(Pause. Jake and Jake Too look at each other.)

JAKE TOO: Better take your sketch pad. Maybe this professor will pose nude for you.

SUSAN TOO: I don't *have* to draw nudes, Jake.

SUSAN: I am drawing trees.

SUSAN TOO: Yes! You may not have noticed, but I am drawing some beautiful trees.

SUSAN: Which Harvey Satterfield would appreciate immediately.

JAKE: *(Starting out.)* Yeah well I got a date tonight.

SUSAN: With your barroom companion?

JAKE: You got it.

SUSAN: Fine. Have a good time.

(Jake starts off, then comes back.)

JAKE: This Vineyard guy. Is he the one who said you were just cheering yourself up?

SUSAN: He's the one…

JAKE: Sounds like a jerk.

JAKE TOO: Well, he's a very nice man.

JAKE: Well, he sounds like a very nice jerk. *(He goes out right.)*

SUSAN: *(Slyly, to Susan Too.)* I think he's actually jealous.

SUSAN TOO: Oh no.

SUSAN: Just a tad.

SUSAN TOO: No, no.

SUSAN: Oh yes yes yes. Now where did I put that beach towel?

(She goes out upstage right. Jake Too stays.)

JAKE TOO: Did you just call him up and say you were coming?

SUSAN TOO: Something like that.

JAKE TOO: Why?

SUSAN TOO: I needed a change of scene.

JAKE TOO: Why?

SUSAN TOO: I just did.

JAKE TOO: Because of me?

SUSAN TOO: No.

JAKE TOO: I'll bet because of me.

SUSAN TOO: No! Not at all. No.

JAKE TOO: Am I getting you down?

SUSAN TOO: Oh no.

JAKE TOO: Staying out half the night, pigging out in the kitchen, overloading the washing machine, forgetting to put gas in the car…No wonder you want to bug out.

SUSAN TOO: *(Crossing to love seat for her book.)* It's not that, Jake. I love having you here. Love it. It's just that I need to be with someone my own age. Just as you do, Jake. With that girl from the bar.

JAKE TOO: I don't like her that much.

SUSAN TOO: Oh now…

JAKE TOO: I don't. She's boring, Mrs. Weatherill.

SUSAN TOO: Well she seems to be boring you pretty nearly every night.

JAKE TOO: That's just sex, Mrs. Weatherill.

SUSAN TOO: Oh come on.

JAKE TOO: I'm talking about, what I'm talking about…You've spoiled me, Mrs. Weatherill. She seems so dumb alongside you.

SUSAN TOO: Oh well…

JAKE TOO: I'm serious. I mean, she's waiting out in the car right now… *(He dashes to the window, waves frantically off right and returns.)* …and I don't even want to go. I'd rather stay here, talking to you.

SUSAN TOO: I think you should let me get going, Jake. *(She edges carefully around him.)* I mean, I'm not Anna. You're not Count Vronsky. *(She goes to close the suitcase.)* We've been living in rather close quarters around here, Jake. It's natural that people might become…well, infatuated. Do you know what that word means? Infatuated? I've recently had occasion to look it up. It means "made fatuous," Jake "Made foolish." The best thing to do is just snap out of it. Get on with it. All that.

JAKE TOO: O.K.

SUSAN TOO: Talk to this girl about "Rock and Roll" or something.

JAKE TOO: Right.

SUSAN TOO: While I'm listening to opera with Harvey on the Vineyard.

JAKE TOO: Right.

(Susan returns with the beach towel, stands listening.)

SUSAN TOO: Otherwise we're just wandering around in the never-never land of infatuation.

JAKE TOO: Right. *(He starts out, stops, turns.)* Still: If I were a professor with a house on Martha's Vineyard, I'd invite you up every weekend. I'd make it an open invitation. And I'd get into bed with you every chance I got. *(Jake Too goes off quickly. Susan looks at Susan Too, then bursts into a sexy version of "Sweet Sue," using her towel as if she were a burlesque queen.)*

SUSAN TOO: *(Trying to stop her.)* Hey. Quit that. Knock it off. Stop! He'll hear you! Susan Weatherill, don't be an absolute fool!

(Susan Too finally gets the towel from her, crosses to the table with Susan imitating her all the way. Susan Too packs the towel in the beach bag, starts off briskly, then stops, and looks at Susan.)

SUSAN TOO: I don't want to go now.

(Susan looks at Susan Too, then takes a pill. They go off either way. Jake Too comes on with a beer and stands leaning against a shelf watching Susan Too go off. Jake comes on from the opposite side. He removes black paint from his hands.)

JAKE TOO: *(Looking off.)* Did she have a good time?

JAKE: She said she did.

JAKE TOO: She came back early.

JAKE: Right.

JAKE TOO: *(Gives Jake a slug of his beer.)* I missed her.

JAKE: Oh God.

JAKE TOO: I missed her more than I thought I could miss a woman.

JAKE: Tell me about it.

JAKE TOO: Do you think she missed me?

JAKE: She said she did.

JAKE TOO: That could've been bullshit.

JAKE: Right…

(Pause.)

JAKE TOO: What should I do about it?

JAKE: Do you want to…?

JAKE TOO: No, I don't want to! I don't know what I want to do.

JAKE: Remember what Dad said: Forget the women and earn the dough.

JAKE TOO: Right.

JAKE: And remember Mom's letter: Change your underwear, and trust in the Lord.

JAKE TOO: Oh Jesus. Maybe I'd just better shove off.

JAKE: Yeah well, whatever you decide, make sure you check it out with Ted.

JAKE TOO: You check it out with Ted, smart-ass. Shit, lot of help *you* are.

(He goes off upstage right, as Susan comes on briskly in an apron from downstage left with cooking ingredients.)

SUSAN: Hi.

JAKE: Hi.

SUSAN: *Black* paint today?

JAKE: We're finishing up the Kaplans' shutters.

SUSAN: Ah. *(She breaks the eggs into the bowl.)*

JAKE: *(Looking at her.)* Making a cake?

SUSAN: From the ground up. If I can remember how to do it.

JAKE: You remind me of my mom.

SUSAN: *(Not pleased.)* Really?

JAKE: She's always in the kitchen baking cakes for the church.

SUSAN: Well of course this is for Ted.

JAKE: Ted?

SUSAN: It's his birthday. Didn't he tell you?

JAKE: No.

SUSAN: Well it is. It's his twenty-first. Didn't he even tell you Nancy was coming to dinner?

JAKE: No.

SUSAN: Well she is. And so is Harvey Satterfield.

JAKE: Harvey Satterfield?

SUSAN: My professor friend. He's coming in especially from the Vineyard.

JAKE: Ted didn't tell me any of that.

SUSAN: Well it's all happening, and we're having his favorite meal, including a homemade cake, *(Looking at an ingredient.)* if I can remember how to do it. And in a few minutes I'm going to ask you to drive down and pick up some of his favorite ice cream.

(Jake sits on the stool downstage to change out of his painting shoes.)

JAKE: I don't think he wants me here.

SUSAN: Ted?

JAKE: He would've told me about the party.

SUSAN: Ted is extremely distracted this summer.

JAKE: I think he'd be just as glad if I shoved off.

SUSAN: Well, you can't, anyway. You haven't finished the Kaplan's house, and you've got that mammoth Victorian of the Millworth's still to go. *(She works on the cake.)*

JAKE: Ted's thinking of subcontracting that job.

SUSAN: Subcontracting? What does that mean, subcontracting?

JAKE: There's this guy Bobby Peretti who's also painting houses this summer. Ted's thinking of subcontracting the job to him.

SUSAN: And why would he want to do that?

JAKE: He wants to take Nancy camping in Vermont.

SUSAN: He wants to do what?

JAKE: Take Nancy camping. Maybe it's a birthday present. To himself.

SUSAN: And will he see his father?

JAKE: Didn't say.

SUSAN: Who lives in a *trailer?* Near *Rut*land? With God knows *what?*

JAKE: Didn't say, Mrs. Weatherill.

SUSAN: But what happens to you? Would you work for this Peretti person?

JAKE: He has his own crew.

SUSAN: But that leaves you high and dry!

JAKE: I could go home. Work in my dad's drugstore.

SUSAN: Why that's outrageous!

JAKE: It's cool.

SUSAN: It is NOT "cool." Ted made a deal to do the Millworth's.

JAKE: It might be better this way, Mrs. Weatherill. Really. Ted and I aren't getting along these days. To be honest with you, we argue about stupid stuff all the time. So maybe it's better to split before we start working on a whole new house.

SUSAN: No! I do not agree with that. No! *(She angrily beats the cake batter, walking around the room.)* We do not make contracts and then walk out on them. No. We do not invite our roommates to visit us for the summer and then suddenly send them packing! No. We do not make very specific arrangements to paint our friends' houses, and then hand things over to a complete stranger! Oh no! I'm sorry. That's something we do not do.

JAKE: Bobby Peretti's very good. He plans to make painting his profession!

SUSAN: I don't care if he's Michelangelo! We stick to our obligations in this family! Honestly. That Ted. He's just like his father. Things get a little difficult, a little emotionally complicated, and he wants to walk away from the whole shebang! *(She returns to the table.)*

JAKE: Look, maybe tonight I should just shove off and eat a pizza.

SUSAN: NO! We are going to have a pleasant meal, tonight, all of us! *(Goes to shelf.)* Now please. Here's ten dollars. Drive down and get some of that ice cream with the Oreos in it, and then come back and change your clothes. Please, Jake. This is very important to me.

JAKE: *(Taking the money.)* O.K.

> *(He goes off right, as Susan puts the batter on the shelf Susan Too comes out center, now dressed for the party. She adjusts her dress as if in front of a full-length mirror.)*

SUSAN: You're not going to wear that, are you?

SUSAN TOO: Why Not?

SUSAN: Don't you think it's a bit much?

SUSAN TOO: *(Looking in the mirror.)* Much?

SUSAN: Much. Much. Do you know what the word means? I've recently had occasion to look it up.

(She exits left as Jake Too enters from behind and watches Susan Too adjusting her dress in the mirror.)

JAKE TOO: Mirror, mirror on the wall…

SUSAN TOO: *(Startled.)* Oh Jake…

JAKE TOO: (Coming toward mirror.) Who is the fairest of them all? Maybe it's Mrs. Weather-all.

SUSAN TOO: Why thank you, Jake.

JAKE TOO: Here's your change from the ice cream.

(He holds out his hands in fists. She slaps his left hand. He opens it. It is empty. He shows her his right containing the money.)

SUSAN TOO: Oh, keep it. Go buy yourself a car.

JAKE TOO: Right. *(Jake Too starts off right. Then stops.)* Could I ask you a serious question?

SUSAN TOO: All right.

JAKE TOO: Did you love your husband?

SUSAN TOO: Oh yes. For a while. Yes.

JAKE TOO: Did he love you?

SUSAN TOO: He said he did.

JAKE TOO: Why did he leave you then?

JAKE TOO: Oh Jake, it's a long story.

JAKE TOO: I think I know why. He thought you were too good for him. I'll bet that was why he split.

SUSAN TOO: Oh God, I hope that isn't true.

JAKE TOO: Or maybe he just thought you were too good-looking.

SUSAN TOO: Thank you, Jake. Do you think I'm wearing too much makeup?

JAKE TOO: *(Looking at her in mirror.)* I like you without any makeup at all.

SUSAN TOO: Well thanks again.

JAKE TOO: Sure. I can appreciate a good antique…Just kidding.

SUSAN TOO: Get dressed, Jake. They'll be here.

(Jake Too goes off right as Jake comes on, now in a jacket.)

JAKE: This O.K.?

SUSAN TOO: Wonderful.

JAKE: Think I should put on a tie?

SUSAN TOO: You look fine. *(Susan Too begins to spread a tablecloth on the drawing table.)*

JAKE: Can I help?

SUSAN TOO: You can get the dishes…I'm pulling out all the stops tonight. My grandmother's silver, the works…This is what is called "putting on the dog."

(Jake helps her set the table.)

JAKE: Woof, woof.

SUSAN TOO: Oh, and Jake…

JAKE: Hmmm?

SUSAN TOO: You and I should make a special effort tonight.

JAKE: To do what?

SUSAN TOO: Not to talk.

JAKE: Not to *talk?* At a *party?*

SUSAN TOO: To each *other,* Jake.

JAKE: Oh.

SUSAN TOO: I mean sometimes you and I get rolling.

JAKE: Sometimes? All the time.

SUSAN TOO: On *Anna Karenina,* for example.

JAKE: *Or* movies. *Or* politics. *Or* even baseball.

SUSAN TOO: You see? Ted says we monopolize the meal.

JAKE: Right.

SUSAN TOO: So we have to be careful, Jake. We have to concentrate on Ted.

JAKE: Right.

SUSAN TOO: Because this is his night, after all. We're all here to tell him that. We all love him, and there's no need for anyone to go running off into the woods.

JAKE: Gotcha, Mrs. Weatherill.

SUSAN TOO: And no need for anyone to run home to Daddy's drugstore, either.

JAKE: Yeah well…

SUSAN TOO: No, I'm serious. We're all in this thing together.

(Susan enters from left with two bottles of wine. She is also dressed up.)

SUSAN: Which does not mean we have to baby him either.

SUSAN TOO: Oh no. I don't mean that.

SUSAN: After all, he is twenty-one years old now. He is a grown-up. Like the rest of us.

SUSAN TOO: Just like you, Jake.

JAKE: Oh I'm older, actually.

BOTH SUSANS: *(Hopefully.)* Really?

JAKE: Yeah. Actually, I'm almost twenty-three.

SUSAN: Hmm…Well…

SUSAN TOO: I see.

SUSAN: Well the point is, we are all mature human beings. And I think it's time to loosen the leash a little.

SUSAN TOO: Give people a little more leeway.

SUSAN: For example, tonight I plan to tell Ted that he can have Nancy sleep over occasionally.

SUSAN TOO: If he wants.

SUSAN: If she wants.

SUSAN TOO: Occasionally.

SUSAN: As long as they're discreet about it.

SUSAN TOO: If it's all right with her family, it's fine with me.

SUSAN: Even if it isn't all right, that's their problem.

SUSAN TOO: Do you agree, Jake?

SUSAN: I mean I can't play policeman for the entire world.

SUSAN TOO: I mean if people want to sleep together, why the hell not?

SUSAN: I might even get Ted a bigger bed.

SUSAN TOO: A bigger bed?

SUSAN: It might just ease the tension around here.

SUSAN TOO: For all of us.

SUSAN: People might stop being so prickly and argumentative.

SUSAN TOO: You might even model for me, Jake.

JAKE: I doubt it, Mrs. Weatherill.

SUSAN TOO: You might.

JAKE: I doubt it.

(The telephone rings.)

SUSAN TOO: I'll get it. *(She goes upstage to answer it.)*

SUSAN: I'll bet poor old Harvey missed the ferry yet again.

SUSAN TOO: It's for you, Jake.

JAKE: Oh yeah?

SUSAN TOO: I suspect it's your little friend from the bar. *(She hands him the phone.)*

SUSAN: Tell her you're tied up, all night long.

(Jake talks with his back to the audience. Jake Too comes on, now similarly dressed up. He carries something behind his back.)

JAKE TOO: Mrs. Weatherill, I've got a present for you.

SUSAN: For me?

SUSAN TOO: This is Ted's birthday, not mine.

JAKE TOO: I don't care. I was going to give it to you when I left, but I decided to do it now. *(He hands it to Susan.)* Maybe it's better than those wimpy flowers I brought when I arrived.

SUSAN: It's a record album!

SUSAN TOO: *(Reading the title.)* "Old Favorites."

JAKE TOO: Read the third selection.

SUSAN: *(Reading.)* "Sweet Sue!"

SUSAN TOO: Where did you find it?

JAKE TOO: In New York. The weekend you went to Vineyard. See? I didn't have an orgy, after all.

SUSAN: *(Reading more titles.)* Oh, and look! Cole Porter, Richard Rodgers, everything.

JAKE TOO: I bought it because it had "Sweet Sue."

(Susan Too taking it to the record player.)

SUSAN: Oh yes!

JAKE TOO: It's a tough song to find, I'll say that. I went to all those old record stores and I finally found it at a place called Bleecker Bob's.

(The music comes up: a lively rendition of "Sweet Sue." Susan begins to sway, then dance. Susan Too follows suit. After a moment.)

JAKE TOO: Want to dance?

SUSAN TOO: Now?

JAKE TOO: Before Ted comes back.

SUSAN: All right.

(Jake Too and Susan start to dance.)

JAKE TOO: I'm not too good at couple-dancing.

SUSAN: You're fine.

SUSAN TOO: *(Watching.)* You're terrific.

JAKE TOO: *(Spinning her off.)* I learned this from my mother.

SUSAN: *(Stopping for a moment.)* Let's forget your mother, shall we? *(She dances closer to him.)*

SUSAN TOO: *(Watching.)* Oh, this brings back such memories. When I was your age, we all used to dance all the time. That's how we got to know a person. By dancing. You'd dance with a man, and you could tell. That's how I met Ted's father. I was at a party, and he cut in on me, and before I knew it, he had danced me right off my feet...

(Susan Too and Jake Too dance well together. Then Jake hangs up the phone and for a moment, watches them dance, then comes downstage.)

JAKE: *(Low, to Jake Too.)* Ask her.

JAKE TOO: *(Low, over his shoulder.)* Not yet.

JAKE: *(Coming down, grabbing his arm.)* You gotta ask her!

JAKE TOO: *(Dancing Susan away.)* I said not *yet*.

SUSAN: What's the matter?

JAKE TOO: Nothing.

(He spins her off. Jake cuts in: to be there when she spins back.)

JAKE: *(After dancing with her for a moment.)* Mrs. Weatherill, could I please borrow your car?

SUSAN: *(Stopping dancing.)* My car?

SUSAN TOO: For when?

JAKE: Tonight.

JAKE TOO: A little later.

JAKE: Right now.

JAKE TOO: Sorry.

   (Pause.)

SUSAN TOO: *(Crossing to record player.)* I'd better turn this thing off.

   (The music stops.)

JAKE: *(Low, to Jake Too.)* Tell her.

JAKE TOO: *You* tell her.

SUSAN: Hey. What's going on?

JAKE: Mrs. Weatherill, when I was down getting the ice cream, I met this girl.

SUSAN TOO: What girl?

JAKE TOO: She mixes the Oreos into the ice cream.

JAKE: I asked her out, Mrs. Weatherill.

SUSAN: *Tonight?*

JAKE TOO: So I wouldn't be a drag around here.

JAKE: And she just called and said yes.

JAKE TOO: She's waiting for me.

JAKE: So I need a car.

SUSAN TOO: But the party.

JAKE TOO: I'd be a fifth wheel here, really.

JAKE: Oh hey lookit, Mrs. Weatherill. I was planning to shove off tomorrow.

JAKE TOO: I planned to give you that record tomorrow, and split.

SUSAN TOO: I see.

JAKE: But this girl…

JAKE TOO: Elaine…

JAKE: …She changes everything. I mean it was dynamite! We connected immediately!

JAKE TOO: We had a really good conversation even while she was getting the ice cream!

JAKE: And when she called just now, we were so eager to talk we could hardly get off the phone!

JAKE TOO: So I decided to give you that record tonight, Mrs. Weatherill.

JAKE: I want to stay here this summer.

JAKE TOO: I want to try to develop this relationship.

JAKE: And you know what, Mrs. Weatherill? There could be a whole different atmosphere around here now. This could be a whole new ball game.

JAKE TOO: If I can just have your car.

(Susan looks at Susan Too, then indicates to Jake Too that the keys are on the table behind the love seat.)

SUSAN: All right.

JAKE TOO: Oh thanks, Mrs. Weatherill. *(He rushes out, tossing the keys in the air.)*

JAKE: Thanks. Really.

(He kisses Susan impulsively on the cheek, then goes out too. Susan stands looking after them, holding her cheek. Pause.)

SUSAN: It's hot in here.

SUSAN TOO: Something's burning.

SUSAN: Yes.

SUSAN TOO: Oh Lord, it's the cake!

SUSAN: No it's not. I'm burning. It's me.

(Quick Curtain)

END OF ACT I

ACT II

The stage looks the same as it did at the beginning of Act I. Only this time it is Jake Too who is posing in the nude on a stool, while Susan Too, in jeans and a smock, draws him at the drawing table. Susan stands upstage, looking out the window.

SUSAN TOO: *(As she sketches.)* This might have been the way to end it, Jake.

JAKE TOO: I doubt it, Mrs. Weatherill.

SUSAN TOO: Oh come on. It might have solved everything.

JAKE TOO: What about Ted, Mrs. Weatherill?

SUSAN TOO: Ted? Who's Ted?

JAKE TOO: Six-foot three? Likes brownies?

SUSAN TOO: Oh that Ted.

JAKE TOO: That Ted.

SUSAN TOO: Ted understands I'm an artist. He used to pose for me all the time.

JAKE TOO: Yeah, but not like this!

SUSAN TOO: He'd understand I'm trying to grow in my work. It wouldn't bother Ted.

SUSAN: *(From window.)* Dreaming again?

SUSAN TOO: Trying to.

SUSAN: Talk about dreams, the boys are playing Frisbee on the lawn. What a beautiful game!

SUSAN TOO: *(To Jake Too.)* You see? You and Ted are getting along fine these days.

JAKE TOO: Since Elaine.

SUSAN TOO: Elaine?

JAKE TOO: My girl.

SUSAN TOO: Ah. Miss Heavenly Hash.

SUSAN: *(At window.)* It's as if they were in perpetual slow motion.

SUSAN TOO: *(To Jake Too.)* Does Ted like Elaine?

JAKE TOO: He likes it that I like her.

SUSAN: No rules, no lines, no one keeping score...

SUSAN TOO: *(To Jake Too.)* Well it's nice to know we've appeased Ted.

SUSAN: *(Coming downstage.)* I think everyone in the world should play Frisbee. It's the solution to world peace. *(To Susan Too.)* Do the Russians play?

SUSAN TOO: I have no idea.

SUSAN: Well they should. We should send great batches of Frisbees to the

Russians and South Africa. I think the Ayatollah Khomeini should be forced to play Frisbee.

SUSAN TOO: Would you be quiet, please? I am trying to draw.

SUSAN: *(She returns to the window.)* Now they've stopped, anyway. Oh I hate to see it end. But they're probably hungry again.

(She goes off right. Jake Too wraps his towel around himself.)

SUSAN TOO: Now what's the matter?

JAKE TOO: I keep worrying about Ted. *(He gets up.)* Maybe I should put on a bathing suit or something.

SUSAN TOO: Don't be silly. Sit down. Please.

(Jake Too does, reluctantly, with the towel wrapped around him. Susan Too tries to continue drawing.)

SUSAN TOO: Just forget about Ted. After all, Ted forgets about us. Or will, before too long. He'll graduate next year, he'll be gone, and I'll be lucky if I get a call from him once a month. Fine. That's life. Goodbye, Ted. He's free, I'm free, that's that. *(She draws frantically, then stops.)* Ted, Ted, Ted. Why does Ted brood over my life, like some God? Are we doomed to be forever at the mercies of our own children? Will there never be a time when we're free? *(She gets up, crosses to the drawing table, erases what she has drawn.)* One of the reasons I got married so young was to get out from under the disapproving frowns of my parents. Am I now to spend the rest of my days kowtowing to my kids? Oh sure, when they were growing up, I was responsible. I couldn't go tearing around. I couldn't afford to send them reeling onto the couches of the local psychiatrists. But now they're old, they're on their own, they're fine. I've got a daughter living with a twice-divorced Italian in California. I've got another involved in some bizarre menage in New York. And now Ted's shacking up right here, right under my nose. I don't pry, I don't criticize. I don't burst through that constantly closed bedroom door and scatter moral disapproval all over the rug. He has his life, why can't I have mine? Why the hell can't I take pencil in hand, and draw a few sketches of a naked man? Good Lord, am I doomed to be Sweet Sue until the day I *die*? *(She resumes her seat, tries to draw again.)*

JAKE TOO: I don't know, Mrs. Weatherill.

SUSAN TOO: And why can't you ever call me Susan?

JAKE TOO: I'll try, Mrs. Weatherill. I mean I'll try, Susan.

(Susan re-enters quickly.)

SUSAN: Because I'll tell you frankly, Jake, I doubt I'll ever create a major work of art knowing I'll end up signing it Mrs. Weatherill.

SUSAN TOO: We need a little music here.

SUSAN: Opera? Again?

SUSAN TOO: No, it doesn't work. Play "Sweet Sue."

SUSAN: No, I'm trying to get *away* from "Sweet Sue."

SUSAN TOO: *(To Jake Too.)* Did I ever tell you how I got hooked on that song?

SUSAN: My father had the sheet music. He used to keep it on the piano.

SUSAN TOO: And whenever I'd get upset or angry…

SUSAN: Why he'd call me into the living room, and sit me down at the piano bench beside him…

(Susan Too sings quietly underneath.)

SUSAN: You see, I used to be a terrible little girl…

JAKE TOO: Oh come on.

SUSAN: No I was. I was a complete hellion. I used to wander around the house, causing trouble. But if my father were home, he'd sit me down beside him on the piano bench, and play.

SUSAN TOO: *(Singing quietly.)* "Every star above
Knows the one I love…"

SUSAN: "Sweet Sue, just—" *(She stops, snaps out of it.)* And that would calm me down, so I could do my homework.

SUSAN TOO: He's dead now. And now I'm a little too old to be crooned to.

(She hands the drawing to Susan who takes over.)

JAKE TOO: Well I guess you don't get upset much any more, anyway.

SUSAN: Oh I do.

SUSAN TOO: You don't know.

SUSAN: Don't be snowed by all this Sweet Sue stuff.

SUSAN TOO: Why do you think I take those pills?

SUSAN: Sue's sweetness is sometimes chemically induced.

SUSAN TOO: And carefully maintained with appropriate doses of white wine.

SUSAN: Underneath, there's a very different person.

SUSAN TOO: Or twenty different people, frantic to get out.

SUSAN: I think that's why I like opera so much. All those different voices singing at the same time.

SUSAN TOO: In harmony…

SUSAN: Sometimes in harmony…

SUSAN TOO: *(At window.)* They're shooting baskets now.

SUSAN: Not the same thing as Frisbee.

SUSAN TOO: Ted looks more and more like his father. Remember how he liked to shoot baskets.

SUSAN: Remember how I kept telling him to grow up?

SUSAN TOO: Take charge…

SUSAN: Be responsible…

SUSAN TOO: Be like me. Be like Sweet Sue.

SUSAN: No wonder he ran for the woods.

SUSAN TOO: *(Looking out.)* They'll be hungry. I'll fix them something.

SUSAN: I already did.

SUSAN TOO: Then I'll get them a beer.

SUSAN: Leave them alone, why don't you.

SUSAN TOO: I can get my own son a beer, can't I? I can at least do that.

> *(She goes off. Jake Too gets up and starts to follow.)*

SUSAN: Hey, hey, hey! Where do you think you're going?

JAKE TOO: To get that beer.

SUSAN: But you're modeling for me.

JAKE TOO: No way.

SUSAN: But you—

JAKE TOO: It's just your fantasy, Mrs. Weatherill. I keep telling you, I'd never do that.

SUSAN: *(Calling after him.)* But I want…I want to…

> *(Jake Too goes out as Jake comes in. Susan turns to him.)*

SUSAN: I want to see you, Jake.

JAKE: That's what Ted said.

SUSAN: *(Beginning to set up her drawing implements.)* Yes, I need your help. Ted very kindly gave me permission to ask you.

JAKE: Ask me what?

SUSAN: Ask your opinion, actually. Sit down please. It's a professional question. It seems that Hallmark is trying to expand its market. They want to go a little beyond hearts and flowers these days. They want to reach out more to your generation.

JAKE: Bridge the tragic gap?

SUSAN: Exactly. And apparently your generation likes to buy cards with a sense of humor. You like to express yourselves with some sort of joke.

JAKE: Oh, I don't know much about greeting cards.

SUSAN: Yes you do. You're young. You're in tune with these things. I'm not. Actually, they rejected my last two ideas. They said Sweet Sue had fallen into a rut.

JAKE: Come on…

SUSAN: No, it's true. I'll admit it. I'll also admit the Dartmouth tuition has gone up another eight and a half percent. And my daughter on the West coast is threatening to get married. So frankly, sir, I am somewhat on the line.

JAKE: *(Settling down.)* O.K. Shoot.

SUSAN: Well, all right now. Lately I've been thinking about…life. *My* life, our life, in these United States. And I want to say something about it in my work. I mean, maybe I can do more this summer than simply draw trees. Maybe I can say something significant, and still get paid for it, by "those who send enough to care the very best."

JAKE: Good idea.

SUSAN: All right. So what I'm proposing to do is a series of cards—seven actually—based on the seven American holidays.

JAKE: Sounds good.

SUSAN: Now wait. These cards would be organized around a specific theme.

JAKE: Go on.

SUSAN: I'm proposing to connect these seven American holidays with the Seven Deadly Sins.

JAKE: Sins?

SUSAN: Sins. Sweet Sue is turning to sin in her old age. What do you think?

JAKE: I don't know the Seven Deadly Sins, Mrs. Weatherill.

SUSAN: Well you don't have to, really…

JAKE: I'm Presbyterian, not Catholic.

SUSAN: You're a human being, Jake. You have human…flaws, like everyone else.

JAKE: I'll say.

SUSAN: All right then. Bear with me. I'll start with the three obvious ones. Christmas, for example, is Greed, or Covetousness. All that grabbing for presents. See?

JAKE: I'll buy that.

SUSAN: And Thanksgiving is Gluttony.

JAKE: That's for sure.

SUSAN: And Labor Day is Sloth, Jake. Laziness. Everyone sitting around.

JAKE: O.K.

SUSAN: Now we get trickier. What's the Fourth of July?

JAKE: Ummm…

SUSAN: Pride. False pride. Waving the flag.

JAKE: What so proudly we hail…

SUSAN: Exactly. All those stupid, chest-thumping speeches…

JAKE: I'm with you.

SUSAN: Now, Easter. Or Passover. What do you think of there?

JAKE: I think of Fort Lauderdale…

SUSAN: Or churches…

JAKE: Or beaches…

SUSAN: Spring clothes…

JAKE: Beer…Burgers…Bodies…

SUSAN: Jake, pay attention. Easter is envy.

JAKE: Right. I envy the guys who go to Fort Lauderdale.

SUSAN: There you are! And I envy the girls who go with them.

JAKE: O.K.

SUSAN: *(Crossing to the other side of him.)* Let's try the next one the other way around. What goes with Anger?

JAKE: Anger?

SUSAN: What holiday?

JAKE: Let me think…Anger…anger…anger *(He thinks.)*

SUSAN: Jake, Anger is New Year's.

JAKE: *New* Year's? New Year's Day is Anger?

SUSAN: Anger that you drank too much. Anger that another wasted year has gone by. Anger that you're getting older by the minute.

JAKE: I don't look at New Year's that way, Mrs. Weatherill.

SUSAN: That's because you're young.

JAKE: I thought these cards are supposed to *be* for the young.

SUSAN: You're right. I'll have to re-think New Year's. *(She returns to her drawing board.)*

JAKE: I'm not much help to you on this, Mrs. Weatherill.

SUSAN: No you are, you are. I'm learning a lot.

JAKE: I think I'm just messing you up.

SUSAN: No, really. There's one more, Jake. I've only given you six.

JAKE: I wasn't even counting.

SUSAN: I was. I saved it for last. What have we missed, Jake? Think. I'll bet we agree on this one…

(Pause. He thinks.)

SUSAN: I'll give you a hint. It's not technically a holiday.

JAKE: Got it! Mother's Day.

SUSAN: *Mother's* Day?

JAKE: And the sin is Possessiveness.

SUSAN: I wasn't thinking of Mother's Day, Jake.

JAKE: You weren't?

SUSAN: No, I'm thinking of Valentine's Day.

JAKE: Valentine's Day? But what sin goes with Valentine's?

SUSAN: I thought lust.

JAKE: Lust?

SUSAN: Lust, Lechery, Sex. Oh I know they keep giving us hearts and flowers, but underneath it all is lust.

JAKE: Wow, Mrs. Weatherill.

SUSAN: That's what I think, anyway. That's what started me off on the whole series. That's what Freud thinks, too.

JAKE: I used to think that.

SUSAN: But you don't now?

JAKE: I'm trying not to.

SUSAN: Well I'm trying to open a few doors for people. I think if we recognize these things, it's easier to deal with them. So do you like the idea?

JAKE: Of lust?

SUSAN: Of the whole thing. The Seven Deadly Sins.

JAKE: Sure.

SUSAN: You do?

JAKE: Sure.

SUSAN: Would you buy one of these cards?

JAKE: I might. Depending on what they looked like.

SUSAN: Of course. I understand that.

JAKE: I mean, what would you draw for Lust?

SUSAN: What would I draw?

JAKE: I mean, would you draw people...doing it?

SUSAN: I might. Discreetly, of course.

JAKE: Doing it *discreetly?*

SUSAN: Yes. You can suggest these things, Jake. There's a painting in the Louvre of this woman, and this swan...

JAKE: I don't know, Mrs. Weatherill. I'm trying to get away from that stuff.

SUSAN: Now wait a minute...

JAKE: *(Backing away.)* I mean, I threw out all my copies of *Playboy*...

SUSAN: But I'm talking about...

JAKE: No, really. When I send Elaine a valentine, I think I'll just send her hearts and flowers. *(He goes out quickly upstage right.)*

SUSAN: *(Starting to follow him.)* No, but wait—
(Susan Too enters quickly from upstage left. She carries a checkbook and envelopes.)

SUSAN TOO: Cool it.

SUSAN: But he made it sound all wrong.

SUSAN TOO: Didn't I tell you? It's dangerous to play with children. Now rise above it.

SUSAN: I'll work on New Year's.

SUSAN TOO: That's it. He goes his way, we go ours. Cool's the word.

(Susan returns to her drawing table. Susan Too pulls up a stool at the end as if it were a desk, and starts making out checks. Jake Too's voice is heard calling from offstage.)

JAKE TOO: *(Offstage.)* Mrs. Weatherill!

SUSAN: Get that. Now that *is* childish.

SUSAN TOO: Instant gratification. We didn't hear it, did we?

SUSAN: No. We don't hear people who yell from way downstairs.

JAKE TOO: *(Offstage.)* Mrs. Weatherill!

SUSAN TOO: *(Finally, quietly and calmly.)* I'm up here, Jake.

SUSAN: That's it. Just…chill out.

SUSAN TOO: *(Making out another check.)* Put our wagons in a circle.

(Jake Too comes hurriedly into the room.)

JAKE TOO: Did I get a call yesterday?

SUSAN TOO: A call?

JAKE TOO: A telephone call. From Elaine.

SUSAN TOO: Elaine?

JAKE TOO: My girl.

SUSAN TOO: Ah, Miss Fudge Ripple.

SUSAN: *(To Susan Too.)* That's a good one. I like that.

SUSAN TOO: Thanks.

JAKE TOO: Did she call?

SUSAN TOO: I don't remember.

JAKE TOO: She said she called.

SUSAN TOO: Well, maybe she did.

JAKE TOO: She said she gave you a message. I was supposed to call her back.

SUSAN TOO: I remember now.

JAKE TOO: That was an important call, Mrs. Weatherill.

SUSAN TOO: I am not a social secretary, Jake.

SUSAN: *(To Susan Too.)* Good point.

SUSAN TOO: I think so.

JAKE TOO: Still…

SUSAN TOO: I do not sit by the telephone every minute of the day, taking cryptic messages. Though you may not believe it, Jake, I have other things on my mind. Such as these bills.

JAKE TOO: *(Starting out.)* O.K., Mrs. Weatherill.

SUSAN TOO: Frankly, I thought it was your former little friend from the bar.

JAKE TOO: *(Exploding.)* It was Elaine!

SUSAN TOO: *(Exploding.)* Well how am I supposed to know that? She doesn't say who she is! She doesn't announce herself.

SUSAN: *(To Susan Too.)* Go easy…

SUSAN TOO: I was always taught to say exactly who I was, first thing, on the telephone. It's known as manners.

SUSAN: Touché.

JAKE TOO: You don't like her, do you?

SUSAN TOO: I don't know her.

JAKE TOO: I can tell you don't like her.

SUSAN TOO: I've never met her, Jake. For some reason, you never bring her around.

JAKE TOO: She says you sound very cold on the telephone.

SUSAN TOO: That's her problem.

JAKE TOO: She gets nervous every time she calls.

SUSAN TOO: Well then maybe she shouldn't call quite so often.

JAKE TOO: We have to communicate, Mrs. Weatherill. We have to make plans.

SUSAN TOO: Then perhaps you could try to do that more on your own time.

JAKE TOO: *(Exasperatedly.)* Oh Jesus. *(He walks out upstage right.)*

SUSAN: Well done.

SUSAN TOO: *(Returning to her checks.)* Thank you.

SUSAN: Mayday, Mayday! Here he comes again.

SUSAN TOO: Your turn.

SUSAN: Gladly.

(Jake enters from downstage right.)

JAKE: What have you got against her, Mrs. Weatherill?

SUSAN: *(As she works.)* Who?

JAKE: *Elaine.*

SUSAN: Not a thing.

JAKE: Tell me.

SUSAN: Jake, I've got to get this *done.*

JAKE: I want to know.

SUSAN: All right, Jake: frankly, I think you can do better.

SUSAN TOO: That's good. That's constructive.

JAKE: What does that mean?

SUSAN: Well it might mean that she sounds a little, well, cheap.

JAKE: She goes to *Skid*more College!

SUSAN: I can't help that, Jake. All I know is there's some strange, breathy little voice on the other end of the telephone which I keep thinking is that bar girl you wanted to get rid of.

SUSAN TOO: *(Looking up from her checks.)* Don't overdo it.

SUSAN: Sorry.

JAKE: They are not the same type at all!

SUSAN: Apparently not.

JAKE: This girl is very important to me!

SUSAN: Apparently.

JAKE: I'm becoming very involved with her, Mrs. Weatherill!

SUSAN: Well you see, I didn't know. You didn't tell me. I had no idea your entire future depended on that teeny, tiny little voice.

JAKE: Oh Jesus! *(He storms out right.)*

SUSAN: *(Getting up to follow him.)* I'm sorry, Jake, that was very cruel…

SUSAN TOO: *(Holding her back.)* Hold on…Calm down…

(Jake Too comes in quickly from upstage right.)

JAKE TOO: *(Angrily.)* She didn't call *today,* did she?

SUSAN TOO: Are you speaking to me in that tone of voice?

JAKE TOO: *(Sarcastically.)* A thousand pardons, Mrs. Weatherill, ma'am, but by any chance did Elaine call today?

SUSAN TOO: Today?

JAKE TOO: While I was at work.

SUSAN TOO: I don't know.

JAKE TOO: You don't *know?*

SUSAN TOO: I had to go out, Jake. I had to buy food. I had to take things to the cleaners.

SUSAN: I had to get the toaster fixed. For the second time this summer.

(Jake enters from downstage right.)

JAKE: Didn't you put the answering machine on?

SUSAN: I forgot.

JAKE: I can't *believe* you didn't put the machine on.

SUSAN: I for*got.*

JAKE: Shit.

SUSAN: I do not appreciate that language, Jake.

JAKE: She's been probably trying to get me all afternoon! *(He grabs the telephone, dials, his back to the audience.)*

JAKE TOO: Shit, shit, shit! *(He starts to leave then turns back.)* We have to talk about this.

SUSAN TOO: What else is there to say?

JAKE TOO: We used to get along so well.

SUSAN: I just don't like it, Jake.

JAKE TOO: O.K. I'll tell her not to call here anymore.

SUSAN TOO: That would be helpful.

JAKE TOO: And I'll try to stay out of your way.

SUSAN: That might make sense.

JAKE TOO: I dunno. You and I had such a good thing going. Pisses me off some-how. *(He goes out upstage right.)*

SUSAN: Oh God. *(Starts to follow him.)*

SUSAN TOO: *(Restraining her.)* Leave it alone.

SUSAN: But he—

SUSAN TOO: Leave it *alone!* Just…go about your business…Just keep it…business as usual.

JAKE: *(On telephone.)* O.K.…See you later…You, too. *(Hangs up, turns to Susan.)* She got home all right.

SUSAN: Good. I'm glad.

(Jake starts out.)

SUSAN: Jake…

(He stops.)

SUSAN: I'm sorry if I've been disagreeable. I've been a little tired lately.

JAKE: O.K., forget it, Mrs. Weatherill.

SUSAN: All this is very new to me. Having you here all summer. Nancy coming and going, a lot of doors opening and closing all night long. I've been having trouble sleeping.

JAKE: I didn't know that, Mrs. Weatherill.

SUSAN: Oh I'm all right. I'm fine. I'll survive.

SUSAN TOO: I won't hurl myself under a train like Anna Karenina.

SUSAN: Actually, I had a doctor's appointment. That's really why I went out. He gave me some new pills. Pills continue to be the solution for Sweet Sue. *(She sits down behind the table.)*

JAKE: We'll be quieter, Mrs. Weatherill. I swear.

SUSAN: No, no. It's just that I'm a silly old-fashioned suburban lady without a husband, and I don't always…I'm not used to…Oh dear. *(She tries not to cry.)*

JAKE: *(Going to her, standing behind her.)* Oh, hey, Mrs. Weatherill.
(He puts his hands on her shoulders. She puts her face against his hand. There is a moment. Susan Too is shocked.)

SUSAN TOO: This Elaine. Will you be seeing her tonight?

JAKE: Sure.

SUSAN TOO: Tell you what: Why don't you bring her around?

JAKE: Around?

SUSAN TOO: So I can meet her, Jake. That way, the next time she calls, I'll be able to connect a face with a voice.

SUSAN: I won't feel quite so much like an answering service.

SUSAN TOO: Maybe I've got her all wrong.

SUSAN: I'd love to meet her, Jake.

SUSAN TOO: So bring her around.

JAKE: I don't want to, Mrs. Weatherill.

SUSAN TOO: Why not?

JAKE: I can't put you and Elaine together.

SUSAN TOO: Are you ashamed of her?

JAKE: NO! Not ashamed…! She's the greatest girl I've ever met! *(He goes off upstage right.)*
(Pause.)

SUSAN: *(As they clean up.)* Well. She can't be *that* great. Ted says she's quite short, actually…tiny…minuscule.

SUSAN TOO: Compared to Nancy. *(Pause.)* Who seems gigantic. *(Pause.)* I thought we did very well just then.

SUSAN: Are you losing your marbles?

SUSAN TOO: I thought we did very well. For the most part.

SUSAN: Was that a crack?

SUSAN TOO: Not really.

SUSAN: That was a crack, wasn't it?

SUSAN TOO: I just don't believe in going to pieces.

SUSAN: Oh God.

SUSAN TOO: I suppose you did it so he'd have to touch you.

SUSAN: WHAT? As if I weren't onto all your phony "bring her around" stuff.

SUSAN TOO: I simply wanted to bring her into the picture.

SUSAN: You simply wanted to throttle her with your bare hands.

SUSAN: I will not dignify that remark with an answer.
(Jake Too enters from upstage right and throws himself discouragedly onto the daybed.)

SUSAN: We're not in sync any more, are we?

SUSAN TOO: Not much. No.

SUSAN: I suppose the psychiatrists have a word for it.

SUSAN TOO: Do you think we should see one?

SUSAN: I don't know. He'd probably charge us double.

SUSAN TOO: I know what he'd say anyway.

SUSAN: What?

SUSAN TOO: He'd say we're sidestepping our own feelings. He'd say we're just tossing the ball back and forth between ourselves. He'd say we've done this all summer.

SUSAN: He'd say we've done this all our lives.

SUSAN TOO: Yes…

SUSAN: Well it's not working. I don't know who I am anymore.

SUSAN TOO: I know one thing.

SUSAN: What's that?

SUSAN TOO: I think it's time I got married. *(She goes off upstage left.)*

SUSAN: *(Following her.)* What? When? Who to?

(She goes off as Jake Too turns on the radio by his bed. Rock music, the Talking Heads, comes up loudly. He gets up and dances wildly to it, then Susan Too appears as if at the door.)

SUSAN TOO: Jake? May I come in?

JAKE TOO: *(Embarrassed; throwing himself on the bed.)* It's your studio.

(She comes in hesitantly.)

SUSAN TOO: May I turn off the music?

JAKE TOO: It's your radio, too.

(She turns off the radio; pause.)

SUSAN TOO: Jake, what would you say if I got married?

JAKE TOO: What would Ted say, you mean?

SUSAN TOO: I know what Ted would say. Ted would say fine.

JAKE TOO: *(Sitting up.)* To this guy on Martha's Vineyard?

SUSAN TOO: Harvey Satterfield.

JAKE TOO: You mean he's asked you?

SUSAN TOO: Many times.

JAKE TOO: How come you haven't done it?

SUSAN TOO: I didn't think I loved him.

JAKE TOO: But you do now?

SUSAN TOO: I like him very much. We get along extremely well. If I put one of those ads in the *New York Review of Books* describing exactly what I wanted as a companion, Harvey would fill the bill perfectly.

JAKE TOO: Oh yeah?

SUSAN TOO: *(Coming downstage.)* I just called him, and asked if I could come visit again, and he suggested I stay for a whole week, which means he'll ask me to marry him. If he doesn't, goddammit, I'll ask *him.*

JAKE TOO: *(Getting up.)* Go for it, Mrs. Weatherill.

SUSAN TOO: Think I should?

JAKE TOO: Sure. Go ahead. Make your move.

SUSAN TOO: Maybe you just want to get rid of me, so you can have a huge orgy all over the house.

JAKE TOO: Maybe you'll have your own up there, Mrs. Weatherill.

(Pause.)

SUSAN TOO: I'm not sure I love him, Jake.

JAKE TOO: Do you love anyone else?

SUSAN TOO: No. Of course not…No.

JAKE TOO: Then maybe you love him, and don't know it.

SUSAN TOO: I doubt that, Jake.

JAKE TOO: It can happen, you know. You can be passionate about a person, and not even realize it.

SUSAN TOO: Oh yes?

JAKE TOO: It happened to me. This summer.

SUSAN TOO: With Elaine?

JAKE TOO: With you.

SUSAN TOO: With *me?*

JAKE TOO: With you, Mrs. Weatherill.

SUSAN TOO: How with me?

JAKE TOO: Don't you remember how I got hung up on you the first part of the summer? Don't you remember?

SUSAN TOO: Oh yes.

JAKE TOO: You called it infatuation, but it was more than that. I'd never met a woman like you before. Ever. So intelligent. So complicated. So on top of things.

SUSAN TOO: Oh, that's just because I'm older.

JAKE TOO: You changed my life, Mrs. Weatherill.

SUSAN TOO: How did I do that?

JAKE TOO: Remember I told you I thought of women as sex objects…

SUSAN TOO: I remember…

JAKE TOO: How I'd be trying to make conversation, and take them seriously, when all I really wanted to do was grab their tits.

SUSAN TOO: *(Ironically.)* I believe I recall some such concern.

JAKE TOO: Well that was my problem. I didn't know how to treat a woman. Until I met you.

(Jake enters quickly from upstage right.)

JAKE: And there's one other thing I want to say.

SUSAN TOO: What?

JAKE: For a while I even thought I might be gay.

SUSAN TOO: Gay?

374 A.R. GURNEY

JAKE TOO: Oh not *gay,* really.

JAKE: Or something like it. Because I couldn't deal with women in a real way. I used to go to church every Sunday, and pray like crazy: "Please, God. Straighten me out with women. Don't let me go gay. Don't make me spend my life selling antiques."

SUSAN TOO: Oh I'm sure every young boy…

JAKE: No, it continued. Even at Dartmouth, I thought I might be gay.

JAKE TOO: Not gay, exactly. Jesus, I went out with girls, made out with them, all that.

JAKE: But I wasn't really connecting with them. I was just using them, going through the motions.

JAKE TOO: I mean, I *liked* them.

JAKE: I just liked the guys more.

JAKE TOO: In certain *areas.* Hanging out. Drinking beer. Skiing. Playing football or Frisbee…

JAKE: But whenever girls got involved, they always seemed to mess it up.

JAKE TOO: In those areas, at least.

JAKE: So I secretly thought I might be this closet gay.

JAKE TOO: Well maybe not *gay…*

JAKE: Yes, *gay,* actually. Even at Dartmouth, that's what I thought I might be.

SUSAN TOO: *(Sitting on the stool, downstage.)* What made you decide to focus your orientation?

JAKE TOO: You.

SUSAN TOO: Me?

JAKE: You, Mrs. Weatherill.

SUSAN TOO: Good Lord, what did I do?

JAKE TOO: You took me out to dinner.

JAKE: Up at Dartmouth. On Parents' Day.

JAKE TOO: You took me to the Surf and Turf.

JAKE: You talked to me…

JAKE TOO: You listened… You took me seriously…

SUSAN TOO: Oh well. Big deal.

JAKE: No, I'm serious, Mrs. Weatherill. That's what did it.

JAKE TOO: I thought you were awesome.

JAKE: That's why I came here this summer.

JAKE TOO: I thought I wanted to meet a girl.

JAKE: But now I know it was really just to meet you.

SUSAN TOO: How do you do.

JAKE: I'm serious, Mrs. Weatherill.

JAKE TOO: I'm really serious.

> *(Pause.)*

SUSAN TOO: So you came.

JAKE TOO: Right. And you didn't treat me like a kid, or student…

JAKE: At least most of the time you didn't…

JAKE TOO: I mean, there you were, this gorgeous woman…

JAKE: Who was my roommate's *mother,* for God's sake…

JAKE TOO: But gorgeous…

JAKE: But a mature woman…

JAKE TOO: Not old, though. I don't mean old…

JAKE: Just sort of mellow, actually. Just sort of ripe…

JAKE TOO: But gorgeous. Really gorgeous, sometimes…

> *(Susan Too sways in appreciation.)*

JAKE: So here was this gorgeous woman, coming on to me…

JAKE TOO: Not coming on. I don't mean coming on…

JAKE: Treating me like you *could* come on…

JAKE TOO: Treating me like a man.

JAKE: That's it. Treating me like a man. That's what happened here this summer, Mrs. Weatherill.

JAKE TOO: I fell in love with you this summer, Mrs. Weatherill.

JAKE: Because you treated me like a man.

> *(Pause.)*

SUSAN TOO: Well you are. You are a man. It's not too tough to treat you like one.

JAKE: *(Getting his jacket from behind the love seat.)* Well all I know, Mrs. Weatherill, is that if it hadn't been for you, I'd never have fallen in love with Elaine.

SUSAN TOO: I see.

JAKE: And because of you, I've also decided to get back into the premed program at Dartmouth. I think I can be a decent doctor now, rather than just a rapist in residence. *(With a glance at Jake Too.)*

SUSAN TOO: That's fine, Jake.

JAKE: God, this is incredible! Here I am, making an important career choice and developing an intense new personal relationship! All because of you, Mrs. Weatherill! You've saved my life. It's as simple as that. *(He goes out right.)*

JAKE TOO: *(Looking after him.)* Sometimes I think that's all a crock.

SUSAN TOO: A crock?

JAKE TOO: About me and Elaine. Sometimes I think I'm just glomming onto her so I don't glom onto you.

SUSAN TOO: Oh, Jake… *(She stands up.)*

JAKE TOO: I mean it. That's why I keep you apart. I'm scared if I put you two together, you'd blow her away.

SUSAN TOO: Oh heavens…

JAKE TOO: Yeah well at least you started the ball rolling in the right direction, Mrs. Weatherill.

SUSAN TOO: Toward Elaine.

JAKE TOO: Right. And the same might be true for you and that guy on the Vineyard.

SUSAN TOO: Harvey Satterfield.

JAKE TOO: Right. I mean, you might love him now.

SUSAN TOO: You think so?

JAKE TOO: You might.

SUSAN TOO: And you think you started that ball rolling for me, Jake?

JAKE TOO: Maybe. I could have. I hope I did.

SUSAN TOO: Well. Let's hope you're right.

JAKE TOO: You think you'll marry him?

SUSAN TOO: I think I'd better.

JAKE TOO: Mrs. Weatherill…

SUSAN TOO: Yes?

JAKE TOO: May I kiss the bride?

(Pause.)

SUSAN TOO: All right.

(She stands stiffly. He approaches her. She presents her cheek. He kisses it. She almost holds him, but doesn't finally.)

SUSAN TOO: You'll be late for Elaine.

JAKE TOO: Right.

(He starts off quickly upstage right. She stands in the same spot, enthralled. He stops upstage, comes back down immediately.)

JAKE TOO: Mrs. Weatherill…

SUSAN TOO: DON'T, don't, don't say anything more!

JAKE TOO: *(Whispering.)* Ted's down there. His door is open. I think he heard what we said.

SUSAN TOO: I'd better—talk to him.

(She goes off quickly downstage right. Jake Too follows as Jake enters from upstage right holding a bloody handkerchief to his nose. Susan comes on immediately behind him.)

SUSAN: What happened?

JAKE: I guess he landed one.

SUSAN: I thought you were taking a good long walk together.

JAKE: We got as far as the end of the driveway.

SUSAN: *(Getting a cloth.)* Let me help.

JAKE: Help Ted. He looks worse than I do.

SUSAN: Ted's got Nancy.

JAKE: He asked what the story was.

SUSAN: I *told* him. I said you may have had a little crush on me.

JAKE: I said I'd been in love with you since Dartmouth.

SUSAN: Oh Jake…

JAKE: I said it was over now. Or I hoped it was.

SUSAN: Oh gosh.

JAKE: I'm glad I told him. I felt good telling him.

SUSAN: Oh boy, oh boy.

JAKE: He wanted to know if it was true for you.

SUSAN: What did you say?

JAKE: I said NO! No way! I said you might be just a little infatuated. That's when he hit me. And I hit him back.

SUSAN: I'll talk to him again.

JAKE: He told me to shove off. *(He gets his backpack out from under the daybed.)*

SUSAN: No. No. Now wait. Please. I know I can clear this up.

(Susan goes out downstage right as Susan Too enters upstage right.)

SUSAN TOO: Ted says he's leaving, too.

JAKE: Why?

SUSAN TOO: He wants to visit his father.

JAKE: Oh yeah?

SUSAN TOO: With Nancy.

JAKE: No kidding.

SUSAN TOO: He wants to *stay* there, Jake. He says he's sold his father short.

JAKE: He'll be back.

SUSAN TOO: Who knows? Maybe not.

JAKE: Come on, Mrs. Weatherill.

SUSAN TOO: I've lost him, Jake. I think I've lost him.

JAKE: Oh no.

SUSAN TOO: *(Crossing to drawing table.)* I've lost my job, too. Did you know that? Hallmark called last week and canceled our arrangement.

JAKE: Those bastards.

SUSAN TOO: All because of my Seven Deadly Sins.

JAKE: I liked that idea.

SUSAN TOO: It was dumb, Jake. A dumb idea. How could I be so dumb?
    (Susan comes back in from right.)

SUSAN: I just called up Harvey at the Vineyard and told him I couldn't come.
    He offered me a rain check. Tomorrow, next week, any time. But I won't
    go. *(She sits on the love seat.)*

JAKE: You should, Mrs. Weatherill.

SUSAN: I can't, Jake. It's not a solution.
    (Jake Too comes on from right; he carries a check.)

JAKE TOO: The "boss" just paid me off. *(He hands it to Jake.)*

SUSAN: At least you're speaking.

JAKE TOO: Oh sure. Nancy even made us shake hands.

JAKE: We won't room together next fall, we agreed to that.

JAKE TOO: But at least we exchanged words.

SUSAN: *(Getting up.)* Oh, then maybe we're all jumping the gun.

SUSAN TOO: *(Coming around the table.)* Maybe nobody should leave until we
    talk.

SUSAN: Talk things out.

SUSAN TOO: Yes. Sit down. Have a beer. Say goodbye in a civilized fashion,
    which is what I've wanted all along.

SUSAN: Get Ted and we'll talk.

JAKE TOO: He's gone, Mrs. Weatherill.

SUSAN: Gone?

SUSAN TOO: Without saying goodbye?

JAKE TOO: He'll call from his dad's. He said he had to get out of this house.

JAKE: *(Taking up his backpack.)* He told me to go too.

JAKE TOO: That was part of the deal. *(He goes to dial the telephone.)*

SUSAN: *(To Jake.)* But what about your job?

SUSAN TOO: You have an obligation.

SUSAN: The Millworth's house is only half done.

SUSAN TOO: You can't just walk away from a half-painted house.

JAKE: Bobby Peretti's taking over.

SUSAN: But you need the money! For college!

JAKE: I'll survive.

JAKE TOO: *(On telephone.)* May I speak to Elaine, please?

SUSAN: At least let me drive you to the bus.

JAKE: That's O.K.

SUSAN: I want to do it.

JAKE: *(Starting out upstage right.)* I'm not going to the bus.

JAKE TOO: *(On telephone.)* Hi. *(Turns upstage.)*

SUSAN: Are you going over to her house?

JAKE: I think so.

SUSAN: You mean, stay there?

JAKE: I think.

SUSAN: You mean you'll hang around there the rest of the summer?

JAKE: Maybe I can work for Bobby Peretti.

(Jake Too continues to talk on the telephone.)

SUSAN TOO: Well. Everyone seems to have solved their problems very nicely this summer.

SUSAN: You…Ted…Nancy…Elaine…

(They begin to swirl around Jake.)

SUSAN TOO: Bobby Peretti…

SUSAN: Even Ted's father seems to have come out ahead.

SUSAN TOO: Everyone gets a happy ending.

SUSAN: Except me.

JAKE: Oh, Mrs. Weatherill…

SUSAN: I'm kind of left holding the bag.

SUSAN TOO: Sweet Sue…Just you.

JAKE: Oh hey.

SUSAN: I'm left with a broken washing machine, for example.

JAKE: I didn't break the—

SUSAN: You overloaded it. Twice.

SUSAN TOO: And you spilled beer on the carpet.

JAKE: That wasn't me.

SUSAN TOO: There is a huge spot!

JAKE: I'll pay for it, right now.

SUSAN: It's not the money, Jake.

SUSAN TOO: It's not the money at all.

SUSAN: It's just that I'm beginning to feel a little exploited around here…

SUSAN TOO: I mean, I devoted my summer to you…

SUSAN: Gave you my work space…

SUSAN TOO: Gave you everything you wanted…

SUSAN: Free room. Free board. Free love…

JAKE: Oh now, come on…

SUSAN: And what happens? I lose my job, I lose my son, I'm left here stranded…

JAKE TOO: *(Into telephone.)* Call you back. There's trouble here… *(He hangs up.)*

SUSAN TOO: I mean, what am I? A doormat? A meal ticket? A cleaning woman?

SUSAN: I am an artist! That's what I am! And I've wasted my valuable summer because of you!

SUSAN TOO: And when I asked you do me one favor.

SUSAN: One small favor…

SUSAN TOO: One easy thing, which might help me in my work.

SUSAN: Might help me develop and stretch and grow beyond this grim suburban prison I've been locked in half my life…

JAKE TOO: O.K., O.K.

SUSAN TOO: And for which I offered to pay twenty-five dollars an hour…

JAKE: *(Exploding.)* ALL RIGHT, MRS. WEATHERILL! *(He begins ripping off his clothes.)* I'll model for you! I'll model for you right now! *(He throws off his clothes.)* Here I am! Is this what you want? Want to see me naked, Mrs. Weatherill? Here I am! Draw me! *(He sits on the stool defiantly, facing her, echoing the same position we saw at the start of both acts.)* Go on, Susan! Draw me! Get me down pat!

(Susan hides her face in her hands. Susan Too turns away.)

SUSAN: Oh, Jake.

JAKE TOO: Oh Jesus…I guess I kind of went overboard, didn't I? I guess I kind of freaked out. *(He hurries down, and begins to pick up the scattered clothes, handing them to Jake.)* Here's your pants. Here's your shirt…Here's your shoes. *(To Susan.)* I apologize, Mrs. Weatherill. I want to apologize for my rude behavior. *(He helps Jake get dressed, then kneels beside him.)*

SUSAN TOO: I love you, Jake.

JAKE TOO: Mrs. Weatherill…

SUSAN: No, I do. I love you.

JAKE TOO: Hey, Mrs. Weatherill…

SUSAN: No, I do. I think about you all the time.

SUSAN TOO: I dream about you.

SUSAN: You're on my mind every minute of the day.

JAKE TOO: It's not love, Mrs. Weatherill. It's just infatuation.

SUSAN: Oh is that it? Infatuation…

SUSAN TOO: Not love?

SUSAN: It's not love when I rush to the window to get one last glimpse of you as you leave in the morning. It's not love when I'm waiting at that same window from four-thirty on, peering down the street, waiting for you to come home. It's not love when I hear your voice in the house; and I drop whatever I'm doing to come down and offer you food, beer, anything, so I have an excuse to be in the same room with you. Or when I ask you the silliest questions…

SUSAN TOO: How was your day?

SUSAN: What color paint did you use?

SUSAN TOO: How are the Red Sox doing?

SUSAN: Anything, so we can talk, so I can talk, so I can hold you here a little longer…

JAKE: Mrs. Weatherill…

SUSAN: No, please. Don't stop me now. It took me so long to get started…

SUSAN TOO: Besides I'm learning something…

SUSAN: I'm learning from the younger generation…

SUSAN TOO: I'm learning what love is not.

SUSAN: So it's not love, is it, when all my conversations with my son, my own son, my only son, are always about you.

SUSAN TOO: Tell me about him, Ted. Tell me about his family.

SUSAN: What's he like at school?

SUSAN TOO: Does he have many friends?

SUSAN: Does he have many girls?

SUSAN TOO: Tell me more, tell me all, tell me anything.

SUSAN: But that's not love.

SUSAN TOO: Oh well then, Jake, if it's not love, then after all these years, I don't know what love is. Because this is like nothing I've ever felt before, ever. Not with my poor, lost husband during those sweet first years of our marriage. Not with Bud Wainwright. Not with Harvey Satterfield on the Vineyard this summer. Well, all I know is I'm sick, Jake, I'm falling apart, I'm dying, even though you assure me it's not love.
(Pause.)

JAKE: *(Quietly; sincerely; to Susan.)* Do you want me to sleep with you?

JAKE TOO: *(To Susan Too.)* Do you want me to sleep with you, Susan?
(Pause.)

SUSAN TOO: No thank you, Jake.

SUSAN: Thank you.

SUSAN TOO: But no.
(The sound of a car horn is heard.)

JAKE TOO: There's my ride.

SUSAN TOO: Elaine.

JAKE TOO: Right.

SUSAN TOO: You'd better go.

JAKE TOO: O.K.
(Both Jakes get up. Jake hugs Susan, Jake Too looks at Susan Too.)

JAKE: Think of the alternative, Mrs. Weatherill.

JAKE TOO: I mean, where would it lead?

JAKE: Where would it lead if we got together?

JAKE TOO: Imagine, you and me…

JAKE: You and me…in the future?

SUSAN: Just go, Jake. Please.

SUSAN TOO: Just go.

> *(Both Jakes exit upstage right, Jake grabbing the backpack on the way. Pause.)*

SUSAN: What do I do now?

SUSAN TOO: Suppose you went after him?

SUSAN: Dreaming again.

SUSAN TOO: Suppose you did. Suppose you bridged that tragic gap?

> *(Susan looks at her, then exits quickly right. Susan Too speaks as if to herself.)*

SUSAN TOO: She dashed down the stairs and caught up to him in the front hall. They fell into a mad embrace. They forgot Ted, forgot Elaine, forgot everything but themselves. They made love all day long in her double bed. They met again three times during the rest of the summer: New York, for a delicious weekend; that secluded inn on the water, near New London, for an afternoon; Aunt Esther's apartment in Boston over Labor Day. It was there they decided not to see each other any more. She gave him her drawing of an apple. They took a walk on Newbury Street. She got cold. He bought her a plum-colored sweater to keep her warm.

> *(Susan comes back in from the right wearing a plum-colored sweater.)*

SUSAN: He's gone.

SUSAN TOO: Yes.

SUSAN: I offered him a beer. I said we should at least sit down and share a beer. But he had to go.

> *(Susan Too clears the sheets from the rumpled daybed.)*

SUSAN TOO: Yes.

SUSAN: I said, "Hey look, We should talk. I'm not that old. You're not that young. It doesn't always have to be so *tragic*." But he left.

SUSAN TOO: *(Goes to window, looks out.)* He's gone?

SUSAN: Yes.

SUSAN TOO: Forever?

SUSAN: Yes.

> *(Susan Too gets the sketch pad, sits center, and idly begins to sketch the empty stool where Jake sat.)*

SUSAN TOO: At least I have this.

SUSAN: *(Taking a bottle of pills from her skirt pocket, looking at them.)* Or these.

SUSAN TOO: Don't be silly.

SUSAN: I don't think I can—

SUSAN TOO: *(Singing insistently.)* "Every star above
Knows the one I love…"

SUSAN: How can you work at a time like this? *(Crossing behind her, looking over her shoulder.)* It's not bad, I'll say that.

SUSAN TOO: Thanks.

SUSAN: Quite good, actually.

SUSAN TOO: Thank you very much.

SUSAN: *(Putting the pills on the drawing table, taking up a pencil.)* Doesn't look like him, though.

SUSAN TOO: Better if it doesn't.

SUSAN: *(Leaning over, adding a flourish.)* What if I do this?

SUSAN TOO: Good. Excellent.
(They work together on the drawing.)

BOTH: *(Singing.)* "No one else it seems
Ever shares my dreams…
(They try harmony.)
And without you, dear, I don't know what
I'd do…"

SUSAN: Do you realize this is the first time in my life I've ever drawn a sex organ on anything?

SUSAN TOO: Make it bigger.

SUSAN: Know something?

SUSAN TOO: What?

SUSAN: This is good.

SUSAN TOO: Oh yes?

SUSAN: This is very good.

SUSAN TOO: You think so!
(She gets up quickly, leans the drawing against the stool downstage; they both stand back and look at it.)

SUSAN: This is the best thing I've done.

SUSAN TOO: I think so, too.
(They stand admiring their work, arm in arm, as the lights fade on them and the recording of "Sweet Sue" comes up.)

THE END